I0123590

MĀORI AND ABORIGINAL WOMEN IN THE PUBLIC EYE

REPRESENTING DIFFERENCE, 1950–2000

MĀORI AND ABORIGINAL WOMEN IN THE PUBLIC EYE

REPRESENTING DIFFERENCE, 1950–2000

KAREN FOX

ANU

THE AUSTRALIAN NATIONAL UNIVERSITY

E PRESS

ANU

E PRESS

Published by ANU E Press
The Australian National University
Canberra ACT 0200, Australia
Email: anuepress@anu.edu.au
This title is also available online at http://epress.anu.edu.au

---

National Library of Australia Cataloguing-in-Publication entry

Author: Fox, Karen.

Title: Māori and Aboriginal women in the public eye : representing difference,
                1950-2000 / Karen Fox.

ISBN: 9781921862618 (pbk.) 9781921862625 (ebook)

Notes: Includes bibliographical references and index.

Subjects: Women, Māori--New Zealand--History.
                Women, Aboriginal Australian--Australia--History.
                Women, Māori--New Zealand--Social conditions.
                Women, Aboriginal Australian--Australia--Social conditions.
                Indigenous women--New Zealand--Public opinion.
                Indigenous women--Australia--Public opinion.
                Women in popular culture--New Zealand.
                Women in popular culture--Australia.
                Indigenous peoples in popular culture--New Zealand.
                Indigenous peoples in popular culture--Australia.

Dewey Number: 305.4880099442

All rights reserved. No part of this publication may be reproduced, stored in a retrieval system
or transmitted in any form or by any means, electronic, mechanical, photocopying or otherwise,
without the prior permission of the publisher.

Cover image: 'Maori guide Rangi at Whakarewarewa, New Zealand, 1935',
PIC/8725/635 LOC Album 1056/D. National Library of Australia, Canberra.

Cover design and layout by ANU E Press

This edition © 2011 ANU E Press

Contents

Acknowledgements

This book began its life as a PhD thesis, undertaken at The Australian National University. I wish to gratefully thank my supervisory panel. Ann McGrath was enthusiastic about the topic from the first time I broached it to her, and her perceptive suggestions influenced me throughout the research and writing process. Bronwen Douglas' warm and generous support, her incisive and often challenging insights, and her intellectual rigour continually assisted and inspired me. Tom Griffiths taught me much about writing and performing history, and was always a source of encouragement and inspiration. I greatly appreciated Barbara Brookes' support, and our discussions shaped my thinking in important ways.

I thank my colleagues and friends at the *Australian Dictionary of Biography* and the National Centre for Biography, the Australian Centre for Indigenous History, the School of History, and the Division of Pacific and Asian History at the ANU. In researching and writing this book I benefitted greatly from discussions, workshops, seminars, postgraduate events, social occasions and talks over coffee. For their intellectual input and support, I especially thank Chris Ballard, Nick Brown, Paul D'Arcy, Desley Deacon, Barry Higman, Pat Jalland, Shino Konishi, Melanie Nolan, Peter Read, Tim Rowse, Carolyn Strange and Angela Woollacott. I also thank Karen Smith and Karen Ciuffetelli, whose administrative support was much appreciated. Thank you to my fellow students and friends, past and present, with whom I shared the delights and stresses of a PhD. Special thanks are due to Hilary Howes, for her encouragement and companionship over cups of coffee in cafes around the campus, drinks in Fellows Garden and cocktails on the beach, and to Keri Mills, for wonderful wandering conversations when we were supposed to be practicing our te reo Māori skills.

I wish also to gratefully acknowledge the help of staff at the following institutions: the National Library of Australia, the National Library of New Zealand, the Alexander Turnbull Library, the State Library of Queensland, the Macmillan Brown Library at the University of Canterbury, and the library of the Australian Institute of Aboriginal and Torres Strait Islander Studies. The staff of the newspaper reading room at the National Library of Australia were particularly helpful, graciously processing my many requests for bulky and awkward newspapers held off-site. Permissions to reproduce material were kindly granted by Melanie Collins, Christian Heinegg, Mihi Rurawhe, the National Library of Australia, the Alexander Turnbull Library and the Northern Territory Library. I offer my apologies to any copyright holders I have been unable to identify and locate. Financially, I was assisted in producing this book by an APA scholarship, by the History Program in the Research School of Social Sciences, and by a publication subsidy granted by The Australian National University.

I would like to express my appreciation to the staff of ANU E Press, and to Melanie Nolan, the editor of the ANU.Lives series, for encouragement and support as this book was in preparation. I am also grateful to the reviewers of the manuscript, whose thoughtful comments helped to improve the work. An earlier version of Chapter Two appeared in the *Melbourne Historical Journal* vol. 35, pp. 35-49, as 'An Encounter With the White World of Wimbledon: Evonne Goolagong and Representations of Race and Gender in Australia'. A version of Chapter Five is forthcoming in *Intersections: Gender and Sexuality in Asia and the Pacific*, issue 28 (December 2011), as 'Matriarchs, Moderates and Militants: Press Representations of Indigenous Women in Australia and New Zealand', online at http://intersections.anu.edu.au/issue28/fox.htm. Parts of Chapter Three were originally published as 'Rosalie Kunoth Monks and the Making of Jedda', in *Aboriginal History* vol. 33 (2009), pp. 77-95. Chapter Four draws on a paper published as 'Oodgeroo Noonuccal: Media Snapshots of a Controversial Life' in *Indigenous Biography and Autobiography*, Aboriginal History monograph no. 17 (2008), pp. 57-68.

Last, but certainly not least, I offer thanks to my friends and family who have listened to my ideas, provided support, and helped to distract me when necessary. In particular, my mother, Ngaire, has always supported me in my intellectual life. Most of all, I thank Jamie. His love and faith in me seem boundless, beyond anything I could have imagined.

Abbreviations

ABC	Australian Broadcasting Commission/Corporation
AC	Companion of the Order of Australia
AFL	Australian Football League
AM	Member of the Order of Australia
APA	Aboriginal Progressive Association
ATSIC	Aboriginal and Torres Strait Islander Commission
CBE	Commander of the Order of the British Empire
DBE	Dame Commander of the Order of the British Empire
FCAA	Federal Council for Aboriginal Advancement
FCAATSI	Federal Council for the Advancement of Aborigines and Torres Strait Islanders
MBE	Member of the Order of the British Empire
MMP	Mixed Member Proportional
MP	Member of Parliament
MWWL	Māori Women's Welfare League
NSW	New South Wales
OAM	Medal of the Order of Australia
OBE	Officer of the Order of the British Empire
ONZ	Order of New Zealand
QCAATSI	Queensland Council for the Advancement of Aborigines and Torres Strait Islanders
QSM	Queen's Service Medal
RCES	Royal Commission on the Electoral System
USLTA	United States Lawn Tennis Association
WCTU	Women's Christian Temperance Union

Illustrations

Glossary of Māori Words

aroha	affection or sympathy
haka	traditional dance
hapū	sub-tribe
hui	meeting
iwi	tribe
kapa haka	traditional performing arts
kāwanatanga	governance or government
kiri	skin or bark
kohanga reo	language nest
kuia	elderly woman
mana	prestige or authority
(te) mana (o te) wāhine	the dignity or strength of women
Māoritanga	Māori culture or way of life
marae	meeting place
marae ātea	courtyard in front of the wharenui
pā	fortified village
pahū	bell or gong
Pākehā	New Zealander of European descent
pere	bell
poi	ball attached to string
(te) reo Māori	the Māori language
tangata whenua	people of the land
tangihanga	funeral or mourning
tikanga	custom

(te) tino rangatiratanga	sovereignty or self-determination
tumuaki	head or leader
waiata	song or chant
whānau	extended family
wharenui	big house or meeting house

Note on Usage

A number of decisions about terminology were necessary in the writing of this book. First, although I have used the terms 'Māori', 'Aboriginal', 'Pākehā', 'Indigenous' and 'non-Indigenous' throughout, I wish to problematise them here. Neither 'Māori' nor 'Aboriginal' people existed in a conceptual sense prior to the coming of Europeans to the lands now known as Aotearoa/New Zealand and Australia; rather, a number of iwi and hapū (tribes and sub-tribes) inhabited the former, and many distinct nations the latter. Both 'Māori' and 'Aboriginal' are problematic words in that they are essentialising terms which set up binary oppositions, and the same might be said of the terms 'Pākehā', 'Indigenous' and 'non-Indigenous'. As well, to describe a person as 'non-Indigenous' is to describe them in terms of what they are not, and is thus a negative and often unhelpful description. However, other terms are difficult to suggest and often equally problematic. Moreover, as this is a study of representations in the media, which has been and continues to be dominated by non-Indigenous people, these terms are appropriate. Not only are they commonly used terms in the media and wider popular discourse, they are constructed terms which represent difference in specific ways. For this reason, I have also used 'New Zealand' rather than 'Aotearoa' or 'Aotearoa/New Zealand'. Second, current scholarly consensus considers race to have no biological foundation, but to be socially constructed and ideological. I adopt this understanding of race as, like gender, socially constructed. Inverted commas are implied around race each time the word is used, though for stylistic reasons they are not included except in quotations. Quotations are given as they appear in the original, excepting where changes to initial capitalisation were required for reasons of style. All numbers and percentages have been rounded to whole numbers. Finally, I have not italicised Māori words, because te reo Māori (the Māori language) is an official language of New Zealand, my country of birth.

Introduction

Very few Aboriginal or Māori women became well-known outside their own communities before the middle of the twentieth century. Among those who did become more widely known, two in particular have continued to be remembered, and often to be celebrated. Te Puea Hērangi is frequently remembered as 'Princess Te Puea' for her connection with the second Māori King, Tāwhiao Te Wherowhero, whose granddaughter she was. She, however, repudiated the title as an alien one, unknown in Māoritanga (Māori culture or way of life). Even more erroneously, Trukanini is often remembered as the last of the Tasmanian Aboriginal people, despite this claim being clearly disproved. Te Puea received royal honours for her work as a leader of her people, her life's work thus acknowledged by the Crown. About the time Te Puea was born, in the late nineteenth century, Trukanini's skeleton was exhumed against her dying wishes, later to be displayed as an artefact. Such contrasting lives, and the popular narratives told of them, piqued my interest when I first read of them, and eventually led me to embark on this exploration of the assonances and dissonances evident in depictions of celebrated Indigenous women in Australia and New Zealand. Their stories provide a foundation for comparing media portrayals of Māori and Aboriginal women in the second half of the twentieth century.

Trukanini, Truganini, Trucanini, Trugernanner

Undoubtedly the most famous Aboriginal woman to live and die before 1950 was Trukanini, whose story has been told and re-told, imagined and re-imagined, many times since her death in 1876. In paintings and photographs, in histories and biographies, in poems, novels and plays, in scientific articles and even in song, the story of Trukanini has been repeated and re-shaped.[1] Lyndall Ryan has described her as 'the most famous Aborigine in white Australian history'.[2] Trukanini became known for a tragic story, as the last Tasmanian Aboriginal person, whose death signalled extinction. Though this basis of fame became contested, particularly through the vocal presence of a continuing community of Tasmanian Aboriginal people, the label of 'last of the race' was frequently still attached to Trukanini, often amended to describe her as the last so-called full-

---

1   L. Ryan, 'The Struggle for Trukanini 1830-1997', *Tasmanian Historical Research Association Papers and Proceedings* 44, no. 3 (1997), p. 153; R. Taylor, *Unearthed: The Aboriginal Tasmanians of Kangaroo Island*, revised ed. (Kent Town: Wakefield, 2008), p. 139. Note that I follow Ryan in spelling the name Trukanini, the spelling used currently by the Palawah people of Tasmania. Ryan, p. 153.
2   L. Ryan, 'Truganini', in *The Oxford Companion to Australian History*, eds. G. Davison, J. Hirst and S. Macintyre, Oxford Reference Online, accessed 8 September 2006, available from http://www.oxfordreference.com/views/ENTRY.html?subview=Main&entry=t127.e1478.

blooded Tasmanian Aboriginal person. As Ryan argued, 'the figure of Trukanini has always been a site of struggle for ownership and possession of the colonial past'.[3] Suvendrini Perera has similarly suggested that Trukanini's body became 'the site of competing narratives about power and powerlessness: agent or object, hostage or traitor, final victim or ultimate survivor?'[4] In the process of that struggle, Trukanini the woman was transmuted into a symbol, often lost under the weight of the different meanings ascribed to her story. Such a process of ascribing meaning to lives and achievements is central to the processes of fame, celebration and remembrance, to the phenomenon of becoming a prominent public figure. A brief examination of this process in popular representations of Trukanini and Te Puea is an appropriate beginning to this study, which takes as its central concern these processes of ascribing meanings to the lives and achievements of prominent Indigenous women through the multiple framings of their stories in the print media.

Trukanini lived during a time of tumultuous change for the Aboriginal people of Tasmania, then known by Europeans as Van Diemen's Land. By 1818, the European population already outnumbered the Aboriginal population. Governor George Arthur's efforts to end violence between Aboriginal people and settlers were unsuccessful, and in 1828 he pronounced martial law in relation to Aboriginal people in settled areas. In 1829, George Augustus Robinson travelled to the Bruny Island Aboriginal mission, where he was to take charge of those Aboriginal people already there, and to prepare for those who would be caught in settled areas. He developed the idea of persuading others to join the mission, and, with a group of Aboriginal people and several convicts, set out to do so. In 1835, he told the Colonial Secretary that all Aboriginal people had been taken away from the mainland (though in fact one further group remained outside the mission until 1842). After being brought in, however, Aboriginal people died rapidly. When the establishment was moved from Wybalenna on Flinders Island to Oyster Cove in 1847, only forty-seven people survived to make the trip, and by 1868 only three remained there.[5] Among them was Trukanini.

---

3   Ryan, p. 154.
4   S. Perera, 'Claiming Truganini: Australian National Narratives in the Year of Indigenous Peoples', *Cultural Studies* 10, no. 3 (1996), p. 395.
5   L. Ryan, *The Aboriginal Tasmanians* (St Lucia: University of Queensland Press, 1981).

Figure 1: 'Portrait of Truganini', Charles Woolley.

Photograph. nla.pic-an23795214-v. National Library of Australia, Canberra.

Trukanini's date of birth is given variously, but most often as 1812.[6] Many tellings of her life state that while she was still young, her mother was killed, her sister kidnapped, her uncle shot, and the man she was to have married murdered while trying to protect her from sawyers. She accompanied Robinson on his mission of conciliation, and is said to have saved his life, perhaps more than once. At Wybalenna, she and other inhabitants were subject to 'a rigid daily routine' that was 'designed to expunge their traditional life'.[7] In 1841, while in Port Phillip with Robinson and a group of other Aboriginal people, she and several others robbed shepherds' huts, wounded four stock-keepers and killed two whalers. For these offences, the men were hanged, while the three women were acquitted and returned to Flinders Island. Trukanini spent the last years of her life with the Dandridge family, James Dandridge having been superintendent at Oyster Cove.[8] She died in Hobart on 8 May 1876, afraid to the end that her body would be mutilated as had been the body of William Lanney, the so-called last Tasmanian Aboriginal male. The unpleasant saga of burial, subsequent exhumation and display of her skeleton in the museum of the Royal Society of Tasmania was only drawn to a close with the cremation of the skeleton and the scattering of the ashes in the D'Entrecasteaux Channel in 1976, a century after her death. Over twenty-five years later, the Hobart *Mercury* announced that remains of her hair and skin had been discovered in the museum of the Royal College of Surgeons in England, and were to be returned to Australia for burial.[9]

Early depictions of Trukanini shifted through a variety of meanings, which Lyndall Ryan has explored in detail. Before her death, these included representations as 'the epitome of the "noble savage"', 'a Pocahontas figure who saved the conciliator', and later 'a respected Indigenous citizen of the British empire, a look-alike Queen Victoria, a widow, awaiting her end and that of her people'. The exhuming of her body 'represented a shift to the triumphalist discourse of science'.[10] A central thread in many narratives of Tasmania and its Aboriginal inhabitants, as mentioned, was the idea that Trukanini was the last Tasmanian Aboriginal person, and that at her death Tasmanian Aboriginal people became extinct. This belief was as persistent as it was false, and it was her perceived status as the last Tasmanian Aboriginal person that was the central element in her continuing prominence in white Australian history and memory. In 1976, the year in which her skeleton was cremated at a ceremony attended by a woman claiming to be a descendant, she was still being referred to in the media as the

6   For instance: V. R. Ellis, 'Trucanini', *Tasmanian Historical Research Association Papers and Proceedings* 23, no. 2 (1976), p. 26; Ryan, *The Aboriginal Tasmanians*, p. 217; L. Ryan and N. Smith, 'Trugernanner (Truganini) (1812?-1876)', *Australian Dictionary of Biography*, Online Edition, updated continuously, accessed 8 August 2006, available from http://barney.asap.unimelb.edu.au/adbtest/biogs/ A060326b.htm.

7   Ryan, *The Aboriginal Tasmanians*, p. 184.

8   Ibid., pp. 166, 184, 197, 217-218.

9   B. Wilson, 'Truganini Remains to Come Home', *Mercury*, 1 June 2002, p. 3.

10   Ryan, 'The Struggle For Trukanini', pp. 155, 159.

last Tasmanian Aboriginal person. In the *Mercury* that year, she was described as 'the last of the now extinct native Tasmanians', as a 'magnet of world-wide curiosity' who had 'lost not only her family, but her race' and as 'the sole survivor of the Tasmanian aboriginal race'.[11] Where she was no longer depicted as the last Tasmanian Aboriginal person, she was often referred to instead as the last so-called full-blooded Tasmanian Aboriginal person, despite the offensiveness of such terminology.

A related narrative about Tasmanian Aboriginal people identified by Ryan was that of genocide, which became apparent as the impact of the Holocaust entered public discourse following World War Two. In the *Sydney Morning Herald* in 1976, the treatment of Tasmanian Aboriginal people was termed 'the world's most successful genocide', while the *Mercury* made reference in 2002 to 'planned annihilation' and to Trukanini having 'died in a kind of concentration camp'.[12] The genocide narrative, argued Ryan, was 'a humanist response to scientific discourses of extinction' that 'argued for Aboriginal agency in resisting extermination', but it was 'too limited to acknowledge the survival of Aboriginal peoples'.[13] Trukanini became a 'symbol of [the] extermination' or the 'attempted genocide' of Aboriginal people in Australia.[14] Bernard Smith saw her as the 'spectre' that haunted Australian history.[15] Such narratives of the past also had implications for the present, denying the Aboriginal community in Tasmania their existence, and thus working against potential land rights claims. The film *The Last Tasmanian*, for example, through canvassing what its director saw as 'genocide' and through its failure to recognise the Aboriginality of descendants, stood opposed to Tasmanian land rights claims.[16] Central to such a narrative was an image of Trukanini as a victim, and of her life as tragic. Nicholas Cree, writing in the *Mercury* in 1976, referred to her 'tragic saga' and her 'unusual and tragic life'.[17] Portraying Trukanini as a victim could deny her agency, making her appear a passive object of colonial action.[18] Such depictions echoed wider representations of Aboriginal people as passive, abject or belonging to the past, unable either to adapt to or to resist European settlement.

Contests over the meanings ascribed to Trukanini's life often related to a question about how to best understand her actions in assisting Robinson. Representations

---

11   N. Cree, 'Truganini: 1812-1876', *Mercury*, 13 March 1976, p. 6; 'Truganini – Symbol of Equality', *Mercury*, 6 July 1976, p. 9.

12   B. Turner, 'Making Amends to Truganini', *Sydney Morning Herald*, 8 May 1976, p. 11; Wilson, p. 3.

13   Ryan, 'The Struggle For Trukanini', p. 165.

14   A. Onsman, 'Truganini's Funeral', *Island*, no. 96 (2004), p. 45; Ryan, 'The Struggle For Trukanini', p. 165.

15   B. Smith, *The Spectre of Truganini* (Sydney: Australian Broadcasting Commission, 1980).

16   Onsman, pp. 46-47; T. O'Regan, 'Documentary in Controversy: The Last Tasmanian', in *An Australian Film Reader*, eds. A. Moran and T. O'Regan (Sydney: Currency, 1985), p. 127.

17   Cree, p. 6.

18   See G. Lehman, 'Trukanini', in *The Oxford Companion to Aboriginal Art and Culture*, eds. S. Kleinert and M. Neale (Melbourne: Oxford University Press, 2000), p. 722.

of her actions and motives sometimes placed her as a type of collaborator, a pawn, a dupe or even a traitor who betrayed her own people. The *Canberra Times* in 1974 claimed that Trukanini 'led her people to slaughter' when she 'agreed to requests to bring [them] out of hiding' in the belief that 'a peace pact was to be signed'.[19] Several depictions also sexualised her, representing her as a promiscuous woman and Robinson's lover. One author described her as having been 'infamous as a wench of incredible charm who teased and wiled her way through life', and as one whose 'sexual prowess was a legend among the two races'. The same author stated that she 'had an uncanny way with men' which she 'used' in 'her role as mediatrix between her people and the British'.[20] Trukanini's actions, however, have also been interpreted in a more positive light in some narratives, as a diplomatic effort to halt the bloodshed and ensure the survival of Aboriginal people. A 1977 article in the Sydney *Sun* referred to her setting out with Robinson to 'bring [Aboriginal people] to safety'. In this article, she was depicted as wise and perceptive, and as having been motivated to rescue her people.[21] Trukanini has become a 'cherished' figure to the contemporary Tasmanian Aboriginal community, understood 'as a woman who displayed strength and diplomacy in her struggle to find a way for her people to endure the savage impact of Europeans on her land'.[22] She has also been depicted as a heroine of the resistance to European settlement. Her rebellion was seen as important by those who organised Black Vine, 'a multi-media performance event ... to pay tribute to the heroes and heroines of black Australia'.[23] As this brief discussion demonstrates, Trukanini has become a largely mythical figure, representations of whom are often more revealing of the discourses they are mobilised in aid of than of her own story.

'The Greatest Māori Woman of Our Time'

If Trukanini was the best-known and most often remembered Aboriginal woman who lived and worked before the second half of the twentieth century, Te Puea Hērangi was and is the best-known Māori woman who lived and worked prior to that period. Indeed, Michael King considered her the first Māori woman to become 'a national figure'.[24] At her death in 1952, one author wrote that she had 'won the great admiration and respect of Maori and pakeha [New Zealanders of European descent] alike' through her 'outstanding leadership' and 'untiring and selfless devotion to the interests of her people'.[25] Moreover, Te Puea was an internationally

---

19   'Truganini Burial Unlikely', *Canberra Times*, 1 April 1974, p. 3.
20   'The Tormented Life and Death of Truganini', *Sydney Morning Herald*, 26 February 1976, p. 16.
21   B. Hastings, 'Truganini's Lover Planned Murder', *Sun*, 23 November 1977, p. 64.
22   Lehman, p. 722.
23   M. Mordue, 'Celebrating Black Heroes', *Sydney Morning Herald*, 2 September 1993, p. 21.
24   M. King, *Whina: A Biography of Whina Cooper* (Auckland: Hodder and Stoughton, 1983), p. 179.
25   'Death of Princess Te Puea', *Te Ao Hou: The New World*, no. 2 (1952), p. 33.

known figure. According to media reports, the United States, Australia, India and Tonga were represented at her tangihanga (funeral), which was also attended by members of the New Zealand Parliament, including the Prime Minister, Sidney Holland. Almost 300 'telegrams of condolence' came from around the globe, and tributes to her were broadcast and published in England.[26]

Figure 2: 'Princess Te Kirihaehae Te Puea Hērangi, wearing the CBE she received in 1938'.

Photograph. PAColl-5584-58. Alexander Turnbull Library, Wellington, New Zealand.

---

26 'Sacred Funeral: Tangi For Te Puea', *Te Ao Hou: The New World*, no. 3 (1953), pp. 4-5.

In many narratives, Te Puea was described in terms that set her apart from other Māori women. After her death, she was described in *Te Ao Hou: The New World*, a magazine published by the Department of Māori Affairs, as 'the greatest Maori woman of the last half-century'.[27] In a radio broadcast that was later published in the same magazine, journalist Eric Ramsden called her 'the greatest Maori woman of our time – perhaps of all time'.[28] And before her death, a 1951 article in *People* magazine noted that she was acknowledged by all Māori people to be 'the most remarkable Māori woman living'.[29] Such judgements were frequently repeated in later celebrations of her life. In his two books of famous New Zealand lives, Eugene Grayland included no Māori women besides Te Puea, writing that she had 'achieved more than any other Maori woman in history' and had become 'the foremost Maori woman of her time throughout the country' because of 'her influence for Maori unity and the preservation of tradition'.[30] Many portrayals of Te Puea thus placed her as exceptional, an almost larger-than-life figure.

Born in 1883, Te Puea was the granddaughter of the second Māori King, Tāwhiao Te Wherowhero. She came to be called 'Princess Te Puea', though she herself did not use the title. Indeed, as Ann Parsonson comments, she 'would not have liked' the 'constant references' to her as a Princess, since 'it was a title originally bestowed on her by Pakeha, which she never used herself'.[31] She was sometimes described as 'the power behind' or 'the woman behind' the throne of the Kīngitanga, the Māori King movement established in the mid-nineteenth century.[32] Although her leadership role was not straightforward at first, she became a well-established leader over time, as her successes mounted. Her major achievement was in working 'alongside three successive kings in re-establishing the Kingitanga ... as a central force among the Tainui people' of the central North Island, and 'achieving national recognition' of the movement from both Māori, despite tribal divisions, and Pākehā.[33]

Te Puea's work encompassed all spheres of life as she pursued goals relating to health, social and economic welfare, cultural revival and political recognition. During the 1918 influenza epidemic, she worked to nurse the people, and to care for those left orphaned. She sought to create a hospital where Māori could be cared for in a Māori environment, to alleviate their fears of travelling to hospital, although in this she was blocked by officialdom. After World War One, she took on a long and demanding project to 'rebuild a centre for the Kingitanga'

---

27   'Death of Princess Te Puea', p. 33.

28   E. Ramsden, 'Memories of Princess Te Puea', *Te Ao Hou: The New World*, no. 3 (1953), p. 7.

29   'Princess Te Puea, the Maker of Maori Kings', *People*, 3 January 1951, p. 37.

30   E. Grayland, *Famous New Zealanders* (Christchurch: Whitcombe and Tombs, 1967), p. 147.

31   A. Parsonson, 'Herangi, Te Kirihaehae Te Puea 1883-1952', *Dictionary of New Zealand Biography*, updated 22 June 2007, accessed 2 August 2007, available from http://www.dnzb.govt.nz/dnzb/default.asp?Find_Quick.asp? PersonEssay=3H17.

32   For example: Grayland, *Famous New Zealanders*, p. 147; 'Princess Te Puea', p. 34; Ramsden, p. 8.

33   Parsonson, 'Herangi, Te Kirihaehae Te Puea'.

at Ngāruawāhia, buying and clearing land and building a marae (meeting place), known as Tūrangawaewae. She was deeply involved in negotiating for compensation for the confiscation of land. As well, Te Puea took an important role in reviving Māori culture. A concert party which she established travelled around raising money for the building at Ngāruawāhia. A tour of the North Island was 'not only a financial success, but ... also contributed to a revival of interest in haka, waiata, and poi' (traditional dances and songs). She also sought to revitalise canoe building. The Kīngitanga, and Te Puea, gained 'increasing official recognition', as was evident in the 1938 visit by the Governor-General, then Lord Galway, to open a carved house built for the King, and to invest Te Puea with a CBE (Commander of the British Empire).[34]

Te Puea's status as a Māori woman acting in a position of leadership was sometimes commented upon in popular texts and the media. Sometimes this was positive, as in descriptions of her as a role model for other Māori women. After her death, the *Te Ao Hou* writer who reported on her tangihanga commented that women 'particularly felt the sharpness of their loss' because she 'had, especially, been their leader'. She had 'shown them what a Maori woman could be', the article continued, and 'had been an example to look up to'.[35] Ramsden wrote that she had been 'obeyed ... implicitly in all policy matters', despite the Waikato iwi (tribe) being 'ever jealous of male prerogatives'.[36] At other times, gendered representations of Te Puea were less positive. Ramsden once described her in this way:

> If a woman, and sometimes subject to the vagaries of her sex, Te Puea seldom let her emotions sway her judgement ... Nevertheless, there were times when she could make use of her undoubted charm to achieve her objectives.[37]

Racialised and gendered representations of Te Puea sometimes appeared to imagine her in terms which downplayed the challenge she might pose to Pākehā, or to male, dominance through her visibility as a strong and proud Māori woman. Te Puea spoke of 'the parallel paths of two canoes – Maori and Pakeha' and considered that 'the two peoples should learn to respect one another's cultures so that they could live comfortably together'.[38] Thus, although she was acknowledged to have strengthened Māori political structures and culture, she appears not to have been constructed as a threatening figure. Ann Parsonson has

---

34 M. King, *Te Puea: A Biography* (Auckland: Hodder and Stoughton, 1977), pp. 72-73, 145, 188-190; T. MacDonald and N. Zister, 'Te Puea Herangi', in *The Book of New Zealand Women/Ko Kui Ma Te Kaupapa*, eds. C. Macdonald, M. Penfold and B. Williams (Wellington: Bridget Williams, 1991), p. 665; Parsonson, 'Herangi, Te Kirihaehae Te Puea'.
35 'Sacred Funeral', p. 4.
36 Ramsden, p. 8.
37 Ibid., p. 7.
38 Parsonson, 'Herangi, Te Kirihaehae Te Puea'.

pointed out that, while Te Puea was 'recognised as a remarkable leader', there was 'little recognition … of the poverty and powerlessness that she had spent her life fighting', either during her lifetime or at her death.[39] In a short biographical article in 1936, James Cowan described her 'heroic work of pure unselfishness' for her people.[40] Such a description not only played down the threat she presented to the Pākehā political order, but also placed her within a predominantly Pākehā discourse of selfless womanhood. In many portrayals, Pākehā seemed all too willing to ignore the more challenging aspects of her work, and to celebrate her in non-threatening terms.

Studying Media Representations of Famous Indigenous Women

Clearly, significant differences are evident between Australia and New Zealand in relation to the remembrance and celebration of Indigenous women who lived and worked prior to 1950. Just as there is no equivalent figure to Trukanini in New Zealand, there is no equivalent figure to Te Puea in Australia. Te Puea was born to a position of political and social status within Māoridom, her place in the historical record almost assured by her lineage, though her standing as an influential leader, like her popular fame and celebration, were not thus assured. Trukanini, herself the daughter of a leader, was instead most known and remembered for something apparently unrelated to her social and political situation and largely outside her control, her longevity, though her experiences and actions during her life did augment her fame. Although close together geographically, both imagined as egalitarian settler societies, and sharing many historical experiences, Australia and New Zealand differed considerably in the extent to which Indigenous women of the nineteenth and early twentieth centuries were present in historical memory, and in the nature of the narratives told of those women.

Beginning research on this subject, I wondered if the conspicuous differences between the lives and representations of Trukanini and Te Puea continued to be evident in those of prominent Māori and Aboriginal women throughout the rest of the twentieth century, a period in which Australia and New Zealand were transformed in remarkably similar ways. As parallels in the experiences and depictions of these women began to accumulate, however, it became clear that conceptualising the stories of Te Puea and Trukanini solely in terms of difference also missed something critical. The lives and representations of both women, of

---

39 Ibid.
40 J. Cowan, 'Te Puea Herangi: Princess of Waikato and Leader of Her People', *New Zealand Railways Magazine*, 1 September 1936, p. 17.

course, did and do reflect differences in the nature and impact of colonialism in their respective countries. Memorialised as the last of her people, Trukanini came to symbolise the destruction of Aboriginal people and culture, while Te Puea was celebrated as an architect of Māori cultural and political revival, a leader with significant influence who might be understood as embodying all that Pākehā viewed as best in Māori culture. Yet their stories also display parallels. In the late twentieth century, Trukanini too came to symbolise Indigenous resilience and resistance, while Te Puea's work of renewal was necessary only because of the destruction of Māori life and culture wrought by colonisation. The persistence of certain narratives about these women may thus have as much to do with cherished non-Indigenous beliefs about Australian and New Zealand national identities and narratives of the past, and with deeply buried aspects of the national psyche in these two countries, as with the women's own experiences. Though their lives followed vastly different paths, in different places and times, both Trukanini and Te Puea might perhaps be best understood as strong women who struggled boldly against the ravages of colonisation.

Popular framings of their lives and work represented both women in terms of particular ideas about race and gender. Patricia Hill Collins has argued that women of African-American descent in the United States 'occupy a position whereby the inferior half of a series of ... dichotomies converge', and that 'this placement has been central to our subordination'.[41] In settler societies such as Australia and New Zealand, Indigenous women have been similarly placed at the convergence of a number of dichotomies based on ideas of race and gender, and this positioning has been central to their experiences of marginalisation and oppression. These intersecting dichotomies have shaped portrayals of Aboriginal and Māori people in popular culture, political and academic discourse and the media. For much of the period since European settlement, representations of Māori and Aboriginal people have been largely imposed from outside Māori and Aboriginal communities. Such representations often drew on entrenched stereotypes and imagined racial binaries. Marcia Langton has observed a 'dense history of racist, distorted and often offensive' portrayals of Aboriginal people in Australia, and in New Zealand too non-Indigenous representations of Māori have often been highly problematic.[42] On both sides of the Tasman, racialised representations intersected in complicated ways with gendered representations in depictions of Aboriginal and Māori women.

Representations are neither transparent nor innocent, impacting on actual lives in complex ways. Negative or stereotypical representations have arguably

---

41 P. H. Collins, *Black Feminist Thought: Knowledge, Consciousness, and the Politics of Empowerment* (New York and London: Routledge, 1991), p. 70.
42 M. Langton, *"Well, I Heard it on the Radio and I Saw it on the Television": An Essay for the Australian Film Commission on the Politics and Aesthetics of Filmmaking By and About Aboriginal People and Things* (North Sydney: Australian Film Commission, 1993), p. 24.

been powerfully implicated in the historical dispossession and repression of Indigenous peoples in many parts of the world. Intersecting racial and gender stereotypes have played a part in shaping the situations of non-white women in various social and political contexts. 'Maintaining images of Black women as the Other', Collins has argued, 'provides ideological justification for race, gender, and class oppression'.[43] Media representations, which are the particular focus of this book, can be remarkably powerful, not only reflecting widely-held social beliefs and attitudes, but also playing a constitutive role in the formation and maintenance of those beliefs and attitudes. Writing of the print media in Australia, Ann Curthoys has noted the importance of its roles in creating community, including or excluding groups or individuals, constituting and being constituted by the society in which it operates.[44] The wide reach of the media, its political and social ubiquity and its apparent transparency mean that media representations are a critical subject for historical research.

A growing body of literature now considers representations of gender and race in popular culture and the media. In relation to the press, a major preoccupation has been coverage of women in politics or as world leaders. Repeated elements in depictions of these women included a focus on their appearance, a greater focus on the private and domestic aspects of their lives than was the case in biographical sketches about men holding similar positions, and a tendency to draw on common gendered frames in stories about women as political leaders.[45] Another focus has been the portrayal or framing of the women's movement in the press from the 1960s.[46] Media representations of women involved in specific fields have also been the subject of attention, with a particular emphasis on

---

43   Collins, p. 68.

44   A. Curthoys, 'Histories of Journalism', in *Journalism: Print, Politics and Popular Culture*, eds. A. Curthoys and J. Schultz (St Lucia: University of Queensland Press, 1999), p. 1.

45   On media representations of women in politics, see for example: J. Baird, *Media Tarts: How the Australian Press Frames Female Politicians* (Carlton North: Scribe, 2004); M. Braden, *Women Politicians and the Media* (Lexington: University Press of Kentucky, 1996); S. J. Carroll and R. Schreiber, 'Media Coverage of Women in the 103rd Congress', in *Women, Media, and Politics*, ed. P. Norris (New York: Oxford University Press, 1997), pp. 131-148; S. Dixon, 'The Enduring Theme: Domineering Dowagers and Scheming Concubines', in *Stereotypes of Women in Power: Historical Perspectives and Revisionist Views*, eds. B. Garlick, S. Dixon and P. Allen (New York: Greenwood, 1992), pp. 209-225; C. Jenkins, 'A Mother in Cabinet: Dame Enid Lyons and the Press', *Australian Journalism Review* 25, no. 1 (2003), pp. 181-196; C. Jenkins, 'The More Things Change: Women, Politics and the Press in Australia', *Ejournalist* 2, no. 1 (2002), accessed 27 February 2009, available from http://ejournalist.com.au/v2n1/cathy.pdf; P. Norris, 'Women Leaders Worldwide: A Splash of Color in the Photo Op', in *Women, Media, and Politics*, ed. P. Norris (New York: Oxford University Press, 1997), pp. 149-165; K. Pickles, 'Exceptions to the Rule: Explaining the World's First Women Presidents and Prime Ministers', *History Now* 7, no. 2 (2001), pp. 13-18; J. Ustinoff, 'The Many Faces of Political Eve: Representations of Queensland Women Parliamentarians in the Media', *Queensland Review* 12, no. 2 (2005), pp. 97-106.

46   L. Ashley and B. Olson, 'Constructing Reality: Print Media's Framing of the Women's Movement, 1966 to 1986', *Journalism and Mass Communication Quarterly* 75, no. 2 (1998), pp. 263-277; M. Barakso and B. F. Schaffner, 'Winning Coverage: News Media Portrayals of the Women's Movement, 1969–2004', *Harvard International Journal of Press/Politics* 11 (2006), pp. 22-44; D. L. Rhode, 'Media Images, Feminist Issues', *Signs* 20, no. 3 (1995), pp. 685-710; S. Sheridan, S. Magarey and S. Lilburn, 'Feminism in the News', in *Feminism in Popular Culture*, eds. J. Hollows and R. Moseley (Oxford and New York: Berg, 2006), pp. 25-

sporting women.[47] Moreover, some individual periodicals have been studied for the ways in which they represented women's lives and experiences. Susan Sheridan, Barbara Baird, Kate Borrett and Lyndall Ryan produced a valuable study of the *Australian Women's Weekly*, exploring the 'female-centred world' it created for readers in the middle of the twentieth century, and the ways in which it framed 'ideals of femininity and domestic life' in those years.[48] Many studies of the ways in which women have been represented in the media have, at least implicitly, focused upon white middle-class women, an imbalance which I hope this work goes some way towards redressing.

Considerable work has also been done to examine issues of representation and racial difference in the media.[49] In Australia, this research has revealed a continual silencing of Aboriginal perspectives, a focus on stories which place

40; N. Terkildsen and F. Schnell, 'How Media Frames Move Public Opinion: An Analysis of the Women's Movement', *Political Research Quarterly* 50 (1997), pp. 879-900; E. van Acker, 'The Portrayal of Feminist Issues in the Print Media', *Australian Studies in Journalism*, no. 4 (1995), pp. 174-199.

47   For instance: G. Gardiner, 'Running for Country: Australian Print Media Representation of Indigenous Athletes in the 27th Olympiad', *Journal of Sport and Social Issues* 27, no. 3 (2003), pp. 233-260; J. Hargreaves, *Sporting Females: Critical Issues in the History and Sociology of Women's Sports* (London and New York: Routledge, 1994), especially pp. 162-173; J. McKay, 'Embodying the "New" Sporting Woman', *Hecate* 20, no. 1 (1994), pp. 68-83; J. Nauright, 'Netball, Media Representation of Women and Crisis of Male Hegemony in New Zealand', *ASSH Studies in Sports History*, no. 11 (1999), pp. 47-65; D. Stevenson, 'Women, Sport and Globalization: Competing Discourses of Sexuality and Nation', *Journal of Sport and Social Issues* 26, no. 2 (2002), pp. 209-225; E. H. Wensing and T. Bruce, 'Bending the Rules: Media Representations of Gender During an International Sporting Event', *International Review for the Sociology of Sport* 38, no. 4 (2003), pp. 387-396.

48   S. Sheridan, B. Baird, K. Borrett and L. Ryan, *Who Was That Woman? The Australian Women's Weekly in the Postwar Years* (Sydney: University of New South Wales Press, 2002).

49   See for example: S. B. Banerjee and G. Osuri, 'Silences of the Media: Whiting Out Aboriginality in Making News and Making History', *Media, Culture and Society* 22, no. 3 (2000), pp. 263-284; K. Barclay and J. H. Liu, 'Who Gets Voice? (Re)presentation of Bicultural Relations in New Zealand Print Media', *New Zealand Journal of Psychology* 32, no. 1 (2003), pp. 3-12; K. Bullimore, 'Media Dreaming: Representation of Aboriginality in Modern Australian Media', *Asia Pacific Media Educator*, no. 6 (1999), pp. 72-80; J. Cochrane, 'Media Treatment of Maori Issues', *Sites*, no. 21 (1990), pp. 5-29; D. Fox, 'The Maori Perspective of the News', in *Whose News?*, eds. M. Comrie and J. McGregor (Palmerston North: Dunmore, 1992), pp. 170-180; H. Goodall, 'Constructing a Riot: Television News and Aborigines', *Media Information Australia*, no. 68 (1993), pp. 70-77; J. Hartley and A. McKee, *The Indigenous Public Sphere: The Reporting and Reception of Aboriginal Issues in the Australian Media* (Oxford: Oxford University Press, 2000); D. Hollinsworth, '"My Island Home": Riot and Resistance in Media Representations of Aboriginality', *Social Alternatives* 24, no. 1 (2005), pp. 16-20; A. McKee and J. Hartley, '"Truth, Integrity and a Little Gossip": Magazine Coverage of Aboriginality and the Law in Australia', *Alternative Law Journal* 21, no. 1 (1996), pp. 15-18, 23; M. Meadows, 'A 10-Point Plan and a Treaty: Images of Indigenous People in the Press in Australia and Canada', *Queensland Review* 6, no. 1 (1999), pp. 50-76; M. Meadows, 'Media Images of Indigenous Affairs in Australia', in *Outer Limits: A Reader in Communication Across Cultures*, eds. J. Leigh and E. Loo (Melbourne: Language Australia, 2004), pp. 273-289; M. Meadows, *Voices in the Wilderness: Images of Aboriginal People in the Australian Media* (Westport: Greenwood, 2001); S. Mickler, *The Myth of Privilege: Aboriginal Status, Media Visions, Public Ideas* (South Fremantle: Fremantle Arts Centre Press, 1998); J. Saunders, 'Skin Deep: The News Media's Failure to Cover Maori Politics', in *Dangerous Democracy? News Media Politics in New Zealand*, ed. J. McGregor (Palmerston North: Dunmore, 1996), pp. 166-180; P. Spoonley and W. Hirsh, eds., *Between the Lines: Racism and the New Zealand Media* (Auckland: Heinemann Reed, 1990); I. Stuart, 'Tauiwi and Maori Media: The Indigenous View', *Pacific Journalism Review* 3, no. 2 (1996), accessed 25 February 2009, available from http://www.asiapac.org.fj/cafepacific/resources/aspac/Maori.html; M. Wall, 'Stereotypical Constructions of the Maori "Race" in the Media', *New Zealand Geographer* 53, no. 2 (1997), pp. 40-45.

Aboriginal people in a negative light and distorted representations of events and issues.[50] One focus of attention in studies of representations of Māori people in the New Zealand media has been the inadequacies of press reporting of protest actions, which cast those involved as dangerous radicals, represented Māori voices as a 'minority' instead of as 'equal Treaty partners' and failed to provide adequate information about the historical context of the protests or about the issues involved.[51] Much research into media representations of Indigenous people has focused on hard news, especially stories about Indigenous issues or crime reporting, rather than on soft news, such as human interest stories.[52] Rod Brookes has pointed out that soft news stories are often considered less 'important' than hard news stories and are thus not frequently studied despite forming a large part of the content of many newspapers.[53] As well, many studies of depictions of Indigenous people in the media concentrate on relatively recent events and issues. My focus on representations of famous Indigenous women throughout the second half of the twentieth century contributes to remedying these imbalances.

In the 1990s, scholars began to consider racialised and gendered representations together. A small number of studies in Australia have taken this approach to press representations. Cathy Greenfield and Peter Williams explored stereotypes evident in newspaper articles about Aboriginal women approaching the 1988 Bicentenary, Kathie Muir examined representations of Ngarrindjeri women in reporting on the Hindmarsh Island affair, and Jane Wilkinson investigated portrayals of 'ethnically and socio-economically diverse women leaders' in two Australian daily newspapers in 2001.[54] Mele-Ane Havea investigated the ways that Aboriginal women were represented in the media through an analysis of stereotypes evident in the portrayal of the women involved in the Hindmarsh Island affair and of athlete Cathy Freeman. Utilising the work of Moreton-Robinson, Havea argued that the 'dominant voice of the media is one of "white normality"'.[55] In the title of her article, she advocated further 'critical reflection' on the ways in which the media represents Aboriginal women, a challenge I

50   Banerjee and Osuri, pp. 270-271; Bullimore, p. 75; Meadows, 'A 10-Point Plan and a Treaty', pp. 56-58.
51   Barclay and Liu, p. 10; Saunders, p. 167; Stuart, 'Tauiwi and Maori Media'.
52   This focus on 'hard news' in many studies of media representations of Aboriginal people was also noted by Alan McKee and John Hartley. McKee and Hartley, p. 16.
53   R. Brookes, *Representing Sport* (London: Arnold, 2002), pp. 34-35.
54   C. Greenfield and P. Williams, 'Bicentennial Preliminaries: Aboriginal Women, Newspapers and the Politics of Culture', *Hecate* 13, no. 2 (1987-1988), pp. 76-106; K. Muir, 'Media Representations of Ngarrindjeri Women', *Journal of Australian Studies*, no. 48 (1996), pp. 73-82; J. Wilkinson, 'Do White Girls Rule? Exploring Broadsheet Representations of Australian Women Leaders', *Redress* 15, no. 1 (2006), pp. 16-21. The Hindmarsh Island affair was a controversy over plans to build a bridge from the mainland to the island. A group of Ngarrindjeri women raised objections because of secret women's business relating to the island, and the federal government acted to stop construction. After another group of women claimed the women's business was a hoax, a Royal Commission was called in 1995. It decided that the claims were fabricated.
55   M.-A. Havea, 'The Need for Critical Reflection on Media Representations of Aboriginal Women', *Journal of Australian Indigenous Issues* 5, no. 1 (2002), p. 12.

have taken up here. As these investigations of media representations have largely been contemporary studies located in cultural or media studies, a further aim has been to explore the intersections of race and gender in media representations historically.

I explore print media representations of prominent Māori and Aboriginal women in New Zealand and Australia during the second half of the twentieth century. I do not seek to contrast depictions of celebrated Indigenous women with some underlying reality, or to highlight the gaps and dissonances between the narratives told about these women and the stories the women themselves tell. Rather, I critically explore the representations themselves, and set them within a historical context that can help to explain how they arose and why they carried such continuing power. Representations of celebrated women are a part of a broader context, a historical moment, composed of public discourses, events, government policies and the actions and words of people, including those of the women themselves. There were always different voices, narratives and framings of these famous women and their lives, including those publicly articulated by the women themselves. Equally, there can be no one reading of any particular representation, because different audiences may understand the meanings of representations differently. In the same way that it is always possible to observe several competing representations at any particular time, any textual analysis must also be alert to the potential for texts to be read in a variety of different ways by different audiences. It is not possible in historical research to grasp fully the multiple ways audiences may read representations, but it remains important to analyse the texts themselves, as it is only by analysing common representations that their pervasiveness can be challenged.

This book foregrounds intersections of race, gender and nation in the shifting depictions of well-known Indigenous women in two white settler societies which are located in close proximity to each other, and whose histories have intertwined at many points in the past.[56] Discourses of national identity across the Tasman have historically displayed both deep resonances and sharp dissonances, particularly regarding issues of race relations. As I began to read and think about this subject, I had conversations with many people about trans-Tasman differences, conversations that often suggested an incommensurability in the colonial pasts of Australia and New Zealand. Yet as I sat in libraries reading a variety of Australian and New Zealand newspapers and magazines, I frequently felt there was a disjunction between such popular beliefs about these two colonial settings, which emphasised differences between them, and the tone

---

56 Note that although I focus upon representations of Māori and Aboriginal women in this book, it is important to emphasise that gender should not be understood as an attribute of women rather than men, nor race as an attribute of Indigenous peoples rather than those of white European descent. A study of representations of famous white men could as easily explore ideas about gender and race. Further, both race and gender are socially constructed categories, and should not be accorded a biological reality.

and content of many popular media stories about Indigenous people. I began to notice recurring themes in many depictions of prominent Aboriginal and Māori women, which were at once clearly comparable and yet often vitally different from each other. More than that, both Australia and New Zealand are settler societies which have had to acknowledge repressive colonial pasts in order to move forward into postcolonial futures, a process neither has reached the end of, although New Zealand is arguably further along it. As Katherine Ellinghaus has observed, 'hauntingly analogous stories of indigenous oppression' are evident in such settler societies.[57]

Widely held ideas about New Zealand's superiority in race relations contributed to a myth of racial harmony that formed a significant strand in conceptions of national identity. New Zealanders frequently expressed the view that race relations in their country were better than those in other settler societies. In 1956 an editorial in *Te Ao Hou: The New World*, though advocating greater understanding between Māori and Pākehā, began with the observation that visitors to New Zealand 'frequently express amazement at the excellent relationships they notice between Maori and European'.[58] In 1971 Keith Sinclair assumed the superiority of New Zealand race relations in a comparative article seeking to explain why this was so.[59] Commentators from other parts of the world have sometimes reinforced this relatively positive view of relations between Māori and Pākehā.[60] Such views sometimes seemed to rest both on an assertion that Māori were a superior type of native people than in other places and that Pākehā were a better group of settlers than were found elsewhere (notably Australia, where convicts formed a large part of the early population).

Although it cannot be disputed that Māori experienced much suffering and loss under colonisation, there were reasons for considering race relations in New Zealand to be better than was the case in Australia, as is outlined in Chapter One. As Barbara Brookes has suggested, while New Zealand 'shared with Australia a view of itself as a "white man's country"', Māori were 'included in the definition of whiteness' at least partially and strategically, and were thus not so thoroughly 'excluded from conceptions of the nation' as were Aboriginal people.[61] Nonetheless, significant broader similarities are evident across the

57   K. Ellinghaus, 'Indigenous Assimilation and Absorption in the United States and Australia', *Pacific Historical Review* 75, no. 4 (2006), p. 564.
58   'Race Relations', *Te Ao Hou: The New World* 4, no. 3 (1956), p. 1.
59   K. Sinclair, 'Why are Race Relations in New Zealand Better Than in South Africa, South Australia or South Dakota?', *New Zealand Journal of History* 5, no. 2 (1971), pp. 121-127.
60   For instance: R. Fisher, 'The Impact of European Settlement on the Indigenous Peoples of Australia, New Zealand, and British Columbia: Some Comparative Dimensions', *Canadian Ethnic Studies* 12, no. 1 (1980), pp. 1-14; R. McGregor, 'Looking Across the Tasman: New Zealand Exemplars in Australian Indigenous Affairs, 1920s-1970s', *History Compass* 5, no. 2 (2007), pp. 406-426.
61   B. Brookes, 'Gender, Work and Fears of a "Hybrid Race" in 1920s New Zealand', *Gender and History* 19, no. 3 (2007), p. 502. As Brookes notes, the idea that Māori and Britons had 'a common Aryan heritage' was 'vigorously promoted' in the late nineteenth century in New Zealand. Brookes, p. 502, citing T. Ballantyne,

Tasman with respect to Indigenous-settler relations. Māori and Aboriginal people both suffered the impacts of violence, disease and social change after the arrival of Europeans, and both experienced loss of language and culture under destructive assimilation policies. As Claudia Orange observed, New Zealand in several ways 'has been merely a variation in the pattern of colonial domination of indigenous races'.[62] Moreover, the second half of the twentieth century saw an intensification of Indigenous rights movements in both Australia and New Zealand, and a strengthening of a shared sense of Indigeneity among various groups around the world. In the emergence of what has sometimes been called the Fourth World, it is possible to observe the globalisation of Indigeneity.[63]

The Women: A Stellar Cast

Identifying a number of women who became well-known either nationally or internationally in these years, I explore their lives as renowned, sometimes controversial, public figures. I examine the telling, re-telling and representation of their lives and work in the print media, as well as considering the extent and nature of their own involvement in those processes. In concentrating upon portrayals of famous or celebrated women, I focus upon representations of those Māori and Aboriginal women who were most visible in the public arena during the period. Terms like 'famous', 'celebrated', 'prominent' and 'significant' are often used almost interchangeably in public discourse. I am concerned particularly with the phenomenon of fame. The women whose lives and media portrayals are the subject of this book were or are all prominent or well-known public figures. Not all of them could be described as celebrities, and they are not necessarily those most celebrated within their own communities. But all of them are women who became widely known in Australia and New Zealand, at least for a time, and whose lives and achievements have been publicly celebrated. It was these women who were most frequently featured in the media, and their lives were often lived in public view. Their words, actions and achievements were frequently observed and reported upon, and through that process invested with a variety of meanings. Some were accorded a place within the celebration of famous national figures or national heroes in Australia or New Zealand, their lives and efforts deemed to embody virtues or qualities seen as part of

Orientalism and Race: Aryanism in the British Empire (Houndmills: Palgrave, 2002), pp. 74-77.

62   C. Orange, *The Treaty of Waitangi* (Wellington: Allen and Unwin in association with Port Nicholson, 1987), p. 5.

63   Tim Rowse has used a similar term, 'global indigenism', to describe the 'modern and postcolonial tradition' by which Indigenous groups constitute themselves politically as Indigenous peoples, and through which governments and other organisations acknowledge indigeneity 'as a distinct form of human experience'. T. Rowse, 'Global Indigenism: A Genealogy of a Non-Racial Category', in *Rethinking the Racial Moment: Essays on the Colonial Encounter*, eds. A. Holland and B. Brookes (Newcastle upon Tyne: Cambridge Scholars, 2011), p. 229.

a particular national identity. Others occupied a more ambiguous position as celebrated Australians or New Zealanders, their lives and achievements working rather to unsettle widely accepted national narratives. For the audiences who read about their lives and achievements, all were potentially inspiring figures. Strong, creative, successful Indigenous women with a media presence, they were perhaps able to leave a mark even on those who encountered them only through the highly mediated instrument of the press.

Identifying celebrated Indigenous women was no simple task. A helpful strategy was to identify those included within the pantheon of people celebrated as great Australians and New Zealanders in the past and today. Different people celebrate different figures, for different purposes and at different times. I therefore investigated a range of texts from the present and the past in order to allow some of those differences to be explored, as well as to identify those Indigenous women who were most often publicly celebrated. The texts chosen included official and semi-official publications, dictionaries of biography, popular books of famous Australians and New Zealanders, articles in magazines and newspapers, websites, children's books and other texts. Although largely sharing a focus on well-known people associated with Australia or New Zealand, these texts do not form a coherent genre, varying both in aims and in intended audience. Reading them, I identified those Indigenous women most frequently included as famous or significant Australians and New Zealanders, what they were celebrated for, and in what types of publication they appeared. For practical reasons, and because many women who did not appear so frequently in these texts were also not often featured in the media, I have focused on those most frequently included. Thus, many women known and celebrated by their own communities or in specific contexts may not feature here, though their stories and their achievements undoubtedly deserve greater attention.

Two further issues of definition required addressing: who was Indigenous and who was female? Defining what constitutes Indigeneity and its specific forms is contested terrain, and not part of the project undertaken here. In a practical sense, however, it was necessary to determine a way of identifying Indigenous women among the larger group of celebrated women in Australia and New Zealand. Since I was exploring representations, it seemed expedient to include any women identified as Aboriginal, Torres Strait Islander or Māori by those compiling books, websites and other texts about celebrated Australians and New Zealanders, as well as those who self-identified as Indigenous. Immediately a question arose as to the potential inclusion of women who, while not Indigenous, were discriminated against in similar ways. Faith Bandler, whose father was from Ambrym in Vanuatu, was active in Aboriginal rights organisations and was sometimes identified as Aboriginal in the media. When she was appointed a Fellow to the Senate of the University of Sydney, the *Sydney Morning Herald* described her as an 'Aboriginal author', claiming that she was thought to be 'the first Aboriginal to hold such a position at the university'.[64] A tiny correction notice the next day announced that she was in fact 'of New Hebridean descent'.[65] Similarly, significant Pacific Island communities exist in New Zealand, and women from these communities may sometimes have had parallel experiences of the media to those of Māori and Aboriginal women. I have here focused upon Māori and Aboriginal women, while accepting that this distinction may in some cases be an arbitrary one.

Moreover, a person's claim to Indigeneity may become contested. Such was the case for Roberta Sykes, who was active in the movement for Aboriginal rights and often described as Aboriginal. After the publication of her three-volume autobiography, Sykes was criticised by several Aboriginal women for adopting an Aboriginal identity and totem not her own, and for failing to challenge the frequent media assumption that she was Aboriginal.[66] Lacking much knowledge about her family connections, Sykes often described herself as 'Black', thus 'creat[ing] an ambiguous identity'.[67] Was I to make a determination as to whether women such as Sykes should be considered Indigenous, and therefore be included here? This was both impossible and inappropriate for me, a Pākehā New Zealander, and I have therefore left the position of Sykes as ambivalent as she herself does, through including media reports and stories about her which identified her as Aboriginal. Nor was the category of women an uncomplicated one. Simple biological binaries between men and women are not always workable. Georgina Beyer was born a man, underwent a sex change operation and became New Zealand's first transsexual MP. Was I to include her? Again, I did so through including articles about her as and where appropriate to my discussion of media coverage of Māori women in politics.

Who, then, were the Māori and Aboriginal women most frequently included in books, articles, online lists and other texts about well-known Australians and New Zealanders? In Australia, tennis player Evonne Goolagong appeared most frequently, followed by poet and activist Oodgeroo Noonuccal (formerly Kath Walker), athlete Cathy Freeman, magistrate Pat O'Shane, reformer and public servant Lowitja O'Donoghue and Trukanini. In New Zealand, opera singer Dame Kiri Te Kanawa was most frequently featured, followed by Te Puea Hērangi and fellow Māori leader Dame Whina Cooper, tour guides Rangitīaria Dennan and Mākereti (Maggie Papakura) and politician Iriaka Rātana. (See Tables 1 and 2 below). A large number of other women also appeared in a small number

---

64 'University Post For Aboriginal Author', *Sydney Morning Herald*, 15 November 1978, p. 8.
65 'Correction', *Sydney Morning Herald*, 16 November 1978, p. 2.
66 K. Meade, 'Writer's Snake Claim Speared', *Australian*, 21 October 1998, p. 5; P. O'Shane, 'Sin of Omission', *Australian*, 7 November 1998, p. 29.
67 S. Kurtzer, 'Is She or Isn't She? Roberta Sykes and "Authentic" Aboriginality', *Overland*, no. 171 (2003), p. 50; R. Sykes, 'In the Public Interest?', *Australian*, 24 October 1998, p. 27.

of texts.[68] Although the differences between the two countries in terms of the achievements of celebrated Indigenous women were less striking across the entire list of women identified by this process, the lists of those most frequently mentioned display a marked disparity between Australia and New Zealand. In New Zealand, three of the six women are known for their leadership (within a tribal setting or within government circles) and three for their achievements in arenas in which perceived feminine attributes such as grace and beauty were valued (the performing arts and tour guiding in the thermal areas of New Zealand). In Australia, two of the six women are celebrated for their sporting achievements, three for their path-breaking achievements in various areas and their advocacy for Aboriginal peoples (in different leadership contexts from those reflected in the New Zealand list), and one is remembered as a tragic figure.

Table 1: Aboriginal Women Featured in 63 Texts about Famous Australians

Name	Times included in texts
Cawley, Evonne (nee Goolagong)	18
Noonuccal, Oodgeroo (also known as Kath Walker)	16
Freeman, Catherine (Cathy)	14
O'Shane, Patricia (Pat)	12
O'Donoghue, Lowitja (Lois)	10
Trukanini (Truganini, Trucanini, Trugernanner)	10

Table 2: Māori Women Featured in 45 Texts about Famous New Zealanders

Name	Times included in texts
Te Kanawa, Dame Kiri	19
Hērangi, Te Kirihaehae Te Puea (Princess Te Puea)	16
Cooper, Dame Whina	11
Dennan, Rangitīaria (also known as Guide Rangi)	9
Papakura, Mākereti (also known as Guide Maggie)	8
Rātana, Iriaka	7

---

68 For a full list and further discussion, see K. Fox, 'Representing Difference: Celebrated Māori and Aboriginal Women and the Print Media, 1950-2000' (PhD thesis, The Australian National University, 2009).

Analytical Framework and Outline

Several strategic decisions were necessary in the research and writing of this book. First, I focus on representations of Indigenous women. I seek to contribute to an understanding of the ways in which gender, race and nation have intersected in media representations, rather than privileging race or gender as a category of analysis. It is, however, important to examine whether or not framings of famous Indigenous women were replicated in representations of Indigenous men or non-Indigenous women, particularly those famous for similar achievements. I therefore selectively compare depictions of famous Indigenous women with those of famous Indigenous men and those of famous non-Indigenous women. Readers may notice an absence of discussion of other pertinent categories of analysis, especially class and religion. Practical considerations restricted such discussion. However, although I focus upon the intersections of race, gender and nation in the media representations I discuss, the book is framed with an awareness of other such categories. Ideas about class were often an important element in narratives about famous Indigenous women, such as those depicting their rise to fame as a rags-to-riches tale of success. Religion presents an interesting case, for while important in the lives of some of the women discussed, it was rarely explicitly treated in media portrayals. Hence, though Whina Cooper's Catholicism was a central aspect of her life, and may have played some role in shaping public perceptions of her, it seemed to be largely invisible in press depictions, and hence does not figure in my discussion.

Second, I concentrate on the period between 1950 and 2000. These years witnessed major political and social change in both Australia and New Zealand, enabling the exploration of shifts in representations during a period of great transformation. The embrace of assimilation in its varied forms, its gradual displacement, and the social and political impacts of Indigenous rights and second wave feminist movements on both sides of the Tasman, in particular, both inform and are illuminated by this study of representations. Moreover, many more Māori and Aboriginal women became widely known and celebrated in these years than previously.

I have occasionally consulted oral history interviews conducted by others and published or deposited in libraries and archives. I have not myself carried out interviews, for several reasons which became apparent to me during the research process. A number of practical concerns suggested themselves early on, the most significant being that the women whose media experiences I discuss were based in far-flung parts of Australia, New Zealand and the rest of the world, and that while some were still in the midst of their careers, others had retired or died. Reaching all of them would not be possible, and any interviewing would of necessity be selective. More importantly, these women had throughout their careers been subjected to the glare of publicity and the pressure of being in constant demand to answer questions, many about issues of race and gender. Rosalie Kunoth-Monks, a long-time advocate for Aboriginal people, told her story to Helen Chryssides for *Local Heroes*, published in 1993. Asked to talk about *Jedda*, the 1955 film which made her famous, she replied with a sigh: 'Jedda? Surely everyone knows that story by now'.[69] What would this book gain, I wondered, that would justify my being one more person harassing these women with questions on the same issues, following a well-worn journalistic path? I seek to explore depictions of famous Indigenous women in the public forum of the press, and I have therefore chosen to contrast those depictions with the ways in which the women publicly represented themselves, articulated their own stories and challenged narratives produced in the media. In order to discuss these women's own articulations of themselves and their work whilst allowing them the privacy that the media rarely do, I chose to discuss only their publicly stated opinions and memories. Such a decision also meant I would not privilege private interviews in which I might seek a reality behind the media stories, which is itself a common framing of celebrity stories in the media.

Finally, I focus on the print media, both for its continuing significance throughout the period and for practical reasons of manageability. Similar research could and should be carried out for other forms of media, such as radio, television and film, the aural and visual dimensions of which might add intriguing elements to representations. Is television, for instance, with its very immediate, ephemeral nature, more susceptible to producing stereotypical representations? What difference does the combination of visual and aural elements make? Or the aural nature of radio? More research is badly needed. I explore a variety of genres in the print media, analysing and contrasting representations of celebrated Indigenous women in these different genres, and the resulting narratives of their lives. One such genre is newspapers, focusing on major dailies, and including material from smaller regional newspapers where practical, as these may reveal variations in narratives along local and national lines. Another is magazines, a category within which important genre differences exist. Narratives and representations can vary greatly between current affairs magazines and women's magazines, for example. Women's magazines also display a variety of approaches in their content. While the *Australian Women's Weekly* and *New Zealand Woman's Weekly* have historically promoted the virtues of domesticity and homemaking, feminist magazines and younger women's magazines may take very different approaches. Where relevant, special interest magazines (such as music- or sport-focused periodicals) were also included. Particularly interesting are the genre differences between magazines produced for Indigenous people by government departments and those produced by Indigenous organisations, although work by

---

69   H. Chryssides, *Local Heroes* (North Blackburn: Collins Dove, 1993), p. 175.

Indigenous authors did sometimes appear in the former. Representations in earlier magazines such as *Dawn* and *Te Ao Hou* might differ greatly from coverage in newer Indigenous-controlled publications such as *Deadly Vibe* and *Mana*. Along with analysing stories which appeared in the print media, I have also drawn upon biography, both popular and academic, and autobiography, both collaborative and single-authored, each of which brings its own considerations of voice. Finally, published interviews, both full transcripts and edited texts, provide a genre in which the subject speaks more freely, although also raising issues of memory and recall. The contributions of the women themselves in fashioning their own representations complicates understandings of representations in the media and acknowledges their own agency in constructing images of themselves.

In this book I begin the historical investigation of the multiple ways in which well-known Māori and Aboriginal women were represented, remembered and re-imagined in the period between 1950 and 2000 as they strode a national, or a world, stage. In Chapter One, I provide a brief discussion of the historical contexts in which the representations explored in the rest of the book were created. I focus upon shifts in government policies relating to Māori and Aboriginal peoples' lives, the continuing and changing nature of Māori and Aboriginal protest activity (particularly the intensification of such activity on both sides of the Tasman from the late 1960s) and the ebb and flow of the feminist movement in Australia and New Zealand. As well, I briefly introduce the media landscape in both countries, commenting upon the shifts in media industries which took place during the period.

Chapters Two to Six focus on particular well-known women, analysing the ways in which their stories were told and re-told in the press, and the complex ways in which the women themselves were depicted. The second chapter focuses upon representations of women who became known for their sporting achievements, especially Evonne Goolagong, and the third upon portrayals of women who became prominent in the performing arts, notably Dame Kiri Te Kanawa. Chapter Four signals a shift away from forms of fame in which political issues may be more muted and toward those in which political issues were often inherent. It focuses upon women who became known for their literary or film-making endeavour, especially Kath Walker (later known as Oodgeroo Noonuccal). Chapter Five takes that emphasis further, examining representations of women who were well-known for their efforts in achieving social and political change, particularly Dame Whina Cooper. Finally, Chapter Six investigates representations of Indigenous women who entered the political system as Members of Parliament, focusing upon Māori women in New Zealand.

All chapters consider the ways in which these well-known women publicly constructed and narrated their own stories, as well as the ways in which others imagined them in the media. Throughout, the multivalent nature of the concept of representation is an important theme. As well as being portrayed in the media, these women represented themselves through their own articulations of their lives and work, chose to or were expected to act as advocates for all Māori or Aboriginal people, and frequently engaged in representational practices through the very nature of their work. Each of these aspects of representation forms part of my discussion of 'representing' well-known Indigenous women. In the conclusion, I offer some reflections on the common themes evident in representations of Māori and Aboriginal women in the print media in the second half of the twentieth century, on the sometimes glaring differences between the experiences and representations of Māori women and those of Aboriginal women, and on wider issues about the ways in which race and gender were imagined in constructions of national identity on either side of the Tasman. It is my hope that exploring common depictions of well-known Indigenous women in a comparative way might reveal not only the complex and multiple ways in which concepts of race, gender and nation were understood during these years of transformation, but also many of the ongoing ambiguities, tensions and uncertainties that have been endemic in the national imaginings of settler societies.

Chapter One

In Australia and New Zealand in the second half of the twentieth century, a great deal of social, cultural and political change took place. This is especially true in relation to Indigenous rights and the status of women. While there had been important Indigenous protest movements and groups formed seeking civil or land rights in the past, protest accelerated from the 1960s and entered the mainstream. Around the same time, a second wave of feminist activism from the 1970s, following the first wave in the late nineteenth and early twentieth centuries, impacted upon the status of women. A number of Indigenous women became nationally known in both countries for their activist efforts or political work during this period, as well as for their efforts and achievements in other fields. Tennis star Evonne Goolagong won her first Wimbledon tournament in 1971, the same year Kiri Te Kanawa made her tremendously successful debut in a major operatic role on the Covent Garden stage. Both women are among the best-known Indigenous women in their respective countries, and were among the first to become nationally and internationally celebrated.

The second wave of feminism, the so-called Māori renaissance and the strong Aboriginal civil and land rights movements of the period form the context in which many famous Indigenous women emerged, and the background against which their experiences and achievements were represented in the media. Some prominent women were involved particularly in one movement, others' concerns spanned more than one, and still others wished to focus upon their own field of activity without being politically active. In this chapter I explore the changing policies and approaches to race relations and Indigenous affairs in Australia and New Zealand, the impacts and aims of Māori and Aboriginal protest movements and the rise of the second wave feminist movement. I also discuss the shifts which occurred in the media industry in Australia and New Zealand during the twentieth century, changes shaping the immediate context in which representations of Indigenous women were produced. Readers familiar with this historical background, or eager to begin exploring famous Indigenous women's media experiences, may like to skip ahead to Chapter Two.

Assimilation, Integration, Self-Determination

Many parallels can be traced in past government policies relating to Indigenous peoples in Australia and New Zealand, as well as significant differences. In the nineteenth century, many observers on both sides of the Tasman believed Aboriginal and Māori people to be dying races, their declining population numbers assumed to signal the unavoidable fate of Indigenous peoples after contact with Europeans.[1] In this discourse of extinction, the figure of Trukanini became a central symbol in Australia, as discussed in the Introduction.[2] As I noted there, continuing constructions of Trukanini as representing the demise of her people undercut the claims of the contemporary Tasmanian Aboriginal community for recognition and land rights. Indeed, nineteenth-century beliefs about the inevitability of Indigenous peoples' extinction potentially assuaged settlers' guilt over the appropriation of Indigenous land, the introduction of infectious diseases and the many other ills brought by European settlement. As Anthony Moran observed in the Australian case, questions about the place of Aboriginal people in a white Australian nation could be disregarded or brushed over while it was believed that Aboriginal people would become extinct.[3] Common depictions of Aboriginal people shifted from emphasising their resistance to European settlement by describing them as savage or violent, to stressing the inevitability of their passing. Such notes of sorrow and 'nostalgia' appeared 'in direct proportion to the speed with which [Aboriginal people] were believed to be dying out'.[4] If Trukanini had a place in national imaginings in Australia, as we have seen, it was often as the tragic relic of a lost and primitive people.

Despite similarities in racial thinking that suggested both Māori and Aboriginal peoples would become extinct, policies from the time of settlement differed in important ways in New Zealand from those in the Australian colonies. Post-hoc adoption of the legal principle of *terra nullius* meant that the continent that was to become the Commonwealth of Australia was deemed empty land, able to be settled without consideration of Aboriginal occupation.[5] Settlement was accompanied by significant violence, continuing longest in the more remote areas

---

1   R. Lange, *May the People Live: A History of Māori Health Development 1900-1920* (Auckland: Auckland University Press, 1999), p. 53; R. McGregor, *Imagined Destinies: Aboriginal Australians and the Doomed Race Theory, 1880-1939* (Carlton South: Melbourne University Press, 1997), p. ix; J. Stenhouse, '"A Disappearing Race Before We Came Here": Doctor Alfred Kingcome Newman, the Dying Maori, and Victorian Scientific Racism', *New Zealand Journal of History* 30, no. 2 (1996), pp. 135-136. Note, however, that these parallel discourses about Indigenous extinction in Australia and New Zealand differed in a number of ways. R. McGregor, 'Degrees of Fatalism: Discourses on Racial Extinction in Australia and New Zealand', in *Collisions of Cultures and Identities: Settlers and Indigenous Peoples*, ed. P. Grimshaw and R. McGregor (Melbourne: Department of History, University of Melbourne, 2007), pp. 245-261.
2   In this respect, the figure of Trukanini sometimes symbolised the culpability of European settlers in the annihilation of Aboriginal peoples. Lyndall Ryan and Andrys Onsman have both observed such representations of Trukanini as a 'symbol' of the 'extermination' or 'attempted genocide' of Aboriginal peoples. A. Onsman, 'Truganini's Funeral', *Island*, no. 96 (2004), p. 45; L. Ryan, 'The Struggle for Trukanini 1830-1997', *Tasmanian Historical Research Association Papers and Proceedings* 44, no. 3 (1997), p. 165.
3   A. Moran, 'White Australia, Settler Nationalism and Aboriginal Assimilation', *Australian Journal of Politics and History* 51, no. 2 (2005), p. 172.
4   R. Waterhouse, 'Australian Legends', *Australian Historical Studies* 31, no. 115 (2000), p. 209.
5   The doctrine of *terra nullius* did not apply in Australia before 1889. B. Buchan, 'Traffick of Empire: Trade, Treaty and *Terra Nullius* in Australia and North America, 1750–1800', *History Compass* 5, no. 2 (2007), p. 387.

of Queensland and the Northern Territory.[6] While humanitarian concerns for the welfare of Aboriginal people prompted the adoption of policies of protection, such policies led to the corralling of Aboriginal people on missions and reserves.

In New Zealand too, Māori rights were often trampled in the face of settler hunger for land. Unlike in Australia, however, a treaty was signed with Māori, the Treaty of Waitangi in 1840. Exactly what the Treaty offered Māori remains disputed, largely due to differences between the English text and the Māori text, the latter being the one signed by the majority of the chiefs who chose to sign.[7] The most important question revolves around the issue of sovereignty. According to the English text, sovereignty was ceded to Queen Victoria, while according to the Māori text, the lesser power of 'kāwanatanga' (governance) was ceded. The Māori text also promised Māori the continued exercise of chieftainship ('te tino rangatiratanga') and the continued possession and enjoyment of resources.[8] Yet as the settler population came to outnumber the Māori population, the Treaty proved a small obstacle indeed to the rapid alienation of Māori land, which was accomplished partly through institutions of government such as the Native Land Court. Thus, although Māori did not suffer violence and legal restrictions to the extent that Aboriginal people did, and which continued into the second half of the twentieth century, a legacy of dispossession and disadvantage was created in both Australia and New Zealand by the turn of the century.

Far from being dying races, it became evident in the first decades of the twentieth century that Māori and Aboriginal populations were increasing. In Australia, concern grew in the settler society about the existence of a mixed-descent population. Schemes of biological absorption were sometimes promoted as a solution, particularly in the 1930s in Western Australia and the Northern Territory, the intention being that Aboriginal blood would be diluted until the policy of a White Australia became a reality.[9] In 1937, a national conference of administrators resolved that the 'destiny' of people of mixed descent was 'their ultimate absorption by the people of the Commonwealth', a statement that has sometimes been read as approving biological absorption.[10] Such policy

---

6   A. McGrath, 'A National Story', in *Contested Ground: Australian Aborigines Under the British Crown*, ed. A. McGrath (St Leonards: Allen and Unwin, 1995), p. 18.

7   P. Mein Smith, *A Concise History of New Zealand* (New York: Cambridge University Press, 2005), pp. 47-49.

8   Ibid., pp. 50-51; C. Orange, *The Treaty of Waitangi* (Wellington: Allen and Unwin in association with Port Nicholson, 1987), pp. 40-42.

9   R. McGregor, '"Breed Out the Colour": Or the Importance of Being White', *Australian Historical Studies* 33, no. 120 (2002), pp. 287-290. On ideas of biological absorption, see also: W. Anderson, *The Cultivation of Whiteness: Science, Health and Racial Destiny in Australia*, 2nd ed. (Carlton: Melbourne University Press, 2005), especially Chapter 8.

10   R. Broome, *Aboriginal Australians: Black Responses to White Dominance, 1788-2001*, 3rd ed. (Crows Nest: Allen and Unwin, 2002), p. 165; S. Macintyre, *A Concise History of Australia*, 2nd ed. (Port Melbourne: Cambridge University Press, 2004), p. 188.

decisions were never straightforward, however, and opposing voices suggested instead cultural absorption, or even the retention of culture within a framework of equality.[11]

Intermarriage was both more common and more accepted in New Zealand, and such concerns about the growth of a mixed race population were not evident. The first half of the twentieth century saw the establishment of programmes to improve Māori health and housing, as well as land development schemes for Māori. During the 1920s, while Gordon Coates held responsibility for Native Affairs, efforts were made to support Māori arts and crafts, and several land claims were settled.[12] Māori were to have, according to the Labour Party from the 1930s, 'equality with racial individuality'.[13] Similarly, New Zealand's Governor-General Lord Bledisloe referred in 1934 to New Zealand having 'two peoples' but 'one nation'. While reality did not entirely reflect this utopian vision, Michael King has argued that this 'myth' did provide some safeguard against 'the more extreme manifestations of prejudice' by supplying 'a moral imperative to which at least lip-service was paid'.[14] During these years, Te Puea Hērangi was one of Māoridom's most significant figures, and her influence reached into government circles. She was a strong leader who played a central role in initiating economic, political and cultural revival, particularly for the people of the Waikato. While Trukanini's name was often associated with being last, Te Puea's was connected with the very different concept of renewal.

After World War Two, important shifts began to occur in approaches to Indigenous affairs in both the Australian states and New Zealand. As the horrors of the Nazi regime became clear, racial science ideas fell into disfavour, and efforts were initiated internationally to end racial discrimination. Biological, as opposed to cultural, absorption was no longer seriously promoted. In both Australia and New Zealand, policymaking was potentially shaped by an awareness of international scrutiny in relation to matters of racial discrimination and a concern to differentiate policies from those of the apartheid regime in South Africa. The mid-twentieth century also saw rapid urbanisation of the Māori population and of some sections of the Aboriginal population, leading to shifts in government policies on both sides of the Tasman. In both countries, forms of assimilatory policy were adopted, aiming to absorb Māori and Aboriginal people into Pākehā or white Australian ways of life. Assimilation policies adopted in the 1950s in Australia offered Aboriginal people equal standards of living, rights and opportunities

---

11   See for instance the discussion in: C. Thomas, 'From "Australian Aborigines" to "White Australians"', *Australian Aboriginal Studies*, no. 1 (2001), pp. 22-23.
12   M. King, 'Between Two Worlds', in *The Oxford History of New Zealand*, ed. W. H. Oliver (Wellington: Oxford University Press, 1981), p. 291.
13   C. Orange, 'An Exercise in Maori Autonomy: The Rise and Demise of the Maori War Effort Organisation', *New Zealand Journal of History* 21, no. 1 (1987), p. 157.
14   King, p. 300.

to those of white Australians.[15] Such equality, however, was premised on the destruction of Aboriginal culture. Paul Hasluck, a major architect of Australian assimilation policy, expected that all that would be left of Aboriginal cultures would be, in Russell McGregor's evocative phrase, 'fragments of folklore'.[16] To a large extent the focus was placed on those of mixed descent, as they were considered most capable of being taught white ways of living. In a practical sense, assimilation in Australia meant the continued removal of children from parents and families, the indenture of girls as domestic servants, inspections and surveillance of private lives, and the tying of benefits and civil rights to whether or not Aboriginal people were considered to be living in a European way. Many of the rights of citizenship were only granted to those who became exempted from protection legislation, a humiliating exercise that many refused to undergo.

Assimilation was always a contested term, and debates over its meaning and practice have continued among scholars today. Assimilation could mean simply equality of Aboriginal people with white Australians, or it could mean the disappearance of Aboriginal culture.[17] Russell McGregor has demonstrated that leading advocates of assimilation in Australia had quite different visions of what the policy might mean, and of what level of destruction of culture it implied.[18] Moreover, while many scholars and commentators in Australia have considered assimilation to refer to a particular policy in existence between the 1930s and the 1970s, it can also be understood as a destructive approach which has continued throughout the years since 1788.[19]

As Anna Haebich has suggested, assimilation in Australia was and is 'a powerful act of national imagining'.[20] Such a vision was tied to a view of the nation as constituted in a White Australia. If Aboriginal people had not cooperated in disappearing physically, they were expected to disappear culturally, into a culturally homogenous nation, thus denying the possibility of any contestation over 'who owns, and whose identity is fused with, the land'.[21] A vision of the nation which celebrated cultural homogeneity in this way suggests important implications for the place that high-achieving and famous Aboriginal people might be expected to hold in the nation, and for the ways in which they might be represented in popular culture such as print media. In particular, Haebich has demonstrated that a tendency to uphold Aboriginal people who were successful

---

15 A. Haebich, 'Imagining Assimilation', *Australian Historical Studies* 33, no. 118 (2002), p. 62.

16 R. McGregor, 'Assimilationists Contest Assimilation: T. G. H. Strehlow and A. P. Elkin on Aboriginal Policy', *JAS, Australia's Public Intellectual Forum*, no. 75 (2002), p. 46.

17 R. Kerin, 'Charles Duguid and Aboriginal Assimilation in Adelaide, 1950-1960: The Nebulous "Assimilation" Goal', *History Australia* 2, no. 3 (2005), pp. 85.1-85.2.

18 McGregor, 'Assimilationists Contest Assimilation', pp. 43-50.

19 T. Rowse, 'Introduction: Contesting Assimilation', in *Contesting Assimilation*, ed. T. Rowse (Perth: API Network, 2005), pp. 1-2.

20 Haebich, p. 62.

21 Moran, pp. 169-170.

in white terms as exemplars of assimilation existed in some sectors of official discourse in the mid-twentieth century, as occurred in the case of artist Albert Namatjira.[22] This trope of representation is further pursued in the following chapters. As well as celebrating successful Aboriginal people as assimilated into white Australian life, such a vision of the nation might contribute to the representation of cultural difference as mere exotica, or to the repression of it, in depictions of these figures. These possibilities too are explored in the case studies which follow.

Assimilatory policies in New Zealand were less repressive and intrusive than those in Australia, but still involved significant destruction of culture. Māori people held positions in government and the bureaucracy, and Māori were not subject to the restrictive laws and denial of citizenship rights that many Aboriginal people continued to experience well into the 1960s and even the 1970s. As with Aboriginal people in Australia, however, Māori in New Zealand were expected to adopt a Pākehā way of life, a pressure which led to much hurt and loss. Women and girls were perceived to have an important role in assimilation, or integration, through their roles as mothers and homemakers, as they were in Australia.[23] In 1960, the Hunn report recommended the adoption of a policy of integration in place of assimilation, and outlined this policy vision. Integration was to 'combine' Māori and Pākehā 'elements', thus creating 'one nation wherein Maori culture remains distinct'.[24] The way of life being advocated, the report argued, was not a Pākehā one, but a 'modern' one which other peoples also lived.[25]

In 1962, J. M. Booth and J. K. Hunn made clear in a small pamphlet that integration referred both to 'the physical sense of the mingling of the two populations' and the 'mental and cultural senses'. Referring to 'the dictionary definition' of the verb 'to integrate' as being 'to make whole', they explained that integration denoted 'the making of a whole new culture by the combination and adaptation of the two pre-existing cultures'. Moreover, it was stressed that the policy did not 'imply social uniformity', but instead 'a unification arrived at personally by each individual of a range of cultural elements derived from both Polynesian

---

22 A. Haebich, *Spinning the Dream: Assimilation in Australia 1950-1970* (North Fremantle: Fremantle, 2008), pp. 152, 355.
23 See: F. Bartlett, 'Clean White Girls: Assimilation and Women's Work', *Hecate* 25, no. 1 (1999), p. 11; B. Brookes, '"Assimilation" and "Integration": The Māori Women's Welfare League in the 1950s', *Turnbull Library Record* 36 (2003), pp. 11, 14-15; H. Goodall, '"Assimilation Begins in the Home": The State and Aboriginal Women's Work as Mothers in New South Wales, 1900s to 1960s', *Labour History*, no. 69 (1995), pp. 75-101; A. Haebich, 'Bridging the Gap: Assimilation and Aboriginal Women and Their Households', *Tasmanian Historical Studies* 9 (2004), pp. 4-20; K. Jenkins and K. M. Matthews, 'Knowing Their Place: The Political Socialisation of Maori Women in New Zealand Through Schooling Policy and Practice, 1867-1969', *Women's History Review* 7, no. 1 (1998), pp. 85-105.
24 J. K. Hunn, *Report on Department of Maori Affairs: With Statistical Supplement* (Wellington: R. E. Owen, 1961), p. 15.
25 Ibid., p. 16.

and European cultures'.[26] Australians, both Aboriginal and non-Aboriginal, who supported the drive for equal rights and opportunities but opposed the destruction of Aboriginal culture had sometimes advocated a similar policy of integration in Australia.[27] However, integration too often meant in practical terms an expectation that Māori adapt to Pākehā ways of life, rather than the other way around. If white New Zealanders imagined their nation as constituted by two distinct peoples, the Māori element was expected to contribute only non-threatening cultural performances and exotic emblems.

Significant change in Indigenous affairs occurred in both Australia and New Zealand from the 1960s. Under the impact of growing protest from Aboriginal and Māori peoples, shifting public opinion and international pressures, both countries changed direction, adopting policies of limited self-determination. In New Zealand, important changes occurred in the direction and operation of the Department of Māori Affairs in the late 1970s and early 1980s, with a shift towards a philosophy of community development.[28] Discrimination was legislated against in the 1971 *Race Relations Act*, and an office of Race Relations Conciliator was established. During this period, Whetū Tirikātene-Sullivan became the second Māori woman to be elected a Member of Parliament (MP), following Iriaka Rātana, who was first elected in 1949. Tirikātene-Sullivan became the first Māori woman appointed a Cabinet Minister when Labour took power in 1972, holding the portfolios of Tourism and the Environment, as well as being Associate Minister of Social Welfare. In the House Tirikātene-Sullivan took strong stands on both Māori issues and women's issues, including introducing a Māori Language Bill to promote the use and teaching of te reo Māori, the Māori language, and arguing for women's right to safe and legal abortion during the 1977 debate on the Contraception, Sterilisation and Abortion Bill. In these years too, the Waitangi Tribunal was established to consider Treaty grievances, in 1975, although it only became properly effective after it was given retrospective power in 1985 to consider grievances dating to 1840. Numerous claims have since gone before the tribunal, with several significant settlements resulting. Issues of cultural loss also began to be addressed, as for example in the setting up of kohanga reo centres (language nests) which allow children to spend their early years in a total immersion Māori language environment.

---

26   J. M. Booth and J. K. Hunn, *Integration of Maori and Pakeha* (Wellington: Department of Māori Affairs, 1962).

27   It is important to note that while many have seen little difference between assimilation and integration, activists in the middle years of the twentieth century often did see this difference, in that integration might deliver civil rights without taking culture away. J. Chesterman, *Civil Rights: How Indigenous Australians Won Formal Equality* (St Lucia: University of Queensland Press, 2005), p. 22.

28   On this shift, see: A. Fleras, 'From Social Welfare to Community Development: Maori Policy and the Department of Maori Affairs in New Zealand', *Community Development Journal* 19, no. 1 (1984), pp. 32-39.

In Australia, despite the reluctance of some states (particularly Queensland), repressive policies such as those restricting Aboriginal people's movements were gradually removed. In 1975, the Whitlam government passed a *Racial Discrimination Act*. Larger numbers of Aboriginal people became involved in the bureaucracy, and Aboriginal people achieved greater input into policy development. The establishment of the Aboriginal and Torres Strait Islander Commission (ATSIC), although it was later dismantled, represented a significant step towards self-determination. The founding chairperson of ATSIC was Lowitja O'Donoghue, who had spent many years working in Aboriginal affairs both from within the government and the bureaucracy and from outside these structures, including having served terms as chairperson of the National Aboriginal Conference and, after its abolition, the Aboriginal Development Commission. In the early 1990s, O'Donoghue was considered by some to be a possible choice as Governor-General. Other shifts were occurring as well during the second half of the twentieth century. The Mabo case in the High Court in 1992 overturned the principle of *terra nullius*, recognising the existence of native title and opening the possibility of land claims where native title had not been extinguished. Although this possibility was severely curtailed by legislation brought in by the Howard government in 1998, the recognition of native title remained a significant step.

Indigenous Activism in Australia and New Zealand

Since settlement by Europeans in Australia and New Zealand, Aboriginal and Māori people have continually protested the injustices of colonisation. Māori resisted colonial pressures in many ways, both individually and collectively. One response was the establishment of the Kīngitanga, or Māori King movement. The Kīngitanga arose in the 1850s at the initiative of Tāmihana Te Rauparaha and Mātene Te Whiwhi. Tāmihana Te Rauparaha had travelled to England and met Queen Victoria, returning convinced of the need to create a Māori monarchy which could unify disparate tribes and thus assist Māori in resisting the pressures of colonisation.[29] At the turn of the twenty-first century, the Kīngitanga remained an effective and widely respected force in Māoridom and in wider New Zealand society. Crowned in 1966 and made a dame in 1970, Te Arikinui Te Ātairangikaahu was the sixth Māori monarch and the first woman to hold the Māori throne. She

---

29 M. King, *The Penguin History of New Zealand* (North Shore: Penguin, 2003), p. 212; S. Oliver, 'Te Rauparaha, Tamihana ?-1876', *Dictionary of New Zealand Biography*, updated 22 June 2007, accessed 14 March 2008, available from http://www.dnzb.govt.nz/dnzb/default.asp?Find_Quick.asp?PersonEssay=1T75; W. H. Oliver, 'Te Whiwhi, Henare Matene ?-1881', *Dictionary of New Zealand Biography*, updated 22 June 2007, accessed 14 March 2008, available from http://www.dnzb.govt.nz/dnzb/default.asp?Find_Quick. asp?PersonEssay=1T89.

became a well-respected figure both nationally and internationally, receiving many foreign dignitaries and members of the British royal family on their visits to New Zealand. In the nineteenth century, however, the establishment of the Kīngitanga was one of the causes of conflict leading to the wars fought in the North Island in the mid-nineteenth century, as was conflict over land sales.[30]

Some resistance movements were religious in character, such as the Pai Mārire or Hauhau movement that emerged in the mid-nineteenth century. Begun by Te Ua Haumēne, who in 1862 had a vision in which the Archangel Gabriel instructed him to 'cast off the yoke of the Pakeha', the movement's 'guiding principle' was the 'goodness and peace' of its name (pai mārire).[31] Although Te Ua Haumēne intended the movement to be peaceful, some of his adherents did not share this intention, leading to further warfare between Māori and British troops.[32] One of the best-known moments of peaceful resistance occurred at Parihaka, where non-violent actions such as disrupting land surveying were used, until imperial troops and volunteers arrived in late 1881, demolishing the village and arresting or scattering the inhabitants.[33] During World War One Te Puea also adopted peaceful means of resistance in her leadership of the anti-conscription movement in the Waikato.

In Australia, Indigenous resistance to European settlement was also widespread, although different in nature to that in New Zealand. In Tasmania, Tarenorerer (known to sealers as Walyer) led a band of warriors in attacks against Europeans and their livestock between 1828 and 1830.[34] Writing in 1870, James Bonwick detailed the activities of a woman he called Walloa, who was presumably the same person. He described this woman, who 'rose, like a Joan of Arc ... to deliver her people', as 'this tigress of the north' and 'the dark Semiramis'.[35] Tarenorerer is now remembered and celebrated for her bravery in resisting the invasion of her people's lands.

As well as armed resistance, Aboriginal people wrote letters and signed petitions seeking an end to injustices. In the early twentieth century, organisations began to form demanding Aboriginal rights and improvements in the welfare of

---

30   Governor George Grey considered the Kīngitanga a threat to British control which had to be suppressed. Historians have debated the precise causes of the fighting, as is reflected in the various names given to the wars, as the Land Wars, the Māori Wars, or the more neutral New Zealand Wars.
31   L. Head, 'Te Ua Haumene ?-1866', *Dictionary of New Zealand Biography*, updated 22 June 2007, accessed 14 March 2008, available from http://www.dnzb.govt.nz/dnzb/default.asp?Find_Quick. asp?PersonEssay=1T79.
32   King, *The Penguin History of New Zealand*, p. 217.
33   Ibid., pp. 220-221.
34   V. m. Matson-Green, 'Tarenorerer [Walyer] (c. 1800-1831)', *Australian Dictionary of Biography*, Online Edition, updated continuously, accessed 2 August 2007, available from http://www.adb.online.anu.edu.au/biogs/AS10455b.htm.
35   J. Bonwick, *The Last of the Tasmanians, or, the Black War of Van Diemen's Land* (London: Sampson Low, Son, and Marston, 1870), pp. 219-220.

Aboriginal people. The 'first united politically organised Aboriginal activist group' was the Australian Aboriginal Progressive Association, established in 1924.[36] In the 1930s, organisations such as the Aboriginal Progressive Association (APA) in Sydney and the Australian Aborigines' League in Melbourne were formed. One of the most evocative and well-known actions of protest taken in the early twentieth century was the holding of a Day of Mourning in 1938, as white Australians celebrated the sesquicentenary of British colonisation. This event expressed Aboriginal protest at the 'callous treatment of our people' during those 150 years.[37] Pearl Gibbs, who had been part of establishing the APA and was also involved in the Sydney Feminist Club, was one of the key organisers of that event.[38] She was tireless in the fight for rights for Aboriginal people throughout her life, for instance founding with Faith Bandler and others the Aboriginal-Australian Fellowship in 1956 and setting up a hostel for Aboriginal people in need of hospital care and their families in New South Wales (NSW).[39]

During the middle of the twentieth century, new organisations formed on both sides of the Tasman seeking improvements in the lives of Māori and Aboriginal people. The push at this time was largely for advances in welfare and an end to discrimination, as well as an extension of civil rights to Aboriginal people in Australia. White Australians often worked in organisations alongside Aboriginal people during these years. A national organisation was established in the Federal Council for Aboriginal Advancement (FCAA), later to become the Federal Council for the Advancement of Aborigines and Torres Strait Islanders (FCAATSI). This organisation is perhaps best remembered for its campaign for a referendum on removing two sections of the Constitution perceived as discriminatory: section 51, which prevented the federal government making laws in regard to Aboriginal people, and section 127, which stated that Aboriginal people should not be counted in censuses. Two key figures in the campaign for the referendum were Kath Walker (later to change her name to Oodgeroo Noonuccal) and Faith Bandler. Both women were part of a deputation to Prime Minister Menzies in 1963 which asked that a referendum be called, and Walker made an impression on Menzies when she told him as he gave her a sherry that supplying alcohol to an Aboriginal person in Queensland could see him jailed.[40] When the referendum was held in 1967, a positive vote of over ninety

---

36 J. Maynard, 'Vision, Voice and Influence: The Rise of the Australian Aboriginal Progressive Association', *Australian Historical Studies* 34, no. 121 (2003), p. 91.

37 B. Attwood, *Rights for Aborigines* (Crows Nest: Allen and Unwin, 2003), p. 54.

38 S. Gilbert, '"Never Forgotten": Pearl Gibbs (Gambanyi)', in *Uncommon Ground: White Women in Aboriginal History*, eds. A. Cole, V. Haskins, and F. Paisley (Canberra: Aboriginal Studies Press, 2005), pp. 109-110.

39 Ibid., pp. 120-122.

40 F. Bandler, *Turning the Tide: A Personal History of the Federal Council for the Advancement of Aborigines and Torres Strait Islanders* (Canberra: Aboriginal Studies Press, 1989), p. 98; K. Cochrane, *Oodgeroo* (St Lucia: University of Queensland Press, 1994), p. 67.

percent was returned, and although the significance of the referendum is often misunderstood, it has since assumed the status of 'a famous event in Australia's political history'.[41]

Another well-known act of protest which made visible the extent of discrimination suffered by Aboriginal people was the Freedom Ride in 1965, modelled on a similar event in the United States. Led by Charles Perkins, a group of University of Sydney students travelled through northern NSW in a bus to draw attention to the discrimination faced by Aboriginal people, meeting angry opposition in towns such as Walgett and Moree.[42] As John Chesterman has shown, the achievement of civil rights for Aboriginal Australians was largely due to such activism within Australia, combined with concern on the part of the government to avoid international pressure about Australia's failure to meet international human rights standards, which activists were able to use to their advantage.[43]

In New Zealand, one of the most important national voices for Māori in the mid-twentieth century was the Māori Women's Welfare League (MWWL), Te Rōpū Māori Toko i te Ora. Formed in Wellington in 1951 at a conference which had brought together welfare committees from around New Zealand, the MWWL sought improvements in education, health, housing and employment, particularly focusing on Māori women and children, as well as fostering Māori culture.[44] Such work was vital in the context of the rapid post-war urbanisation of Māori people. The organisation's first Dominion President, Whina Cooper, was to become one of the pre-eminent figures of Māoridom in the second half of the twentieth century and the leader of the 1975 land march, one of the most visible acts of Māori protest during those decades. Michael King observed that Cooper's status as the 'public face' of the league meant that she was soon 'the best-known Maori woman in the country' and 'a frequent subject for newspaper stories and features'.[45] She travelled throughout the country speaking to Māori women about the organisation's objectives, creating and strengthening branches.[46] In April 1954, the organisation had 'at least 3,842 members', forming 303 branches.[47] Cooper initiated one of the MWWL's early major projects, a survey of Māori housing needs in Auckland which was carried out by unpaid members and which

41 Attwood, p. x.
42 Broome, p. 180.
43 Chesterman, pp. 36, 39.
44 T. Rei, 'Te Rōpū Māori Toko i te Ora/Māori Women's Welfare League 1951-', in *Women Together: A History of Women's Organisations in New Zealand: Nga Rōpū Wahine o te Motu*, ed. A. Else (Wellington: Historical Branch, Department of Internal Affairs and Daphne Brasell, 1993), pp. 34-35.
45 M. King, 'Cooper, Whina 1895-1994', *Dictionary of New Zealand Biography*, updated 7 April 2006, accessed 7 May 2007, available from http://www.dnzb.govt.nz/dnzb/Find_Quick.asp?PersonEssay=5C32.
46 I. Byron, *Nga Perehitini: The Presidents of the Māori Women's Welfare League, 1951-2001* (Auckland: Māori Women's Development, 2002), pp. 15-16; M. King, *Whina: A Biography of Whina Cooper* (Auckland: Hodder and Stoughton, 1983), pp. 172-173.
47 A. Harris, 'Dancing With the State: Māori Creative Energy and Policies of Integration, 1945-1967' (PhD thesis, University of Auckland, 2007), p. 100.

revealed the inadequacy of much Māori housing, eventually leading to action to improve the situation by the Departments of Māori Affairs and Housing and the Auckland City Council.[48] During the 1950s and 1960s the league advocated integration, seeking to attain Pākehā standards of living and opportunities without loss of culture, and this led the organisation into the 'contradictory position' of seeking 'to uphold both modernity and tradition'.[49]

After the formation of the Māori Council, then all male, the league lost some of its force as a source of national leadership for Māori.[50] Set up in 1962, the council was treated with some suspicion as a creation of the government, and of the National Party which was then in power, but it addressed similar issues to those focused upon by the MWWL and showed itself willing to oppose the government in the matter of legislative changes relating to Māori land.[51] Like the MWWL, the Māori Council then considered integration, conceived as an end to discrimination, to be a positive approach.[52]

From the late 1960s, new generations of activists arose in Australia and New Zealand, often taking a more militant stance in their demands for change. More than pursuing an end to discrimination or the achievement of civil rights and equality of opportunity, Indigenous organisations in Australia now focused more intently than they had previously done on specifically Indigenous rights, particularly land rights. A young, urban group of Aboriginal leaders used more militant tactics of protest, and the term 'black power' began to be used, adopted from the United States movement.[53] A Black Panther Party was formed, taking inspiration from both the 'programme' and the 'style' of its namesake party in the United States.[54] No longer content to work through white-dominated organisations, this new generation of leaders advocated 'an Aboriginal or black consciousness' more powerfully than previous groups had done, and rejected assimilation or integration in favour of self-determination.[55] These younger leaders were disillusioned by the lack of change they saw following the 1967 referendum, despite the 'high expectations' it had created.[56]

---

48 King, *Whina*, pp. 175-177.
49 Brookes, '"Assimilation" and "Integration"', pp. 12-13, 16; B. Brookes, 'Nostalgia for "Innocent Homely Pleasures": The 1964 New Zealand Controversy over *Washday at the Pa*', *Gender and History* 9, no. 2 (1997), pp. 242-261.
50 Brookes, '"Assimilation" and "Integration"', p. 16; R. Walker, *Struggle Without End/Ka Whawhai Tonu Matou*, revised ed. (Auckland: Penguin, 2004), p. 203.
51 Walker, pp. 205-206.
52 Brookes, '"Assimilation" and "Integration"', p. 16.
53 Attwood, p. 321; Broome, p. 188.
54 Attwood, p. 324.
55 Ibid., pp. 322-323; Macintyre, p. 235.
56 G. Foley, 'Black Power in Redfern 1968-1972', *The Koori History Website*, updated 5 October 2001, accessed 19 May 2008, available from http://www.kooriweb.org/foley/essays/essay_1.html.

One of the most effective acts of protest in the 1970s was the creation of an Aboriginal tent embassy in 1972. Erected as a response to Prime Minister William McMahon's 1972 Australia Day speech refusing to accept land rights, the embassy graphically displayed the feeling of many Aboriginal people that they had become aliens in their own land.[57] Although it later returned, the embassy was removed by police in July of that year, and the violent clash between police and activists was covered on television. Roberta (Bobbi) Sykes was recognised as one of the key leaders in this new generation of activists. Described by Alan Trengove in the *West Australian* in 1974 as 'black, beautiful, angry and articulate', she took a central role in the tent embassy protest, and was arrested when it was removed in July 1972.[58] Throughout these years, a growth in Aboriginal 'pride and identity' was clearly evident, expressed in the emergence of a number of community projects for Aboriginal welfare, in the increase in artistic and cultural productions and groups, and in the development of Aboriginal studies courses.[59] Aboriginal pride and cultural identity was also expressed in the poetry and writing of Oodgeroo, as in the works of other poets, writers, artists and filmmakers.

In New Zealand too, the 1970s and 1980s saw the rise of a new generation of young, urban Māori activists. The MWWL, like many Māori people working in the public service, began to be criticised by this new generation as being too conservative and not assertive enough.[60] Ngā Tamatoa (young warriors) was the first of the new urban-based groups to 'make its influence felt', after it was established in Auckland in the late 1960s, emerging from the Auckland University Māori Club.[61] Although the 'radicals' in the group, who drew inspiration from Black Power leaders in the United States and provoked 'adverse publicity with their rhetoric of brown power, Māori liberation, separate government and even a separate foreign policy' did not control the group, Ngā Tamatoa was willing to take 'radical protest action' as well as to work within the system.[62] Among the aims of the group were the retention and management of Māori land, the cessation of Treaty of Waitangi celebrations and the inclusion of the Māori language in school curricula.[63]

Several major protests over the alienation of Māori land occurred from the 1970s as well. The first of these was the land march through the length of the North

---

57   Attwood, p. 345; B. Attwood and A. Markus, *The Struggle for Aboriginal Rights: A Documentary History* (St Leonards: Allen and Unwin, 1999), p. 174.

58   R. Sykes, *Snake Dreaming* (St Leonards: Allen and Unwin, 2001), p. 386; A. Trengove, 'Bobbi Sykes – Controversial Champion of Her People', *West Australian*, 7 November 1974, p. 46.

59   Broome, pp. 201-203.

60   King, *The Penguin History of New Zealand*, pp. 480-481; Mira Szaszy quoted in V. Myers, *Head and Shoulders* (Auckland: Penguin, 1986), p. 241.

61   King, *The Penguin History of New Zealand*, pp. 484-485.

62   Walker, pp. 210-211.

63   King, *The Penguin History of New Zealand*, p. 485.

Island to Parliament led by Whina Cooper, which brought media attention to Māori grievances in relation to the loss of land. Another media event was the 1977 occupation of Bastion Point (Takaparawhā) by the Ōrākei Māori Action Group, protesting plans to subdivide rather than return land that had been wrongfully taken from Māori. The protest lasted 507 days before the protesters were violently removed by police. Not far away, at Raglan, Tuaiwa (Eva) Rickard led the Tainui Awhiro people's campaign to have land returned which had been taken during World War Two for use as an aerodrome. Following the war, the land was developed as a public golf course rather than being handed back, and a sacred burial site was turned into a bunker. Rickard was arrested in 1978 along with other protesters after occupying the land. The land was eventually returned, and was used as a base for employment programs and for the Māori sovereignty movement. A strengthening of Māori pride was also evident from the 1970s in the emergence of Māori authors, artists and filmmakers such as Patricia Grace, Keri Hulme, Robyn Kahukiwa and Merata Mita, and in efforts to preserve and strengthen te reo Māori, the Māori language. By the end of the decade, some observers had begun to refer to a Māori 'renaissance'.[64]

Antipodean Feminist Movements

Women in the Australian colonies and in New Zealand formed organisations and campaigned for equality for women in the latter part of the nineteenth century and the beginning of the twentieth century. In this first wave of feminism, the focus was on attaining equal rights by legislative change. Prominent among the changes sought by first wave feminists were the removal of discriminatory laws such as those restricting married women's property rights, denying women the franchise, refusing women the right to a divorce in all but extreme cases and favouring men in determining the custody of children. Campaigning for the franchise, women stressed not only their right as adult members of society, many of whom paid taxes to the governments in whose formation they had no part, but also that women would have a purifying influence on politics and on society.[65] Australia and New Zealand were among the first countries in the world in which women gained the vote, in New Zealand in 1893, South Australia in 1894, Western Australia in 1899 and at the federal level in Australia in 1902. In South Australia, women also gained the right to stand for election in 1894, and this was also the case at a federal level in 1902.[66]

---

64   Ibid., p. 487.
65   V. Burgmann, *Power and Protest: Movements for Change in Australian Society* (St Leonards: Allen and Unwin, 1993), pp. 77-78.
66   M. Sawer and M. Simms, *A Woman's Place: Women and Politics in Australia* (St Leonards: Allen and Unwin, 1993), p. 6.

Māori women won the franchise along with Pākehā women in 1893 in New Zealand, while Aboriginal people remained unable to vote in some states of Australia, until as late as 1965 in Queensland.[67] One of those remembered for her efforts towards women's suffrage is Meri Te Tai Mangakāhia, who put a motion to the Kotahitanga (Māori unity movement) Parliament in 1893 that women be able to vote and be elected as members, and who appears to have been the first woman to address the Parliament when she was asked to speak to the motion.[68] While Māori women were sometimes active in women's organisations such as the Women's Christian Temperance Union (WCTU) in New Zealand, such inclusion of Aboriginal women 'as fellow activists' was not imaginable in Australia at the same time.[69]

Although descriptions of the feminist movement as having waves imply the existence of a lull between them, women's organisations were not inactive in the years between the achievement of the franchise and the emergence of women's liberation groups in the 1970s.[70] Women's organisations such as the WCTU and the National Council of Women remained active in both Australia and New Zealand, as did a host of other organisations. These groups continued to campaign for women's rights, pursuing issues such as equal pay, the right for women to act as jurors and the right of married women to paid employment.[71] Some white feminist reformers also pursued goals relating to the social and economic positions of Indigenous women. As Alison Holland has shown in the Australian context, for instance, the WCTU in the mid-twentieth century displayed considerable concern over wider issues of peace, humanitarianism and Aboriginal rights.[72]

---

67 Chesterman, p. 110. The 1902 *Franchise Act* denied Aboriginal people the federal vote, except where they had the state vote and were on the electoral rolls prior to 1901. Electoral officials decided who was deemed Aboriginal for these purposes. Australian Electoral Commission, *History of the Indigenous Vote* (Kingston: Australian Electoral Commission, 2006), p. 5. Although only Western Australia and Queensland ever explicitly denied Aboriginal people the state vote, states such as NSW and Victoria used other methods to prevent Aboriginal people from voting. Chesterman, p. 134.

68 A. Ballara, 'Mangakahia, Meri Te Tai 1868-1920', *Dictionary of New Zealand Biography*, updated 22 June 2007, accessed 14 May 2008, available from http://www.dnzb.govt.nz/dnzb/default.asp?Find_Quick. asp?PersonEssay=2M30.

69 P. Grimshaw, 'Interracial Marriages and Colonial Regimes in Victoria and Aotearoa/New Zealand', *Frontiers* 23, no. 3 (2002), p. 12.

70 Burgmann, pp. 78-79; M. Lake, *Getting Equal: The History of Australian Feminism* (St Leonards: Allen and Unwin, 1999), p. 9.

71 Lake, pp. 9-10.

72 A. Holland, 'To Eliminate Colour Prejudice: The WCTU and Decolonisation in Australia', *Journal of Religious History* 32, no. 2 (2008), p. 259. On WCTU involvement with issues of Aboriginal rights in Australia, see also P. Grimshaw, 'Gender, Citizenship and Race in the Woman's Christian Temperance Union of Australia, 1890 to the 1930s', *Australian Feminist Studies* 13, no. 28 (1998), pp. 199-214. On the WCTU's agenda towards and involvement with Māori women in the late nineteenth and early twentieth centuries, see P. Grimshaw, 'Women and the Legacy of Britain's Imperial "Civilising Mission" in New Zealand, 1894-1914', in *Britishness Abroad: Transnational Movements and Imperial Cultures*, eds. K. Darian-Smith, P. Grimshaw and S. Macintyre (Carlton: Melbourne University Press, 2007), pp. 169-186. For a comparative perspective,

For many women in this period, marriage meant the end of paid employment and the assumption of the roles of mother and homemaker. Although the Second World War had given rise to considerable change in women's social positions, particularly in relation to work, after the war women faced social pressures to return to the domestic life of home and family. During the 1950s, the ideal of the suburban nuclear family prevailed on both sides of the Tasman, promoted by women's magazines such as the *Australian Women's Weekly* and the *New Zealand Woman's Weekly*. This was the ideal which assimilation policies expected Aboriginal and Māori people to adopt, in contrast to traditional communal lifeways.

During the 1960s and 1970s, a second wave of feminism emerged in many Western countries, leading to significant social, political and cultural changes in both Australia and New Zealand. Second wave feminism incorporated a variety of different incarnations of feminism, from radical to socialist to liberal. Newly formed women's liberation groups existed alongside more conservative feminist organisations such as the Women's Electoral Lobby (WEL). Established in Australia in 1972, WEL pursued changes through legislation and lobbying rather than more radical goals, thus remaining closer to the liberal feminist goals of the first wave.[73] On the whole, however, as Christine Dann noted in the New Zealand context, the second wave of the feminist movement saw a surge in women's 'organisation and militancy'.[74]

By 1972, about forty women's liberation groups had been formed in Australia, and about twenty in New Zealand.[75] The aims of the women's liberation movement in New Zealand and Australia were comparable to those espoused in other Western societies, and included equal pay, the cessation of discrimination based on sex, 'autonomy' in relation to the body and 'liberation from the role of "housewife"'.[76] One particularly contentious campaign was for the right to abortion that was both legal and safe. Consciousness-raising groups, conventions and events such as the International Women's Year and the United Nations Decade for Women drew attention to obstacles and inequalities faced by women and emphasised the value of women's contributions and abilities both within and apart from a domestic setting.[77] Many feminists active in this second wave movement sought

see P. Grimshaw, 'Indigenous Women's Voices in Colonial Reform Narratives – Victoria and New Zealand/ Aotearoa', in *Women's Politics and Women in Politics: In Honour of Ida Blom*, ed. S. Sogner and G. Hagemann (Oslo: Cappelen Akademisk Forlag, 2000), pp. 173-196.

73   Lake, pp. 237-239.

74   C. Dann, *Up From Under: Women and Liberation in New Zealand 1970-1984* (Wellington: Allen and Unwin in association with Port Nicholson, 1985), p. 4.

75   G. Bolton, *The Oxford History of Australia: 1942-1988 The Middle Way*, vol. 5 (Melbourne: Oxford University Press, 1990), p. 201; King, *The Penguin History of New Zealand*, p. 462.

76   Mein Smith, p. 237.

77   R. Dalziel, 'Political Organisations', in *Women Together: A History of Women's Organisations in New Zealand: Nga Rōpū Wahine o te Motu*, ed. A. Else (Wellington: Historical Branch, Department of Internal Affairs and Daphne Brasell, 1993), p. 66.

something more than equal rights, advocating instead wider change to society to incorporate perceived feminine values. As Marilyn Lake has pointed out in the Australian context, 'what was revolutionary was the attack on sex roles, and more radically, the family'.[78] The 1970s and 1980s, more so in Australia than in New Zealand, saw the 'institutionalisation' of feminism in government programmes and bureaucratic structures aimed at advancing women's equality and social positions.[79] As was the case in relation to Indigenous activism, feminist concerns thus gained a degree of governmental legitimacy through being implicated in policy shifts and changes in bureaucratic structures.

Indigenous women sometimes became involved in the second wave feminist movement. In New Zealand, activist, businesswoman and MP Donna Awatere Huata (then Awatere) observed that 'in the early days' she and writer and academic Ngāhuia Te Awekōtuku were 'the most visible Maori women in the women's movement'.[80] In Australia, Pat O'Shane was a strong supporter of both Indigenous and women's rights. As she explained in an edited interview with Susan Mitchell in 1984, she found it 'difficult to say I'm black first and a woman second or vice versa'.[81] However, as for many African-American women in the United States, disillusionment often set in as Indigenous women observed that the feminist movement was centred on issues that were predominantly the concern of white, middle-class women. In New Zealand, splits between Māori and Pākehā women, and between lesbian and straight women, had by the 1980s made annual nationwide women's conventions unworkable.[82] Failing to understand that Indigenous women often experienced racism as a greater form of oppression than they did sexism, and that many Indigenous women saw a need to stand with Indigenous men in fighting racism, non-Indigenous feminists generally viewed Indigenous and migrant women as simply suffering additional 'degrees of oppression'.[83] Māori and Aboriginal women in the 1970s and 1980s often felt that their energy must first go to the struggles of their people. As O'Shane wrote in *Refractory Girl* in 1976, for Aboriginal women 'our major fight is against racism'.[84]

As well, the aims and perspectives of the feminist movement did not always sit easily with Indigenous cultural values. One example of such a conflict is evident

---

78 Lake, p. 232.
79 Ibid., p. 253.
80 D. A. Huata, 'Walking on Eggs', in *Heading Nowhere in a Navy Blue Suit and Other Tales From the Feminist Revolution*, eds. S. Kedgley and M. Varnham (Wellington: Daphne Brasell, 1993), p. 122.
81 S. Mitchell, *Tall Poppies: Nine Successful Australian Women Talk to Susan Mitchell* (Ringwood: Penguin, 1984), p. 153.
82 King, *The Penguin History of New Zealand*, p. 462.
83 On this issue in Australia, see: H. Goodall and J. Huggins, 'Aboriginal Women Are Everywhere: Contemporary Struggles', in *Gender Relations in Australia: Domination and Negotiation*, eds. K. Saunders and R. Evans (Marrickville: Harcourt Brace Jovanovich, 1992), pp. 401-402; Lake, pp. 249-250.
84 P. O'Shane, 'Is There Any Relevance in the Women's Movement For Aboriginal Women?', *Refractory Girl*, no. 12 (1976), p. 33.

in the number of Māori women who upheld the prohibition in some iwi (tribes) against women speaking on the marae ātea (the meeting place courtyard, where visitors are welcomed and issues debated), a prohibition frequently attacked by white observers as being discriminatory. The emergence of new feminist thought such as postcolonial feminism and women of colour feminism was a response to the inadequacies of Western forms of feminism which tended to universalise the experiences of women. Māori and Aboriginal women sometimes developed forms of feminist thinking tied to their own cultures. For Māori women, this is sometimes expressed in the phrase 'mana wāhine' (the dignity or strength of women). Te Awekōtuku observed that there was a common view that 'being Maori and feminist must be a contradiction' since 'feminism is some imported Pakeha idea', but that she did not take this view herself since 'feminism is what we make it'. She advocated being feminist in 'a Maori way' and 'reclaiming and celebrating what we have been, and what we will become'.[85] Sometimes asked if there could be 'a unique form of Maori feminism', social reformer and thinker Mira Szaszy observed that she could not find a corresponding word in Māori, pointing instead to the goddesses of legend and the 'dignity' of women in Māori culture as the 'closest' parallels she could find to Western ideas of feminism. Within the MWWL, she observed a 'spirit' among the women as they 'worked without self for the good of the whole' which she thought 'the nearest I can get to a Maori definition of feminism'.[86] The rise of a second wave of feminism and the varied engagements of Māori and Aboriginal women with the movement were an important part of the social, cultural and political contexts within which media representations of famous Indigenous women were produced and disseminated.

The Media Industry in New Zealand and Australia

Dramatic shifts have also occurred in the media industries since the first newspapers were published in the Australian colonies and in New Zealand in the nineteenth century. From those few newspapers have developed media conglomerates, publishing magazines as well as newspapers, producing radio and television broadcasts, and generating web-based news and entertainment sites. While some publications, such as the *Sydney Morning Herald* and the *Age*, have existed throughout that period of change, others appeared and vanished relatively quickly, and still others experienced a variety of incarnations as they were taken over, renamed, merged or redesigned. By the middle of the twentieth

85   N. Te Awekōtuku, *Mana Wahine Maori: Selected Writings on Maori Women's Art, Culture and Politics* (Auckland: New Women's Press, 1991), p. 10.
86   M. Szaszy, 'Opening My Mouth', in *Heading Nowhere in a Navy Blue Suit and Other Tales From the Feminist Revolution*, eds. S. Kedgley and M. Varnham (Wellington: Daphne Brasell, 1993), p. 84.

century, a flourishing print media industry had developed in both Australia and New Zealand, with major daily newspapers situated in the capital cities of the Australian states and the main centres of New Zealand, and a range of magazines publishing on a regular basis. The *Bulletin* in Australia, which was to be reinvented as a modern current affairs magazine in the 1960s, had been published since 1880. The *New Zealand Listener*, a magazine of news and entertainment, had been published since 1939. Women's magazines like the *Australian Women's Weekly* and the *New Zealand Woman's Weekly* had been published since the early 1930s. These long-established publications have sometimes experienced shifts in orientation and emphasis under the influence of changing editorial and managerial leadership, as well as wider social changes, while also displaying some continuities in focus.

Over the years, these long-running and well-established publications were joined by new titles, sometimes short-lived, which often aimed to cater for particular audiences or to provide different perspectives from those evident in the mainstream press. The shifts in the social and political positions of women and of Indigenous people in the second half of the twentieth century began to be reflected in shifts in the media industries as well. During the 1950s, magazines such as *Dawn* (later *New Dawn*), published by the NSW Aborigines' Welfare Board, and *Te Ao Hou: The New World*, published by the New Zealand Māori Affairs Department, came into existence. Both magazines ceased publication in the mid-1970s, by which time *Aboriginal and Islander Identity* was being published in Australia, providing an outlet for Aboriginal voices. New feminist magazines such as *Broadsheet* in New Zealand and *Mejane* in Australia began publication in the 1970s, part of a longer tradition of feminist publications stretching back into the nineteenth century. At the same time, new magazines, such as *Cleo* and *Cosmopolitan*, emerged aimed at younger, single, working women. From the 1970s, a proliferation of Māori and Aboriginal newspapers and magazines appeared. Such publications were part of a long history of Indigenous writing in both countries. In New Zealand, especially, Māori adopted modern media forms early in the colony's existence, with a number of Māori language newspapers being published in the nineteenth century.[87] The Mana News Service was established in New Zealand in 1990, and began producing a high quality glossy magazine, *Mana*, in 1993. *Mana* in New Zealand and *Deadly Vibe* in Australia are only two of the newspapers and magazines established in the late twentieth century which continue the tradition of Māori- and Aboriginal-controlled publications providing a voice for Māori and Aboriginal peoples. The media landscape at the end of the twentieth century thus appeared very different from that in the 1950s.

---

87 On these publications, see J. Curnow, N. Hopa and J. McRae, eds., *Rere Atu, Taku Manu! Discovering History, Language and Politics in the Maori-Language Newspapers* (Auckland: Auckland University Press, 2002).

Yet on both sides of the Tasman, the media industries remained dominated by non-Indigenous voices and structures well into the 1980s, and at the end of the twentieth century Indigenous perspectives often continued to be expressed in forums outside the mainstream media. In Australia, the creation of an Indigenous media sphere was in large part prompted by an awareness on the part of many Aboriginal people that the non-Indigenous media had not served Aboriginal people well, and by a corresponding belief that one way to challenge the failings of the mainstream media was through the growth of an 'indigenous media network' which Aboriginal people 'control and produce'.[88] In New Zealand too, mainstream media organisations remained dominated by Pākehā values, philosophies and structures, and often failed to incorporate Māori perspectives. The constructed 'dichotomy' between hard and soft news, for instance, often places stories about Māori and about women as soft news, and the 'focus on the present and the urgent … contrasts with Māori viewpoints'.[89] Many small Māori-controlled publications have experienced a lack of funding, resources, advertising and sales, as well as a more general lack of governmental support.[90] Indeed, suggestions have been made by some involved in publishing these small periodicals that the Ministry of Māori Affairs/Te Puni Kōkiri competes with them through publishing its own periodical, *Kōkiri Paetae* (later *Kōkiri*), a professionally-produced publication focusing on 'cheerful' stories of Māori success rather than covering more negative issues.[91] At the same time, Māori editors and journalists may practice 'self-censorship' in publications controlled by iwi authorities, or through avoiding producing stories which show Māori people in a negative light, given the frequency with which such stories appear in the mainstream media.[92] Despite these and other issues involved in the re-shaping by Indigenous communities of European communication mediums, the proliferation of Indigenous-controlled publications is clearly a crucial means of challenging the domination of non-Indigenous structures and values in the media industries.

Although this book concentrates on the print media, it is important to note that the advent of new technologies such as radio, television and the internet have produced changes in the ways in which information is delivered and received. More than the print media, television in particular is focused on providing entertainment. Famous Indigenous women in the second half of the twentieth century were increasingly portrayed on television as well as in print, as for instance in the coverage of Goolagong's second Wimbledon win

---

88 M. Rose, ed., *For the Record: 160 Years of Aboriginal Print Journalism* (St Leonards: Allen and Unwin, 1996), p. xx.
89 E. Taira, 'Māori Media: A Study of the Māori "Media Sphere" in Aotearoa/New Zealand' (PhD thesis, University of Canterbury, 2006), p. 22.
90 Ibid., p. 66.
91 Ibid., pp. 71-72.
92 Ibid., pp. 74-76.

in 1980. Televised representations may differ from representations in the print media, owing to the different production processes and the visual nature of the medium. New technologies also impacted negatively on the dominance of the print media. The emergence of television in Australia contributed to a drop in advertising in newspapers, a fall in circulation, and a decline in the number of papers published.[93]

As in the case of the print media, Indigenous people have adopted these new technologies and begun to produce their own representations of themselves and their communities. In the late twentieth century, radio stations, internet sites and television programmes controlled by or catering for Indigenous peoples began to be established on both sides of the Tasman, and these often provide an alternative to mainstream media organisations. The visual and aural nature of television and radio have made these mediums particularly attractive to Indigenous communities in Australia and New Zealand, as they are more obviously suited to adaptation for uses drawing on oral traditions than is the print media. Significantly, a nationwide Māori television channel was established in New Zealand in 2004, which has been highly successful.

Understandings of the role of the media have also shifted over time, and these changes too might have an impact on the ways in which people, events and issues were presented. In the newspapers of the nineteenth century, political points of view proliferated openly in reporting. By the middle of the twentieth century, this approach had been replaced by a drive for objectivity, which proved an elusive goal as critics continued to detect political bias, selective reporting and misrepresentations in the press. The political and social change that occurred in Australia in the 1960s and 1970s revealed the 'limits of neutrality and passive objectivity' and contributed to a revival of investigative reporting, after a postwar period of conservatism and press support for the establishment.[94] The latter part of the twentieth century also saw a rise in the amount of analysis and comment included in broadsheet newspapers in Australia, allowing for deeper analysis of events and issues.[95] The ideal of detached, objective writing was also challenged by many who were writing for small, Indigenous-controlled publications. In New Zealand, Eliana Taira has observed that reporters working for these publications frequently wrote from a more involved standpoint than the supposedly objective one promoted in the mainstream press.[96] Just as shifts in

---

93   E. Morrison, 'Newspapers', in *The Oxford Companion to Australian History*, eds. G. Davison, J. Hirst and S. Macintyre, Oxford Reference Online, accessed 8 November 2006, available from http://www.oxfordreference.com/views/ENTRY.html?subview=Main&entry=t127.e1074.

94   J. Schultz, 'The Press', in *The Media in Australia: Industries, Texts, Audiences*, eds. S. Cunningham and G. Turner (St Leonards: Allen and Unwin, 1997), pp. 29-30.

95   M. Ricketson, 'Newspaper Feature Writing in Australia 1956-1996', in *Journalism: Print, Politics and Popular Culture*, eds. A. Curthoys and J. Schultz (St Lucia: University of Queensland Press, 1999), pp. 176-177.

96   Taira, pp. 83-85.

these generally accepted beliefs about the social and political role of the media may shape media representations of people and events, so too may shifting codes of practice and ethical guidelines. The Australian Journalists' Association first promulgated a code of ethics to guide journalists in 1944, and this was revised in 1984. The 1984 revisions included the addition of a section stating that 'unnecessary emphasis' ought not to be put upon a person's race, gender, marital status and so on.[97] However, negative framings of both Indigeneity and gender continue to be apparent in media portrayals of Indigenous people and of women.

Any analysis of media texts must also take into account the commercial imperatives and production processes of the media as an industry, as these impact upon the packaging of news and features. During the twentieth century, considerable shifts occurred in media ownership. In Australia, the names of Murdoch, Packer and Fairfax loom large in the history of the media industries, and the companies begun by these families had come to dominate the market by the last years of the twentieth century. In New Zealand, Independent Newspapers Limited (INL) and Wilson and Horton had come to own many of the country's newspapers by the late twentieth century. Both were 'New Zealand-controlled ownership blocs', until Wilson and Horton was purchased by the Australian APN News and Media in 1998 and INL was sold to another Australian company, Fairfax Media, in 2003.[98] Critics in Australia observed that the concentration of ownership, and cross-ownership of different areas of media such as television and newspapers, might adversely affect the level of diversity in views and coverage.[99] The nature of the media as a commercial industry also means that a focus on commercial realities may play a role in determining what is considered news- or feature-worthy, or in shaping the angle taken on specific issues and events.

Systemic constraints in the industry similarly play an important part in the selection and presentation of news and features. In the production of newspapers in particular, two such factors are the existence of deadlines, the requirement that the paper appear on time, and the 'news hole', the space in the paper remaining for news after advertisements have been placed.[100] Newspapers also often rely upon services such as Reuters in the gathering of news, meaning that very similar stories often appear in newspapers across Australia and New Zealand. At the same time, individual editors and journalists may sometimes help determine the ways in which news and features are selected and reported. For much of the twentieth century, Australian journalists' work was subject to close control

97   D. Bowman, 'The AJA Code', in *Issues in Australian Journalism*, ed. J. Henningham (Melbourne: Longman Cheshire, 1990), p. 54.
98   G. Hannis, 'The New Zealand Press Association 1880-2006: The Rise and Fall of a Co-Operative Model for News Gathering', *Australian Economic History Review* 48, no. 1 (2008), p. 61.
99   B. Bonney and H. Wilson, *Australia's Commercial Media* (South Melbourne: Macmillan, 1983), p. 66.
100   R. Tiffen, 'The Press', in *The Media in Australia: Industries, Texts, Audiences*, eds. S. Cunningham and G. Turner (St Leonards: Allen and Unwin, 1997), p. 195.

by employers.[101] However, this approach had weakened by the 1980s as 'an extensive network of managers' appeared who often gave less attention to issues of content than owners and editors had done in the past, and editors and journalists started to stress their freedom in the line taken on issues and events.[102] The interplay of commercial, systemic and individual factors in the shaping of media representations of people, events and issues is a complicating factor in any analysis of those representations.

Conclusion

The second half of the twentieth century was a time of great social, cultural and political transformation. In both Australia and New Zealand, an upsurge in Indigenous activism played an important part in bringing about a shift in policies towards Indigenous affairs. Although there were differences in the implementation of policies across the Tasman, it is clear that in the twentieth century a drive towards assimilation was followed in both countries by an official acceptance of self-determination, at least to some degree, although this was significantly reversed in Australia by the Howard government. Similarly, a second wave feminist movement emerged in the 1970s, bringing in its wake significant changes to the social and political positions of women. This period of change was paralleled by the continuation of change in the media industries, as new technologies appeared, and ownership was further consolidated in a small number of large companies. This web of dramatic changes shaped the contexts in which women like Goolagong and Te Kanawa became known to the public, and inevitably shaped the ways in which they were represented in the media. If particular discursive formations hold greater sway than others at particular times, transitions such as occurred in the second half of the twentieth century can subordinate them to new ones. Throughout these years of transformation, competing discourses about assimilation, self-determination, Indigeneity, gender roles and feminism appeared and reappeared in representations of famous Indigenous women, revealing as much about the social and political formations in which they were created as about their ostensible subjects.

---

101   Schultz, pp. 41-42.
102   Ibid., p. 42.

Chapter Two

When Evonne Goolagong won the Wimbledon ladies' singles competition in 1971, newspapers around Australia announced the result with sensationalist headlines and hyperbole. Aged nineteen and a newcomer on the world stage of tennis, Goolagong defeated the reigning champion, fellow Australian Margaret Court. What was it that made Goolagong's win such a media sensation? Was it her youth, rural Australian background and unexpected bursting into international success? Was it her beauty, in a sport where a woman's media profile was and is heavily influenced by her appearance and sexuality? Or was it that she was of Aboriginal descent, the heroine of a classic rags-to-riches tale of triumph? In this chapter, I explore representations of Aboriginal and Māori women who became famous for their sporting achievements during the second half of the twentieth century, focusing particularly on Goolagong. I consider the common portrayal of sport as a road to overcome discrimination and social disadvantage, the recurring representation of Indigenous sportspeople as natural athletes and the often ambivalent depictions of sporting women, making a particular comparison with representations of Court, to date Australia's only other winner of the Wimbledon ladies' singles tournament. Throughout the chapter, I also discuss the ways in which Indigenous sportswomen themselves reflected on and attempted to shape their own public biographies. Finally, I consider the ways in which the complicated intersections between dominant discourses of femininity, Indigeneity and national imaginings were both echoed and forgotten in representations of a new generation of Indigenous sportswomen by the last decade of the twentieth century.

Indigenous Women in Sport

In the late nineteenth and early twentieth centuries, Indigenous men in Australia and New Zealand sometimes achieved great success and even fame in sport, despite the barriers of racism, exclusion and poverty which existed in both countries (particularly Australia). Indigenous women's participation in sport, however, was considerably more limited. Women have historically been restricted and marginalised in sport, confined to sports perceived as female-appropriate and ignored or stereotyped in the media. Approaching the twenty-first century, it remained the case that more attention in academic scholarship, popular writing and the media was focused upon men's experiences of sport than upon those of women. Such gender discrimination intersected with racial discrimination to further marginalise Indigenous women in sport on both sides of the Tasman. Scholars of Australian sports history have observed that Aboriginal women historically experienced greater marginalisation in sport than either Aboriginal men or non-Aboriginal women.[1] As Colin Tatz wrote in 1995, 'if white women are having difficulty getting to first or second base in sport, then by comparison their black sisters are not coming within cooee of the ballpark'.[2] While Māori women in New Zealand were perhaps more able to participate in organised sport than were Aboriginal women in Australia, owing to the legal restrictions and relatively greater level of social prejudice faced by Aboriginal women, few reached the upper levels of their chosen sports, and even fewer became well-known for their sporting achievements.

Nonetheless, a small number of Aboriginal and Māori women did succeed in reaching state or national representative level in the first half of the twentieth century. In Australia, cricketers Edna Crouch (later Newfong) and Mabel Campbell (later Crouch) played for Queensland against England during its 1934-1935 tour.[3] Faith Coulthard (later Thomas) was also a successful cricketer. Remembered as the first Indigenous woman to represent Australia internationally in cricket, Coulthard played against England in 1958.[4] She later remembered that reporters sought to interview her as the 'native nurse' on the team. Because the captain, vice captain and managers 'wanted to be in the news', the interview did not eventuate, which Coulthard considered 'was good anyway, because I didn't know what to bloody well say'.[5] In New Zealand, Meg Matangi captained the national netball team which toured Australia in 1938.[6] Another who competed outside New Zealand during these years was endurance swimmer Katerina Nehua. She broke the world record in a contest in Sydney in 1931, and again later that year in Brisbane.[7] Yet her achievements were sometimes imagined in terms of feminine domesticity, as when she was reported to have entered an event in Manly during the Depression because she needed the money to give her unemployed husband and four young children a better life.[8] Following these and other forerunners, increasing numbers of Māori and Aboriginal women achieved fame and success in sport during the second half of the twentieth century. One woman stands out, however, as having reached heights of international success

---

1   For example: M. K. Stell, *Half the Race: A History of Australian Women in Sport* (North Ryde: Angus and Robertson, 1991), p. 236; C. Tatz, *Obstacle Race: Aborigines in Sport* (Sydney: University of New South Wales Press, 1995), pp. 6, 269-270.

2   Tatz, p. 270.

3   Ibid., p. 271.

4   Ibid., p. 272; B. Whimpress, 'The First Aboriginal Test Cricketer', *The Journal of the Cricket Society* 20, no. 4 (2002), p. 9.

5   F. Thomas, 'From the Shoulder', in *Women of the Centre*, ed. A. Pring (Apollo Bay: Pascoe, 1990), p. 38.

6   J. Nauright, 'Netball, Media Representation of Women and Crisis of Male Hegemony in New Zealand', *ASSH Studies in Sports History*, no. 11 (1999), p. 63.

7   P. Goldstone, 'Nehua, Katerina 1903-1948', *Dictionary of New Zealand Biography*, updated 22 June 2007, accessed 6 August 2007, available from http://www.dnzb.govt.nz/dnzb/default.asp?Find_Quick. asp?PersonEssay=4N4.

8   C. Daley, 'Women Endurance Swimmers: Dissolving Grease Suits and Decentring New Zealand History', *Sporting Traditions* 21, no. 2 (2005), pp. 35, 41.

and fame not matched by another Indigenous sportswoman in Australia or New Zealand until the 1990s. Evonne Goolagong (later Cawley) was twice winner of the Wimbledon ladies' singles competition, as well as winning the ladies' singles competition four times in the Australian Open and once in the French Open.

Figure 3: 'Evonne Goolagong Relaxes at Kooyong Between Tournament Matches', 1 February 1971, Eric Wadsworth.

Australian Information Service. Photograph. nla.pic-vn3050389. National Library of Australia, Canberra.

Sport and the Rags-to-Riches Myth

To many observers, it seemed a long way from Goolagong's early life in the small town of Barellan in New South Wales (NSW) to her position in the top ranks of women's tennis in the 1970s and 1980s. Her background, variously imagined as being in the outback, the bush or the rural heartland of NSW, was frequently referenced in representations of her as a fairytale success. Wrote one journalist in 1965: 'I saw yesterday a sight that will stay in my mind forever – a slim brown aboriginal girl from the bush, playing tennis on a posh North Shore court, her face alive with delight'.[9] Some years after her retirement, another commented that

---

9   F. Margan, 'Wimbledon is Her Real Goal', *Daily Telegraph*, 12 January 1965, p. 14.

'the little girl from the back streets of Barellan made the big time'.[10] Following Goolagong's first victory in the Wimbledon ladies' singles in 1971, her youth and rural origins were emphasised along with her Aboriginality in the media sensationalism of her achievement. As the Hobart *Mercury* announced, 'Miss Goolagong, the part aboriginal from the New South Wales outback, beat the defending champion and three times winner', Margaret Court, to take the title.[11] The *Age* similarly declared that 'the part-Aboriginal girl from a little outback NSW town today dethroned the reigning champion'.[12] In portraying Goolagong as the girl from the outback, such statements greatly exaggerated Barellan's remoteness, and at the same time failed to acknowledge Court's upbringing in the rural city of Albury in NSW. Moreover, despite the persistence of such narratives about Goolagong's early life, much of her adolescence was spent in Sydney, where she went to develop her tennis after her coach, Victor Edwards, invited her to live there with his family.

Where media narratives of Goolagong's life made reference to her extended stay with the Edwards family, Victor Edwards was usually imagined as a mentor or guardian to whom her parents had entrusted her so that she might have a chance to reach tennis success. Analogously to the experience of the land, white people discovered Goolagong's talent, and interceded to develop it. In one recurring narrative, it was this discovery that was central to her success. She was 'just another underprivileged outback child, the daughter of a shearer – until a tennis coach noticed her ability to pound a tennis ball'.[13] Edwards' agency in her rise to the top was also stressed in the *Daily Telegraph* after her first Wimbledon win: 'The little part-Aboriginal girl, discovered by coach Vic Edwards on a tennis court at Berellan [sic] … ten years later is queen of the tennis world'.[14] Goolagong herself was once quoted explaining her belief that 'some people think that Mr. Edwards plucked me out of Barellan and, presto, I became a Wimbledon champion', an idea that gave her 'no credit as a person'.[15] In an autobiography co-authored with Phil Jarratt in 1993, she observed another distorting facet of this framing of her life. 'I have been painted many times in the media as an Eliza Doolittle,' she wrote, 'an Aboriginal urchin who was saved from the savages and taught civilised ways by the Edwards family'.[16]

Sometimes such narratives of success were manufactured deliberately. An Australian Broadcasting Commission programme produced after Goolagong's

---

10   G. Roberts, 'Evonne's Greatest Return', *Good Weekend*, 16 January 1993, p. 8.

11   'Evonne Storms Way to Title – Great Win', *Mercury*, 3 July 1971, p. 42.

12   P. Stone, 'Evonne is Wimbledon's Darling!', *Age*, 3 July 1971, p. 28.

13   A. Trengove, 'You'll Be Right, Sport', *Sun News-Pictorial*, 7 August 1971, p. 21.

14   M. Gibson, 'Evonne – Queen of Tennis', *Daily Telegraph*, 3 July 1971, p. 1.

15   P. Bodo, *The Courts of Babylon: Tales of Greed and Glory in a Harsh New World of Professional Tennis* (New York: Scribner, 1995), p. 110.

16   E. G. Cawley and P. Jarratt, *Home! The Evonne Goolagong Story* (East Roseville: Simon and Schuster, 1993), p. 115.

1971 Wimbledon win upset not only Goolagong, who observed the film crew's attempt to 'illustrate beyond any shadow of doubt the rags-to-riches element of my story', but also other residents of Barellan, who considered that the depiction of the Goolagong family as poor and ostracised was demeaning.[17] While narratives of non-Aboriginal sportspeople sometimes shared a similar rags-to-riches framing, there were thus important differences of tone and emphasis in narratives of Goolagong's life, centring on her Aboriginality. Goolagong's 'extraordinary appeal' with Australian spectators was explained in the NSW Aborigines Welfare Board publication *Dawn* in 1968 as due to her being seen 'not only as a rising champion, but also as an Aborigine who has made good'.[18] Likewise, stories about world champion boxer Lionel Rose that appeared in the press after his sporting career sometimes made reference to his having risen to fame and success from a poor background living in a dirt-floored shack, although also often considering that he had later lost the fairytale.[19] Embedded in narratives of a rags-to-riches transformation was this subtext of salvation, which could assuage white guilt about past injustices when referencing Aboriginal individuals.

Sport has often been considered a field of opportunity in which racial prejudice might be overcome. In an article in the *Sun News-Pictorial* in 1971, Alan Trengove wrote that sport was 'the one arena in which the aboriginal has had *almost* an equal opportunity to display those qualities that the white man admires'.[20] Sport was, he wrote, 'a great leveller', and encouraged 'social integration' and closeness between people.[21] Mark Ella, a successful Aboriginal rugby player, made a similar point in 1989, although he also noted the difficulties that Aboriginal people faced in seeking to 'make it'.[22] Historians have sometimes agreed that sport might be a path to social equality. Richard Broome has argued that Indigenous men 'experienced moments of dominance' in boxing and running performances that 'endured in the minds of all Australians', thus 'modifying the power of white racial dominance'.[23] Likewise in New Zealand, it was sometimes suggested that rugby union was inclusive, an arena in which Māori (men) could easily participate and

---

17 Ibid., pp. 208-209.

18 'Two Years Till Wimbledon?', *Dawn* 17, no. 3 (1968), p. 1. Peter Kell made a similar point when he suggested that the media liked Goolagong and Rose for their 'heartwarming' rags-to-riches stories. P. Kell, *Good Sports: Australian Sport and the Myth of the Fair Go* (Annandale: Pluto, 2000), p. 44.

19 For instance: P. Fitzsimons, 'Rose's Tale Worthy of the Movie Treatment', *Sydney Morning Herald*, 10 February 1990, p. 66; G. Kieza, 'The Rose Tragedy: Real Life Fairytale Turns Sour', *Daily Telegraph*, 17 June 1983, p. 13.

20 Trengove, p. 21, emphasis in original.

21 Ibid., p. 21.

22 Mark Ella, 'Foreword' in B. Harris, *The Proud Champions: Australia's Aboriginal Sporting Heroes* (Crows Nest: Little Hills, 1989), p. 5.

23 R. Broome, 'Enduring Moments of Aboriginal Dominance: Aboriginal Performers, Boxers and Runners', *Labour History*, no. 69 (1995), p. 171.

which was thus a spur to integration or to harmonious race relations.[24] As Geoff Watson noted, the involvement of Māori in sports lent weight to the longstanding view that race relations in New Zealand were better than elsewhere, particularly when Māori players represented New Zealand.[25] However, several scholars have contested these beliefs, often pointing to the barriers faced by Indigenous sportspeople as constituting partial or total refutation of the idea that sport could be a route to social and economic equality.[26] While sport has sometimes provided a means of escaping poverty and a measure of social acceptance, it has also been subject to restrictions on Indigenous participation that have limited this possibility. Indigenous sportspeople who have reached the top of their respective sports have been few. Moreover, the celebration of those who did become sports stars often involved the repetition of racialised and gendered narratives that could reinforce stereotypical understandings of Indigenous peoples and cultures.

The Natural Athlete: Indigeneity and Physicality

Behind the idea that sport was one of few routes to success and recognition for Indigenous peoples seems to lie a continuing belief in their possession of greater natural talent for sport than that possessed by white people. In 1971, the year Goolagong first won Wimbledon, Trengove stated in the Melbourne *Sun News-Pictorial* that Aboriginal people were usually good at sport, and that many 'seem naturally endowed with speed-of-foot and quick reflexes'.[27] Scholars of race and sport have observed this myth of innate athletic ability in framings of Indigenous sportspeople on both sides of the Tasman, particularly in relation to men playing Australian Rules football (AFL) in Australia and rugby union in New Zealand.[28] As Darren Godwell has suggested, failing to question the myth of the natural athlete could result in Aboriginal people becoming 'typecast in

---

24 See for instance: T. McLean, *All Blacks Come Back: Terry McLean Looks at New Zealand and World Rugby* (London: Pelham, 1975), p. 15; S. Zavos, *The Gold and the Black: The Rugby Battles for the Bledisloe Cup: New Zealand vs Australia 1903-94* (St Leonards: Allen and Unwin, 1995), pp. 13-15.

25 G. Watson, 'Sport and Ethnicity in New Zealand', *History Compass* 5, no. 3 (2007), p. 783.

26 D. Booth and C. Tatz, *One-Eyed: A View of Australian Sport* (St Leonards: Allen and Unwin, 2000), p. 3; R. Cashman, *Paradise of Sport: The Rise of Organised Sport in Australia* (Melbourne: Oxford University Press, 1995), pp. 149-150; Kell, pp. 39-41; J. McKay, 'Enlightened Racism and Celebrity Feminism in Contemporary Sports Advertising Discourse', in *Sport, Culture and Advertising: Identities, Commodities and the Politics of Representation*, eds. S. J. Jackson and D. L. Andrews (London and New York: Routledge, 2005), p. 88.

27 Trengove, p. 21.

28 For instance: S. Coram, *The Real and the Unreal: Hyper Narratives of Indigenous Athletes and the Changing Significance of Race* (Altona: Common Ground, 2007), p. 19; D. Godwell, 'Playing the Game: Is Sport as Good For Race Relations as We'd Like to Think?', *Australian Aboriginal Studies*, no. 1-2 (2000), p. 13; C. Hallinan, T. Bruce and J. Bennie, 'Freak Goals and Magical Moments: Commonsense Understandings about Indigenous Footballers', paper presented at The Australian Sociological Association Conference, La Trobe University, 8-11 December 2004, p. 5, accessed 18 October 2007, available at http://www.tasa.org. au/conferencepapers04/docs/LEISURE/HALLINAN_BRUCE_BENNIE.pdf; B. Hokowhitu, 'Tackling Maori

life as sportspeople', as well as reinforcing existing 'racial inequities in power relations'.[29] Further, the emphasis on natural athleticism and physicality often implicitly downplayed Indigenous sportspeople's hard work and suggested that they were closer to nature than were white athletes. Victory for black sportspeople was thus sometimes interpreted as stemming from a 'natural advantage' that was 'often linked to "animal" ability and cunning', while in the case of a white athlete it could be considered a triumph of 'intellect and strategy over brutish instinct'.[30] The discourse of natural athletic talent was thus linked to discourses which constructed Indigenous people as primitive, closer to the animal world than white people; their natural talent in sport was 'socially acceptable savagery'.[31] Such representations of innate athletic ability were not confined to Indigenous sportsmen. Writing in 1994, Jennifer Hargreaves identified similar depictions of black sportswomen as natural athletes, although she did not discuss the experiences of Aboriginal women in Australia or Māori women in New Zealand.[32]

A narrative of natural talent was evident in some representations of Goolagong. In the *Australian*'s coverage of her two victories in the ladies' singles competition at Wimbledon, particularly that by Murray Hedgcock, the myth appeared implicitly several times. After defeating Billie Jean King in the 1971 semi-final, she was said to have an 'extraordinary athletic ability' which 'made her the most intriguing tennis player in the world' at the time.[33] Her play in the 1971 final was described as 'one of the finest displays of natural tennis ability ever seen at Wimbledon', and she was described after her victory in the 1980 semi-final as 'the world's most naturally gifted tennis player'.[34] She was described in the *National Times* in 1982 as having been 'universally accepted as one of the most naturally gifted athletes tennis has known'.[35] Descriptions of her playing style as fluid and natural similarly implied an innate skill rather than one which had been developed through hard work. 'Evonne is the most natural of players,' stated George McGann in the *Bulletin* in 1978.[36] It was this natural talent which enabled the fairytale of her success, according to many framings of her story, although

Masculinity: A Colonial Genealogy of Savagery and Sport', *The Contemporary Pacific* 16, no. 2 (2004), pp. 268-272; M. Wall, 'Stereotypical Constructions of the Maori "Race" in the Media', *New Zealand Geographer* 53, no. 2 (1997), p. 42.

29   Godwell, pp. 16, 19.

30   L.-A. Hall, 'Gesture, Symbol and Identity', in *The Oxford Companion to Aboriginal Art and Culture*, eds. S. Kleinert and M. Neale (Melbourne: Oxford University Press, 2000), p. 438.

31   Hokowhitu, pp. 268-270; Wall, p. 42.

32   J. Hargreaves, *Sporting Females: Critical Issues in the History and Sociology of Women's Sports* (London and New York: Routledge, 1994), p. 255.

33   M. Hedgcock, 'The Day Billie-Jean Was Just an Accessory', *Australian*, 2 July 1971, p. 20.

34   M. Hedgcock, 'Evonne Cures Sick Wimbledon: The Kid From Barellan in Fifth Final', *Australian*, 4 July 1980, p. 14; 'I Knew She'd Win, Says Evonne's Mum', *Australian*, 3 July 1971, p. 1.

35   D. Hickie, 'The Millionairess: How the Quiet Evonne Goolagong Became the Rich and Worldly Mrs Cawley', *National Times*, 19 December 1982, p. 7.

36   G. McGann, 'Evonne Smashes Back Into the Big-Time', *Bulletin*, 7 February 1978, p. 36.

only through the agency of benevolent non-Indigenous figures, particularly Edwards. Hedgcock framed the 'Goolagong story' in this way when he wrote of 'the part-Aboriginal girl from Barellan showing amazing flair for tennis [who] was brought to Sydney to become part of the family of coach Vic Edwards'.[37] Recurring portrayals of Edwards as the mentor who shaped raw talent into a champion suggest the apparently masterly media skills of Edwards himself. Goolagong observed in her 1993 autobiography that Edwards was 'a master at using the media to further his own ends', and several times referred to him as having shaped her story into a legend through his feeding of the media.[38] She quoted him referring to her in a monthly newsletter for his coaching school as 'the person I raised from obscurity to world fame'.[39] Emphasising Goolagong's innate ability and the role of Edwards in shaping that ability denied the centrality of her own determination and hard work in her success. In telling her own story in 1993, Goolagong sought to disrupt these earlier glowing narratives of Edwards' role in her life and career, giving a much more critical account of her relationship with him.

The myth of natural talent also appeared in representations of other Indigenous sportswomen in Australia and New Zealand. Ruia Morrison, a Māori tennis player who competed at Wimbledon four times from 1957 and reached the quarterfinals once, was considered naturally talented by some observers. Profiling her in 1956 for the Māori Affairs Department publication *Te Ao Hou: The New World*, Michael Lindsay termed her 'a "natural"', whose 'graceful, effective style can be traced directly to her Maori lineage'. She had, he wrote, 'an inborn sense of rhythm and a fluid swing controlled by the supple muscles so typical of the Maori'.[40] A much later retrospective article, in 1995, described her as having had 'a natural rhythm and keen eye'.[41] Morrison herself was once quoted commenting, however, that what was termed being a 'natural' stemmed from having learnt much of tennis from her childhood habit of 'swishing' at things with a stick. She was quoted observing that 'I didn't move fast on the court but I had this ability called anticipation'.[42] Such a quality, although arguably 'natural', suggested that contrary to the stereotype, she was indeed a 'thinking' player. Similarly, in *Mana* in 1995, Vanessa Bidois wrote that Morrison was successful as a tennis player despite being small and lacking 'power' in part because of her ability to 'read play exceptionally well' and to 'anticipate'.[43] Morrison was also once quoted, however, saying that there had 'always been good Maori players since I've been

37 M. Hedgcock, 'Our Evonne Comes Bouncing Back', *Australian*, 7 July 1980, p. 7.
38 Cawley and Jarratt, pp. 99-100, 107, 114.
39 Ibid., p. 284.
40 M. Lindsay, 'I Shall Play Tennis All My Life', *Te Ao Hou: The New World*, no. 14 (1956), p. 52.
41 'Morrison's Moment', *New Zealand Sport Monthly*, February 1995, p. 28.
42 M. Romanos, 'Ruia Morrison', *Tu Tangata*, no. 30 (1986), pp. 46-47.
43 V. Bidois, 'You Want to Come Back', *Mana*, no. 8 (1995), p. 67.

around because of their natural co-ordination skills'.[44] Indigenous sportspeople's own articulations of their success in terms of the myth of natural talent add a complicating layer to understanding representations of race and gender in the media.

More than merely downplaying Indigenous athletes' hard work, representations of them as naturally talented could be linked to narratives of them as disinclined to work and train hard. Brendan Hokowhitu noted that Māori men playing rugby were subject to representation as naturally talented but 'lazy', having the talent but not the discipline.[45] In an edited interview, world champion squash player Leilani Joyce (earlier Marsh, later Rorani) remembered: 'I grew up with the stereotype that Maori people have got the talent but they don't have the guts'.[46] In the case of Aboriginal sportspeople, a variation of this theme was the oft-repeated suggestion that they would go 'walkabout' when competing. 'Going walkabout' was perceived as a 'natural' Aboriginal trait. The phrase was used in relation to Aboriginal workers on cattle stations going away for a period, giving time for seeing kin, holding ceremonies and educating children in traditional ways. In this sense, it could be considered positive. Yet the term also conjured up images of directionless wandering, and employers disapproved of a perceived tendency for Aboriginal workers on pastoral stations to leave and go back to their own people and way of life for a while. Aboriginal boxers in the mid-twentieth century were sometimes described in the press as 'inconsistent performers who went "walkabout"'.[47] Rod Humphries' suggestion in the *Sydney Morning Herald* in 1971 that Lionel Rose had the 'ambition' to be a champion again but 'none of the dedication' that he had had the first time likewise implied natural talent that was not harnessed to the necessary determination and diligence.[48] Similarly, Aboriginal footballers were routinely cast as lacking reliability and diligence as well as having natural flair and ability, and were often excluded from positions on the field demanding they be leaders or quick thinkers.[49] Aboriginal netballer Marcia Ella was also reportedly the subject of 'racist slurs' in the 1980s for her 'inconsistent form'.[50]

This image can first be seen in relation to Goolagong in the reported comments of Faith Martin, one of the instructors who noticed her tennis ability at a coaching clinic in Barellan and informed Edwards of her potential. In a 1975 publication claiming to be Goolagong's autobiography, Martin was quoted

44   Romanos, p. 47.
45   Hokowhitu, pp. 271-272.
46   K. Douglas, *Living Life Out Loud: 22 Inspiring New Zealand Women Share Their Wisdom* (Auckland: HarperCollins, 2001), p. 58.
47   Broome, p. 178.
48   R. Humphries, 'What's Happened to Lionel Rose? Like Most Men of 22 He Wants to … Eat, Drink and be Merry', *Sydney Morning Herald*, 2 March 1971, p. 19.
49   Coram, pp. 61-69, 81, 89; Hallinan, Bruce and Bennie, pp. 5-6.
50   Stell, p. 239.

saying that a child might not 'maintain the interest year to year'. 'And with the Goolagongs being Aboriginals', she added, 'you wouldn't count on their not moving somewhere else'.[51] Importantly, there is doubt over the genesis of this publication, as Goolagong hints in her 1993 collaborative autobiography that the earlier book was actually not an autobiography, but was the creation of Edwards and an American journalist, Bud Collins.[52] The author(s) of the book discussed the use of the 'walkabout' image in relation to Goolagong's moments of lost concentration while playing. Supposedly in Goolagong's voice, they explained:

> When this happens, ... most spectators nod knowingly, "Evonne's gone walkabout".
>
> ... I've accepted the expression "walkabout" for my spells, but the word didn't come from me. It came from Mr Edwards. Though I know he wasn't being condescending, it is an expression that irritates many Aborigines ...[53]

The description of her times of lost concentration as 'spells' implied that there was something wrong with her.

The phrase was used more in newspapers during her 1980 Wimbledon campaign, by which time many writers considered that she had not dominated world tennis to the extent that commentators in 1971 had expected. There were eighteen references to this tendency in forty-eight articles from Australian newspapers in 1980, as opposed to seven references in thirty-seven articles in 1971, almost a doubling of their frequency. Lenore Nicklin noted in one match report in the *Sydney Morning Herald* that Goolagong 'appeared to go on her habitual "walkabout"' part way through the match, and commented in another that she 'went walkabout in the second set', playing terrible shots.[54] A play on the idea was made in the headline of one report of her 1980 victory: 'Evonne goes winabout'.[55] More disturbing is the anecdote sometimes told of an unnamed Australian Premier remarking in 1980 of his hope that she 'wouldn't go walkabout like some old boong' in the final.[56] Writing on Australian Wimbledon champions in 1995, Allan Kendall noted that although Goolagong was seen as 'a bit of a perhaper' because she might at any time lose concentration, her record of reaching the final in the Grand Slam events that she played was very steady.[57] It was often taken for granted that her times of lost concentration meant that she did not win

---

51 E. Goolagong and B. Collins, *Evonne! On the Move* (New York: E. P. Dutton, 1975), p. 49.
52 Cawley and Jarratt, pp. 84, 134, 213.
53 Goolagong and Collins, pp. 32-33.
54 L. Nicklin, 'Battle of Singles Warms Up', *Sydney Morning Herald*, 1 July 1980, p. 36; L. Nicklin, 'Evonne is No Irene Buckley', *Sydney Morning Herald*, 4 July 1980, p. 30.
55 S. Jobson, 'Evonne Goes Winabout', *Sun-Herald*, 6 July 1980, p. 1.
56 Tatz, p. 276.
57 A. Kendall, *Australia's Wimbledon Champions* (Sydney: ABC, 1995), pp. 241-242.

as often as she could have. In a book on Australian sportspeople, Terry Smith commented that 'of course, she would have won many more major events but for her famous "walkabouts"'.[58] This stereotypical image of Aboriginal people was thus redeployed in relation to lapses in concentration that all sportspeople are presumably susceptible to, diluting Goolagong's supposedly unbeatable natural ability to explain why she did not win more consistently. Goolagong herself observed in her 1993 autobiography that 'saying that I went "walkabout" was just another way of implying that Aborigines were underachievers who lacked the will to win'.[59]

Goolagong's Aboriginality was also called on to explain her perceived carefree, innocent nature, particularly in relation to her approach to tennis. During her first Wimbledon competition in 1970, Jim Webster wrote in the *Sydney Morning Herald* that 'sophisticated Wimbledon, with all its pompous trappings, was softened yesterday by the endearing simplicity of Evonne Goolagong'.[60] In both 1971 and 1980, a significant number of Australian newspaper articles discussed Goolagong's grace, charm or cheerful nature. On court she was often described as being calm and happy, rather than aggressive, particularly in reports during the 1971 Wimbledon tournament. Described as 'the smiling Evonne' in the Melbourne *Herald* in 1970, she was termed 'the happy little Australian' in the *Sydney Morning Herald* in 1971, and in the *Australian* the same year was described as exhibiting 'girlish enthusiasm'.[61] These depictions demonstrate the intersection of gender and race in representations, as they are both gendered and raced, suggesting a purportedly feminine frivolity as well as a supposedly Aboriginal childlike naturalness. Morrison, although not described as lacking the killer instinct, was similarly described as having a 'sparkling personality' and as being known for her 'good natured impishness'.[62] While these traits were often admired, ascribing them to a basic racial nature infantilised a champion and evoked European images from the time of early contact of Indigenous peoples as childlike. As well as race and gender, however, Goolagong's perceived cheerful and innocent nature and relaxed approach were sometimes ascribed to her country beginnings. In a 1975 children's book, Linda Jacobs wrote that Goolagong's experiences during her career meant 'the quiet country life will never again be for her', but that it could still be seen in her innocence, 'joy of playing' and 'level-headed view of life'.[63] Representations such as these suggest the importance of multiple stereotypes in media representations and caution against racial over-determination.

---

58   T. Smith, *The Champions: Australia's Sporting Greats* (North Ryde: Angus and Robertson, 1990), p. 216.
59   Cawley and Jarratt, p. 141.
60   J. Webster, 'Evonne is a Success', *Sydney Morning Herald*, 25 June 1970, p. 11.
61   A. Chave, 'A "Social" Game for Evonne', *Herald*, 24 June 1970, p. 35; 'Evonne Sweeps Into Final at Wimbledon', *Sydney Morning Herald*, 1 July 1971, p. 13; M. Hedgcock, 'Magnificent Evonne!', *Australian*, 3 July 1971, p. 28.
62   'Morrison's Moment', p. 28; Romanos, p. 46.
63   L. Jacobs, *Evonne Goolagong: Smiles and Smashes* (St Paul: EMC, 1975), p. 38.

The Exotic Other in the White World of Tennis

The image of Wimbledon as a world apart from Goolagong's was often evident in narratives of her life, related to the rags-to-riches myth and a narrative of her as a sort of Cinderella to whom Edwards played the fairy godmother. Hedgcock wrote in the *Sunday Australian* that her 'early background was about as far in distance and style from a gala Wimbledon finals day as it would be possible to imagine'.[64] Developed from indoor tennis, lawn tennis had roots in that 'game of kings', as it was in sixteenth-century France and England. Yet unlike in Europe, public tennis courts were available to the majority of the Australian population, and tennis in the 1950s was not constrained by class distinctions to the extent that it was, for instance, in the United States, so that it was possible for champions to emerge from rural backgrounds as well as urban. Graeme Kinross-Smith considers that it was in the 1950s and 1960s, about the time that Goolagong was a young player, that tennis became 'open ... to a wider spectrum of the Australian population'; moreover, 'traditions of country competition' existed in a number of states, including NSW, which contributed to the rise of strong players despite their 'being distanced in their formative years from coaching and regular top-level competition'.[65] Goolagong was not the first Australian tennis champion to emerge from a less than wealthy rural background.

Tennis was also a predominantly white game for much of its existence. Colin Tatz, writing in 1987, included tennis among sports in Australia that did not have a history of Aboriginal participation, Aboriginal role models, or support networks.[66] Bud Collins wrote in the prologue to the 1975 purported autobiography that it was 'a very white game, with a few exceptions', and Goolagong herself noted that 'tennis in Australia in 1961 was truly the whitest of worlds'.[67] Similarly in New Zealand, the president of the Aotearoa Māori Tennis Association, Dick Garratt, was reported in 1998 to have cited lack of resources and social restrictions on Māori as reasons why fewer successful Māori players emerged in earlier years. Ruia Morrison, he said, reached the level of success she did 'more as a fluke because she was so clever'.[68] Even the clothing that competitors were to wear was white. Before Goolagong appeared on the famous showground of Wimbledon's Centre Court in 1970, her clothing was checked to ascertain that it 'complied with the "predominantly white" regulation'.[69] In a sense, Goolagong was performing whiteness through her dress. She herself made reference to this in 1996, when she was quoted in the press defending

---

64 M. Hedgcock, 'Will Success Spoil Her?', *Sunday Australian*, 4 July 1971, p. 42.
65 G. Kinross-Smith, 'Lawn Tennis', in *Sport in Australia: A Social History*, eds. W. Vamplew and B. Stoddart (Cambridge: Cambridge University Press, 1994), pp. 143-145.
66 C. Tatz, *Aborigines in Sport* (Bedford Park: The Australian Society for Sports History, 1987), p. 58.
67 Cawley and Jarratt, p. 79; Goolagong and Collins, p. 10.
68 A. Sanders, 'Maori Dominate at the Net', *Sunday Star-Times*, 29 March 1998, Sport section, p. 6.
69 Cawley and Jarratt, p. 158.

Cathy Freeman's decision not to carry the Aboriginal flag at the Atlanta Olympic Games. Some controversy had been caused when Freeman carried it along with the Australian flag at the 1994 Commonwealth Games in Victoria in Canada (as I discuss further below), and she was aware that to do so in the Olympic Games might lead to disqualification. Goolagong was quoted in the *Australian* saying that 'it's like I can't wear a black dress at Wimbledon, so that's the rule'.[70]

Wimbledon was the most elite and tradition-bound tournament of all; to play at Wimbledon was to be in the centre of the elite white world of tennis. Goolagong made her first appearance on Wimbledon's prestigious Centre Court in 1970, and lost the match. After the game she spoke to reporters, describing the interview in her 1993 collaborative autobiography. 'I had been thrashed in a second round match by a player who wouldn't be going much further in the tournament either,' she said, but the press conference was 'jam-packed'. The reporters 'didn't want to know about my tennis, they wanted me to speak in Wiradjuri or throw a boomerang or something'. Among the questions she remembered were several telling ones:

> Did I feel proud to be the first Aborigine to play Wimbledon? What did I think of apartheid? Was there racial discrimination at home?[71]

Goolagong's Aboriginality, particularly in the first years of her career before she won major international titles, was a key factor in making her newsworthy. Indeed, Australian newspapers gave considerably more coverage to the 1971 ladies' singles final at Wimbledon than had been the case when Court had won, as expected, the previous year. While Goolagong's youth, supposed outback background and beauty all contributed to the newsworthiness of her win, the sensationalist announcements of her victory in 1971 assuredly owed much to her status as the first Aboriginal tennis star.

As Lee-Anne Hall has argued, Aboriginality can act as 'a reason to be noticed, a journalistic angle [and] a sponsor's delight'.[72] Writing with Jarratt in 1993, Goolagong herself observed that 'my race made me different and therefore newsworthy'.[73] A similar observation was made in the autobiography of world champion boxer Lionel Rose, written collaboratively with Rod Humphries. A tentative suggestion was made that the excessive publicity he experienced might have had 'something to do with being the first Aboriginal to become a world champion at anything and with my assimilation into the white community'.[74]

---

70   J. Ellicott, P. Jenkins and P. Atkinson, 'Cawley Flies the Flag for Freeman', *Australian*, 2 August 1996, p. 2.
71   Cawley and Jarratt, p. 158.
72   Hall, p. 438, emphasis removed.
73   Cawley and Jarratt, p. 13.
74   L. Rose and R. Humphries, *Lionel Rose: Australian: The Life Story of a Champion* (Sydney: Angus and Robertson, 1969), p. 124.

Certainly, several press reports of his world championship victory in 1968 noted that he was the first Aboriginal person to win a world title.[75] Much earlier, Katerina Nehua's being Māori was a point of interest in the media when she competed in Australia in the early 1930s. Caroline Daley argued that as 'a non-indigenous indigenous person' Nehua had 'offered the Australian journalists an exotic allure that the white contestants lacked'.[76] On rare occasions, journalists themselves made astute observations as to the reasons for Goolagong's media appeal. Before her 1971 Wimbledon win, Denis O'Brien asked in the *Bulletin* whether she was 'tennis box-office' because she was 'a genuine whizz', or whether it was also partly because she was 'part-Aboriginal'.[77]

As with other Indigenous sportspeople, Goolagong's Aboriginality was frequently referenced in the media. Such references ranged from descriptions of her as an Aboriginal or part-Aboriginal tennis player, rather than as an Australian tennis player or simply a tennis player, through allusions to a mystical cultural heritage, to descriptions of her physical appearance. Mike Gibson described her in the *Daily Telegraph* in 1971 as a 'frizzy-haired little piccaninny', although knowing Goolagong would not like it, because he thought 'that is what she looked like'. In the same article, he also described her as having 'blood from the Dream Time running through her veins'.[78] Goolagong once commented in an edited interview that when she first went to Sydney 'news clippings used to annoy me a bit, because it would be "Aboriginal Evonne Goolagong", and that's all they'd put'.[79] In the early twentieth century, Katerina Nehua was similarly identified in the press by her ethnicity. Caroline Daley observed that 'the fact that she was Māori was a frequent refrain', and that she 'was rarely referred to as a New Zealander, even in the New Zealand press'.[80] Jennifer Hargreaves noted in 2000 that 'racialised accounts of Aboriginal superstars' that treat them 'as the "Other"' appeared 'commonplace' in the Australian and Canadian medias.[81] The same might be said of the New Zealand media. Stella Coram similarly observed that in newspaper pieces about Aboriginal AFL players, one 'defining feature' was that 'indigenous athletes are known by their Aboriginality', which 'explains everything from their successes to their challenges'. Newspaper articles about Aboriginal athletes, she argued, 'reify race logics' and are 'essentialist' in that 'they determine that indigenous athletes are different in cultural and racial

---

75   For example: 'Champion on Way Home: Rose Has Big Choice of Challengers', *Sydney Morning Herald*, 29 February 1968, p. 13; R. Mitchell, 'A Dedicated Boy Who Hitched a Ride to World Crown', *Australian*, 29 February 1968, p. 15.
76   Daley, p. 44.
77   D. O'Brien, 'Evonne Goolagong: A Touch of TNT', *Bulletin*, 27 February 1971, p. 32.
78   M. Gibson, 'A New Queen Aces King', *Daily Telegraph*, 2 July 1971, p. 39.
79   S. Mitchell, *Winning Women: Challenging the Norms in Australian Sport* (Ringwood: Penguin, 1985), p. 69.
80   Daley, p. 44.
81   J. Hargreaves, *Heroines of Sport: The Politics of Difference and Identity* (London and New York: Routledge, 2000), p. 91.

terms'.[82] Such a focus on race in framing narratives of Indigenous athletes set them apart from non-Indigenous athletes and irrevocably marked them as different.

Yet while her Aboriginality was often exoticised, Goolagong was sometimes also written of in ways that repressed her Aboriginality. Once she had become internationally successful, she began to be described slightly less often as Aboriginal than had been the case in the early years of her career. She herself was quoted in *Deadly Vibe* magazine in 2001 observing that although she did not follow what was written about her when she was playing, 'I did notice that the more successful I became, the whiter I seemed to become'.[83] New Zealand hockey and tennis player Margaret Raureti Hiha made a similar point in an edited interview given after her retirement from competitive sport. 'You're a Maori until you succeed,' she said, and after that 'you're a New Zealander or perhaps a New Zealand Maori'. As well as opera singers Kiri Te Kanawa and Inia Te Wiata, she argued that such a pattern was obvious in descriptions of tennis player Kelly Evernden, who 'was a Maori when he was young, and … became a New Zealander when he became world class in tennis'.[84] Closely tied to such representations were imaginings of the nation, and of the sometimes ambivalent place of Indigenous people within it. By 1980, Goolagong had become thoroughly Australian, celebrated as one of Australia's sporting heroes, and her Aboriginality was often elided. Like Freeman later, she was sometimes referred to as belonging to an imagined Australian nation: 'our Evonne'.[85] In one article in the Melbourne *Herald* in 1980, she was described as 'our Evonne, with her Aussie smile and nonchalance'.[86] Particularly when a competitor in international tournaments, Goolagong both actually and metaphorically represented the Australian nation.

There was potentially more to such descriptions than a simple embrace of her tennis achievements. Kell argued that Goolagong's 'media success' and 'acceptance [by] mainstream Australian society' was built partly on repressing Aboriginal identity and not being seen as 'radical'.[87] Goolagong was featured in the *Australian Women's Weekly* after her 1971 Wimbledon win. In a recent study of that publication between 1945 and 1971, Susan Sheridan, Barbara Baird, Kate Borrett and Lyndall Ryan argued that Aboriginal people were 'named as individuals' in the magazine only when being included as 'success stories', that

---

82 Coram, pp. 155-156.
83 'All About Evonne', *Deadly Vibe*, no. 47 (2001), p. 8.
84 A. Brown, ed., *Mana Wahine: Women Who Show the Way* (Auckland: Reed, 1994), p. 89.
85 M. Gawenda, 'Evonne, So Fan-Tastic!', *Herald*, 3 July 1980, p. 38; Hedgcock, 'Evonne Cures Sick Wimbledon', p. 14; Hedgcock, 'Our Evonne Comes Bouncing Back', p. 7.
86 B. Matthews, 'Mr Nasty and Mr Nice', *Herald*, 27 June 1980, p. 13.
87 Kell, p. 44.

is, as 'successes of assimilation'.[88] Goolagong does not appear to have been explicitly described in such terms in the *Women's Weekly*, but the celebration of her as successfully assimilated was sometimes implicit in media treatment of her. Perhaps the most obvious example was an advertisement which appeared in the official publication *New Dawn* in 1974. Readers could write in for a copy of a booklet produced by the Department of Labour in which young Aboriginal people were shown doing a variety of jobs, along with information on how to obtain a similar job. Goolagong's words from the introduction of the booklet were quoted at the top of the advertisement, and a picture of her was used to illustrate it.[89]

Goolagong herself considered that when Aboriginal people were successful in any field, 'there is a tendency, perhaps unconscious, for Australians to say, "See, we're not holding them back, we give them every opportunity"'. She suggested that the fact that she was given 'a ticker-tape parade through the streets of Sydney and a Lord Mayoral reception' while multiple Wimbledon winners Court and John Newcombe had not received such an honour reflected the tension in 'racial politics' in Australia in 1971 and 'a kind of racial relief' at her win, 'a feeling that somehow my achievements proved that Australia was a land of equal opportunity'.[90] The enthusiastic embrace of 'our Evonne' perhaps carried echoes of this relief. A concept of 'enlightened racism' is useful in understanding such framings. Representing an Indigenous figure in ways which emphasised him or her as successful in the terms of the dominant white culture allowed non-Indigenous admiration for the person's achievements, while also implying that such success was open to all who had the will to achieve it, denying the existence of systemic barriers.[91] Framings of Indigenous athletes that repressed their Indigenous identity might thus be as problematic as those which exoticised it.

Around the time that Goolagong rose to international prominence, a strong Aboriginal protest movement was visible in Australia (as discussed in Chapter One). Within this context, Goolagong was sometimes criticised by Aboriginal people for remaining unpoliticised, or for turning herself white and failing to make sufficient efforts to assist her people. That is, she was reproached for not actively representing Aboriginal people in a political sense. She was publicly criticised by Charles Perkins, who said that he 'couldn't care less' about her sporting successes because she 'didn't care about [her] race', and in an angry

---

88 S. Sheridan, B. Baird, K. Borrett and L. Ryan, *Who Was That Woman? The* Australian Women's Weekly *in the Postwar Years* (Sydney: University of New South Wales Press, 2002), p. 146.

89 'New Aboriginal Employment Booklet Available', *New Dawn* 5, no. 2 (1974), p. 6.

90 Cawley and Jarratt, pp. 204-205.

91 McKay, p. 83. For the original articulation of this concept of 'enlightened racism', see S. Jhally and J. Lewis, *Enlightened Racism: The Cosby Show, Audiences, and the Myth of the American Dream* (Boulder: Westview, 1992), especially pp. 93-98.

poem by poet Kevin Gilbert.[92] The poem, published after her win in 1980, was a bitter attack on her for not using her prominence to call attention to the hardships suffered by Aboriginal people.[93] In her collaborative autobiography, Goolagong's response was, partly, that she did more for Aboriginal people by playing at the top of her sport than she might have 'with a hundred soapbox speeches'. While people in Australia protested about apartheid and the prospect of racial disturbances was raised, she wrote, 'a black Australian curtseyed before royalty, then went on to prove that Aborigines could make it to the top'.[94]

Goolagong received much criticism when she agreed to play in South Africa in 1971, including from prominent Aboriginal people who felt that she should not go and that she was letting down her people. In her 1993 autobiography, her comments about this incident included that she did not know very much about South Africa or apartheid, but that once criticism began, she was glad of the chance to 'show white South Africans just what a black athlete could do'.[95] Goolagong thus appears to have considered herself a role model and example rather than a political spokesperson. Playing tennis, she could represent Aboriginal people at the same time as she represented Australia, and she could fulfil such a representative role without being overtly political. Moving back to Australia later in life, Goolagong became involved in tennis development for young people and in Indigenous sports programmes, such as the Goolagong National Development Camp for Aboriginal children. Her autobiography was also produced after her return to Australia, co-authored with Jarratt. Throughout her career, she emphasised, she was always 'a proud Aboriginal woman, a Wiradjuri Koori' who had 'stayed close' to her 'Aboriginal roots'. Becoming a champion required 'sacrifices', she stressed, and if she had 'shut out certain things that others thought were obvious', tennis 'was only a part' of her life. 'If I hadn't become a champion', she asked, 'who would listen to me now?'[96] Answering her critics, and demonstrating that she had not lost touch with her Aboriginal heritage, appear to have been crucial imperatives in Goolagong's decision to write her own story.

Beauty, the Body, Feminism and Sport

Women's position in sports during the twentieth century was contested and shifting. In this context, Indigenous sportswomen were represented in the media not only in terms of narratives about race, but also about gender, and the two

---

92   Cawley and Jarratt, pp. 337-339; 'Perkins Fires Evonne a Volley', *Daily Telegraph*, 9 July 1980, p. 3.

93   K. Gilbert, 'To My Cousin Evonne Cawley', *Bulletin Literary Supplement*, 30 September 1980, p. 2.

94   Cawley and Jarratt, pp. 205, 339.

95   Ibid., pp. 174-177.

96   Ibid., pp. 12, 16.

intersected in crucial ways. On her return to Australia after winning Wimbledon in 1971, Goolagong was received as a celebrity. As well as the parade and reception in Sydney, she attended dinners and functions, appeared on a television show and was present at a parade and 'Wimbledon Ball' held in Barellan. A photo spread appeared in the *Australian Women's Weekly*. Three pictures showed her in action on the court, while a larger picture took up the full second page, showing her at the Wimbledon Ball, with a caption telling the reader that 'happy Evonne' wore a 'slim-fitting gown' in 'gold-and-silver lame'.[97] A later article, in September 1971, reported that she had purchased many clothes while overseas, including the outfit she was wearing that day. Mention was made of her beauty and glamour, and that she 'looked very attractive and outstanding among the crowd that swirled around her'.[98] In these articles, and in the images which accompanied them, Goolagong was placed within discourses of femininity that were common to women's magazines at the time. Images of Goolagong published in women's magazines were also more likely to show her as part of a family unit than were images published in newspapers, which most frequently pictured her within a tennis context. Such textual and visual depictions of her were in many ways not different from the 'consistent portrayal of white women as active, glamorous and sexually desirable' which was evident in the *Australian Women's Weekly* at the time. Aboriginal women appeared in the magazine between 1945 and 1971 'only if they conformed to such ideals of white femininity'.[99] Clearly, Goolagong could be depicted in just such ways.

Likewise, Māori women who featured in the *New Zealand Woman's Weekly* were often depicted in ways that focused on domestic details, fashion and beauty. In 1990, an article appeared about the marriage of New Zealand netball captain Waimarama Taumaunu, and another article described lawn bowls player Millie Khan as a 'modest mother of seven'.[100] Outside of sport, similar portrayals of Māori women were also evident. Opera singer Dame Kiri Te Kanawa, for instance, was often quoted discussing the centrality in her life of home and family, or her approach to motherhood and marriage.[101] Indeed, articles about Te Kanawa in the *New Zealand Woman's Weekly* throughout her career often elided racial difference in a focus on shared gender experiences.

While women's magazines such as these were vitally implicated in delineating ideals of femininity, Indigenous sportswomen were also represented in similar ways in other print media texts. Goolagong was often described as a 'girl' in

---

97 D. Brook, 'Triumph of Evonne Goolagong', *Australian Women's Weekly*, 21 July 1971, pp. 8-9.
98 G. Newton, 'Evonne Goes Home', *Australian Women's Weekly*, 8 September 1971, pp. 8-9.
99 Sheridan, Baird, Borrett and Ryan, p. 114.
100 'Cards and Letters Just Kept Coming', *New Zealand Woman's Weekly*, 2 April 1990, p. 13; P. Neville, 'Netball Star's Finest Match', *New Zealand Woman's Weekly*, 29 January 1990, p. 10.
101 For instance: A. Lord, 'Dame Kiri: "If I Lost My Voice …"', *New Zealand Woman's Weekly*, 15 July 1991, pp. 12-14.

reports of Wimbledon in 1971.[102] Though she was young at the time, such descriptions also echoed common representations of sporting women as 'girls' or as behaving in 'girlish' ways.[103] In other familiar representations of dominant ideals of femininity, she was described in 1971 as 'vivacious' and as a 'pretty, petite 19-year-old', and despite its being irrelevant to her tennis ability, her choice in fashion was detailed.[104] She was 'Wimbledon's sweetheart', 'Australia's darling of the courts' and 'Wimbledon's darling'.[105] Playing after the birth of her first child, she was described in reports of the Wimbledon tournament in 1980 as 'the world's favourite tennis mum' by former Australian Wimbledon champion John Newcombe, writing with John Thirsk in the *Daily Telegraph*, as 'Supermum' by Trengove in the *Sun-Herald* and as 'happy Evonne Cawley, contented wife and mother' by Hedgcock in the *Australian*.[106] Similarly gendered representations sometimes appeared in print media stories about Māori sportswomen, as indeed was the case in stories about non-Indigenous sportswomen on both sides of the Tasman and more widely. In 1995, reporter Chris Fogarty asked in the *Sunday Star-Times* whether or not a male rugby player would be asked 'similar questions about the demands of family, work and sporting career' as were asked of New Zealand netballer Noeline Taurua-Barnett.[107] Awareness of this issue did not, however, stop Fogarty from including mention of Taurua-Barnett's partner and daughter in the article.

A focus on domestic details, clothes and beauty emphasised attributes perceived as feminine, and this focus has been common in media representations of sportswomen during the twentieth century. As Marion Stell argued, 'reassurance that a champion athlete is still a normal woman is a continuing need in our society'.[108] Jim McKay has observed that scholars approaching the study of sport from a 'feminist/cultural studies perspective' have demonstrated that the media 'naturalise hegemonic definitions of "real men" and "real women" in sport'.[109] Several scholars have observed the continuing frequency of reporting on sportswomen's domestic lives, particularly in relation to marriage and

---

102   For example: A. Chave and M. Bingham, 'Evonne Is New Queen', *Herald*, 3 July 1971, p. 4; Hedgcock, 'Will Success Spoil Her?', p. 42; 'Moochi Is the Wonder Girl of World Tennis', *Age*, 3 July 1971, p. 1.

103   E. H. Wensing and T. Bruce, 'Bending the Rules: Media Representations of Gender During an International Sporting Event', *International Review for the Sociology of Sport* 38, no. 4 (2003), pp. 388, 392-393.

104   'Evonne's a Winner On Court and Off', *Age*, 2 July 1971, p. 26; C. Pritchard, 'Tennis Queen Dances All Night to Celebrate', *Sun-Herald*, 4 July 1971, p. 5; P. Stone, 'Smashing Win to Evonne', *Age*, 1 July 1971, p. 28.

105   M. Gawenda, 'Tearific – That's Champ Evonne', *Herald*, 5 July 1980, p. 1; J. Newcombe and J. Thirsk, 'Our Only Hope', *Daily Telegraph*, 23 June 1980, p. 6; Stone, 'Evonne is Wimbledon's Darling!', p. 28; R. Yallop, 'Borg's Biggest Battle', *Age*, 23 June 1980, p. 11.

106   M. Hedgcock, 'Evonne Plans to Defend Her Title', *Australian*, 7 July 1980, p. 1; J. Newcombe and J. Thirsk, 'She Can Win', *Daily Telegraph*, 4 July 1980, p. 64; A. Trengove, 'Supermum is Kelly's Hero ...', *Sun-Herald*, 6 July 1980, p. 65.

107   C. Fogarty, 'Taurua-Barnett Times It Right', *Sunday Star-Times*, 18 June 1995, p. B14.

108   Stell, p. 180.

109   J. McKay, 'Embodying the "New" Sporting Woman', *Hecate* 20, no. 1 (1994), p. 69.

motherhood, and of narrative framings that trivialise their achievements or emphasise their (hetero)sexuality.[110] In being framed in such ways in the print media, Goolagong and other Indigenous sportswomen shared in representations common to all sportswomen and to which sportsmen, Indigenous or non-Indigenous, were not subject.

Narratives of white Australian champion Margaret Court's life were similar to those told of Goolagong. Court also came from a 'little country town', and was once described as the 'girl from Albury who became a tennis legend'.[111] She was said to have had 'a poor and tough upbringing in the backblocks' of Albury, making her story almost as much a rags-to-riches tale as Goolagong's.[112] An oft-repeated story about both Court and Goolagong is of their having used pieces of wood as their first rackets when children.[113] Also like Goolagong, Court was discovered as a talent while still young, moving to Melbourne aged fifteen under the patronage of a former champion, Frank Sedgman, who was once said to have 'plucked' her from her hard life in Albury.[114] Court was considered to be 'athletic' by several commentators, and was described as 'a natural athlete before she went near a gym' by Allan Kendall.[115] Importantly, she was also known for being subject to nerves affecting her game, particularly on the Centre Court at Wimbledon.[116] Indeed, in one book of famous Australian sportspeople, it was stated that she would 'undoubtedly have had an even more impressive record but for her "big match" nerves'.[117] The difference, of course, was that in Court's case this weakness in her game was not blamed on race or discussed in racially loaded terms.

It is this very invisibility of whiteness, that allows it to be imposed as a norm, that has contributed to the continuation of historical inequalities in power relations. While white feminists have begun to write about and analyse whiteness, Aileen Moreton-Robinson has argued that, rather than 'white race privilege' being

---

110   A. Burroughs and J. Nauright, 'Women's Sports and Embodiment in Australia and New Zealand', in *Sport in Australasian Society: Past and Present*, eds. J. A. Mangan and J. Nauright (London: Frank Cass, 2000), p. 198; P. Heaven and D. Rowe, 'Gender, Sport and Body Image', in *Sport and Leisure: Trends in Australian Popular Culture*, eds. D. Rowe and G. Lawrence (Sydney: Harcourt Brace Jovanovich, 1990), p. 60; McKay, 'Embodying the "New" Sporting Woman', pp. 70, 77-78; Stell, p. 233; D. Stevenson, 'Women, Sport and Globalization: Competing Discourses of Sexuality and Nation', *Journal of Sport and Social Issues* 26, no. 2 (2002), p. 212; Wensing and Bruce, pp. 387-388.

111   Kendall, p. 206; H. Schmitt, 'After the Baby – Back to Tennis', *Herald*, 10 February 1972, p. 13.

112   P. Wilson, 'Mrs Tennis Court', *People*, 4 February 1981, p. 19.

113   See for instance: 'Australian Revolutionised Women's Tennis', *Daily Mirror*, 27 May 1977, p. 50; Kendall, p. 232.

114   For instance: 'A Grand Slammer', *Daily Mirror*, 5 November 1984, p. 38; Wilson, 'Mrs Tennis Court', p. 19.

115   Kendall, p. 211. For descriptions of her as 'athletic', see: 'Margaret Court Wins Easily', *Age*, 2 July 1970, p. 24; L. Tingay, 'All Time Greats: Margaret Court', *Tennis World*, July 1984, p. 37.

116   'Australian Revolutionised Women's Tennis', p. 50; Hedgcock, 'Magnificent Evonne!' p. 28; Kendall, pp. 216-217, 219; Tingay, p. 37.

117   M. Andrews, *101 Australian Sporting Heroes* (Frenchs Forest: Child and Associates, 1990), p. 27.

'interrogated as a form of difference', it 'is an invisible omnipresent norm'.[118] As she observes, the 'white cultural system … exists as omnipresent and natural, yet invisible', and race exists as 'a categorical object … deemed to belong to the other'.[119] For Court, while print media representations of her sometimes made visible her position as a woman in the male-dominated realm of sport, no reference was made to her as white. She was often described in terms related to gender or age, as a 'woman player', a 'girl', a '30-year-old Perth mother' or as 'Mrs Court'.[120] Yet she was only ever described as an 'Australian' tennis player, while Goolagong was also sometimes tagged as Aboriginal or part-Aboriginal, though less often by 1980. Goolagong was represented as different, Other, the only Aboriginal woman playing international tennis. Court was part of the 'invisible omnipresent norm' in her whiteness, if still marginalised by her gender.

It is important also to consider the context of sport in general and tennis in particular at the time. As David Rowe and Jim McKay argue, 'the relationship between sport and hegemonic masculinity is both deep and enduring'. They suggest that 'one reason that sport is such a resonant symbol of hegemonic masculinity is that it literally *embodies* the seemingly natural superiority of men over women'.[121] Some debate exists among scholars as to the extent and timing of the impact of the second wave feminist movement upon women's participation in sport, but it is clear that the movement did have at least some impact by the 1980s.[122] Tennis has been, as Deborah Stevenson has argued, 'a site where debates on women and sport have flourished'.[123] In the early 1970s, considerable protest took place against women's tennis receiving less attention and less prize money than men's tennis. A split developed between the United States Lawn Tennis Association (USLTA) and a new Women's Pro Tour, the Virginia Slims circuit, after the latter was set up in 1970 with larger monetary prizes by Gladys Heldman from *World Tennis* magazine. In 1973, when the USLTA held a women's pro tour competing with the Virginia Slims tour, two groups of female players had formed, with Goolagong in the USLTA faction.[124] Tennis, in particular, has also been a sport in which players were represented in terms of gender stereotypes and their

118   A. Moreton-Robinson, 'Troubling Business: Difference and Whiteness Within Feminism', *Australian Feminist Studies* 15, no. 33 (2000), p. 348.

119   Ibid., p. 349; A. Moreton-Robinson, 'Whiteness, Epistemology and Indigenous Representation', in *Whitening Race: Essays in Social and Cultural Criticism*, ed. A. Moreton-Robinson (Canberra: Aboriginal Studies Press, 2004), p. 76.

120   For example: 'Australian Revolutionised Women's Tennis', p. 50; 'Grand Slam is Maggie's Target', *Advertiser*, 20 June 1973, p. 18; Schmitt, p. 13; J. Thirsk, 'Aussies on the Ball: Grand Slam Tennis Mum', *Daily Telegraph*, 4 July 1973, p. 24.

121   D. Rowe and J. McKay, 'A Man's Game: Sport and Masculinities', in *Male Trouble: Looking at Australian Masculinities*, eds. S. Tomsen and M. Donaldson (North Melbourne: Pluto, 2003), pp. 200, 206, original emphasis.

122   On this issue see: Booth and Tatz, p. 11; Heaven and Rowe, p. 59; Stell, pp. 233, 251-252.

123   Stevenson, p. 212.

124   G. M. Heldman, 'The Women's Pro Game', in *The Encyclopedia of Tennis*, ed. M. Robertson (New York: Viking, 1974), pp. 68-70.

physical appearance and dress scrutinised. As Stevenson argues, 'in contrast to other high-profile sports such as track and field and swimming, where such an image has never been hegemonic, the image of the fit, yet feminine, tennis player persists' even in the early twenty-first century. Tennis, she states, 'is a sport where assumptions about hegemonic femininity have been challenged, an arena where the media mediate the negotiation of sexuality, image, and the sporting woman'.[125] Media depictions of Goolagong during her career in tennis can only be thoroughly understood within this context.

By the time of her second win in 1980, Goolagong was sometimes represented as a feminine player who was different from the manly women supposedly then appearing on the circuit. Writing in the *Sun-Herald*, Sandra Jobson felt that what 'really won the applause from the British' was Goolagong's 'calm femininity', at a time when female tennis players were supposedly 'neurotic', had '"prune faces"' or were allegedly lesbians. She and fellow-finalist Chris Evert-Lloyd, Jobson noted, were 'two of the most popular and attractive girl players', as well as being 'happily married'.[126] Another reporter, Michael Gawenda, described Goolagong in the Melbourne *Herald* in 1980 as having 'grace and charm' and 'sheer femininity'.[127] The familiar representation of Goolagong as cheerful, innocent and lacking a killer instinct was also a feminised image, in that she was not seen to be implicating her gender by playing tennis. Similarly, Court was described in the *Australian* in 1970 as a powerful athlete, stronger than some men, but 'recognisably – thank God – a woman'.[128] This focus on femininity is particularly important in the context of a widespread belief in tennis that the best female players played 'like men'.[129] In an echo of the dichotomy that female athletes have continually struggled with over the years, Goolagong's defeat of Court in 1971 was 'thought to be the triumph of grace over power'.[130] Moreover, Angela Burroughs and John Nauright have observed the growth of a 'new focus on the "heterosexiness" of female players' arising 'through changes in media representation' approximately over the period of Goolagong's tennis career. They argue that a 'heterosexy hegemony' arose in Australia and New Zealand that 'has worked to position female athletes in opposition to male athletes and to valorise femininity in women's sport'.[131] Writing of the period between 1970 and 1990, Marion Stell has observed that as 'competition got tougher and sportswomen needed to train harder, longer and with more emphasis on strength, so too did

125   Stevenson, pp. 209, 212.
126   Jobson, p. 2.
127   M. Gawenda, 'Martina's Price of Fame', *Herald*, 21 June 1980, p. 21.
128   A. Cooke, 'Margaret – Powerful, Charming, Sentimental Favourite', *Australian*, 1 September 1970, p. 20.
129   Stevenson, p. 218.
130   Stell, p. 262.
131   Burroughs and Nauright, p. 189.

the pressure to conform to society's image of a real woman'.[132] Indigenous sportswomen were not immune to such pressures, and representations of them in the print media often combined these gendered tropes with the racialised ones discussed earlier.

Freeman and Reconciliation: Race, Gender, Nation and Sport in the 1990s

Many Indigenous women have made their mark in a variety of sports on both sides of the Tasman since Goolagong's retirement from the tennis circuit in the early 1980s. Women such as Nova Peris and Cathy Freeman in Australia, and Leilani Joyce in New Zealand reached great sporting success and became well-known nationally and internationally. Yet like all women in sport, Māori and Aboriginal sportswomen continued to be represented in gendered ways in the print media, at least at times, and often continued to struggle for recognition in comparison with sportsmen. Neither did media representations entirely cease to frame Indigenous sportswomen as racial Others. Toni Bruce and Christopher Hallinan suggest that representations of Freeman in the print media in the late twentieth and early twenty-first centuries were little different from those evident in media narratives about Goolagong. Among other framings, Freeman was represented as a 'natural runner' and as 'unmotivated', as well as being represented in ways which emphasised perceived ideals of femininity.[133] One article which referred to her 'natural talent', printed in the *Sun-Herald* in 1994, was titled simply 'The Natural'.[134] Another, in the *Daily Telegraph* in 1996, commented that her 'spritely charm' at the Atlanta Olympic Games would 'long be remembered'.[135] At the same time, one sign of new departures in media representations of sportswomen was the frequency with which Freeman was represented as similar to machines in her ability.[136] Some representations of Freeman made explicit comparisons with Goolagong. Writing in the *Sydney Morning Herald* in 1995, Jeff Wells described Freeman and Goolagong as both having 'a fine Aboriginal grace in their movement and their mien'.[137] After Freeman's silver medal win in Atlanta in 1996, Richard Yallop wrote that Goolagong's 'charm' was that 'she carried her extraordinary talent so naturally and with such unaffected spontaneity', and that

---

132   Stell, p. 258.
133   T. Bruce and C. Hallinan, 'Cathy Freeman: The Quest For Australian Identity', in *Sport Stars: The Cultural Politics of Sporting Celebrity*, eds. D. L. Andrews and S. J. Jackson (London and New York: Routledge, 2001), pp. 264-265.
134   B. Holmes, 'The Natural', *Sun-Herald*, 13 March 1994, pp. 68, 85.
135   'Cathy Has the World at Her Feet', *Daily Telegraph*, 31 July 1996, p. 10.
136   G. Gardiner, 'Running for Country: Australian Print Media Representation of Indigenous Athletes in the 27th Olympiad', *Journal of Sport and Social Issues* 27, no. 3 (2003), p. 248.
137   J. Wells, 'Cathy The Colossus? You're Kidding!', *Sydney Morning Herald*, 12 August 1995, p. 62.

'it was exactly the same when Cathy Freeman, Evonne's natural successor, wrote her name into Olympic history at Atlanta stadium'.[138] Like Goolagong, Freeman was herself aware of her position as embodying Aboriginal prowess in the face of racism and exclusion. She recalled that when she won gold in the 400m at the Commonwealth Games in 1994 and carried the Aboriginal flag along with the Australian flag on her victory lap, she 'wanted to shout, "Look at me, look at my skin. I'm black and I'm the best"'.[139]

Figure 4: 'Cathy Freeman, Commonwealth Games, Victoria, British Columbia, Canada, 1994', Melanie Collins.

Photograph. nla.pic-an22839269. National Library of Australia, Canberra.

Similar to representations of Goolagong, an imperative towards narrating sporting achievements in terms of salvation was sometimes evident in later framings of Freeman and of hockey player and runner Nova Peris (earlier Peris-Kneebone). After Peris won gold as a member of the successful Australian hockey team at the Olympic Games in Atlanta in 1996, the win was described in the *Age* as particularly great 'for someone who has overcome the disadvantages of isolation and lack of opportunity', as well as having had a child at a young age.[140] In this rags-to-riches narrative, racism appears to feature rarely as a barrier to success. Greg Gardiner noted this tendency in relation to an article about Peris in the

---

138   R. Yallop, 'Cathy's Charm Has a Silver Lining', *Australian*, 31 July 1996, p. 1.
139   C. Freeman and S. Gullan, *Cathy: Her Own Story* (Camberwell: Penguin, 2004), p. 81.
140   R. Hinds, 'Unbridled Joy Over Gold Win', *Age*, 3 August 1996, p. A1.

Australian in 1998, in which she was represented as having overcome much hardship, type unspecified. Where racism was mentioned, he observed, it was conceived of as merely 'an "obstacle" to overcome'.[141] After her silver medal victory in Atlanta, Freeman's 'road to the top' was similarly described in the *Age* as having 'been rockier than most', and although it was acknowledged that 'behind every athlete's Olympic medal is struggle and hardship', it was suggested that 'perhaps Cathy Freeman's story – and that of her mother, Cecilia, – are among the most poignant'.[142]

Peris and Freeman themselves both sometimes gave weight to such interpretations of their successes. Each suggested in their respective collaborative autobiographies that they desired their stories to encourage people, especially young Aboriginal people, and that dreams could be achieved.[143] Although such representations of Peris and Freeman emphasised their own hard work and determination to a greater extent than was the case in representations of Goolagong, they remained problematic. Stressing hard work and tenacity as a way in which systemic problems of poverty, exclusion or racism might be overcome potentially implied that failure to overcome those barriers was the fault of the individual concerned themselves.

Representations of Indigenous sportswomen also, however, encapsulate threads of discourse other than those of race and gender. Throughout this discussion, the intricate relationships that exist between discourses of race and gender and those of nation have been apparent. Indeed, ideas of nation have been central to discourses about sport. Sporting events, particularly international events, are 'a key arena in which particular versions of nation are expressed'.[144] Rod Brookes is right to argue that it 'is difficult to envisage sportswomen being held up by the media as being representative of the nation in the way that, for example, male soccer or rugby teams are'.[145] Yet as Bruce and Hallinan argue, 'highly mediated images of Aboriginality and sport have become integral to an understanding of what it means to be Australian'.[146] Echoes of similar intersections between race and nation were sometimes evident in New Zealand as well. The comment was made in the *New Zealand Herald* in 1991, for example, that 'no truer-bluer Kiwi than Wai [Taumaunu] ... could be chosen' to captain the New Zealand netball side.[147] Caroline Daley has noted a tendency in New Zealand sports history for Māori sportspeople 'to be whitewashed to become Brown Britons' or

---

141 Gardiner, pp. 241-242.
142 G. Roberts, 'The Pride Of Being Cathy's Mum', *Age*, 21 September 1996, Saturday Extra, p. 3.
143 Freeman and Gullan, p. 80; N. Peris and I. Heads, *Nova: My Story: The Autobiography of Nova Peris* (Sydney: ABC, 2003), pp. 300-301.
144 Bruce and Hallinan, p. 260.
145 R. Brookes, *Representing Sport* (London: Arnold, 2002), p. 130.
146 Bruce and Hallinan, p. 260.
147 McLean on Sport, 'Taumaunu Displays Mana on Court', *New Zealand Herald*, 2 May 1991, section 2, p. 7.

for 'their presence in team sports [to be] noted as evidence of harmonious race relations'.[148] As is clear in the transformation of Indigenous sportspeople in the press from Aboriginal and Māori athletes to Australian and New Zealand athletes, Indigenous sportspeople have been represented in ways which bear sharply on imaginings about the nation in Australia and New Zealand. Media portrayals of Indigenous sportswomen are thus tightly implicated in representing particular versions of the nation. Representing Australia on an international sporting stage, Goolagong could be depicted as an exotic novelty, an assimilation success or a symbol that all was well in Australian race relations.

Most obviously, race and nation were deeply embedded in media narratives about Cathy Freeman, possibly the most famous Aboriginal sportswoman yet. Scholars have begun to closely analyse media representations of Freeman, particularly in relation to two highly symbolic events in her career: her decision to carry the Aboriginal flag as well as the Australian flag in her victory laps at the 1994 Commonwealth Games, and her victory in the 400m at the Sydney Olympics in 2000. Freeman was a hugely popular athlete, and her victory in 2000 was celebrated across Australia. Larissa Behrendt argued that this public embrace of Freeman was 'not of [her] Aboriginality per se', so much as it was of 'the type of Aborigine' that she appeared to exemplify, which was one who was 'non-confronting, amiable, modest and successful in the dominant culture'.[149] Yet Freeman was also a more confronting figure sometimes, as when she carried the Aboriginal flag on her victory laps, and at such times she became a less acceptable figure.

Freeman has also been framed in the media as a 'symbol of national reconciliation'.[150] Indeed, Bruce and Hallinan have suggested that, in her position as a successful Aboriginal person who represented Australia internationally in a sporting sense, Freeman appeared to be an embodiment of the possibility of reconciliation. 'Embracing Freeman,' they argued, could therefore be 'an easy way out for Australians who, without having to take any action, can believe: *We are not racist: We love Cathy*'.[151] Perhaps because of the perceived necessity of representing her as 'an "Australian"', common gendered ways of representing sportswomen were less evident in stories about Freeman.[152] In depictions which sought to articulate particular versions of an Australian nation, race was perhaps more central than was gender, suggesting a continuing uninterest in viewing women as being able to represent the nation. At the same time, it was the

---

148 Daley, p. 44.
149 L. Behrendt, 'Cathy Freeman and the Politics of Sport', *Journal of Australian Indigenous Issues* 4, no. 1 (2001), p. 28.
150 C. Elder, A. Pratt and C. Ellis, 'Running Race: Reconciliation, Nationalism and the Sydney 2000 Olympic Games', *International Review for the Sociology of Sport* 41, no. 2 (2006), pp. 181-200; Gardiner, pp. 245, 249-251; McKay, 'Enlightened Racism and Celebrity Feminism', p. 90.
151 Bruce and Hallinan, pp. 261, 267, original emphasis.
152 Wensing and Bruce, pp. 393-394.

particular conjunction of political and social factors, as well as the specificities of Freeman's own story and person, which made such representations both frequently articulated and compelling.

Conclusion

Representations of racial difference were deeply embedded in many media stories about Goolagong, and she was reflective about those representations. Her profile as an Aboriginal sportsperson was the most evident depiction, both in her playing days and more recently. Her Aboriginality was often framed as a key defining characteristic in narratives of her life and career. Naming her as Aboriginal or part-Aboriginal, referring to her as possessing natural talent or liable to go walkabout, or describing her physical features all framed her as different, as racially Other. Yet she was also subject to media representation in relation to her youth, rural background, beauty and positioning as a feminine woman who was also a strong and fit sportsperson. Sometimes the key factor in framing representations was gender, as when her perceived femininity was celebrated by commentators in the context of feminist pressures for change in women's tennis and the application of negative stereotypes to many female players. Discourses of gender thus intersected with discourses about race in shaping narratives about Goolagong, as in narratives about other Aboriginal sportswomen in Australia and Māori sportswomen in New Zealand. Gendered depictions, however, might be elided in framings which focused on representing particular versions of an Australian or New Zealand nation, and representations of race often fell into accepted parameters as exotic Others, authentic Kiwis and Aussies, or symbols of harmonious race relations or reconciliation. Demonstrating the multiple and complex nature of representation, women such as Goolagong and Freeman could be framed as representing ideas about race, gender and the nation at the same time as they represented Australia in a more practical sense in international sporting competitions. No longer whitewashed as assimilated by the end of the twentieth century, Indigenous sportswomen were nonetheless often represented in the print media in ways which marked them as different in both racial and gendered terms, and depictions which placed them as representing the nation on an international stage frequently remained deeply ambivalent.

Chapter Three

Besides sports, Indigenous people in New Zealand and Australia sometimes became famous in another area of performance before and during the second half of the twentieth century: the performing arts. In music, singing, acting and other fields of entertainment, a small number of Māori and Aboriginal women became nationally, and sometimes internationally, known. Although this path to success was more well-trodden in New Zealand than it was in Australia, it became more common in Australia from the 1950s. As these women attained success in their chosen fields, their careers and personal lives were often written about in the media, as was the case for those who succeeded in the sporting arena. In this chapter, I explore patterns in depictions of Māori and Aboriginal women who became prominent in a variety of performing arts over the second half of the twentieth century, focusing particularly on narratives about New Zealand soprano Dame Kiri Te Kanawa. Several recurring threads of representation were evident in print media narratives about these well-known women, often resonating with ways of framing Indigenous women who had become well-known for their sporting successes. Within the context of broad social and political change, and of significant shifts in the entertainment industries themselves over this half-century, such patterns of representation were both maintained and transformed.

Māori and Aboriginal Women in the Performing Arts

As in other forms of entertainment and spectacle, in sport it was possible for Indigenous people to become well-known and celebrated before the second half of the twentieth century, particularly in New Zealand. Māori concert parties had showcased Māori musical talent and culture since the nineteenth century. Te Puea Hērangi organised a group, Te Pou o Mangatāwhiri, which toured the North Island raising money to build a marae (meeting place) at Ngāruawāhia and contributed to a cultural revival. Women such as Tuini Ngāwai, a prolific composer and songwriter, her niece Te Kumeroa Ngoingoi (Ngoi) Pēwhairangi, a songwriter remembered also for her efforts in advancing the Māori language, and orator Whaia McClutchie, were familiar names in relation to music and kapa haka (traditional performing arts). Individual singers also met with success, both within New Zealand and internationally. Fanny Howie, known on the stage as Princess Te Rangi Pai, performed to great acclaim in Britain at the beginning of the twentieth century. Perhaps the earliest commercial recording of Māori music was made in 1927, of Ana Hato and her cousin Deane Waretini.[1] New Zealand's first Māori film stars also appeared early. In the 1925 classic *The Romance of Hinemoa*, the cast was entirely Māori, with Maata Hurihanganui in the title role. Ramai Hayward, who as Ramai Te Miha was the star of the 1940 film *Rewi's Last Stand*, pursued a long career in film and television with her husband, filmmaker Rudall Hayward.

A number of Māori women also became nationally and internationally famous through their work as tour guides around the thermal areas found in the central North Island. Often also members of concert parties, guides entertained tourists as well as informing them, and performed Māori culture for visitors. As early as the 1860s women took tourists to see the renowned Pink and White Terraces at Lake Rotomahana. The 'hospitable reception of visitors' remained 'primarily a women's responsibility', according to Ngāhuia Te Awekōtuku, and by 1870 'guiding as a female occupation was established'.[2] One of the best-known of these early guides was Sophia (Te Paea) Hinerangi, who in Rotorua was 'the most famous woman of her time'.[3] After the Tarawera eruption destroyed the terraces in 1886, tourist guiding became centred around the thermal village of Whakarewarewa. There, two sisters, Maggie (Mākereti) and Bella Thom, became particularly prominent as guides. Guide Maggie Papakura, as she was known to tourists, gained international status when in 1901 she guided the Duke and Duchess of Cornwall and York. Another guide who became famous was Rangitīaria Dennan, better known as Guide Rangi. Born at the end of the nineteenth century, she was as a child a member of a concert party, organised by Mākereti, which visited Australia.[4] During her guiding career, she escorted many notable people, receiving the MBE (Member of the Order of the British Empire) for her work in 1957. Newspapers across the country lamented her passing when she died in 1970.

In Australia, a rather different entertainment landscape prevailed. Aboriginal music was not embraced by European settlers as Māori music was in New Zealand. Although bands or choirs which gave popular performances were sometimes formed on missions in the late nineteenth and early twentieth centuries, such as at Yarrabah in Queensland, these groups appear not to have been well-known nationally. Few Aboriginal performers made recordings during the 1950s and

---

1   J. M. Thomson, *The Oxford History of New Zealand Music* (Auckland: Oxford University Press, 1991), p. 203.

2   N. Te Awekōtuku, *Mana Wahine Maori: Selected Writings on Maori Women's Art, Culture and Politics* (Auckland: New Women's Press, 1991), pp. 77-78.

3   J. Curnow, 'Hinerangi, Sophia 1830-1834?-1911', *Dictionary of New Zealand Biography*, updated 7 July 2005, accessed 28 March 2006, available from http://www.dnzb.govt.nz/dnzb/default.asp?Find_Quick. asp?PersonEssay=2H37.

4   C. Parekowhai, 'Dennan, Rangitiaria 1897-1970', *Dictionary of New Zealand Biography*, updated 7 July 2005, accessed 28 March 2006, available from http://www.dnzb.govt.nz/dnzb/default.asp?Find_Quick. asp?PersonEssay=4D12.

1960s, and while an increase in recordings by Aboriginal men was evident in the 1970s, only four Aboriginal women seem to have recorded their music in that decade.[5] No Aboriginal people starred in films until the Charles Chauvel film *Jedda* in 1955, which featured Rosalie Kunoth-Monks and Bob Wilson, billed as Ngarla Kunoth and Robert Tudawali, in the lead roles. Indeed, during the 1960s and 1970s, 'the dominant belief was that there were no Indigenous actors' in Australia, and even after that view began to shift in the 1970s and 1980s, Indigenous actors continued to be viewed as 'amateurs'.[6] Moreover, it was not common practice in Australia for Aboriginal women (or men) to act as tour guides.

As John Ramsland and Christopher Mooney have noted, however, it was sometimes possible for Aboriginal people to reach national prominence in the performing arts before the 1950s, as it was in sport.[7] Betty Fisher's fame as a singer was fleeting, but it was Australia-wide. After she was evacuated from Croker Island Mission to Otford in New South Wales (NSW) during World War Two, Fisher appeared on radio 2UW's 'Australia's Amateur Hour'.[8] Considerable publicity came her way, including a feature in the *Australian Women's Weekly* in 1946, in which it was observed that a meeting was to be held to consider her 'future' and that 'offers of subscriptions for her training' had been forthcoming.[9] Fisher, however, returned to Croker Island, and although she continued to perform in the Northern Territory, her moment of national fame appeared to be over. Blues and jazz singer Dulcie Pitt, who performed as Georgia Lee, had a long and successful career in music. She first performed with her sisters and brother, before going on to a successful solo career, with her first recording appearing in 1949. During several years in London, Lee became known across Britain, due in particular to her performances with Geraldo's Orchestra in its weekly BBC radio broadcasts. After returning to Australia in 1957, she continued her musical career, becoming in 1962 'the first female Aboriginal vocalist to produce an album', *Georgia Lee Sings the Blues Downunder*, and continuing to perform until 1978.[10]

---

5 K. Barney, '"Women Singing Up Big": The Growth of Contemporary Music Recordings by Indigenous Australian Women Artists', *Australian Aboriginal Studies*, no. 1 (2006), pp. 44-45.

6 M. Casey and L.-M. Syron, 'The Challenges of Benevolence: The Role of Indigenous Actors', *JAS, Australia's Public Intellectual Forum*, no. 85 (2005), pp. 100, 102.

7 J. Ramsland and C. Mooney, *Remembering Aboriginal Heroes: Struggle, Identity and the Media* (Melbourne: Brolga, 2006), p. 319.

8 B. Fisher, 'Talking History', *Land Rights News* 2, no. 13 (1989), p. 30.

9 'Her Future – Island Mission or Concert Hall?', *Australian Women's Weekly*, 23 March 1946, p. 19.

10 Ramsland and Mooney, pp. 320-323.

Dame Kiri Te Kanawa

Within the long line of Māori musical success, a young singer appeared in the 1960s who rapidly became a well-loved celebrity in New Zealand. Kiri Te Kanawa reached a level of international fame far greater than any Māori singers or musicians before or since. Her life has been chronicled in three biographies, countless newspaper and magazine articles, and several television programmes. Yet although basic biographical details are easily obtained, her very fame obscures many details of her story. Born in 1944 in Gisborne, on the east coast of the North Island, she was adopted shortly after by Tom and Nell Te Kanawa. At this point, so early in her life, the mythology begins. Numerous accounts state that she was named 'Kiri' by the Te Kanawas and that this means 'bell' in Māori.[11] Such foreshadowing of singing success, however, is not evident in definitions of the word given in Māori dictionaries.[12] Te Kanawa began singing at a young age and was encouraged by her mother. The family moved to Auckland so that she could receive proper training for her voice and she attended St Mary's College for Girls, where she was taught by (Dame) Sister Mary Leo, one of New Zealand's most successful singing teachers. After several competition successes, including in Australia, she left New Zealand to study at the London Opera Centre, having been awarded a grant from the Queen Elizabeth II Arts Council of New Zealand.

Most biographical sketches of Te Kanawa note that star status quickly followed after her highly successful debut as the Countess Almaviva in the Mozart opera *Le Nozze di Figaro* at Covent Garden in 1971. Her United States debut, as Desdemona in Verdi's *Otello*, occurred in 1974 and it too was enthusiastically praised in reviews, although she had replaced a fellow singer with only a few hours' notice. A further highlight of her career often mentioned in biographical accounts was her singing of Handel's 'Let the Bright Seraphim ' at the wedding of Prince Charles and Lady Diana in 1981, shortly after which she received the DBE (Dame Commander of the Order of the British Empire). Te Kanawa began to give large outdoor concerts, including one for the Australian bicentennial in 1988, Opera in the Outback, and three free concerts for the New Zealand sesquicentennial in 1990, billed as Kiri's Homecoming. Later in her career, Te Kanawa set up a foundation to assist young New Zealand singers, the Kiri Te Kanawa Foundation.

---

11   For instance: D. Fingleton, *Kiri Te Kanawa: A Biography* (Clio: Oxford, 1982), p. 6; K. Frost, 'Kiri – The Name Means "Bell"', *Thursday*, 8 June 1972, p. 18; A. Simpson and P. Downes, *Southern Voices: International Opera Singers of New Zealand* (Auckland: Reed, 1992), p. 220.
12   Translations of 'kiri' include 'skin' or 'bark', while 'bell' is translated as 'pere' or 'pahū'. See: P. M. Ryan, *P.M. Ryan's Dictionary of Modern Maori*, 4th ed. (Auckland: Heinemann, 1994), pp. 28, 114-115.

Figure 5: 'Kiri Te Kanawa, Wearing a Concert Gown of White Crepe', 5 February 1967.

Photograph. EP/1966/0479-F. Dominion Post Collection. Alexander Turnbull Library, Wellington, New Zealand.

Humble Beginnings and Natural Talent

Several narratives of Te Kanawa's life presented her rise to stardom from humble beginnings as an adopted Māori child in the rural New Zealand city of Gisborne as a rags-to-riches tale reminiscent of narratives of Evonne Goolagong's path to tennis success. Writing in the *New Zealand Herald* in 1990, Jane Phare referred to Te Kanawa as 'the Kiwi diva who rose from nothing to international acclaim'.[13] The next year, Jane Sweeney observed in the lifestyle magazine *Next* that Te Kanawa had 'come a long way from the baby girl whose adoptive parents said no to her at first because they wanted a boy'.[14] Of course, narratives of humble beginnings are not restricted to Indigenous performers. Joan Sutherland, one of Australia's most famous opera singers, was described early in her career as having made a similar journey from a humble early life to world fame. 'The glorious voice of a former Woollahra typist has conquered the world of opera', the *Sun-Herald* proclaimed in 1961. The author, Margaret Jones, noted that Sutherland's success was 'all a long way from Sydney, a job in an office, and lessons at the Conservatorium'.[15] Framings that emphasised class mobility could thus be as important in media portrayals of the famous as narratives that centred on ideas of gender or race.

However, such framings of Te Kanawa's path to success sometimes made reference to her Māori ancestry, implying that being Māori had made her rise to fame more improbable. In 1978, John Ross wrote in the *New Zealand Herald* that 'the Maori girl who arrived in London 12 years ago is now an international celebrity'.[16] Phare remarked that Te Kanawa's success and fame were 'not bad for an adopted Maori kid from a poor background with a potential to sing well'.[17] More recently, the *New Zealand Woman's Weekly* ran an article in 2002 in which the author, Alice Fowler, stated that 'the great opera diva grew up in conditions which today would be called, at best, socially deprived'.[18] Indeed, Te Kanawa herself has framed her story this way. In a speech to the Rotary Club of Auckland in 2004, she said that she had been 'born in Gisborne and came from very humble beginnings'. She spoke of her adoption and of growing up as a Māori child in New Zealand in the mid-twentieth century, recalling once 'being sent home from a birthday party by a school friend's mother – because I was Maori'. She had, she said, been able to 'pull myself up' only 'because of my mother and the pride of my father'.[19]

Bass-baritone Inia Te Wiata, who had a successful operatic career in London until his death in 1971, was also occasionally described as an unlikely star who had risen from a poor background. Ziska Schwimmer, in a profile of Te Wiata published in 1958 in the Māori Affairs Department publication *Te Ao Hou: The New World*, wrote that there had been 'little in [his] early background to lead

13   J. Phare, 'Swansong for a Songbird', *New Zealand Herald*, 26 September 1990, section 2, p. 1.

14   J. Sweeney, 'Prime Times', *Next*, no. 6 (1991), p. 86.

15   M. Jones, 'The Glorious Voice of a Former Woollahra Typist has Conquered the World of Opera: The Joan Sutherland Story', *Sun-Herald*, 3 December 1961, p. 43.

16   J. Ross, 'Kiri's New Role', *New Zealand Herald*, 27 May 1978, section 2, p. 1.

17   Phare, section 2, p. 1.

18   A. Fowler, 'Kiri – The Diva Opens Her Heart', *New Zealand Woman's Weekly*, 24 June 2002, p. 8.

19   K. Te Kanawa, 'Kiri Te Kanawa Speech to the Rotary Club of Auckland', updated 2008, accessed 25 February 2008, available from http://www.kiritekanawa.org/pdf/2004_02_02_ rotary_speech.pdf.

him to world fame or the life of a professional artist'.[20] A similar rags-to-riches narrative can also be observed in the Australian media in relation to famous Aboriginal singers and entertainers, both men and women. In a profile which appeared in the NSW Aborigines Welfare Board magazine *Dawn* in March 1952, well-known tenor Harold Blair was imagined as having once been 'a barefooted little aboriginal boy' on an Aboriginal reserve who 'never dreamed, even in his wildest flights of imagination, that one day he would stand on the concert platforms of the world, to receive the enthusiastic applause of tremendous audiences'. It had been, the article opined, a 'meteoric rise from the canefield labour to the concert platforms of the world'.[21] Georgia Lee was described in an article in the Brisbane *Courier-Mail* in 1955 as 'a £2000-a-year London "blues" singer' who had once lived 'in a crowded native hut in Cairns'.[22] Similarly, but decades later, the success of singer Maroochy Barambah was contrasted with the poverty of her childhood home, Cherbourg Aboriginal Settlement in Queensland, which was described as 'one of the most deprived towns in Australia'.[23] For both Indigenous and non-Indigenous performers, singing could thus be seen, like sport, as a field of achievement that could provide opportunities for social and economic mobility for those who were successful.

As was the case for those successful in sport, such an escape from disadvantage was sometimes represented as resulting from the good fortune of having natural talent. Narratives of natural gifts are not uncommon in biographical material about musicians, actors and other performers. In Te Kanawa's case, many of the profiles which appeared in newspapers and magazines throughout her career made reference to her voice as a natural gift or God-given talent. As Katie Pickles has observed, Te Kanawa's achievements were thus 'often constructed as determined by the "gift" of a pleasant voice box', rather than through her own hard work and resolve.[24] Indeed, Te Kanawa's success was frequently ascribed to a combination of natural attributes: her beauty, singing voice and acting talent. Sue Miles wrote in *50 Famous New Zealanders* that Te Kanawa's 'exceptional voice', 'considerable acting ability' and the fact that she was 'strikingly good looking' were 'a combination that carried her on to international fame'.[25] In 1976, in the *Bulletin* in Australia, she was said to have a 'beautiful voice and … equally beautiful person', the 'fame' of which 'kept spreading', meaning that she was always in demand.[26] The repetition of such representations in narratives of Te Kanawa's life gave her little credit for her own successes in the competitive world of international opera.

---

20 Z. Schwimmer, 'Inia Te Wiata', *Te Ao Hou: The New World*, no. 23 (1958), p. 10.

21 'A Dream Came True! Our Singing Ambassador', *Dawn* 1, no. 3 (1952), pp. 8-9.

22 'From Native Songs to English Variety', *Courier-Mail*, 4 January 1955, p. 3.

23 R. Milliken, 'Songlines', *Good Weekend*, 20 January 1996, p. 15.

24 K. Pickles, 'Kiwi Icons and the Re-Settlement of New Zealand as Colonial Space', *New Zealand Geographer* 58, no. 2 (2002), p. 13.

25 S. Miles, *50 Famous New Zealanders: Portraits and Biographies of 50 of the Most Famous New Zealanders* (Auckland: Burnham House, 1985), p. 96.

26 B. Hoad, 'Heavenly Voice, Feet on the Ground', *Bulletin*, 4 September 1976, p. 44.

Narratives of natural talent could sometimes, for Indigenous performers, take on an added dimension of ethnicity. Natural musical ability is a continuing feature of stereotypes about Māori people, if not about Aboriginal people. Peter Downes, writing about Howard Morrison and the Howard Morrison Quartet in 1979, commented: 'Put any four Maori boys together, give them guitars and ask them to sing, and the results almost certainly will be musical and entertaining'.[27] *Mana* magazine, which is produced by a Maori-controlled media organisation, contributed to this idea, publishing in 1996 a story called 'What Makes Them Sound So Great?', which profiled some of the 'marvellous singers' whom Māori family groups 'keep producing'.[28]

This recurring belief sometimes appeared in writing about Te Kanawa early in her career. In the programme for her Wellington farewell concert in 1966, the organiser and manager, Gladstone Hill, described having once heard Māori people singing 'in one of those spontaneous outbursts of song, so typical of the Maori people', and commented that listening to Te Kanawa brought back memories of that event.[29] The same year, in a feature about Te Kanawa, who had recently arrived in England to study at the London Opera Centre, the London *Times* observed that 'to be the daughter of a Maori father is to be a singer'. The writer continued that according to 'one New Zealander who is writing Kiri's biography: "The Maoris don't know how to sing a wrong note"'. Te Kanawa was quoted saying 'Let's say we're musical – full stop'. The article's author then observed that it appeared that 'all Maoris can harmonize without being taught', and that 'one New Zealand surgeon has suggested that the construction of the Maori throat is quite different from that of Europeans'.[30] Much later, in 1991, a resource for schools noted that Te Kanawa 'reflects the finest qualities of the Maori people in singing, graceful movement, relaxed and fun loving humour'.[31] Such representations of Māori as naturally musical are complex, reflecting both the importance of music as a form of expression within Māori culture and a sometimes cherished identity as musical people, and less positive stereotypes of Māori as musical, cheerful and childlike entertainers.

While Aboriginal people were not often depicted as having natural musical talent, narratives of natural talent were evident in relation to the acting abilities of Rosie Kunoth (as she then was) and Bob Wilson when they starred in *Jedda* in 1955. In promotional material, Chauvel described Kunoth as 'beautiful, intelligent

27 P. Downes, *Top of the Bill: Entertainers Through the Years* (Wellington: A. H. and A. W. Reed, 1979), p. 86.

28 W. Harawira, 'What Makes Them Sound So Great?', *Mana*, no. 12 (1996), p. 15.

29 Programme for farewell concert, Wellington, 1966, ephemera collection, National Library of Australia, Canberra.

30 'Maori Girl Studies Opera Here', *Times*, 31 May 1966, p. 13.

31 M. Leyden, *Celebrating New Zealanders* (Auckland: Michael Leyden, 1991), p. 81.

and a born actress'.[32] Reviewing the film in the *News-Weekly*, E. S. Madden thought Kunoth and Wilson both had 'the instinctive sense of the dramatic so characteristic of their race'.[33] M. S. in the *Weekly Times* stated that they were 'like most Australian natives … born mimics' whose 'almost flawless portrayals … show how their natural talents have responded to clever direction'. M. S., in fact, suggested that Kunoth might be able to 'wrest the best actress "Oscar" from Hollywood's darling, Grace Kelly'.[34] This was high praise of Kunoth's acting in the film, but it was not praise of her professional skill and hard work; instead the praise was in large part for the direction, which had skilfully utilised her natural ability. The *Film Weekly* reviewer went further, commenting that 'through sheer animal magnificence, Robert Tudawali emerges as a strong screen personality'.[35] This remark equated the Aboriginal actors with nature and the animal world, giving Wilson no credit for any acting craft. These understandings of the work of Aboriginal actors as stemming from natural ability resonate with later narratives in the 1970s, 1980s and early 1990s identified by Maryrose Casey and Liza-Mare Syron. During this period, Aboriginal actors were often understood as being 'amateurs (however gifted)' rather than as professionals, and their acting as being natural in the sense that they were being themselves, witnessing to their own experiences.[36] Kunoth herself, however, remembered her acting as having been natural in a rather different way. Her experience of filming *Jedda* was in many ways a negative one, and she observed in an interview later in life that since 'most of the emotions' she was asked to act 'were fear anyway' her performance 'was natural'.[37]

As with stereotypes which considered Indigenous people to have natural sporting ability, suggestions that Māori or Aboriginal success in music or acting was due to natural ability could operate to downplay the skill and hard work required to succeed. Such an implication could sometimes sit alongside a further stereotype of Māori people: that they were lazy. Te Kanawa has reportedly confessed to being fun-loving and disinclined to work hard when first studying at the London Opera Centre.[38] Narratives that connected this aspect of her life story with her ethnicity (rather than, for instance, her youth) could operate to reinforce these negative stereotypes of Māori. In her book *Diva: Great Sopranos and Mezzos Discuss Their Art*, Helena Matheopoulos commented that Te Kanawa had a

---

32 *Eve in Ebony: The Story of "Jedda"*([Sydney]: [Columbia Pictures Proprietary], [1954]), National Library of Australia, Canberra.

33 E. S. Madden, '"Jedda" Could Begin a New Australian Era', *News-Weekly*, 12 October 1955, pp. 7-8.

34 M. S., 'Best Australian Film So Far', *Weekly Times*, 7 September 1955, p. 92.

35 'Reviews', *The Film Weekly*, 12 May 1955, p. 13.

36 Casey and Syron, pp. 102-103.

37 R. Kunoth-Monks, interview with R. Hughes, conducted 10 July 1995, in *Australian Biography* series, accessed 27 February 2008, transcript available from http://www.australianbiography.gov.au/subjects/ kunothmonks/ interview3.html, tape 3.

38 For instance: R. Jacobson, 'Dame Kiri', *Opera News* 47, no. 12 (1983), p. 14; V. Myers, 'Candid Kiri', *New Zealand Listener*, 5 August 1991, p. 16.

'calm, placid side' to her character that was 'given to bouts of lethargy', which 'those who know these latitudes consider typically Maori'.[39] Yet Te Kanawa has stressed that she worked very hard to succeed after that early period at the Opera Centre, and this hard work was often acknowledged in accounts of her life alongside comments upon her less rigorous approach when she first arrived. As Jane Sweeney wrote in *Next* magazine in 1991: 'Those initial lazy ways at the London Opera Centre have long gone'. Te Kanawa, by then, was described as 'follow[ing] a strict routine held together by a well-planned schedule'.[40] The teaching resource previously mentioned also commented upon the effort that had been required for Te Kanawa to achieve what she had, stating that her life was 'a splendid example for young people that natural talents and hard work can bring great success'.[41] Such narratives of her life thus combined reference to stereotypes of Māori as both naturally musical and lazy with admiration for the hard work required to become an internationally successful opera star. As in the case of sports stars, narratives which framed Te Kanawa's success as providing an example of the rewards of hard work could also carry potentially negative implications. If determination and hard work, along with natural talent, were represented as the route by which obstacles might be overcome and success reached, one potential implication was that this route was open to all who chose to follow it, thus denying the existence of entrenched disadvantage in the lives of Indigenous people.

Exoticism and Glamour in the Performing Arts

During the 1950s and 1960s, and earlier, media representations of famous Indigenous women in the performing arts often combined fascination with them as exotic and primitive with depictions of them as glamorous and part of a modern world. In a 1969 article in the New Zealand young women's magazine *Thursday* about the recent success of 'coloured' women in modelling, Joan Scott wrote that 'coloured models' were 'glamour incarnate with a bit of primitive mystery thrown in', as well as being naturally 'graceful and feminine'.[42] Thirty years before, the pictorial magazine *Pix* had published a series of posed photographs of guide Lena Hamana, in which she was mostly shown dressed in 'ancient Maori dress' rather in than her usual 'modern clothing'. In these photographs, Hamana was imagined to be enacting the daily life of a 'Maori maid' of three centuries earlier. Described as a 'glamor girl' in whom 'ancient Maori culture' remained alive, she was said to have '[thrown] off the mantle that civilisation has given her race'

---

39   H. Matheopoulos, *Diva: Great Sopranos and Mezzos Discuss Their Art* (London: Victor Gollancz, 1991), p. 211.
40   Sweeney, p. 88.
41   Leyden, p. 79.
42   J. Scott, 'Black Is Beautiful', *Thursday*, 10 July 1969, p. 13.

to pose for the photographs.[43] Fiona Paisley has argued that when Mira Szaszy (then Petricevich) attended Pan-Pacific Women's Association conferences in the 1950s, she was 'admired because of the combination of western modernization and "traditional" life she managed so glamorously'. Szaszy belonged to the newly-formed Māori Women's Welfare League, and was a recent runner-up in the Miss New Zealand contest. Central to the standing she and others like her gained at these conferences, Paisley contended, was the facility to 'appear one day in traditional dress and the next in fashionable suits'.[44]

These two threads of representation were both evident in a booklet produced in 1962 about Maureen Kingi, who was chosen as Miss New Zealand that year. Throughout the booklet, photographs showed Kingi performing her duties as a beauty queen, either elegantly dressed in the style of the day, or dressed in the piupiu (flax skirt).[45] Although the piupiu was at the time New Zealand's national costume for international beauty contests, Spencer Jolly suggested some years later that Kingi could 'rightfully claim' it 'as her national dress' while other winners of the title had 'mixed feelings' about it.[46] On the front cover of the booklet, Kingi was pictured seated neatly in a traditionally carved window-frame, wearing a stylish dress and a string of pearls. This posed photograph encapsulates the juxtaposition of ancient and modern which was also evoked in the written text. The unnamed author(s) noted that 'her performances with the triple and double long pois as well as singing made her an unusual and interesting personality' when she toured the North Island.[47] Similarly hinting at exotic difference, Jolly wrote in 1974 that the crowd at the 1962 final had been 'captivated by the smile and lovely eyes of a dark skinned girl from Rotorua'.[48] Kingi's appeal thus lay both in her being Māori, and therefore an exotic and unusual winner of the competition, and in her being perceived as a modern girl. In her position as Miss New Zealand, both threads of representation were important, as she was able to be seen as both an authentic New Zealander who embodied the romantic appeal of Māori culture, particularly when she was overseas, and as a sophisticated and modern New Zealand girl.

Indigenous film stars in Australia and New Zealand were also portrayed in such contradictory ways. Looking back at Ramai Hayward's career in film, Jacqueline Amoamo wrote in the *New Zealand Listener* in 1993 that photographs used for publicity for *Rewi's Last Stand* (1940) showed Hayward as 'an exotic beauty as

---

43 'Day in Maori Maid's Life', *Pix*, 22 July 1939, p. 24.

44 F. Paisley, 'Glamour in the Pacific: Cultural Internationalism and Maori Politics at Pan Pacific Women's Conferences in the 1950s', *Pacific Studies* 29, no. 1/2 (2006), p. 76.

45 *The Story of Maureen Kingi: Miss New Zealand 1962* (Dunedin: Joe Brown Enterprises, [1962]), National Library of New Zealand, Wellington.

46 S. Jolly, *The Miss Parade* ([n.p.]: Southern Press, 1974), p. 105.

47 *The Story of Maureen Kingi*. A poi is a ball attached to a string, either short or long, which is swung and twirled whilst singing and dancing.

48 Jolly, p. 89.

striking as many of the current crop of Hollywood starlets'.[49] In Australia, in a phrase that neatly captured the appeal of the combination of exotic difference and glamorous modernism in the mid-twentieth century, Georgia Lee was termed the 'Dusky Bombshell' by media in Melbourne.[50] A number of accounts of the 1955 premiere of *Jedda* in Darwin described Rosie Kunoth's dress and appearance, placing her within the discourse of glamour surrounding a movie star and a premiere. Kunoth 'looked very charming', thought the *Northern Territory News*, while Chauvel's wife and filmmaking partner Elsa felt she 'looked a dream of a girl' and that 'her quite simple deportment gained the admiration of all'.[51] Kunoth herself recalled the 'beautiful white frock with straps' that she had worn, and that she 'looked like a princess, or a queen'.[52] The glamorous discourse Kunoth was placed within in media reports was what might be expected for a white film star, and she herself did not consider it entirely negative. She stated in a later interview that 'it became almost glamorous to be an Aboriginal person'. 'There was an Aboriginal girl standing up there looking nearly as good as Marilyn Monroe', she remembered.[53]

Kunoth's attractive appearance was often mentioned in the media around the time the film was released. Several references were made to her skin colour, as 'a brown-skinned beauty', a 'comely chocolate heroine' or as having 'dark loveliness'.[54] These comments called upon her descent from an ancient tribe to add mystery to the glamour. However, such representations were significantly outnumbered by comments on her prettiness that did not mention her colour, subsuming her race under a focus on beauty and femininity. Part of Kunoth's appeal was also the shyness sometimes reported. M. S., writing in the *Weekly Times*, referred to her 'shy, unspoilt charm' and her 'soft accent'.[55] Soft voices and timidity had sometimes been considered attractions of Aboriginal women in the earliest days of contact. Such images imagined Aboriginal women within 'European aesthetic traditions'.[56] Descriptions of Kunoth in the media in the 1950s positioned her within Hollywood aesthetic traditions, even while deploying the idea of the exotic as part of her appeal. Liz Conor has shown that in the 1920s 'Aboriginal and Islander women were systematically constructed as premodern or "primitive" precisely through their perceived failure to *appear* modern'. Aboriginal women, Conor argued, 'were cast … as illegitimate and

49   J. Amoamo, 'In On the Action', *New Zealand Listener*, 11 September 1993, p. 33.
50   Ramsland and Mooney, p. 321.
51   'Jedda Night Caught the Imagination', *Northern Territory News*, 6 January 1955, p. 5; E. Chauvel, *My Life with Charles Chauvel* (Sydney: Shakespeare Head, 1973), p. 146.
52   H. Chryssides, *Local Heroes* (North Blackburn: Collins Dove, 1993), p. 187.
53   Ibid., p. 189.
54   J. B. Glen, 'On the Rugged Trail of "Jedda"', *New York Times*, 31 January 1954, p. 5; '"Jedda's" Spectacular Premiere!', *The Film Weekly*, 13 January 1955, p. 12; B. McArdle, 'Jedda Opens New Cinema Field', *Age*, 24 August 1955, p. 2.
55   M. S., p. 92.
56   A. McGrath, 'The White Man's Looking Glass: Aboriginal-Colonial Gender Relations at Port Jackson', *Australian Historical Studies* 24, no. 95 (1990), pp. 197-199, 202.

unassimilable objects in the modern scene'.[57] By the 1950s in Australia, and apparently earlier in New Zealand, the construction of Indigenous women as exotic and primitive could sit alongside constructions of them as able to be assimilated into modernity, to become modern girls like their white counterparts.[58]

Figure 6: 'Rosalie Kunoth-Monks', Steve Lorman.

Photograph. PH0141/0169. Northern Territory Library, Darwin.

Throughout her career, both in the media and in publicity material, Te Kanawa's being Māori was sometimes framed as adding interest to her story or as making her more exotic. Alan Armstrong, a reviewer for *Te Ao Hou*, suggested in 1967 that Te Kanawa's 'appeal' lay partly in 'her Maori ancestry', and he noted that she was 'unique' because she was 'the first Maori female singer of serious music to stand at the threshold of fame and fortune overseas'.[59] In the first biography

---

57 L. Conor, *The Spectacular Modern Woman: Feminine Visibility in the 1920s* (Bloomington: Indiana University Press, 2004), pp. 12, 206, original emphasis.

58 For an illuminating discussion of the ways in which ideas of exoticism and modernity intersected in the 'racially ambiguous ... feminities' constructed by three Australian women in the first half of the twentieth century, see A. Woollacott, *Race and the Modern Exotic: Three 'Australian' Women on Global Display* (Clayton: Monash University Publishing, 2011).

59 A. Armstrong, 'Review of *KIRI, Music and a Maori Girl*, by Norman Harris in association with Kiri Te Kanawa', *Te Ao Hou: The New World*, no. 58, March 1967, p. 58.

published about Te Kanawa, an adulatory book written by Norman Harris when she was still in her early twenties, her Māori heritage formed a point of interest. The book began with a mythical story about Te Kanawa, 'a warrior' and 'commanding' leader, and ended with a description of her farewell from her 'own people'.[60] This narrative of her life was written before it became widely known that she was adopted, which she revealed on British television in a BBC profile about her in 1975.[61] Like other narratives written before this revelation, Harris presented her as a descendant of Māori aristocracy, adding to the exotic aura surrounding her. Pickles has observed this invention of 'noble warrior connections' for Te Kanawa, and the recurring transformation of such 'chiefly connections' into an aristocratic background.[62] Te Kanawa herself sometimes reportedly referred to her Māori descent as making her exotic. In 1983 she was quoted in the *New Zealand Listener* stating that 'I'm exotic because I have two cultures on my side'.[63] Almost a decade later, she reportedly said that she had come to understand her mother's view that her Māori descent was the best part of her descent, and was quoted explaining that 'it's unique to be Maori, to sing opera, have a fantastic name; it's all rather exotic and interesting'.[64] In 2008, biographical information provided on the website for the Kiri Te Kanawa Foundation continued to describe her as having 'the exotic blood of native Maori aristocracy'.[65]

Te Kanawa's beauty was frequently mentioned in media reports about her, often with overtones of fascination with her colour. Pickles noted that Te Kanawa's Māori descent was sometimes represented as giving her an exotic beauty.[66] In the *New Zealand Woman's Weekly* in 1974 she was described as having 'dark beauty', and in 1980 as being a 'dark-eyed, part-Maori beauty'.[67] The Christchurch *Press* in 1981 described her as 'tall and slender, with the good looks that go with her part-Maori ancestry'.[68] This fascination was particularly evident in some profiles of her published in the international media. In the *San Francisco Chronicle* she was described in 1990 as a 'handsome woman with enormous brown eyes and copper-tone skin inherited from her Maori father'.[69] Descriptions of Te Kanawa

---

60   N. Harris, *Kiri: Music and a Maori Girl* (Wellington: A. H. and A. W. Reed, 1966), pp. 7, 57-59.

61   Fingleton, pp. 154-155.

62   Pickles, p. 14.

63   T. Reid, 'Kiri: Giving Something Back', *New Zealand Listener*, 15 January 1983, p. 14.

64   Myers, 'Candid Kiri', p. 21.

65   'Kiri Te Kanawa Bio', updated 2008, accessed 27 February 2008, available from http://www.kiritekanawa. org/ kiri+te+kanawa.

66   Pickles, p. 14.

67   A. Gordon, 'Film of the Mozart Opera "Don Giovanni" Brings Kiri Te Kanawa Close to Home', *New Zealand Woman's Weekly*, 7 April 1980, p. 6; D. Webster, '"Sundays are for Cycling"', *New Zealand Woman's Weekly*, 18 November 1974, p. 6.

68   K. Coates, 'Kiri's Royal Wedding Performance Will Have a World-Wide Audience', *Press*, 11 July 1981, p. 15.

69   R. Stein, 'Daily Doings of a Down-to-Earth Diva: Kiri Te Kanawa Featured in San Francisco's "Capriccio"', *San Francisco Chronicle Datebook*, 21 October 1990, p. 21.

which imagined her beauty in these ways echoed earlier imagery of Māori women used on postcards in the early twentieth century. Jacqui Sutton Beets has shown how the 'Māori maidens' on these postcards were those whose beauty matched European ideals, while at the same time retaining the exotic allure of the 'Other'. Those who were chosen for photographing often had, for instance, 'large eyes', 'flowing dark hair' and 'olive (not black) skin'.[70] Written descriptions of Te Kanawa's beauty often drew attention to her big brown eyes, golden skin or dark hair. In Australia, for instance, she was described as 'a knockout' in the *Courier-Mail* in 1987, with 'golden brown skin, smooth as an egg', 'fabulous' eyes which were 'large, limpid brown', and 'marvellous, thick glossy chestnut' hair.[71] In the United States magazine *Opera News*, Lady Antonia Fraser extolled her skin as 'the healthy color of a smooth brown egg', and her 'enormous' eyes, which were 'chestnut like her thick and glossy hair'.[72] Publicity shots, and the carefully posed photographs which accompanied many articles in the print media, also sometimes highlighted these features of her appearance. Pickles has written that Te Kanawa was 'objectified in a number of ways as a modern Maori Maiden'.[73] Like Kingi, Te Kanawa was thus sometimes imagined in ways which placed her as the modern embodiment of the romantic Māori maiden whose image had been so often used on the postcards of the early twentieth century.

Being thought to have exotic looks perhaps contributed to the recurring depiction of Te Kanawa as a woman who was particularly lovely within the already glamorous world of opera. Although she was often portrayed as having remained a down-to-earth and modest New Zealander, particularly during the 1980s and early 1990s, she was also often referred to as glamorous or as a diva. The latter is a common description of women who become internationally known as opera singers, particularly sopranos, and is a word that has come to carry both positive and negative connotations. Both the glamorous image and the down-to-earth image appear to have been encouraged by the marketing machine which was inextricably part of Te Kanawa's career. Photographs in concert programmes were usually very glamorous, while those in magazines such as the *New Zealand Woman's Weekly* showed her both in extravagant operatic costume or elegant dress and relaxing in casual clothes.[74] In the United States music magazine *Fanfare* in 1989, Nick Rossi observed the intertwining of these themes in Te

---

70 J. S. Beets, 'Images of Māori Women in New Zealand Postcards After 1900', in *Bitter Sweet: Indigenous Women in the Pacific*, eds. A. Jones, P. Herda and T. M. Suaalii (Dunedin: University of Otago Press, 2000), p. 18.
71 F. Hernon, 'Kiri Gives Her Regards to Broadway', *Courier-Mail*, 29 August 1987, weekend section, p. 4.
72 A. Fraser, 'My Heroine', *Opera News* 51, no. 7 (1986), p. 21.
73 Pickles, p. 13.
74 See for instance: A. Barrowclough, '"I Can Inspire True Passion"', *New Zealand Woman's Weekly*, 13 April 1992, p. 8; J. Davies, '"Sometimes I Just Have to be Alone"', *New Zealand Woman's Weekly*, 9 November 1992, p. 21; programme for An Evening Quayside with Kiri, Auckland, 1994, ephemera collection, National Library of Australia, Canberra; programme for Victoria State Opera Foundation Gala Benefit, 1985, ephemera collection, National Library of Australia, Canberra.

Kanawa's image as a star. Her life, he wrote, was 'a contradiction of parts' in that she was 'a consummate vocal artist *and* a devoted mother, an opera star of the first magnitude *and* a very warm, friendly, down-to-earth person'.[75] In 1991, writing in the Wellington *Evening Post*, Kate Coughlan detailed Te Kanawa's concern that photographs accompanying the story be beautiful, quoting her as stating that 'the glamour image is important to my career'.[76] At the same time, in an article in Brisbane's *Sunday Mail Magazine* in 1992 titled 'The reluctant diva', Te Kanawa was quoted observing that she was unlike many other singers in that she did not need a large retinue. 'I don't need all the glamour', she commented.[77]

Te Kanawa's continuing popularity in New Zealand appeared to rest in part upon the representation of her as retaining an unpretentious and down-to-earth New Zealand attitude despite her fame and wealth. This was particularly evident in women's magazines such as the *New Zealand Woman's Weekly*, in which Te Kanawa was often depicted approvingly as an ordinary wife and mother, implicitly sharing something of the experience of the readers.[78] Slightly more than a quarter of the images published in articles about Te Kanawa collected from women's magazines showed her with her family or within a relaxed domestic setting, compared to just over six percent of the images which accompanied articles collected from newspapers and other magazines. Te Kanawa was often quoted in the *New Zealand Woman's Weekly* talking at length about her family life with her husband and two adopted children.[79] In 1991, Angela Lord began an article in the magazine by describing Te Kanawa 'in between' international tours as 'at home making a cup of tea and compiling a shopping list' in her kitchen.[80] Such articles often implied that they gave a privileged view into her life, revealing the real woman beneath the star persona. Lord observed that Te Kanawa was generally 'prepared to let the outside world see only the polished image of the Diva, carefully hiding the woman, wife and mother under the glamorous facade', and an article by Alice Fowler in 2002 was titled 'Kiri – the diva opens her heart'.[81] Te Kanawa's great appeal, then, was the result of a combination of factors: her glamorous occupation and her beauty, her supposedly exotic looks and name, and her down-to-earth persona. If the latter was particularly important in the media in New Zealand, the glamour and mystery of her being a Māori opera singer was perhaps more central to many representations of her in the international media, particularly early in her career.

---

75 N. Rossi, 'An Interview With Dame Kiri Te Kanawa', *Fanfare* 13, no. 1 (1989), p. 499, original emphasis.
76 K. Coughlan, 'Dame Kiri: Behind the Scenes', *Evening Post*, 7 September 1991, p. 21.
77 G. Barrett, 'The Reluctant Diva', *Sunday Mail Magazine*, 1 November 1992, p. 17.
78 The trend in media narratives to locate Te Kanawa in the domestic sphere has also been observed by Katie Pickles. K. Pickles, 'Colonisation, Empire and Gender', in *The New Oxford History of New Zealand*, ed. G. Byrnes (South Melbourne: Oxford University Press, 2009), pp. 239-240.
79 For example: Barrowclough, p. 8; A. Lord, 'Dame Kiri: "If I Lost My Voice ..."', *New Zealand Woman's Weekly*, 15 July 1991, pp. 13-14.
80 Lord, p. 12.
81 Fowler, pp. 8-11; Lord, p. 12.

Representing Race, Representing Nation

Framings of famous Indigenous women in the media might market more than simply their own work. In the 1950s and 1960s, successful Māori women and men were sometimes represented as displaying the harmonious race relations believed to exist in New Zealand, and the success of the assimilation and integration policies, both to international and to New Zealand audiences. In the sporting arena, tennis player Ruia Morrison was once quoted saying that on one overseas trip she had made, she thought in hindsight that she 'usually got the front berth socially to show we were racially integrated'.[82] Joe Brown, who held the franchise for the Miss New Zealand pageant in 1962, was keen to impress upon the government the value of Kingi's involvement in an international beauty contest, and her scheduled appearance on television in the United States, for promoting New Zealand as a tourist destination overseas.[83] Visiting the United States, Kingi was not just a 'Beauty Delegate' but also an 'Ambassadress of friendship and goodwill for her country'. In the booklet about Kingi produced by Joe Brown Enterprises, a quote from a camera operator at the international pageant stated that Kingi's appearance on the television show 'Who in the World' had done 'more good for New Zealand than anyone, anything ever done before'.[84] Across the Tasman, Miss Australia too was expected to act as an ambassador for her country. In 1961, the winner was Tania Verstak, a young woman who had been born in China, the child of Russian refugees, and who had arrived with her family in Australia in 1952. After her win, she was not only depicted in the media as 'a glowing example of modern Australian womanhood', but was also portrayed by the federal government as an 'example of the success of its immigration policy' and of the success of the assimilation process which immigrants were to go through.[85]

In her overseas travels, Kingi might in a similar way represent to international audiences the successful and harmonious nature of race relations at home. Ensuring this image of racial harmony was potentially an important concern given international interest in the subject in relation to Australia and South Africa. When she spoke in California at the International Beauty Congress in 1962, Kingi spoke in part upon this theme. In New Zealand, she explained, 'we pride ourselves in the concord and harmony in which we live with each other'. 'I am an example of this integration', she asserted, 'for my mother is European and my father is Maori'.[86] The unnamed author(s) of the 1962 booklet portrayed

---

82 D. Simons, *New Zealand's Champion Sportswomen* (Auckland: Moa, 1982), p. 237.
83 Jolly, p. 90.
84 *The Story of Maureen Kingi*, emphasis removed.
85 J. Ustinoff and K. Saunders, 'Celebrity, Nation and the New Australian Woman: Tania Verstak, Miss Australia 1961', *JAS, Australia's Public Intellectual Forum*, no. 83 (2004), pp. 68-70.
86 *The Story of Maureen Kingi*.

Kingi and her family as exemplars of integration. Her Māori father was 'a highly esteemed member of the staff of the Maori Affairs Department in Rotorua, a licensed interpreter (first grade) and a clerk of the Maori Land Court'. One brother was a carpenter, singer and entrant in male pageants, another brother was 'one of only three or four Maoris holding a Bachelor of Commerce degree' and 'an accountant in Wellington' studying for his Masters, and her sister was 'employed by the Social Security Department and … studying for her B.A. degree'. Kingi herself was 'a student radiographer'. Prior to winning the competition, Kingi had been involved in Māori concert parties and had 'participated in filmings and photographs for the publicity of Rotorua and New Zealand overseas'. She had been, the booklet noted, 'photographed for post-cards and slides and … filmed by the National Film Unit'.[87] As a modern embodiment of the exotic Māori maidens whose images were so popular on postcards early in the century, Kingi's image was thus used to market New Zealand as an international tourist destination both before and after she won the Miss New Zealand competition. At the same time, her success, like that of her family, could be mobilised both to demonstrate overseas the superiority of race relations in New Zealand and to illustrate domestically the success of the integration policy.

Representations of Te Kanawa could also operate to show that integration was proceeding apace, and benefiting all, as well as that New Zealand had harmonious race relations. In the souvenir programme produced for her farewell concert in Wellington in 1966, Gladstone Hill hailed the concert as 'an opportunity to show the world that in New Zealand the Pakeha would work for, and with, the Maori in the same manner and to the same extent as he would do for a fellow Pakeha'. In the farewell concert, he continued, 'the Pakeha and the Maori combined and co-operated to honour this talented Maori girl in her pursuit of the highest honours in the world of song'. The concert programme also contained a copy of a letter from the office of the Minister of Māori Affairs, which expressed similar sentiments:

> With a Pakeha mother and Maori father, Kiri represents all that is best in New Zealand … As the Minister of Maori Affairs, Mr Hanan, mentioned to you, the developing pattern of full integration in New Zealand is admirably typified in Kiri …[88]

Te Kanawa thus appears to have been publicly embraced and presented as a symbol of New Zealand's good race relations. Katie Pickles noted that in one early image of Te Kanawa as a young woman the 'integration of Maori and Pakeha worlds' was clearly evident in the 'juxtaposition' of the 'traditional cloak' which she wore with 'modern hair and make-up'. Te Kanawa represented, Pickles suggested, 'a national and international ambassador for New Zealand

---

87   Ibid.
88   Programme for farewell concert, National Library of New Zealand, Wellington.

race relations', someone who could be read 'both as an example of integration and of assimilation'.[89] Unlike Kingi, Te Kanawa was not sent overseas explicitly to market New Zealand, but she was nevertheless depicted in ways which suggested that she too was imagined at least in part as an advertisement for her country.

If Australia did not pride itself on its exemplary race relations as New Zealand did, those Aboriginal people who did reach fame in the performing arts were nonetheless sometimes represented as exemplars of assimilated Aborigines. In 1962, *Dawn* reported on the events marking National Aborigines' Day in Sydney, at which singers and musicians such as Lorna Beulah, Jimmy Little and Col Hardy had performed. Little and Hardy were pictured with soccer player Charlie Perkins and 'singer-actor' Candy Williams, and the group described as a 'credit to their race'.[90] Harold Blair was likewise termed 'a credit to himself, his people and his country' in a profile which appeared in *Dawn* in 1952.[91] Similarly, despite the anti-assimilation slant of *Jedda* itself, publicity material and articles about the film in 1954 and 1955 sometimes depicted Rosie Kunoth and Bob Wilson as assimilation successes, implicitly if not explicitly. Wilson was profiled in a publicity booklet, *Eve in Ebony*, under the headline: 'Robert Tudawali – Civilised Savage'.[92] *Dawn* described the stars as 'two typical Australians, hard working and good living' and 'a credit to their race'.[93] Kunoth knew little about films when she was cast as Jedda.[94] Yet *Dawn* claimed she had a 'favourite film star', Stewart Granger, just like 'white girls her age'.[95] Such depictions sat uneasily alongside portrayals of her as exotic, different or primitive, which were also evident in promotional material in the 1950s. *Eve in Ebony* ended its profile of her with the comment that she 'retains the age-old, primitive emotions of her race' and would 'always be a somewhat unknown quantity with her charming will-o'-the-wisp quality'.[96]

Kunoth was to some degree unusual, as an Aboriginal woman who became nationally visible in the press in the 1950s and 1960s, since at that time such celebrity was for the most part focused upon a small number of Aboriginal men. Those men included her fellow actor Tudawali, artist Albert Namatjira, boxer Dave Sands and singers Little and Blair. As Anna Haebich has argued, media coverage of their achievements and personal lives was shaped by ideas about assimilation then circulating, and they were represented both as embodying

---

89 Pickles, 'Kiwi Icons', pp. 13-14.
90 'Crowds Stood Still in Heart of Sydney', *Dawn* 11, no. 8 (1962), pp. 1-4.
91 'A Dream Came True!', p. 9.
92 *Eve in Ebony*.
93 'Jedda is YOUR Film', *Dawn* 3, no. 9 (1954), p. 10.
94 Chryssides, pp. 180-181.
95 'Jedda is YOUR Film', p. 9.
96 *Eve in Ebony*.

assimilation and as struggling to achieve it, as assimilated Aborigines and as men who lived 'between two worlds'.[97] Namatjira, before his tragic death, was 'promoted by the government as the public face of assimilation' in a documentary produced by the Commonwealth Film Unit in 1947.[98] Yet although the appropriation of such figures as embodying the success of the government's assimilation project resonates with representations of Kingi and Te Kanawa as exemplars of integration, what was perhaps most different in New Zealand was that there was not a history of significant debate as to whether Māori were able to be assimilated, as there was about Aboriginal people in Australia.

Successful Aboriginal people in Australia were also sometimes presented as having a potential role as ambassadors, able to show white Australians the capabilities of Aboriginal people, and perhaps also their ability to assimilate. Writers of promotional material for *Jedda* in the 1950s forecast a future for Kunoth in which she would represent the abilities and worth of Aboriginal people to white society. The writer(s) of *Eve in Ebony* declared that 'Ngarla Kunoth, beautiful aborigine girl, has become a proud ambassadoress of one of the greatest aborigine races in the world'.[99] *Dawn* also took up this refrain, contending that having 'proved herself a very talented actress as well as a charming young Australian woman', there was 'no doubt' that she would 'bring a great deal of very favourable publicity to the aboriginal people'.[100] The possibility of well-known Māori women fulfilling such a role as ambassadors for Māori appears not to have been publicly articulated in New Zealand, perhaps because any such statements might potentially have undermined the widely-held belief that New Zealand's race relations were harmonious.

At the same time, however, Māori women were sometimes represented as performing an ambassadorial role for all of New Zealand, both overseas in the case of Kingi and Te Kanawa and within New Zealand in the case of the Māori women who guided foreign and domestic tourists around the thermal areas. Te Kanawa was described in Auckland's *Metro* magazine in 1990 as 'our most prominent international ambassador'.[101] Rangitīaria Dennan, who was best known as Guide Rangi, was widely known and celebrated for her work as a guide, and guided a number of dignitaries and celebrities during her career. At her death, an editorial in the *New Zealand Herald* stated that she would be remembered, among other reasons, for having 'served New Zealand very well'.[102] She was described in an editorial in the *Dominion* as 'an internationally renowned New Zealander'

97 A. Haebich, *Spinning the Dream: Assimilation in Australia 1950-1970* (North Fremantle: Fremantle, 2008), p. 353.
98 Ibid., p. 355.
99 *Eve in Ebony.*
100 'Our Cover', *Dawn* 3, no. 10 (1954), contents page.
101 P. Shaw, 'Kiri: Another Opinion', *Metro*, no. 105 (1990), p. 150.
102 'Guide Rangi', *New Zealand Herald*, 15 August 1970, p. 8.

who had 'personified this country more than anyone of the age'.[103] As a figure who could be perceived both as embodying Māori cultural heritage and as being integrated into Pākehā ways of life, Guide Rangi could be an ambassador for New Zealand to the rest of the world.

The appropriation of Māori women as ambassadors for the nation held echoes of the familiar appropriation of Indigenous images to symbolise the nation and to express its unique nature. Yet strong and successful women were not unaware of the potential for using their prominent position to promote their own message, and were sometimes able to undermine images of racial harmony and to reveal the struggles faced by Indigenous peoples. In a letter written to the readers of *Te Ao Hou* in 1962 around the time she gave her speech at the International Beauty Congress, Kingi wrote not about the harmonious nature of New Zealand's race relations, but about the need for Māori to ensure their language and culture survived. She exhorted older people to help those who were younger to speak the Māori language, and younger people to seek an education as well as to keep the cultural arts alive.[104]

Dennan clearly used her position as a guide to comment upon the situation of the Māori people after colonisation, as well as to argue for the retention of Māori culture and custom. Ngāhuia Te Awekōtuku argued that Māori women were used to promote tourism for more than a century, whether or not they were aware of it, and suggested that women such as Dennan had 'dignified and also used the image'.[105] During her guiding career, Dennan 'achieved wide recognition as a cultural ambassador', as Cushla Parekowhai observed, communicating aspects of Māori life and custom to tourists as she guided them.[106] During a radio interview with her recorded in the 1950s, the interviewer observed that she had 'long since been accepted by both our races as a spokesman for her own Maori people' and that she knew 'just how to interpret the way of the Maori to the Pakeha'.[107] In an autobiography she co-authored with Pākehā journalist Ross Annabell, Dennan recalled that she had realised when she began guiding that 'most of the visitors were interested in Maoris as well as the geysers and the mud' and that a guide 'could well become an ambassador, serving by example to show visitors the true worth of our race'.[108] As she once stated, 'I had one goal in life, to get the world to appreciate the name of a guide and a Maori.'[109] If she was sometimes appropriated as an ambassador for New Zealand to the rest of

103   'Death of Rangi', *Dominion*, 15 August 1970, p. 12.

104   M. Kingi, 'A Letter From Maureen', *Te Ao Hou: The New World*, no. 40 (1962), p. 3.

105   Te Awekōtuku, p. 94.

106   Parekowhai, 'Dennan, Rangitiaria'.

107   S. Barnett and J. Sullivan, eds., *In Their Own Words: From the Sound Archives of Radio New Zealand* (Wellington: GP Books in association with Radio New Zealand Sound Archives, 1988), p. 28.

108   R. Dennan and R. Annabell, *Guide Rangi of Rotorua* (Christchurch: Whitcombe and Tombs, 1968), p. 74.

109   Barnett and Sullivan, eds., p. 27.

the world, Dennan also succeeded in subverting that appropriation, apparently considering that Māori were in need of an ambassador of their own. In this sense, Dennan and others like her were sometimes able to play a role analogous to that of the cultural mediator or interpreter, a role that scholars have suggested some Indigenous women played in frontier situations in the Americas.[110]

Changing Times in the Performing Arts

In the years following the late 1960s, Indigenous performers more frequently used their public roles to impart political messages, speaking out against discrimination, advocating change in the entertainment industries or promoting cultural revival. Using their fame in such a way became more possible in part because of wider social and political changes, such as the so-called Māori renaissance and the upsurge of protest activity by Māori or the growth in the Aboriginal rights movement, and in part because of changes in the entertainment industry itself. Film stars, for instance, gained greater independence from production companies in the last decades of the twentieth century and became more able to have a public voice apart from their film roles and establish a public persona. As well, different films began to be made, including by Indigenous directors and producers, and different television programmes to be screened, such as *Women of the Sun* in Australia, which told Indigenous stories. In Australia, Katelyn Barney noted some growth in the number of Indigenous women releasing recordings in the 1980s, and a 'dramatic increase' in this number in the 1990s.[111] Women such as Moana Maniapoto-Jackson in New Zealand and Justine Saunders in Australia were part of a new generation of artists, actors, musicians and singers from the 1970s who spoke out more vocally about the many injustices suffered by Māori and Aboriginal peoples. Depictions of women in the performing arts as exotic entertainers or exemplars of integration and harmonious race relations appeared in the media less often, and were sometimes replaced by portrayals as radicals or activists.

Moana Maniapoto-Jackson, a qualified lawyer who also worked in talkback radio and television, became known for her political views as well as her music, some of which was itself seen as political. Her commitment to utilising music to send 'positive messages' to Māori sometimes meant that she was 'labelled as a radical'.[112] She was described by Rosa Shiels in the Christchurch *Press* in 1996 as 'well known for her stance on social issues and her talking-head television

---

110 See for example: F. Karttunen, *Between Worlds: Interpreters, Guides, and Survivors* (New Brunswick: Rutgers University Press, 1994); C. S. Kidwell, 'Indian Women as Cultural Mediators', *Ethnohistory* 39, no. 2 (1992), pp. 97-107.
111 Barney, p. 45.
112 W. Nissen, *Filling the Frame: Profiles of 18 New Zealand Women* (Auckland: Reed, 1992), p. 22.

appearances'.[113] Another reporter, Michelle Cruickshank, commented in the *Sunday Star-Times* in 1998 that Maniapoto-Jackson 'is known as much for her mouth as her music' and 'uses every opportunity ... as a platform to promote her convictions'.[114] Maniapoto-Jackson was once quoted commenting that 'it's amazing how people embroider things, misquote you and give you labels like "Maori rights singer"'.[115] In Australia, Ruby Hunter sang of the struggles and survival of Aboriginal people, and of her own experiences as a member of the Stolen Generations. Justine Saunders was open about the struggles she faced as an Aboriginal woman in her acting career, and spoke out publicly about problems of discrimination in the industry. As she recalled, she had 'to fight the stereotype, the white interpretation of the Black story' that had seen her play characters who were 'raped and murdered', or 'the white man's fantasy' wearing 'a lap-lap' and having 'a bit of a love affair with the white man', which usually ended after her character died.[116]

As well, artists such as Maniapoto-Jackson and Maroochy Barambah promoted Indigenous music and language in their work. Barambah was described in 1995 as having become a 'torch-bearer for Aboriginal culture'. She organised a Barambah Beltout Festival in 1994, after a return to Cherbourg to speak to children about Aboriginal music led her to formulate an idea for 'an Aboriginal initiated multicultural festival'.[117] Barambah was quoted in 1996 saying that 'I see myself as a pioneer of Indigenous music', something that had not been 'easy' given 'all the discrimination' in Australia.[118] Similarly, Maniapoto-Jackson was sometimes quoted observing discrimination in the music industry, or commenting that it was difficult to advance Māori music. A particular problem she had faced was reportedly that songs with Māori language lyrics were more difficult to succeed with in a mainstream arena.[119] Despite these difficulties however, the increasing numbers of Māori and Aboriginal women in the performing arts, and their increasing ability and willingness to speak on political matters, constitute a significant shift.

Rosie Kunoth-Monks, on the other hand, left the performing arts behind after the end of her role in *Jedda*. She entered a convent, and during those years learned more about the experiences of Aboriginal people.[120] Leaving the convent, she took a job as Aboriginal Liaison Officer in the Department of Aboriginal Affairs

113   R. Shiels, 'Sounds of the World', *Press*, 9 February 1996, p. 21.
114   M. Cruickshank, 'The Power of Language is Moana's Political Weapon of Choice', *Sunday Star-Times*, 15 February 1998, Revue section, p. 3.
115   Nissen, p. 22.
116   R. Sykes, *Murawina: Australian Women of High Achievement* (Sydney: Doubleday, 1993), p. 142.
117   C. Baker, 'Maroochy Barambah Belts it Out', *Artforce*, no. 89 (1995), pp. 6-7.
118   N. Wallace, 'A Voice from the Wilderness', *Courier-Mail*, 25 April 1996, 'What's On' liftout, p. 6.
119   Shiels, p. 21.
120   R. Kunoth-Monks, interview with R. Hughes, conducted 11 July 1995, transcript available from http://www.australianbiography.gov.au/subjects/kunothmonks/interview4.html, tape 4.

in Melbourne. Her return in 1977 to Alice Springs to operate the Ayiparinya Aboriginal Hostel brought another awakening, as she saw great change since she had left, which she described as 'cultural genocide', wrought by alcohol, loss of culture and country, racism and bureaucratic problems in Aboriginal Affairs.[121] She increasingly spoke out about the issues she observed. Kunoth-Monks became involved with the Country Liberal Party, and twice ran unsuccessfully for office in the Northern Territory seat of Macdonnell. Hindsight made her 'glad' later in life to have lost these elections, as she had 'discovered ... that the policies of the party control you'.[122]

Kunoth-Monks' involvement with government continued in her time as Ministerial Officer to Paul Everingham, the first Chief Minister of the Northern Territory, until a plan to flood a sacred site made it impossible for her to continue. She held many positions relating to Aboriginal matters, including in the Aboriginal Development Commission, the Central Australian Aboriginal Legal Aid Service and the Aboriginal Deaths in Custody Royal Commission. Her return to the film industry came later in life and in a position of greater strength. She did not act again, taking instead a role behind the scenes, as a 'co-ordinator' for Aboriginal people involved in movies.[123] Later still, she returned with her family to her birthplace, Utopia Station, to live a traditional life, focusing on her responsibilities for preserving and passing down culture and land. Speaking on the Australian Broadcasting Corporation television programme *Message Stick* in later life, she noted that she was 'not an actress', and that her 'purpose now is to retain our language and our land' and to 'hold onto our corroboree and our rituals'.[124] As she matured and increasingly spoke out about the problems she observed, representations of her began to shift, from depictions of a pretty, charming and shy young glamour girl to portrayals of a confident, outspoken or even formidable woman. In the *Bulletin* in 1990, for example, she was termed 'an eloquent spokesperson for Aborigines' who was 'impossible to ignore' when she had 'a full head of steam'.[125] Yet she did not escape *Jedda*, as her starring role in the film was frequently referenced in the media to remind readers of her 1950s fame outside the Northern Territory.

Te Kanawa's career has spanned these years of change, and her periodic returns to New Zealand for concerts or holidays have been to a changing society. Throughout her career Te Kanawa has acknowledged her Māori heritage, and has at times promoted Māori culture, language or music. In *Opera for Lovers*,

---

121 Chryssides, p. 196; R. Kunoth-Monks, interview with R. Hughes, conducted 11 July 1995, transcript available from http://www.australianbiography.gov.au/subjects/kunothmonks/interview5.html, tape 5.
122 Chryssides, pp. 196-197.
123 Ibid., pp. 175, 197-199.
124 R. Maza and R. Kunoth-Monks, 'Rosalie's Journey', updated 29 April 2005, accessed 27 February 2008, available from http://www.abc.net.au/message/tv/ms/s1307580.htm.
125 'A Legend Laments', *Bulletin*, 12 June 1990, p. 46.

a book she co-authored with Conrad Wilson in 1996, she commented that 'although I was raised differently from other Maori kids – I was brought up white – I am Maori in every other sense'.[126] She produced a book of Māori stories in 1989, observing in the foreword that she had 'had a very happy childhood surrounded by many Maori friends and relations' and that the stories contained in the book were 'my recollection of those tales that I remembered and loved best as a child'.[127] In 1999, she recorded an album of Māori songs, similarly stating in the album notes that the songs it included 'were the background to my childhood in New Zealand', and expressing her pleasure that she could 'share these wonderful and unique sounds with people from around the world'.[128] In an article in the *New Zealand Herald* that year, she was quoted saying that the songs on the album were 'ethnically correct' and 'as authentic as we can get', whereas those she had recorded at the beginning of her career in the 1960s had been 'more stylised'.[129] As well, Te Kanawa was more than once reported to have said that she hoped to be a role model for Māori. In 1987, she was quoted in the *New Zealand Listener* saying that 'being Maori' involved 'being a reasonable role model'.[130]

After leaving New Zealand in 1966, Te Kanawa lived overseas, returning to New Zealand only for short periods. For the major part of her international career, she was usually labelled in the media in terms of her New Zealand-ness, rather than her Māori-ness. After she travelled to London to study and work she began to be frequently described in the media as a 'New Zealand soprano' or 'New Zealand singer'. Te Kanawa was sometimes quoted declaring that she represented New Zealand, rather than specifically representing Māori people. In 2004, she was quoted in the *Dominion Post* observing that New Zealanders who became famous were 'spreading the good word about New Zealand and New Zealanders' and 'represent our country in the best and most positive way we can'.[131] This statement echoes earlier depictions of famous Māori women as ambassadors for New Zealand as a whole on the international stage.

Te Kanawa remained largely apart from political issues during the majority of her career, focusing instead on her operatic work. In terms of 'representation' as advocacy, she might be said to have focused upon representing New Zealand, and upon representing classical music to an audience unfamiliar with it, rather than upon representing Māori or Māori concerns. Asked by a reporter for the *New Zealand Listener* in 1983 if her 'international reputation' meant that 'she

126 K. Te Kanawa and C. Wilson, *Opera for Lovers* (Sydney: Hodder Headline, 1996), p. 250.
127 K. Te Kanawa, *Land of the Long White Cloud: Maori Myths, Tales and Legends* (London: Pavilion, 1989), pp. 7-8.
128 K. Te Kanawa, 'Kiri: Maori Songs' (Auckland and London: EMI Records, 1999).
129 D. Sampson, 'Now is the Hour', *New Zealand Herald*, 20-21 November 1999, p. D1.
130 P. Stirling, 'The Diva Will Decide', *New Zealand Listener*, 22 August 1987, p. 18.
131 R. McLean, 'One Cool Dame', *Dominion Post*, 11 December 2004, p. 4.

might have a bigger opportunity – to speak loudly on behalf of the Maori's push for equality', she was quoted responding that she had not felt 'pressure of that sort', that she was 'brought up to be a singer and a small ambassadress for New Zealand', and that she felt herself to be 'a different sort of spearhead'.[132] In a 1991 article in the *New Zealand Woman's Weekly*, she was quoted distancing herself from 'activists', explaining that 'campaigning' was 'their mission in life', and that her 'mission is music'.[133] In relation to those who had tried to press her into acting as a spokesperson for Māori issues, she was quoted in 1993 as saying: 'I tell them, if you want to advance my cause, then you will advance classical music'.[134]

In recent years, Te Kanawa has occasionally commented on Indigenous issues. Her comments have not always been well received by Māori leaders in New Zealand, however. In 2000, she reportedly said that women should be able to speak on the marae ātea (the courtyard in front of the wharenui, or meeting house). The iwi (tribe) chairman of Ngāti Porou, Api Mahuika, was quoted in the *Dominion* stating that Te Kanawa 'cannot dictate what rights should apply to women from other tribal areas' and that she had 'no right to speak for other iwi' than her own. She should, he was quoted saying, return to New Zealand and learn about the situation before she spoke publicly on the matter.[135] The biggest controversy occurred in 2003, after she gave an interview to Melbourne's *Herald Sun*. She was quoted saying that too many Māori lived on government benefits, did not work hard and had no pride. 'I wish there were more Maori people with my sort of attitude', she reportedly said, 'but there are not'.[136] Several Māori leaders were reported to be 'upset', with many Māori Members of Parliament (MPs) reportedly seeing her views as lacking knowledge because she did not live in New Zealand, and as lacking understanding of Māori culture.[137] While several Māori MPs agreed that welfare dependency was a problem, such criticisms were particularly bitter coming from a fellow Māori, a woman who was extremely wealthy in contrast to the poverty and disadvantage that many Māori people faced, and someone who had lived much of her life overseas rather than in New Zealand working to improve the situation.[138] Te Kanawa's position as a Māori performer has thus been in many ways different from that of other Māori people in the performing arts, both in the extent of her fame and in the lack of status she has had within Māoridom.

---

132   Reid, p. 14.
133   Lord, p. 14.
134   J. Moir, 'Dame Kiri at the Crossroads', *Sydney Morning Herald*, 28 December 1993, p. 18.
135   J. Milne, 'Kiri Backs Women on Maraes', *Dominion*, 3 January 2000, p. 1.
136   R. Berry, 'Lazy Maori Lack Pride, Says Kiri', *Dominion Post*, 28 February 2003, p. A1.
137   'Dame Kiri Raised Leadership Issues for Maori, Minister Says', New Zealand Press Association, 28 February 2003, accessed from Factiva, 29 July 2008.
138   See reported comments in: R. Berry, 'Critics Hit Back at Dame Kiri Over Māori Work Ethic Claim', *Press*, 1 March 2003, p. A3; R. Berry, 'Kiri's Concerns Valid, Says Peters', *Dominion Post*, 1 March 2003, p. A3.

The Diva Effect

A much greater international celebrity than other women discussed in this chapter, and largely without leadership status within the Indigenous community, Te Kanawa was in many ways represented differently in the media as well. Portrayals of Te Kanawa were in some ways more like those of Sutherland, and of other international operatic sopranos, than they were like those of other Māori performers. Like Te Kanawa, Sutherland was sometimes depicted as an awe-inspiring diva with a lovely voice, although not generally as being physically beautiful as was Te Kanawa, and at the same time was often portrayed as a modest and friendly woman who retained the down-to-earth disposition often perceived as characteristic of both Australians and New Zealanders.[139] Moreover, available material about Te Kanawa's life and career displays the impact of a marketing machine much greater than that wielded by lesser celebrities. Journalists themselves sometimes commented on this marketing machine even as they perpetuated representations that drew on the accepted Te Kanawa legend or attempted to dismantle it. In 1994, one journalist observed in the *New Zealand Listener* that Te Kanawa's was a 'tenderly nurtured image' and argued that 'the Kiri we see [is] a confection created by more than 25 years of careful manipulation of performances, contacts and publicity'.[140] Magazine and newspaper features continually reported the same details of her career, narrated her life in similar ways and quoted her saying similar things in answer to the same questions. No other woman discussed in this book appears to have been the subject of marketing to the same extent.

Yet through the marketing it seems clear that Te Kanawa remained part of an earlier generation of Māori women who had become prominent in the performing arts. While a new generation of performers were increasingly vocal about discrimination in the entertainment industries, and in society more generally, depictions of Te Kanawa remained remarkably similar throughout her career. It was in the emergence of a new generation of more outspoken performers that Indigenous experiences of the performing arts in New Zealand and Australia converged most strongly. While New Zealand is backed by a longer and more numerous lineage of Māori success in the performing arts, parallels in the concerns of Indigenous performers from the 1970s, and in their ability to speak out, are evident across the Tasman.

---

139 For examples of these and similar depictions, see: 'Australia Awaits Joan Sutherland', *Woman's Day with Woman*, 15 January 1962, p. 8; A. Goddard, 'Opera Star Who is Still "Just Joan"', *Sydney Morning Herald*, 14 August 1965, p. 13; M. Prerauer, 'La Stupenda is Back! And Despite All the Fame and Fortune, She is Still Our Joan at Heart', *Sunday Telegraph*, 30 June 1974, p. 37; D. Riseborough, 'After 25 Years Still a Voice of Spun Gold', *Woman's Day*, 12 January 1976, p. 2; J. Yeomans, 'Our Modest La Stupenda', *Courier-Mail*, 29 June 1976, p. 5.
140 K. Stewart, 'Party on, Diva', *New Zealand Listener*, 2 April 1994, p. 44.

Conclusion

Te Kanawa emerged as a singer and celebrity within a long tradition of Māori musical success in New Zealand and internationally. Unlike figures such as Kunoth or Blair in Australia, there was no sense that her success was unique, surprising or a manifestation of a new phenomenon. Yet despite the different histories of Indigenous involvement in the performing arts in New Zealand and Australia, print media depictions of those Māori and Aboriginal women who did become famous in the performing arts evinced certain parallels. Whether it was as exotic beauties, as glamorous modern women or as models of successful assimilation, representations of these women did often echo each other. During the 1950s and 1960s in Australia, successful Aboriginal performers like Kunoth and Blair were often appropriated as public symbols of the success of the assimilation project. In New Zealand, performers such as Te Kanawa and Kingi were likewise depicted as embodying integration, although these depictions were not underlaid by a history of significant debate over whether or not Māori could be assimilated as were depictions of Aboriginal performers in Australia. Representations of both Māori and Aboriginal women often combined a fascination with exoticism with portrayal in the terms of modern and sophisticated (white) femininity. Māori women such as Kingi and Te Kanawa were sometimes imagined as representing New Zealand's harmonious race relations and successful policy of integration to the world, and to this extent were imagined as national representatives who could embody that nation to an overseas audience. Aboriginal women such as Kunoth had first to gain acceptance within Australia as having been assimilated into a homogenous, white Australian nation, a nation which by its very whiteness continued to exclude them. As a new generation of Indigenous performers emerged in both Australia and New Zealand in the 1970s and 1980s, and a new generation of activists became visible, New Zealand's comfortable image became increasingly tarnished. On both sides of the Tasman, the assimilationist dream began to appear lost.

Chapter Four

Works of literature, films, artworks and other products of creative endeavour are often read and analysed in terms of the messages their creators might have attempted to convey through them. In such fields of achievement, where art and politics frequently collide, how were successful and prominent Indigenous women and their works depicted in the print media? How did they represent themselves and their work? What discursive threads were common between depictions of writers and those of filmmakers, and which were different? In this chapter I examine representations of Indigenous women celebrated for their literary and filmmaking achievements, focusing in particular on Oodgeroo Noonuccal (formerly Kath Walker). While many Indigenous women have authored or co-authored autobiographical texts as well, particularly in Australia, I focus here upon fiction writers. For the most part, fiction writers and their works have become more prominent than have the authors of autobiographical texts (although Sally Morgan is a notable exception). I explore depictions of these women as firsts or curiosities, discuss discourses of authenticity and assimilation, and consider contests over the place of politics in creative work, an issue that was particularly potent for Indigenous writers, filmmakers and artists. I discuss shifts in these trends of representation, especially relating to the emergence of Indigenous women in filmmaking. Throughout, I draw comparisons with the experiences and media depictions of Indigenous men and non-Indigenous women in the creative arts.

Indigenous Women and the Literary World

Māori and Aboriginal peoples told stories long before the arrival of Europeans, creating vibrant cultures of oral literature. After Europeans arrived, forms of written literature in English also began to be adopted, and adapted. In the second half of the twentieth century, written literature in English by Aboriginal and Māori authors proliferated, often retaining elements of the earlier oral forms, and becoming a rich field of literature which is now widely studied. Some Māori and Aboriginal women whose work was part of this development became nationally prominent and celebrated. In both Australia and New Zealand, this proliferation of published Indigenous voices writing fiction in English occurred alongside and as part of a wider phenomenon of social and political change. As Adam Shoemaker has pointed out, Oodgeroo began writing and publishing poetry within this context. Shoemaker suggested that the 'heightening of Aboriginal pride, resolve and socio-political involvements' during the 1960s 'helped to provide the impetus for cultural expressions of Aboriginality, as well as for public campaigns'. One aspect of Aboriginal resistance to the official policy of assimilation, he argued, was through 'the assertion of Aboriginal individuality, protest and pride which Noonuccal's poetry represents'.[1] Similarly, the publication of Patricia Grace's fiction in New Zealand during the 1970s and 1980s was part of what was sometimes termed a Māori renaissance. Whether or not this term is an appropriate one, there was undoubtedly an intensification of Māori demands for social and political change, and a strengthening of assertions of cultural identity, during those years. The work of Indigenous authors, like that of Indigenous filmmakers, artists and songwriters, often challenged non-Indigenous representations of Indigenous peoples and cultures.

At the same time, the second half of the twentieth century also saw a proliferation of writing by women, building on a long history of women's creative endeavours. This flowering of literature by women was connected to the second wave feminist movement, which sought to 'reclaim the value and importance of women's interests', and therefore of the issues women wrote about.[2] In a book of interviews with New Zealand women authors published in 1989, Sue Kedgley observed that a number of women began writing after a feminist awakening of some form enabled them to find their voice.[3] While such an understanding of 'women's writing' was essentialist, as was a categorisation of writing by Indigenous people as 'Indigenous writing', the literature produced by women and by Indigenous people was advanced by, and contributed to, the assertions of identity made through feminist and Indigenous rights movements.

Oodgeroo, Fame and the Media

When she died in 1993, the woman who had become famous as Kath Walker was known as Oodgeroo of the Noonuccal tribe, and as the custodian of Minjerribah, the sand island in Brisbane's Moreton Bay (Quandamooka) that was named Stradbroke Island by Europeans.[4] It was on this island in 1920 that Oodgeroo was born and named Kathleen Jean Mary Ruska. Her first collection of poems, *We Are Going*, was published in 1964, and she became famous more or less immediately. If it was on her poetry that her fame was first based, however, her writing was seen to be deeply entwined with her activist efforts on behalf of Aboriginal people, and she became well-known nationally for this work as well. Oodgeroo was deeply involved in the Aboriginal civil rights movement for much of her life. She was secretary of the Queensland Council for the Advancement

1   A. Shoemaker, *Black Words White Page* (Canberra: ANU E Press, 2004), pp. 5, 182.
2   S. Kedgley, *Our Own Country: Leading New Zealand Women Writers Talk About Their Writing and Their Lives* (Auckland: Penguin, 1989), p. 13.
3   Ibid.
4   I refer to her throughout this chapter as Oodgeroo, the name she herself chose.

of Aborigines and Torres Strait Islanders (QCAATSI), became involved with the Federal Council (FCAATSI) and was a key figure in the campaign for the 1967 referendum. Her writing thus went alongside and was part of her political efforts on behalf of Aboriginal people, in a period when Aboriginal issues became more visible to the wider population. In her terms, perhaps, her writing was part of her project of educating the white population of Australia.[5] Oodgeroo later returned to Stradbroke Island to live, running a cultural and education centre, Moongalba. Over 8000 children visited the centre between 1972 and 1977, staying in tents and learning Aboriginal approaches to gathering food.[6]

Figure 7: 'Portrait of Oodgeroo Noonuccal', Australian Overseas Information Service.

Photograph. nla.pic-an11618802. National Library of Australia, Canberra.

---

5   Rhonda Craven noted after Oodgeroo's death that she had 'utilised every skill she had to educate' and had preferred to be termed an 'Educator'. R. Craven, 'Oodgeroo: An Educator Who Proved One Person Could Make a Difference', *Australian Literary Studies* 16, no. 4 (1994), p. 122.
6   K. Cochrane, *Oodgeroo* (St Lucia: University of Queensland Press, 1994), p. 93.

Not all writers and filmmakers are equally prominent. After the publication of *We Are Going*, Oodgeroo had considerably more public visibility than most other Indigenous women writers and filmmakers. Fame extending beyond literary circles has often been linked to involvement in non-literary public activities, such as Oodgeroo's activist work. Writers and filmmakers could also become nationally prominent through receiving prestigious national or international recognition for their work. Keri Hulme seems to have become better-known than fellow New Zealander Patricia Grace, presumably because she was the first New Zealand writer to win the Booker Prize, which she received in 1985 for her novel *the bone people*. Hulme's win prompted a spike in media interest in her and her work around the time of the award. Outside of moments such as these, writers and filmmakers are usually not large-scale celebrities in the way sportspeople, actors or musicians may be, sometimes being well-known in literary circles and almost entirely unknown outside of them. Writers such as Hulme and Grace did not make public gestures of protest, and controversy was rarely attached to them. These writers appeared in the press largely only in relation to reviews of their work, reports of prizes they had won, or events that they took part in. Oodgeroo, on the other hand, was a public person who often appeared in the media, and her protest activities made her more prominent. Indeed, her later educative work appears not to have been so well-known as her early poetry and activism.

As a public person, Oodgeroo had a sometimes ambiguous relationship with the media. Roberta Sykes remembered her having been angry about sometimes being 'misquoted' and 'betrayed' by the press.[7] At the same time, the media provided a channel to convey her message to the wider population. Many of her speeches and gestures of protest over the years were reported in newspapers throughout Australia. For example, several newspapers in late 1970 reported the possibility that she might emigrate. She was quoted in the *Australian* explaining that she felt her poetry had done nothing but 'cause the Australian people to duck for cover with a guilty conscience', and she felt unable to remain and 'wait for the Aboriginal to die'.[8] In another example, the *Australian* reported in 1979 that she had 'given her new book to a German publisher as a protest at Australia's treatment of Aborigines' and the country's policies relating to uranium.[9] One of her most visible and widely commented upon gestures of protest related to the celebration of the Bicentenary in 1988. Made a Member of the Order of the British Empire (MBE) in 1970, Oodgeroo had reportedly suggested that very year that she might return the award.[10] At the end of 1987, she did so, at the same time changing her name from Kath Walker to Oodgeroo of the

---

7 R. B. Sykes, 'While My Name is Remembered …', *Australian Literary Studies* 16, no. 4 (1994), p. 38.
8 '"I Won't Watch the Aboriginals Die Out": Kath Walker Talks About Deserting', *Australian*, 21 November 1970, p. 5.
9 'Kath Closes the Book on Local Publishers', *Australian*, 5 October 1979, p. 2.
10 'May Return MBE, Says Native Leader', *Age*, 27 July 1970, p. 10.

Noonuccal tribe (sometimes written Oodgeroo Noonuccal). A piece appeared in the *Age* explaining that 'as a protest against what the Bicentenary "celebrations" stand for', she could 'no longer, with a clear conscience, accept the English honour of the MBE', and would therefore return it. Seeing the Bicentenary as an anniversary of '200 years of rape and carnage', she asked, 'what is there to celebrate?'[11] Oodgeroo's use of the media as a channel for her messages about Aboriginal rights contributed to her having experienced greater levels of media attention than authors and filmmakers might usually expect.

'An Aborigine Who is Also a Poet': Being Exceptional and Being First

Oodgeroo and Patricia Grace, like many other Indigenous women featured in this book, were hailed as having achieved a 'first' in their work (see Chapter Six). After the publication of *We Are Going*, it became a common refrain that Oodgeroo was the first published Aboriginal poet, or the first Aboriginal person to have a book published.[12] She was described in the *Canberra Times* in 1966 as 'Australia's first aboriginal poet to be published' and as 'the first writer of aboriginal blood to publish a volume of verse', which made her 'unique'.[13] A retrospective article in 1999 referred to her as 'the first of her race to have a book of poems published', defining her not only as a literary first, but also in the earlier biological language of race.[14] A little over ten years after Oodgeroo's first book was published, Grace's first collection of short stories, *Waiariki*, was published in 1975. Grace had begun writing fiction while teaching and raising seven children. Her work was first published in magazines such as *Te Ao Hou: The New World* and the *New Zealand Listener*. After *Waiariki*, she published a novel in 1978 (*Mutuwhenua: The Moon Sleeps*), and has since produced a long list of short story collections, novels and children's books. Grace was acclaimed as the first Māori woman to publish a collection of short stories when *Waiariki* appeared, and to publish a novel when *Mutuwhenua* appeared. Although others had previously published individual stories, David McGill described her in the

---

11   O. Noonuccal, 'Why I Am Now Oodgeroo Noonuccal', *Age*, 30 December 1987, p. 11.
12   See, for instance: D. Rowbotham, 'Brisbane Woman Compared With a Top Negro Writer', *Courier-Mail*, 9 May 1964, p. 2; 'There's Rhyme in Her Reasoning', *Sunday Truth*, 9 October 1966, p. 59; D. Warnock, 'Kath Walker – Poet With a Cause', *West Australian*, 21 April 1971, p. 8, biographical cutting files, National Library of Australia, Canberra. Such statements often tended to obscure the earlier literary efforts of David Unaipon, whose published work included legends, a life story and poetry. P. Jones, 'Unaipon, David (1872-1967)', *Australian Dictionary of Biography*, Online Edition, updated continuously, accessed 19 January 2009, available from http://www.adb.online.anu.edu.au/biogs/A120339b.htm.
13   T. I. Moore, 'Aboriginal Poet: Technique has Matured', *Canberra Times*, 17 December 1966, p. 13; 'Prophet in Her Country', *Canberra Times*, 18 October 1966, p. 14.
14   'Great Australian Poets Part Eight: Oodgeroo Noonuccal (1920-93)', *Sunday Herald Sun*, 25 July 1999, p. 51.

New Zealand Listener in 1975 as the 'first Maori woman writer'.[15] Hulme's *The Silences Between (Moeraki Conversations)* was similarly described at least once when it appeared in 1982 as the first poetry collection by a Māori woman published in New Zealand.[16]

Indigenous men whose creative work was published were likewise sometimes portrayed as having achieved a 'first'. After the publication of Hone Tuwhare's *No Ordinary Sun* in 1964, R. S. Oppenheim described it in the *Journal of the Polynesian Society* (*JPS*) as 'the first publication of a volume of poems by a Maori writer'.[17] In the same journal a decade later, Oppenheim reviewed Witi Ihimaera's 1972 short story collection *Pounamu Pounamu*, describing Ihimaera as 'New Zealand's first recognisably Maori writer'.[18] Those who were first were sometimes viewed as role models or path-breakers, both by commentators in the media and by other Indigenous writers. Sykes considered that Oodgeroo opened a way for others, and that it was a 'duty' for them to 'push the boundaries' until 'they break and fall away'.[19] Similarly, Hulme noted in one interview that becoming a writer was 'easier' for her because of the example of Grace, as 'another woman with a dual background' whose work had been published.[20]

Being first, or being acclaimed as first, was not necessarily positive, however (as is also discussed in Chapter Six). For writers and filmmakers, it could give rise to the belief that the success of a work was at least partly due to the curiosity of the public, rather than to the quality of the work. Just as Evonne Goolagong felt that she received greater press coverage than she otherwise would have because of her Aboriginality, Oodgeroo was quoted in interviews several times suggesting that her Aboriginality had increased interest in her poetry, at least to begin with. In a 1966 *Canberra Times* article discussing the sales success of *We Are Going*, she was quoted saying, 'I am aware that its success was due to its curiosity value as the work of an Aboriginal, rather than any greatness in my verse'.[21] She made a similar comment in the foreword to *The Dawn is at Hand*, her second book of poetry which was published in 1966, and she repeated the suggestion in later interviews.[22] Literary critics sometimes made similar comments. In a review of *We Are Going* in the *Australian* in 1964, Ian Turner wrote that he considered

---

15   D. McGill, 'Unassuming Grace', *New Zealand Listener*, 11 October 1975, p. 21. Those who had published individual short stories included Arapera Blank, J. C. Sturm and Rose Denness.

16   D. Long, 'A Conversation With Keri Hulme', *Tu Tangata*, no. 7 (1982), p. 2.

17   R. S. Oppenheim, 'Review of *No Ordinary Sun*, by Hone Tuwhare', *Journal of the Polynesian Society* 74, no. 4 (1965), p. 525.

18   R. S. Oppenheim, 'Review of *Pounamu Pounamu*, by Witi Ihimaera', *Journal of the Polynesian Society* 84, no. 4 (1975), p. 506.

19   Sykes, 'While My Name is Remembered', p. 41.

20   Kedgley, p. 100.

21   'Prophet in Her Country', p. 14.

22   G. Turcotte, 'Recording the Cries of the People', in *Aboriginal Culture Today*, ed. A. Rutherford (Sydney: Dangaroo, 1988), p. 19; E. Smith, 'Are You Going to Come Back Tomorrow?', *The Queensland Writer* 2, no. 1 (1990), p. 13; K. Walker, *The Dawn is at Hand* (Brisbane: Jacaranda, 1966), foreword.

Oodgeroo to be 'like the late Albert Namatjira … having a *succes de surprise*', although he thought that was 'a reflection on the audience, not on the poet'.[23] Later, fellow poet Judith Wright wrote that *We Are Going* 'had a high success for its curiosity value, but in fact it was a good book anyway'.[24]

Such comments were also made in relation to work by Indigenous men. Author and critic Bill Pearson contended that Ihimaera's writing ability was 'obscured by the initial acclaim from reviewers and by the publisher's promotion of him as "the first Maori novelist"'. He observed 'an undercurrent of muttering' from some Pākehā commentators suggesting that Ihimaera's success was due to 'the commercial exploitability of his Maoriness'.[25] Pearson quoted Oppenheim, who in his rather negative review of *Pounamu Pounamu* in the *JPS* had implied that the book was achieving success due to 'the adulatory and unintentionally patronising Pakeha public which is thirsty, just now, for a deep draft of ethnicity'.[26] Conceptualising the success of Indigenous writers in such ways gave them little credit for their literary skill and success.

Occasionally, comments by critics extended to a suggestion that the work actually lacked merit, or that the writer had been exploited by publishers as a curiosity. In 1971, Hal Colebatch paid Oodgeroo a back-handed compliment in a review of *My People* in the *West Australian*, admiring her 'achievement' in having 'produced several books of poetry' with 'no more than an elementary formal social education' and 'frightful social handicaps', but contending that it was 'impossible to pretend that the general standard of the poetry is high'. Colebatch suggested that Oodgeroo was acclaimed more by 'guilt-ridden white liberals than by Aborigines'. Yet, he argued, it was not the 'fault' of Oodgeroo that the work was 'not high class', as the 'blame' was upon 'those who have exploited her by promoting all her work, however trivial, as that of an important, serious poet'.[27] Similarly, David Norton suggested in 1976, reviewing *Waiariki*, that Grace had 'probably been hurried into producing a book before she [was] ready' and that the publisher was 'guilty of inverted prejudice in publicizing her as the "first Maori woman author", as if she is to be read because she is unique and because this was International Women's Year'. Unlike Colebatch, however, Norton considered this a problem because Grace ought to be seen as one who 'can be read because she can write well'.[28] Some years later, Hulme stated in an interview in 1982 that she had had a 'nasty feeling' that her work was 'being looked at through a different pair of spectacles: "This is a Maori woman writing … we'll give it a little more time than … if it was just a Pakeha woman"'.

---

23 I. Turner, 'Colour Seeks Justice', *Australian*, 26 September 1964, p. 13.

24 J. Wright, 'Creating a New Dreamtime', *National Times*, 14-19 June 1976, p. 46.

25 B. Pearson, 'Witi Ihimaera and Patricia Grace', in *Critical Essays on the New Zealand Short Story*, ed. C. Hankin (Auckland: Heinemann, 1982), p. 167.

26 Ibid., quoting Oppenheim, 'Review of *Pounamu Pounamu*', p. 507.

27 H. Colebatch, 'Lights and Shades in Aboriginal Poetry', *West Australian*, 6 March 1971, p. 20.

28 D. A. Norton, 'Not All Loners and Losers', *Landfall* 30, no. 2 (1976), p. 152.

For Hulme, while such attention was 'an advantage' in terms of drawing attention, she wanted 'to be acknowledged … as a writer … and not for it to be the performing dog'.[29]

Assimilation, Authenticity and Art

Indeed, these writers were frequently described in the media in terms of their Indigenous descent, rather than simply in terms of their occupation. In the first decades after the publication of *We Are Going*, Oodgeroo was often described as an 'Aboriginal poet' or 'Aboriginal poetess', rather than simply as a poet. In fifteen articles published between 1965 and 1969, twelve references were made to Oodgeroo as an 'Aboriginal poet' (or 'poetess'). One review of her work, published in *Hemisphere* in 1964, was simply titled 'Aboriginal Poet' in large letters.[30] This description became far less common in articles about her from the mid-1980s, perhaps because she was by then very well-known, or perhaps because her name change made her Indigeneity evident without need for elaboration. In one article in the *Australian* in 1969, she was termed '*the* Aboriginal poet', a description that also served to emphasise representations of her as a first and a path-breaker.[31] Grace was often described as a 'Maori writer' or 'Maori woman writer' in the years following the publication of her first book. This thread of description continued throughout her career, although as she became more established as a writer she was also sometimes described as a 'New Zealand writer', in local terms as a 'Wellington writer' or 'Plimmerton writer', or simply as a 'writer'. Whether this shift reflected changing standards about how people ought to be described or a more frequent claiming of her as a New Zealander as she became more acclaimed (reminiscent of Goolagong's being described as an 'Australian' tennis player) is not clear. That it might be the latter is suggested by the fact that Hulme was often described as a 'Kiwi author' or 'New Zealand author' at the time of her Booker Prize win, when she gained international prominence and brought literary glory to the nation.

Depiction in terms of Indigeneity was also common for many male Indigenous authors. Writing in 1978, Ihimaera observed that even when a Māori author did not view himself or herself as having 'a dual role as a writer and a Maori and a dual responsibility to his craft and to his people' it was certain that 'other people do and indeed are very eager to cast him in various roles'. A Māori author would, he wrote, 'suffer patronisation because people are often more interested in him

---

29 Long, p. 5, emphasis removed.
30 J. Hellyer, 'Aboriginal Poet', *Hemisphere* 8, no. 12 (1964), p. 17.
31 'Aboriginal Poet Sees Black Revolt as Inevitable', *Australian*, 17 September 1969, p. 2, my emphasis.

as a Maori and not as a writer'.[32] In Ihimaera's own case, such labels became more complicated when he wrote a novel in which the central character was a married Pākehā man struggling with his homosexuality. As Mark Amery noted in a profile of Ihimaera in 1995, he was suddenly 'in a position to be labelled a gay writer, to watch people try to put him within the bounds of another "genre"'.[33] As this remark suggests, the interests and identities of authors are often more fluid than such labelling allows.

Non-Indigenous women writing fiction also sometimes had to contend with being labelled in biologically deterministic ways. In 1969, poet Judith Wright was described in the *Australian* as perhaps 'Australia's greatest woman poet', a statement which qualified her status as a poet, implicitly suggesting that Australia's best poets must be men.[34] Pākehā author Fiona Kidman was one of nine 'women-poets' whose work was reviewed in *Islands*, a New Zealand journal of 'arts and letters', in 1976.[35] She commented in 1979 that she wanted 'to do without the "woman writer" label', but added that 'if it's still *necessary* in order to get recognition, we'll just have to use it'.[36] Indeed, reflecting on the 1975 publication of her first collection of poems, *Honey and Bitters*, she suggested that it and other books by women had been more readily accepted by publishers that year, due to their commercial utility during International Women's Year.[37]

Moreover, as Anne Else has suggested, women's writing could be received by critics in different ways to that of men. Else has discussed the masculinism evident in New Zealand literature from the 1930s into the 1970s, which marginalised women's writing and led to negative assessments of their work.[38] Kidman's first novel, the 1979 *A Breed of Women*, was subjected to just such negativity by some reviewers. She recalled in a later interview that the book was 'absolutely rubbished' by critics despite selling well, and that it was described in one review as 'the thinking woman's Mills and Boon'. Such unfair criticism greatly upset her, and she suggested that she was 'treated more harshly' because it was her book that 'started to turn the tide for women writers' in New Zealand, because she was 'the first' and because she was doing something 'different'.[39] Such negative assessments of women's writing continued into the 1980s, Else argued,

32 Witi Ihimaera in P. Grace and W. Ihimaera, 'The Maori in Literature', in *Tihe Mauri Ora: Aspects of Maoritanga*, ed. M. King ([Wellington]: Methuen, 1978), p. 85.

33 M. Amery, 'Witi Ihimaera: Stepping Out', *Quote Unquote*, no. 20 (1995), p. 15.

34 G. Williams, 'The Calm Miss Wright Fights to Save Reef', *Australian*, 26 November 1969, p. 3.

35 S. Cauchi, 'Feminine Persuasive Force', *Islands* 5, no. 1 (1976), p. 102.

36 A. Else, 'Fiona Kidman', *Broadsheet*, no. 75, November 1979, p. 35, quoted in A. Else, 'On Shifting Ground: Self Narrative, Feminist Theory and Writing Practice' (PhD thesis, Victoria University of Wellington, 2006), p. 70.

37 Kedgley, p. 163.

38 A. Else, 'Not More Than Man Nor Less: The Treatment of Women Poets in *Landfall*, 1947-61', *Landfall* 39, no. 4 (1985), pp. 431-446.

39 Kedgley, pp. 166-167. The review in question was: W. S. Broughton, 'Review of *A Breed of Women*, by Fiona Kidman', *Landfall* 34, no. 4 (1980), p. 367.

as authors 'continued to receive the kind of critical response which took it for granted that not only was their gender the most salient issue to address, but [that] it had a predetermined and harmful significance'. In such 'masculinist' critical responses, women's literary work was deemed either 'feminine' or 'feminist' (and either way of little critical import), or was 'found to have redeeming "masculine" and/or "universal" qualities'.[40] For Māori and Aboriginal women, however, it was first their Indigeneity which was deemed the crucial issue to address in reading their work, and only secondly if at all their gender. When Māori and Aboriginal women who wrote fiction were described in terms of gender, it was in generally in tandem with descriptions which emphasised their Indigeneity. Describing writers in such biologically deterministic ways denied them the opportunity to be considered solely as authors, making their Indigeneity and/or their gender appear central to their work in a way that they themselves may not have considered it to be.

Aboriginal and Māori women writers sometimes resisted labelling as Indigenous authors. While Oodgeroo was a strong advocate of Aboriginal rights and felt that her poetry gave a voice to Aboriginal people, she also wished to be considered as an individual writer without such labels being applied.[41] She commented that:

> When I'm written up in the papers or the media or whatever, they always call me an "Aboriginal poet"; they always tag me with that. And I don't see myself as an "Aboriginal poet" ... I see myself as a poet who is proud to be of Aboriginal descent.[42]

Similarly, Grace said in an interview in 2003:

> We don't give these labels to ourselves. Other people do that. I don't object to them – woman writer, Maori writer, New Zealand, Pacific or Oceanic writer, short story writer, novelist. The only adjective I would use for myself is "fiction," that is "fiction writer."[43]

However, Grace has also observed that there is a point at which 'you do realize ... that you're not in the mainstream' and that 'there are lots of things you have in common' with the work of other Maori writers which 'makes it legitimate to say there is such a thing as Maori writing'.[44] Although she stressed that 'Maori people are all different from each other', she observed that 'these varied backgrounds

---

40 Else, 'On Shifting Ground', p. 77.
41 Shoemaker, p. 188.
42 Personal interview with Oodgeroo Noonuccal, conducted by Cliff Watego, Stradbroke Island, August 1982, quoted in Shoemaker, p. 188.
43 P. F. Calleja, 'An Interview With Patricia Grace', *Atlantis* 25, no. 1 (2003), p. 112.
44 T. E. Tausky, '"Stories That Show Them Who They Are": An Interview with Patricia Grace', *Australian and New Zealand Studies in Canada*, no. 6 (1991), p. 95.

may have some things in common', and that 'themes could be similar'.[45] In one interview in 1985, Ihimaera commented that his relationship with the label of 'Maori writer' had undergone shifts over his writing career. While he still considered himself 'a Maori writer', he felt that he had become 'a little bit more selfish' following the emergence of greater numbers of Māori authors. 'I am becoming less and less a person who is writing on behalf of a culture', he stated, and 'more a writer who is articulating selfish concerns'. These new concerns, however, were his own personal perceptions of 'being Maori' and were perhaps even more 'pro-Maori' than was his previous writing.[46] Racially-based labels thus had ambiguous meanings for writers themselves, sometimes acting as a vehicle for asserting identity and at other times pigeonholing their work and restricting potential readings of it.

A common thread in representations of Indigenous authors and their work thus related to a concept of 'Aboriginal writing' or 'Māori writing', that is, to discourses of Aboriginalism and issues of authenticity and assimilation. Similarly to Said's concept of 'Orientalism', the discourse of 'Aboriginalism' in Australia as discussed by Bob Hodge and Vijay Mishra displays both a deep interest in Aboriginal culture and a refusal to allow that Aboriginal people can properly represent themselves.[47] One consequence of this discourse 'was to create the illusion that there is an "Aboriginal voice", spoken by a unitary Aboriginal subject'.[48] Reviews and commentaries about the work of Indigenous writers occasionally suggested that they might be considered authentic Indigenous voices. In 1966, T. Inglis Moore wrote that Oodgeroo was 'the authentic voice of the Aborigine', in a review of *The Dawn is at Hand* for the *Canberra Times*.[49] Almost a decade later, a comment in the *New Zealand Listener* suggested that while New Zealand writers of short stories often drew from 'childhood experience', Grace's stories were different in that 'she is Maori and a woman and so offers a new insight'.[50] More perceptively, in the literary journal *Landfall* in 1984, Bernard Gadd wrote of a Tuwhare poem that it had a 'totality' which captured 'the entire complex of the Maoritanga [cultural practices and beliefs] that breathes within Tuwhare's poetry even when it is not ostensibly Maori at all'.[51] The emphasis placed on this idea of authenticity illustrates clearly the multiple meanings of the concept of representation. Authors' fictional portrayals of Indigenous experiences could be endowed with greater representational weight if they themselves were considered authentically Indigenous.

---

45 Calleja, pp. 111-112.
46 J. Wilkinson, 'Witi Ihimaera', *Kunapipi* 7, no. 1 (1985), p. 103.
47 B. Hodge and V. Mishra, *Dark Side of the Dream: Australian Literature and the Postcolonial Mind* (North Sydney: Allen and Unwin, 1991), p. 27.
48 Ibid., p. 107.
49 Moore, p. 13.
50 M. Duckworth, 'The Warm', *New Zealand Listener*, 25 October 1975, p. 63.
51 B. Gadd, 'Hone Tuwhare in His Poetry', *Landfall* 38, no. 1 (1984), p. 86.

At other times, the work of both male and female Indigenous writers could be denigrated as not sufficiently authentic because they were considered to be assimilated, urban, distanced from their culture and language or of mixed descent. Or, to put it another way, the author's being perceived as assimilated could provoke suggestions that his or her depiction of Indigenous lives was an inadequate representation of those lives. Hodge has observed that Oodgeroo's poetry was criticised when it appeared as 'not Aboriginal enough', and noted that 'earnest white critics who claimed to understand Aboriginality better than she did said that they would have liked the work better if it had been more obviously Aboriginal'.[52] Similarly, Penny van Toorn observed the way in which 'essentialist beliefs about Aboriginality' placed Oodgeroo's poetry in a bind: she was in the eyes of some commentators 'too modern to be authentically Aboriginal' and in the view of others too 'old-fashioned and rhetorical to be a proper poet'.[53] In the first two pages of a 1977 *Meanjin* article about the work of Aboriginal poets, John Beston commented on the extent to which Oodgeroo, Jack Davis and Kevin Gilbert were assimilated. Oodgeroo had 'quite forgotten the language of her ancestors', he stated, and like Davis and Gilbert was not 'a fullblood Aboriginal' nor 'really familiar with the oral literature of [her] tribe', although the three authors were 'sufficiently steeped in Aboriginal culture' to make reference to 'myths' or 'heroes from the past or present' and to 'reproduce Aboriginal English'.[54] As van Toorn has noted, Indigenous and 'other non-Anglo-Celtic Australian writers' were often 'required to prove their authenticity and put their cultural identity on display'.[55] Criticisms of Aboriginal authors as not being authentically Aboriginal were a clear manifestation of the discourse of Aboriginalism.

Ironically, however, being considered assimilated (and thus not authentically Indigenous) could also result in praise for a writer's work. Oodgeroo sometimes implied that she was acceptable to white Australians because she could be considered assimilated. When being interviewed about her new exhibition of artwork in 1985, she was quoted in the *Australian* saying, 'I am acceptable, because I've made the grade and it makes them feel comfortable', presumably referring to white Australians.[56] Criteria used in reviewing the work of Indigenous authors also sometimes implied that literary acceptance was only possible through being assimilated and adopting European literary conventions. Writing of the work of Oodgeroo, Davis and Gilbert, Beston observed that 'the question

---

52 B. Hodge, 'Poetry and Politics in Oodgeroo: Transcending the Difference', *Australian Literary Studies* 16, no. 4 (1994), p. 67.

53 P. van Toorn, 'Indigenous Texts and Narratives', in *The Cambridge Companion to Australian Literature*, ed. E. Webby (Cambridge: Cambridge University Press, 2000), p. 30.

54 J. Beston, 'The Aboriginal Poets in English: Kath Walker, Jack Davis, and Kevin Gilbert', *Meanjin* 36, no. 4 (1977), p. 447.

55 van Toorn, p. 41.

56 A. L. Urban, 'Kath Walker is Finding Solace in Sea Creatures', *Australian*, 21 November 1985, p. 16.

was inevitably raised, whether the *ordinary* standards of literature should be applied to their work'.[57] In this comment, ways of evaluating literature that were culturally specific to a European literary lineage were assumed to be the norm against which any other approach to writing might be understood. Yet regardless of whether Indigenous authors were praised for adopting European forms or criticised as being inauthentic, discussing a concept of 'Indigenous writing' and questioning how to evaluate such writing constructed these authors as Other to an imagined norm of the writer that was both white and male.

Questions of authenticity also reared their heads in relation to the work of Māori authors in New Zealand, both men and women. Reviewing *Pounamu Pounamu* in the *JPS* in 1975, Oppenheim made reference to other reviewers who had suggested that the book's 'folk language with its carefully unitalicised Maori phrases sounds about as authentic as stage Irish'.[58] Almost a decade later, in an essay on the stories of Ihimaera and Grace, Pearson described Grace as 'an urban Maori imperfectly acquainted with the language and myths of her ancestors'.[59] And when Hulme won the Pegasus Prize for Māori Literature for *the bone people* in 1984, New Zealand writer and critic C. K. Stead drew on similar ideas in a scathing article about the book and about Hulme's win. He argued that the novel ought not to have won the prize, because Hulme did not qualify as a Māori writer, having 'only' one great-grandparent who was Māori, not having been raised speaking the Māori language, and having included in the book elements of Māori 'language and mythology' which Stead considered 'willed, self-conscious, not inevitable, not entirely authentic'. He considered *the bone people* 'a novel by a Pakeha which has won an award intended for a Maori', though he argued that this was not the 'fault' of Hulme, but a result of the existence of an award for Māori writers which he considered ill-conceived. Moreover, he suggested that the literary merit of the novel was over-estimated because it was considered to be the work of a Māori woman.[60] As Margery Fee has contended, the 'demand for "authenticity" denies Fourth World writers a living, changing culture'.[61] Debating the authenticity of Indigenous writers in the media and in literary journals raised doubt as to whether their success and fame was deserved, while representing them as assimilated negated the politically uncomfortable aspects of their work and rendered them no longer threatening.

---

57   Beston, p. 460, my emphasis.
58   Oppenheim, 'Review of *Pounamu Pounamu*', p. 506.
59   Pearson, p. 166.
60   C. K. Stead, 'Keri Hulme's "The Bone People," and the Pegasus Award for Maori Literature', *Ariel* 16, no. 4 (1985), pp. 102-107.
61   M. Fee, 'Why C. K. Stead Didn't Like Keri Hulme's *the bone people*: Who Can Write as Other?', *Australian and New Zealand Studies in Canada*, no. 1 (1989), p. 17.

Politics in Writing: Contesting Literary Merit

Linked to debates about authenticity was thus an uncertainty about the political messages perceived to be carried in writing by Indigenous authors. Such uncertainty was clearly evident in reviews both in literary magazines and in newspapers. Where writing communicated a political message, or could be seen to do so because of its subject matter, the literary merit of the work was sometimes contested. Indeed, it might be said that Indigenous writers were sometimes criticised for making representations on behalf of Indigenous people through their fiction.

In reviewing Oodgeroo's poetry, critics appeared caught between a desire to praise the first published Aboriginal poet, a perceived need to applaud her political message, and a rejection of the poetry as lacking literary worth precisely because of its clearly political nature. Her poetry was often dismissed as being without literary merit, termed mere propaganda, as Shoemaker has observed.[62] Poet and author Jill Hellyer, reviewing *We Are Going* for *Hemisphere* in 1964, considered that the best poems in the volume were those written 'from experience and observation' and that the writing became 'weak when it moralise[d]'. Hellyer insisted that Oodgeroo should 'take her more serious poems less seriously', as her 'pleadings' for Aboriginal people were 'most powerful when they do not become obvious' and the poems were weaker when 'an attitude of preaching' entered them. Oodgeroo's focus on 'the theme of her race', argued Hellyer, 'must limit her eventually unless she ceases to regard herself as a propagandist for her people'.[63] A year later, Bruce Beaver was even more dismissive, writing that the 'literary merit' of Oodgeroo's poetry was 'slight enough but the appeal of a propagandizing talent with a racial chip on the shoulder so close to home [was] acknowledged by a considerable audience of serious readers as well as the sentimentally inquisitive'.[64]

Such negative critical assessments of her poetry remained in evidence in reviews of her later volumes of poetry. In 1971, S. E. Lee wrote that both Oodgeroo and Davis produced 'too many polemical pieces, too much didactic social comment on issues like assimilation and integration, prejudice and racism'.[65] Notwithstanding this comment, Oodgeroo's poetry appears to have often been criticised more harshly than were the works of other Aboriginal authors. In the

---

62   Shoemaker, pp. 182-185.
63   Hellyer, pp. 17-18.
64   B. Beaver, 'Australian Letters', *Landfall* 19, no. 4 (1965), p. 370.
65   S. E. Lee, 'Old Verse', *Southerly* 31, no. 3 (1971), p. 234.

Adelaide *Advertiser* in 1971, for instance, Katherine England suggested that it would be 'difficult to compare [Oodgeroo] seriously with poets of the calibre of Jack Davis'.[66]

Oodgeroo was herself at times dismissive of her poetry as simple and as propaganda. In an interview in 1990, she was quoted agreeing with the interviewer that her poems were 'propaganda' and explaining that this was because of the need to get 'seventh generation white Australians' to listen, a task which required 'shock tactics'. 'I'd rather hit them with my words', she said, 'than pick up a gun and shoot them'.[67] However, Oodgeroo did not always take the same view on what was political or what was propaganda as the critics did. In the foreword to *The Dawn is at Hand*, her second book of poetry, she observed that fellow poet James Devaney had 'suggested to me that "propaganda-like stuff" which might be all right for my campaigning addresses … is not necessarily good in poetry'. Therefore, she wrote, there was only one such poem in the new volume.[68] Reviewing the book for the literary journal *Southerly* in 1967, Lee sneered that clearly Oodgeroo was 'unable to understand' Devaney's 'good advice', since several other poems in the volume were 'all crudely and rhetorically propagandist'.[69] As Judith Wright later noted, 'if there was one forbidden territory in poetry' during the era in which Oodgeroo began writing, 'it was "propaganda and protest" literature, especially in verse'.[70] Wright herself became known later in her career as a conservationist and a champion of Aboriginal rights as well as for poetry, and at least one review of her work considered it political. Reviewing *Fourth Quarter* for the *Sydney Morning Herald* in 1977, Robert Gray observed that the book included some 'angry political poems', and contended that Wright had not 'written well out of anger and despair'. Ironically, part of his problem with those poems was that she had not 'quite gone all the way' in her protest, but had attempted unsuccessfully to maintain 'something of the literary motive'.[71] Oodgeroo transgressed the edict against politics in poetry boldly and unapologetically, and often found her work consigned to a literary dustbin, assessed as having only historical interest as the first Aboriginal poetry published, or social utility as a cry from the dispossessed.

Moreover, Oodgeroo's work could be condemned as politically motivated on other grounds. Early in her writing career, she had joined the Realist Writers' Group in Brisbane. Such groups of left-wing or communist authors existed throughout Australia, and envisioned themselves as the literary voice of the working classes. Established following the Second World War, the groups aimed

---

66   K. England, 'Kath Walker: A Fighter in Verse', *Advertiser*, 1 May 1971, p. 26.
67   Smith, p. 14.
68   Walker, *The Dawn is at Hand*, foreword.
69   S. E. Lee, 'Poetic Fisticuffs', *Southerly* 27, no. 1 (1967), p. 64.
70   J. Wright, 'The Poetry', published in Cochrane, p. 168.
71   R. Gray, 'Poet in Politics', *Sydney Morning Herald*, 30 April 1977, p. 19.

'to promote the discussion and production of socialist realism in literature'.[72] As well, Oodgeroo first became politically active through involvement with the Communist Party, the only party not to support a White Australia policy, though she left when she discovered that other members wished to write her speeches for her. These associations may have led to increased criticism of her poetry based on its clear political and social messages as her deep involvement in the Aboriginal civil rights movement appears to have done. As she recalled in a speech given in 1993, one of the early criticisms of her poetry was that it was not her work, but that a 'well-known Communist' was 'writing it for her'.[73] Likewise in New Zealand, Hone Tuwhare's membership of the Communist Party led to his being denied publication in the Māori Affairs Department magazine *Te Ao Hou*. Interestingly, Tuwhare stated in one interview in 1988 that for his poetry to 'really mean something' it ought to 'have some relationship' to his 'working class background'.[74] His emphasis of his class background in this instance, rather than of his Māoriness, illustrates the complex and multifaceted nature of personal identities and political views.

No review claimed that Oodgeroo's message was either untrue or unnecessary, but dismissing the poems as poetry effectively attempted to tame or silence that message. Criticising the poems as political or as mere propaganda suggested that if Oodgeroo wanted to be a poet, she would have to leave her political message to other arenas. In other words, if it was acceptable for her to represent Aboriginal people in her poetry through being an authentic Indigenous voice, it was far less acceptable for her to use her writing to represent them in a political sense. Nearing the end of the twentieth century her poetry began to be reassessed, as significant shifts occurred both in literary critique and in society as a whole, including the emergence of Aboriginal critics. Cliff Watego, for instance, argued in relation to Oodgeroo's poetry that 'what might be termed protest poetry is merely the poetic expression of black perceptions of the social incongruities present in Australian society'.[75] Recognition of the political messages in the poetry is now far more integral to celebration of the poetry.

Such a contest over literary merit was more muted in New Zealand. Tuwhare, apart from the *Te Ao Hou* incident, appears not to have met with criticism on these grounds. Like the work of Grace and Ihimaera, his poetry was generally received more enthusiastically by reviewers than was Oodgeroo's writing. Indeed, in one review in the *Journal of New Zealand Literature* in 1984, his poetry was said

---

72   J. McLaren, *Writing in Hope and Fear: Literature as Politics in Postwar Australia* (Cambridge: Cambridge University Press, 1996), p. 33.
73   O. Noonuccal, 'Writers of Australia, "I dips me lid"', Goossens Lecture, delivered at the Sydney Opera House, 9 June 1993, reprinted in Cochrane, p. 229.
74   B. Manhire, 'Ready to Move: Interview with Hone Tuwhare', *Landfall* 42, no. 3 (1988), pp. 271-273.
75   C. Watego, 'Aboriginal Poetry and White Criticism', in *Aboriginal Writing Today*, eds. J. Davis and B. Hodge (Canberra: Australian Institute of Aboriginal Studies, 1985), p. 82.

to display 'aroha', or 'human warmth and affection', which gave 'depth and validity' to its 'strong political currents'.[76] Reviews of Grace's work far less often considered it to be political, or suggested that the literary merit suffered because of a political message. Perhaps this is partly because, unlike Oodgeroo, Grace was not actively involved in campaigns for Māori rights. One profile, in the art and literary magazine *Quote Unquote* in 1994, introduced her as being 'as modest as she is talented', and stated that she 'doesn't wage public campaigns, engage in literary debates or air her opinions on [radio station] *The Edge*', but 'simply writes fiction'.[77] Most reviews of Grace's work were positive, with very little criticism. She was often praised for her ability with language, and for her sensitivity and perception. One reviewer even suggested in the *Sunday Star-Times* in 1995 that *Collected Stories* might be too positive, asking where 'life's larger conflict and tragedy' figured, and if life was 'so untroubled and easily affirmed'.[78] A decade earlier, Beston had argued that 'her wish to avoid dealing with interracial tensions' had restricted her writing.[79] Similarly, Pearson had observed in his 1982 essay that Ihimaera's early short stories had 'disappointed some Maori political activists who think writing by Maoris should advance the cause of Maori rights', and that Ihimaera had sometimes been referred to as an '"uncle Tom", "middle-class Maori" [and] "pakeha pet"'.[80] While Goolagong was criticised by some Aboriginal people for remaining uninvolved in political issues, and Te Kanawa's occasional political statements sometimes stirred controversy among Māori commentators, the earliest Indigenous writers in New Zealand were complimented by literary critics, almost all of whom seem to have been non-Indigenous, for their lack of overt political involvement.

Critics generally considered that Grace's work became more political in later publications, and it was in relation to her later books that most criticisms of her work as being marred by political intentions were made. Michelle Keown and Karen Sinclair have both observed that during the 1980s Grace's writing became less engaged with celebrations of rural life, nostalgia for a past way of life or encouraging understanding of Māori culture, and more concerned with the political issues facing Māori.[81] When *Potiki* was published in 1986, the book's 'more aggressive political stance' was apparent to a number of reviewers.[82] Grace herself recalled an attempt by some parents to have the novel banned from one school where it was studied, because they considered it 'written to incite racial

---

76 R. Cooper, 'Recent New Zealand Poetry', *Journal of New Zealand Literature*, no. 2 (1984), p. 37.

77 N. Cox, 'Living in Both Worlds', *Quote Unquote*, no. 12 (1994), p. 9.

78 M. Morrissey, 'Tang of Salt Anchors Stories', *Sunday Star-Times*, 1 January 1995, p. D4.

79 J. Beston, 'The Fiction of Patricia Grace', *Ariel* 15, no. 2 (1984), p. 50.

80 Pearson, p. 167.

81 M. Keown, 'Interview with Patricia Grace', *Kunapipi* 22, no. 2 (2000), p. 54; K. P. Sinclair, 'Maori Literature: Protest and Affirmation', *Pacific Studies* 15, no. 4 (1992), p. 284.

82 R. Robinson, 'Grace, Patricia', in *The Oxford Companion to New Zealand Literature*, eds. R. Robinson and N. Wattie, Oxford Reference Online, accessed 30 April 2007, available from http://www.oxfordreference.com/views/ENTRY.html?subview=Main&entry=t200.e472.

tension and create social disharmony'.[83] She argued that actual events, such as at Bastion Point and the Raglan Golf Course, had 'legitimised' the novel, which had been criticised for being 'farfetched' in its depiction of the lengths to which white developers would go to gain Māori land, although the book 'takes things a bit further'.[84] In a *New Zealand Herald* review of *Cousins*, the novel which followed *Potiki*, Penelope Carroll contended that when one of the characters became involved in Māori rights concerns, 'the story [became] somewhat lost in political polemic', and that the writer's voice intruded in place of the character's.[85] However, another review of the novel, which appeared in the current affairs magazine *North and South*, commented that there was 'a refreshing absence of stridency' in the writing and that the novel 'only towards the end ... become[s] clearly, and effectively, political'.[86] In Grace's next novel, *Baby No-Eyes*, David Eggleton considered that Grace was 'the writer as activist'. Writing in the liberal *New Zealand Listener*, he termed the novel a 'polemical' one, although he did not argue that this detracted from the book.[87]

For the most part, indeed, reviewers agreed that Grace made points without lessening the literary merit of the writing. Philip Tew described her in 1995 as 'a warm writer but not a cosy one', whose stories 'don't come blustering up to you demanding your attention' but instead 'creep up and surprise you with their force'.[88] Similarly, Pauline Swain noted in 1998 that Grace had 'a deceptively light touch with material that in other hands could be bombastic or preachy'.[89] If political messages in writing had become more acceptable by the last years of the twentieth century, they were still to be softly framed. Although no literature is entirely without political import, many non-Indigenous reviewers appeared to prefer work which could be read in non-political ways and often harshly criticised work which did not leave them that option.

Literature, Activism and Representation

Observations of political themes in the works of the earliest Indigenous women writers could be echoed by representations of them in the media as activists or radicals. Shoemaker noted that in the case of Australia, 'the white public spokespersons are, by and large, not authors', whilst 'amongst the Black Australian community, public spokespersons far more frequently are writers,

83   V. Hereniko, 'An Interview with Patricia Grace', *Contemporary Pacific* 10, no. 1 (1998), p. 160.
84   Keown, p. 55.
85   P. Carroll, 'Window on Maori Life', *New Zealand Herald*, 5 September 1992, section 2, p. 6.
86   G. Lay, 'Graceful Relations', *North and South*, November 1992, p. 119.
87   D. Eggleton, 'A Child Reclaimed', *New Zealand Listener*, 28 November 1998, p. 40.
88   P. Tew, 'Warm But Not Cosy', *Press*, 18 February 1995, p. 10.
89   P. Swain, 'Vintage Storytelling', *Dominion*, 19 September 1998, p. 20.

or are influenced by them'.[90] This linkage, as was shown above, often led to disparagement of Indigenous writers' work by largely non-Indigenous critics. It also sometimes led to the potentially negative depiction of writers as outspoken radicals. For Oodgeroo, whose prominence was based upon her role as an activist as well as upon her status as a poet, such threads of representation were often evident in descriptions of her in newspapers and magazines. As well as being described as a poet, she was also often depicted as an 'activist', civil and land rights 'campaigner', 'fighter' for Aboriginal rights, or in other such terms. Similarly, she was often labelled both poet and activist in texts collecting the stories of famous or prominent Australians. In Susan Mitchell's collection *The Matriarchs*, for instance, she was described as a 'Poet and Aboriginal Activist'.[91] Aboriginal men who both wrote fiction and struggled for Aboriginal rights might also be depicted in similar ways. An interview with Jack Davis in the *Sydney Morning Herald* in 1988 began by describing him as 'a curious mix of black revolutionary and mild-mannered liberal', while an article in the *West Australian* the same year termed him a 'political activist' as well as an 'Aboriginal poet [and] playwright'.[92] Kevin Gilbert was also sometimes termed an 'activist' as well as being described with phrases such as 'Aboriginal poet' or 'Aboriginal writer'.[93] For other Indigenous writers, however, who were for the most part not actively involved in activist work or members of activist organisations, most articles appearing in magazines and newspapers focused on their literary work. Descriptions of them likewise generally focused on their work in these fields. Hulme, for instance, was usually described in newspapers simply as an 'author', 'writer' or 'poet', as was Grace.

A related set of representations of Oodgeroo also centred on her activist work. She was known for her fire as a spokesperson, and fire-related terms were sometimes used to describe her. Even in a story which described her as having 'become more a doer than a shouter', this perception of her was evident:

> Put down poet and civil rights person Kath Walker's lack of fire yesterday to one of those dreaded Melbourne colds. ... That's not to say the fires have gone out – with just a minimum of stoking she can flare up as she has done so often ... [94]

---

90   Shoemaker, p. 14.
91   S. Mitchell, *The Matriarchs: Twelve Australian Women Talk About Their Lives to Susan Mitchell* (Ringwood: Penguin, 1987), p. 195.
92   B. Evans, 'Jack Davis Smells Change on the Wind', *Sydney Morning Herald*, 20 February 1988, p. 74; M. Pritchard, 'WA Playwright Honoured', *West Australian*, 12 February 1988, p. 16.
93   See for instance: K. Childs, 'Aboriginal Poet Rejects "Blood Money" For Anthology of Blacks' Work', *Age*, 6 August 1985, p. 1; B. Evans, 'Grants Aid Art's Creative Force', *Sydney Morning Herald*, 8 October 1992, p. 14; R. Hefner, 'Nation's Disgrace Burns Within', *Canberra Times*, 15 May 1988, p. 7.
94   G. Bicknell, 'Kath's Fire Still Has Heat', *Daily Telegraph*, 19 July 1977, p. 13.

Throughout her career, newspaper and magazine articles which profiled Oodgeroo or reported upon her work and public statements often employed words such as 'fierce', 'intense', 'outspoken' or 'forthright' to describe her. One article in the *Herald* in 1969 referred to her 'tirades about the white Australians' treatment of the aboriginal'.[95] Such descriptions were evident in many newspapers across Australia, despite their different contexts and political leanings. Such a depiction of her also appeared in other analogies. Shelly Neller wrote in the conservative *Bulletin* in 1980 that Oodgeroo 'brandishes her passionate views with the force and accuracy of a stockwhip'.[96] In another example, Oodgeroo's tolerance and understanding for the Palestinians who hijacked a plane she was travelling on in 1974, though tempered by her statement that she would not 'condone what they did', was presented by the reporter, Greg Roberts, as evidence of her 'undying political radicalism'.[97] She herself both observed in one interview that she was 'very angry' in the years in which her early poems were written and 'used to have to tone myself down a lot', and remarked in another that 'I've been called an Activist but I think I'm fairly conservative'.[98] Yet other forces could also be at play in these representations. Shoemaker observed that Kevin Gilbert's angry verse was published rather than his love poems, arguing that it appeared it was 'commercially more profitable to publish a militant Aboriginal writer', and thus that publishers in this way 'dictated the public image with which well-known Aboriginal authors have been cloaked'.[99] This observation reveals the contingent nature of representations, which may sometimes be shaped as much by commercial or political imperatives as by particular ideas about race or gender.

As well as being fiery, however, Oodgeroo was sometimes also described, in more gendered portrayals, as dignified and graceful, and her dislike of violence in protest was reported on several occasions.[100] When she received the award of Aboriginal of the Year in 1985, she was described by the *Sun-Herald* as receiving it 'with her accustomed soft-spoken grace, edged with hard-nosed home truths about the lot of her race in Australia'.[101] Moreover, it has been observed that Oodgeroo's positive vision of civil rights and hope for the future may have endeared her to readers who would not have appreciated a more militant stance. Eva Rask Knudsen suggested that Oodgeroo was embraced by some critics:

---

95 R. Rule, 'Reforms First', *Herald*, 12 July 1969, p. 26.
96 S. Neller, 'Kath Walker, Activist, Artist, Finds a New Medium For Her Cause', *Bulletin*, 3 December 1985, p. 90.
97 G. Roberts, 'Kath Walker Makes a Stand in the Sitting-Down Place', *Good Weekend*, 28 February 1987, p. 19.
98 Mitchell, p. 203; Smith, pp. 13-14.
99 Shoemaker, p. 197.
100 'Poet Hits at "Black Power" Violence', *Sydney Morning Herald*, 1 December 1971, p. 11.
101 M. Barnes, 'Kath's Devoted Herself to Survival', *Sun-Herald*, 15 September 1985, p. 53.

almost as a cherished national treasure or as their own symbol of redemption because her conciliatory poems gave them the chance to exorcise their own guilty feelings about a very racist Australia ...[102]

As in some representations of Goolagong and Cathy Freeman, Aboriginal success and supposed assimilation could thus be appropriated as a sign that all was well in race relations in Australia. At her death Oodgeroo was lauded as 'an outstanding Australian', 'one of Australia's finest citizens', 'a battler' and 'a national treasure'.[103] Such tributes, however genuine, potentially transformed her from a controversial figure and a challenger of society into an embodiment of an idealised nation and one of its canonised heroes. This representational transformation is emblematic of the ways in which representations may shift after the death of a person, a trend which is considered in relation to Whina Cooper in the next chapter.

Providing A Voice? Motivations for Writing

How, then, did Indigenous women writers represent themselves? How did they conceive their position and objectives, and what were their publicly articulated intentions in their work and lives? Did these women understand themselves to be spokespeople for the concerns of Indigenous people, or seek to represent the experiences and struggles of Indigenous people from a privileged position as insiders? In one interview in 1977, Oodgeroo explained that in writing she was 'putting [Aboriginal people's] voices on paper', and that she did not view *We Are Going* as 'my book' because 'it was the people'.[104] Ten years later, in another interview, she remembered having felt that it was 'time we recorded the cries of the people and gave them a book they could call their own'.[105] She considered herself a 'spokeswoman' for Aboriginal people, though only one of a number, since different groups had different representatives.[106] As well, she clearly viewed her work as part of a wider role as an educator, and deliberately communicated a strong political message in her poetry. Her approach to her writing is further illustrated by her comments in a review which she wrote of a book of essays on Aboriginal affairs in 1970. 'Every Aboriginal,' she stated, 'when given the

---

102   E. R. Knudsen, 'From Kath Walker to Oodgeroo Noonuccal? Ambiguity and Assurance in *My People*', *Australian Literary Studies* 16, no. 4 (1994), p. 108.

103   F. Hamilton, 'Oodgeroo Buried Beneath the Paperbarks: Tributes Flow for "Grand Old Lady"', *Canberra Times*, 21 September 1993, p. 3; Minister for Aboriginal and Torres Strait Islander Affairs Robert Tickner, quoted in 'Nation Mourns Tenacious Mother Figure', *Australian*, 17 September 1993, p. 2; Queensland Premier Wayne Goss, quoted in D. Smith, 'Goss Leads Tributes to "Remarkable Australian"', *Gold Coast Bulletin*, 17 September 1993, p. 2.

104   J. Davidson, 'Interview: Kath Walker', *Meanjin* 36, no. 4 (1977), pp. 428-429.

105   Turcotte, p. 18.

106   R. Shiels and C. Leimbach, 'Stradbroke Dreamtime and Beyond ... Conversations With Kath Walker at Moongalba', *Simply Living*, no. 17 (1981), p. 63.

opportunity should spell out the humiliation, contempt and discrimination' that Aboriginal people experienced due to 'the clash of culture, the denial of human and legal rights, the ignoring of the true voice of the Aborigine, and the covering-up of basic rights'.[107] While she wished to be considered as a poet independent of her Aboriginality, Oodgeroo also clearly saw her poetry as another avenue through which to articulate her message about Indigenous rights.

For Grace, on the other hand, any political motivation in the process of writing appeared to be secondary to the desire to create stories, and she sometimes resisted being categorised as a political writer. In a 1998 interview, she remembered that she began writing simply desiring to write, and that she had had 'no real social motivation at all'. While she thought she had put on the back of the book that she wished 'to communicate who we are to other people', she recalled that she had not considered that as a driving force whilst actually working on the stories.[108] In another interview in 1992, she stated that her work was 'mainly a challenge to myself' and that she 'set out to tell a story' without 'thoughts of changing the world or of enlightening people'.[109]

At the same time, however, she noted more than once that she felt many representations of Māori produced by non-Māori writers had been problematic and that she wished to supplement them with different representations, while also wanting to address the shortage of literature to which Māori could relate.[110] Asked in 1994 if there were 'political themes' in her work, she responded that she had known when she began writing that 'there were people who hadn't been written about' and 'lives that hadn't been described', which she wanted to write about, but that she did not then view such writing as 'political'. However, she recalled that she 'came to see that when you write about people who don't have power, whose mana [prestige or authority] has been eroded, then it is political'. She concluded that although she had not 'set out to be a political writer', she was 'happy if people see my writing that way'. As she explained:

> Good writing needs to describe the human condition, and a writer will write from her own background, her own experience, her own standpoint, her own view of life, her own realities.[111]

As these comments suggest, the distinction between representing Indigenous lives in an artistic sense and representing them in an advocacy sense was often fine indeed. While Grace acknowledged in one interview that her later stories

---

107   K. Walker, 'Aboriginals: The Smell of Frustration', *Politics* 1 (1970), p. 90.

108   A. Sarti, *Spiritcarvers: Interviews With Eighteen Writers From New Zealand* (Amsterdam: Rodopi, 1998), p. 45.

109   J. McRae, 'Patricia Grace', in *In the Same Room: Conversations With New Zealand Writers*, eds. E. Alley and M. Williams (Auckland: Auckland University Press, 1992), p. 292.

110   Patricia Grace in Grace and Ihimaera, pp. 80-83; Kedgley, pp. 55, 64.

111   A. Goslyn, 'Patricia Grace on Politics and People', *Broadsheet*, no. 202 (1994), p. 54.

were 'more political' than her earlier writing, she remarked that even those were 'not real outbursts of anger', since she had 'never been convinced that people listen to outbursts' and thought it was probably 'better to sneak up on people'.[112] Hulme has also spoken of being concerned to tell a story, rather than to make a political point. Asked if she had 'a quest' in her writing, she answered that she wrote 'for myself', although noting that 'I do try to look earnestly and deeply into certain social situations in New Zealand, because this place fascinates the hell out of me'.[113] Like Grace, she stated that 'your Maoriness, like everything else, is intimately part of you and it will normally show through your writing as well'.[114]

Questions asked of Grace in several published interviews addressed the issue of the place of politics in literature, often seeming to refer specifically to political issues affecting Māori. Similar questions were not often asked in interviews with Oodgeroo, perhaps due to her clear stance as an activist. In an interview published in 2003, Grace was asked if she felt that 'Maori writing has to be political'. She answered in the negative, saying that it need neither 'engage in political themes' nor 'define Maori culture', although she qualified this by suggesting that 'in another way it always will define Maori culture', and that 'in a way ... all of our writing is political'.[115] In another interview, she acknowledged that she had felt 'some pressure' to write about issues of race relations, but thought it 'natural' to write about such issues because one wrote 'from your own background and experience'.[116] Ihimaera similarly once noted that he had been 'accused of not being "political" enough or critical enough of our Pakeha-dominated society'. He commented that he felt his writing was 'political because it is exclusively Maori' and that 'the criticism of Pakeha society is implicit in the presentation of an exclusively Maori values system', but he professed himself 'more concerned with the greatest problem we have – that of retaining our emotional identity'.[117] While Indigenous writers were well aware that their writing might articulate messages about the social and political worlds in which they lived and wrote, such imperatives were often not as central to their work as reviewers and critics expected.

---

112   Kedgley, p. 56.
113   Sarti, p. 62.
114   Long, p. 5.
115   Calleja, p. 113.
116   Hereniko, p. 159.
117   Witi Ihimaera in Grace and Ihimaera, p. 84.

Entering the Film Industry: Indigenous Women and Filmmaking

Slightly later than in the literary field, a number of Indigenous women began to be known as filmmakers in the last decades of the twentieth century. While New Zealander Ramai Hayward had been making films with her husband Rudall from the 1950s, her contribution was often subsumed under that of her husband in accounts which placed her as his wife or 'assistant'.[118] Particularly from the 1970s under the impact of the second wave of feminism, films began to appear which could be understood as carrying feminist messages, and increasing numbers of women began to make their own films. Māori and Aboriginal people also increasingly sought to represent themselves on film and to tell their own stories, no longer accepting representations by outsiders. In the 1970s and 1980s, Essie Coffey and Tracey Moffatt in Australia and Merata Mita in New Zealand were part of this shift in the film industry. Moreover, such assertions of identity could overlap. Jocelyn Robson and Beverley Zalcock noted that films by Indigenous women united 'an interrogation of issues related to both race and gender'.[119] While filmmakers have often been represented in similar ways to those in which authors were represented, it is important to bear in mind the particularities of the film industry itself. Producing a film generally requires significantly greater resources than does producing literary work. Mita has noted that when Māori people choose to make a fiction film, they need to 'satisfy the demands of the cinema, the demands of their own people, [and] the criteria of a white male-dominated value and funding structure', including demonstrating 'what Americans call "crossover potential"' and raising 'about one third of the projected budget'.[120] The differences within the industry itself, while not obviously impacting on the ways in which Indigenous women filmmakers were represented in the media, were an important part of the economic, political and cultural contexts in which those representations were produced.

As in literature, so in film being first could act as a stimulus to fame. Arguably the most well-known Indigenous women in filmmaking in Australia and New Zealand, Moffatt and Mita, were both recognised as having achieved such 'firsts'. Mita's 1988 feature film *Mauri* was the first made by a Māori woman and, slightly later, Moffatt's 1993 film *Bedevil* became the first feature film made in Australia by an Aboriginal woman. However, by the time of Mita's and Moffatt's first feature films, comment upon their success as being due to their curiosity value appears to have become much less common. In 1988, Moffatt

---

118 D. Shepard, *Reframing Women: A History of New Zealand Film* (Auckland: HarperCollins, 2000), p. 12.
119 J. Robson and B. Zalcock, *Girls' Own Stories: Australian and New Zealand Women's Films* (London: Scarlet, 1997), p. 59.
120 M. Mita, 'The Soul and the Image', in *Film in Aotearoa New Zealand*, eds. J. Dennis and J. Bieringa (Wellington: Victoria University Press, 1996), p. 49.

felt able to say that she thought her work was 'receiving attention and awards not just because it is dealing with Aborigines or because I am an Aborigine but because I am experimenting with different film forms'.[121] At the same time, she was quoted in the *Sydney Morning Herald* in 1992 commenting that there was 'automatic interest' in her work because she was Aboriginal, and that she had been concerned in the past that she was chosen for survey exhibitions 'as the token black'.[122]

Although these women were still sometimes labelled in the media in racial terms, such labels were less common by the late 1980s. The revised Australian Journalists Association code of ethics which emphasised that undue stress should not be placed upon ethnicity, or other such attributes, had been in place since 1984, and was perhaps having some impact on media practices. However, such labels persisted sufficiently often in media profiles and critical commentaries to rouse protest from Moffatt. In an interview published in the New Zealand feminist magazine *Broadsheet* in 1993, she stated that she would prefer not to be labelled an Aboriginal filmmaker or photographer. 'Sometimes I wish they would forget I'm Aboriginal and just look at the work', she said, because it ought to 'stand on it's [sic] own'.[123]

Indigeneity also remained central to depictions of Indigenous women in the film industry in other respects. Despite Moffatt's often-voiced opposition to her work being read in terms of her Aboriginality and her background growing up as a foster child in a white family, discussions of her work sometimes persisted in reading it in these terms. In a 1993 article in the *Sydney Morning Herald*, Anabel Dean commented that Moffatt's films were 'influenced by her background', and in an article in the *Age* in 2002 Geoff Masien remarked that she was 'clearly influenced in her work by her experience of growing up female and Aboriginal in a predominantly white, working class suburb'.[124] Even after observing that Moffatt did not want to be seen as an 'Aboriginal artist', Jane Mills remarked in an article in *RealTime*, a journal of contemporary arts, that it was 'hard to see why she insists on the disclaimer', as her films had 'a strong political sensibility in which her Aboriginality, like her feminism, is impossible to ignore'.[125]

By the late 1980s, some commentators were also beginning to shift their stance on the place of politics in artistic endeavour. The choice to make representations for or against a political cause in literary or artistic work appeared to have

---

121   A. Rutherford, 'Changing Images', in *Aboriginal Culture Today*, ed. A. Rutherford (Sydney: Dangaroo, 1988), p. 155.
122   H. O'Neill, 'From Personal to Universal', *Sydney Morning Herald*, 25 March 1992, p. 18.
123   M. Rupa and A. Tsoulis, 'Indigenous Filmmakers', *Broadsheet*, no. 199 (1993), p. 35.
124   A. Dean, 'The Ghosts in the Family', *Sydney Morning Herald*, 28 October 1993, p. 20; G. Masien, 'Something More? Try a $250,000 Bid', *Age*, 5 February 2002, The Culture section, p. 4.
125   J. Mills, 'A (Filmic) Space Between Black and White', *RealTime + OnScreen*, no. 44 (2001), p. 17.

become more widely viewed as acceptable. Indeed, Moffatt sometimes faced pressure to be more political in her work, which she resisted. In an interview in 1988, she stated that:

> I didn't feel I had to set out to make films about the struggle for Land Rights, mining on Aboriginal land, issues dealing with racism which people automatically think that that's what you're going to do because you're a black film maker.

She observed that while 'statements need to be made', she was attempting to 'say them in a more interesting way'.[126] When asked in a 1999 interview whether or not there was 'a political intention' underlying her photographic work, she commented that she wished to 'create a world' rather than to 'make some grand statement on race', although she had made 'political films'.[127] Moreover, she explained that she did not wish to work in a realistic or ethnographic style, as documentaries and dramas with Aboriginal subjects usually did. She recalled having encountered some negative reactions from Aboriginal people over her depiction of Aboriginal women in her short film *Nice Coloured Girls*, because she was 'an Aboriginal film maker'. 'From certain members of the Aboriginal scene,' she said, 'you are pressured into always having to present a positive view of Aboriginal life which I find really annoying'. Moffatt noted a generational difference, explaining that she was 'not the generation that set up the tent embassy in 1972 and fought the Land Rights battle' and other struggles. Instead, she was:

> of the generation who have benefitted from the work of Kath Walker and so many others like her. We're a different generation, a generation that feels comfortable in talking about Aboriginal society whether it be through film or writing or art.[128]

Such a generational difference could lead both to a determination on the part of a filmmaker to resist being categorised as a political artist, and to criticism from others for failing to make political statements.

Essey Coffey and Merata Mita were both overtly and intentionally political in at least some of their filmmaking. The documentary *My Survival as an Aboriginal*, directed by Coffey, was described in the Melbourne *Herald* in 1979 as Coffey's 'cry of anger, defiance and protest'.[129] For Coffey, the urge to make the film was linked inextricably to a message that she wanted heard. Knowledge about the legacies of the stolen generations had brought her to a decision that Aboriginal

---

126   Rutherford, p. 153.
127   G. Matt, 'An Interview with Tracey Moffatt', in *Tracey Moffatt*, ed. M. Snelling (Brisbane: Institute of Modern Art, 1999), p. 67.
128   Rutherford, pp. 148, 152, 155.
129   B. Wilson, 'Her Cry For Survival', *Herald*, 29 August 1979, p. 4.

people needed to use mass media in order to gain recognition.[130] Coffey was sometimes described in newspaper stories as an 'activist' or 'campaigner' for Aboriginal rights, as well as being described as a film-maker or singer.[131] In at least one newspaper report she was termed 'outspoken', and she was also described that way in an article in *Deadly Vibe*, a magazine aimed at Aboriginal youth.[132]

Mita's documentaries *Bastion Point – Day 507*, about the removal of land protesters from Bastion Point by police in 1978, and *Patu!*, about protests against the Springbok tour of New Zealand in 1981 and the police response, also dealt with clearly political issues. She faced opposition from authorities, such as the police, in making both films. In one edited interview published in 1986, she noted that 'if a film I make causes Maori people to feel stronger about themselves and lose some of their inferiority, then I'm achieving something worthwhile for the revolution'. At the same time, Mita observed that she had been 'stereotyped as a radical political film-maker', although she did not see herself that way. Rather, she saw herself 'as representing what already exists – representing the truth' and 'exposing a Maori viewpoint'. She suggested that 'because I'm a Māori woman' such an endeavour was 'seen as dangerously radical'.[133] As in the case of literature, there thus appeared to be an expectation on the part of some reviewers that films made by Indigenous filmmakers would be partial and political. Through her filmmaking, Mita also sought to challenge previous filmic representations of Māori by outsiders. In 1989, discussing *Mauri*, she stated that she had 'really wanted to destroy the massive sentimental view of Māori people' and 'to break out of a particular characterisation that Māori people find themselves in', especially on film. In the same interview, she spoke about a 'Māori way of telling stories', arguing that 'we've got a tradition so we should be building on it'.[134] *Mauri*, however, was criticised by 'Pakeha reviewers' because it 'did not conform to mainstream narrative conventions'.[135] As had been the experience of many Indigenous authors, non-Indigenous reviewers could be highly critical of film work that did not fit a Western norm.

---

130 Essie Coffey interviewed by Hazel de Berg, 1980, DeB 1154, ORAL TRC 1/1154, Hazel de Berg collection, National Library of Australia, Canberra.

131 See for instance: M. Ansara, 'Bush Queen Focused on Inequality', *Australian*, 9 January 1998, p. 11; 'Farewell for Essie', *Daily Telegraph*, 9 January 1998, p. 15; J. Freebury, 'Any Reel Progress?', *Canberra Times*, 28 February 1998, 'Panorama' liftout, p. 21.

132 See for instance: Ansara, p. 11; 'Essie Coffey', *Deadly Vibe*, no. 37, p. 12.

133 V. Myers, *Head and Shoulders* (Auckland: Penguin, 1986), pp. 66, 71.

134 C. Parekowhai, 'Kōrero ki Taku Tuakana: Merata Mita and Me', *Illusions*, no. 9 (1989), pp. 24, 26.

135 Shepard, p. 121.

Gender, Indigeneity and the Politics of Feminism

Thus far, my focus has largely been upon common framings of race in depictions of prominent Indigenous women writers and filmmakers. In this section, the spotlight turns to common framings of gender, and to the intersections evident between racialised and gendered representations. These women, as well as being positioned as Indigenous writers, were sometimes also positioned as women writers, and their work considered as such by critics. Such a consideration was evident, for example, in the inclusion of both Grace and Hulme in a collection of interviews with other New Zealand women writers edited by feminist Sue Kedgley.[136] Reviewers also occasionally made mention of women-centred themes in their work. Reviewing Grace's novel *Cousins*, Ngāhuia Te Awekōtuku wrote that the portrayal of women waiting for their men to return from war made it 'a women's novel, a view from a uniquely female place'.[137] Grace herself once suggested that women's writing was 'more finely detailed' than that of male writers, and that women 'tend to write about children and relationships in a closer and more understanding way'.[138] Hulme similarly saw a difference between the writing of men and women, as she did between the writing of Māori and Pākehā, since 'everything writers write is coloured and informed by their own perspective and background'.[139]

None of the women whose media representation is discussed in this chapter appear to have been actively feminist through organisational membership, yet closeness to feminist concerns seemed to be assumed by several interviewers. These women were sometimes questioned about whether or not they were feminist, questions which would clearly not have been asked of male authors and filmmakers, Indigenous or non-Indigenous. Such questions were particularly asked within the context of publications with feminist perspectives which focused on the life stories of successful women. While Oodgeroo's work was rarely, if ever, discussed as the work of a woman, perhaps because her political voice was so clearly attuned to Aboriginal issues, she was several times asked if she was a feminist. In an interview with Susan Mitchell published in 1987, Oodgeroo stated that:

> I don't believe in Woman's Lib. ... I was liberated the day I was born. ... Even in the Aboriginal movement I will not join women's groups. I don't even fight for Aboriginals either. I fight for all people.

---

136 Kedgley, *Our Own Country*.
137 N. Te Awekōtuku, '"Journeys ... Expectations, ... Self-Awakenings"', *New Zealand Listener*, 5 September 1992, p. 52.
138 Kedgley, p. 64.
139 Ibid., p. 98.

Further, Oodgeroo argued that women should not 'fight' men, but 'educate them'.[140] In her view, feminist concerns were of less relevance in an Aboriginal setting. Asked in one interview if she had been concerned that there were 'certain rules women must observe' or 'things they can't do' relating to women's position in Aboriginal society, when she herself was 'a driving force in the Aboriginal movement and ... extremely vocal', she responded that she had not been concerned 'because the same applies to the men'. Women, Oodgeroo stated, had 'more than enough freedom in the Aboriginal world'.[141] At the same time, she once explained to an interviewer that 'the mother of life, the Rainbow Serpent – in our world God is a woman', and commented that this demonstrated 'how wise the Aboriginals were, to realise that the woman has the strength'.[142]

Grace too was often asked about her relationship with feminism. If she drew on her experiences as Māori in her writing, interviewers seemed to want to know if she did the same as a woman. In an interview published in the collection edited by Kedgley, Grace commented that while she was never 'actively' involved in the feminist movement, she became 'more and more aware of the position of women' during the 1970s, as she listened to what was being said. She 'started to realise a lot about the lives of women and especially about their expectations', and recalled realising that she 'could easily understand what feminists were saying, because of my awareness of racial oppression'. Asked if she identified as feminist, she replied that she had not 'heard anyone call me a feminist', but that she was. She explained that she believed that 'all people should realise their own potential in their own way, and support each other' to do so, concluding that she could be seen as 'a pro-child, pro-family feminist'.[143] Much later, in 2003, when asked if she would describe herself as 'a feminist writer', she responded 'I sometimes don't know what to say when people ask me if I am a feminist writer because I am not well-versed in feminist theory'. However, she continued:

> that does not mean that I don't understand the position of women in society. In some ways I regard myself as a feminist activist in that I am a *woman* and I have always *acted*.[144]

She remarked that she felt 'very comfortable when ... writing about women, especially ... about strong Maori women characters', and that 'I come from a culture where women are strong'.[145] When asked if she wished to reveal women's lives in her writing, as she did Māori lives, she answered that she did not 'consciously set out to do that' and that she wrote from her 'experience

---

140 Mitchell, pp. 198, 209.
141 C. Baker, ed., *Yacker 2: Australian Writers Talk About Their Work* (Sydney: Pan, 1987), p. 289.
142 Davidson, p. 436.
143 Kedgley, p. 66.
144 Calleja, p. 111, original emphasis.
145 Ibid.

and background'.[146] Like Oodgeroo, Grace suggested that feminist issues for Indigenous women were linked to the legacies of colonisation. Once asked to talk about the status of Māori women, she stated that problems such as 'the abuse of women' or 'the low status of women' were 'not something that came from the old society' but 'a modern phenomenon that has come with colonisation'.[147] Women, she said, needed to 'take our place, the place that we had in the beginning, our rightful place in contemporary society', and 'reclaim our status, our mana, our leadership roles'.[148]

Hulme was also asked if she was a feminist in an interview published in the collection edited by Kedgley. She replied with vigour that 'I'm a feminist because I was born female' although she had 'never belonged to a feminist group' and was 'not a joiner'. Asked if she was 'reluctant to be described as a "women's writer"', she stated that she was 'happy to be described as a woman writer and women's writer', but qualified that by noting that she felt 'some diffidence' in being so identified, 'because of the widespread confusion between sex and gender'. Hulme explained that 'my sex is female but my gender is neuter, which leaves me uncertain as to what kind of a woman I am', but that her 'commitment' was 'to the female side of life – to values which are commonly regarded as female ones' and that there were 'experiences which are unique to being a woman, even to someone who perceives herself to be a neuter woman'.[149]

Among filmmakers, Mita was also conscious of facing repression in terms of gender as well as in terms of race. In one interview, she commented that 'my battles with sexism and racism have been constant'. She recalled having come 'into conflict with traditional Maori thinking' because 'lots of things I've done are contrary to how a Maori woman should traditionally behave'. As well, she saw her film work 'as a way of emancipating Maori women', since 'where I come from women don't have speaking rights on the marae [meeting place]', and film and television were able to 'speak to many more people'.[150] Nevertheless, in both critical discussions and interviews, the focus was more often upon the position of Indigenous women writers and filmmakers as Indigenous than it was on their position as women. Likewise, representations in the media drew more often on common discourses surrounding Indigeneity than upon tropes of femininity.

---

146   Kedgley, p. 65.
147   Goslyn, pp. 54-55.
148   Ibid., p. 55.
149   Kedgley, pp. 98, 102-103.
150   Myers, pp. 56-57, 64.

Reflections on Trans-Tasman Difference: Postcolonial Artistry

By the 1990s, Aboriginal and Māori women were taking a strong place in all areas of the creative arts. Surveying depictions of Indigenous women writers and filmmakers in the media, and their own public articulations of their lives and work, several parallels are evident across the Tasman. As assertions of Māori and Aboriginal identity were made increasingly strongly from the late 1960s, and as movements for civil, language and land rights intensified, Indigenous women's voices increasingly appeared in published prose and poetry and, slightly later, in film. Grace once suggested that, while there were other Māori women who wrote short stories before her, 'the time was not right for their stories to come out in book form', and that the publication of her work and of Ihimaera's was 'part of the movement'.[151] Indeed, these women's work has often been analysed academically as part of a postcolonial literature or postcolonial film industry. Placing the work of these women in this context of social and political change perhaps contributed to the continual interpretation of it as political, and to a repeated expectation that they would act as spokespeople for Aboriginal or Māori people. As Fee observed, 'white writers' may have been able to 'choose to write as whatever they like', but such a choice was less available for 'minority writers', who were often 'forced into the position of speaking for their minority'.[152]

As a concept, 'representation' impacted upon the lives and careers of Indigenous women writers and filmmakers in multiple ways. Besides being portrayed in particular ways in the media, these women both represented Māori or Aboriginal worlds through their fiction writing or filmmaking, and were frequently expected to, or chose to, use their work to represent the political concerns of Māori or Aboriginal people. At the same time, media representations were by no means monolithic, often different for different women or at different times. Such differences sometimes stemmed from the level of political involvement of the women themselves and from their own aims. While not able to entirely escape having their work viewed in political terms, these women made choices which affected how they were represented, and how their work was understood both in the popular press and in literary journals. Moreover, changing trends in literary criticism and appreciation as well as wider social and political changes at times led to shifting understandings of their work. Nevertheless, the work of Indigenous women writers and filmmakers on both sides of the Tasman

---

151   P. Della Valle, 'The Wider Family: Patricia Grace Interviewed by Paola Della Valle', *The Journal of Commonwealth Literature* 42, no. 1 (2007), p. 135.
152   Fee, p. 15.

was persistently viewed through a lens of difference. In depictions as firsts, as authentic or inauthentic, as assimilated or as activists, ideas of racial difference remained central, far more so than did ideas of femininity and gender.

Conclusion

Although filmmaking was in many respects a different industry from that of fiction writing, representations of filmmakers displayed many similar tropes and drew upon similar discourses about Indigeneity. Literature and films were not always viewed as political, but they were necessarily more ambiguous in this sense than were other types of achievement, because they were always read as saying something. Particularly in the 1960s and 1970s, sports stars and performing artists were more often conscripted as symbols upon which meaning could be inscribed than were writers and filmmakers, who spoke for themselves by the very nature of their work. Indigenous women writers such as Oodgeroo and Grace emerged at around the same time as did Goolagong and Te Kanawa, but had a much different experience in relation to the ways in which they were represented in the media. Far from being represented as naturally talented, their abilities in such an intellectual endeavour were sometimes questioned. Rather than being persistently depicted as symbolising harmonious race relations or reconciliation, they were sometimes treated as too political or too radical, and depiction as assimilated more often served to question their authenticity as Indigenous artists than to set them up as role models. While gender was sometimes important in portrayals of these writers and filmmakers, and in understandings of their work, it was not as central as was the case in sport, where female participation and image were more contested, or in the performing arts, where feminine glamour was often treated as central to women's fame and success. In representations of Indigenous women writers and filmmakers, both in the print media and articulated by the women themselves, discourses around Indigeneity often proved more central. Discourses about the nation were also less central in depictions of writers and filmmakers than in those about sportspeople and performing artists, perhaps because they did not perform so clearly upon an international stage, or because it was potentially more difficult to inscribe ideas of national identity upon them. Where ideas of nation might become relevant was in the possibility for these writers and filmmakers to be celebrated as legitimating the image of the nation as a postcolonial one, a possibility that was much less open to reviewers of Oodgeroo's poetry than it was to reviewers of less clearly political writers.

Chapter Five

Dame Whina Cooper was, wrote Michael King, 'the country's best known matriarch'.[1] An *Otago Daily Times* editorial after her death in 1994 lamented the 'loss' of 'both a significant figure and an important symbol', someone who in 'this age of the celebrity' satisfied the desire of 'wider New Zealand, both Maori and pakeha' for 'a special figure to respect and love'.[2] Cooper's national prominence developed through her lifetime of struggle for Māori people and her visibility as a leader within Māoridom. It is such prominence, accrued through leadership and through social and political institutions, which is the focus of this chapter. Particularly from the 1970s, a number of Māori and Aboriginal women became nationally known in New Zealand and Australia for their leadership and activism. Some worked for change from within the institutions of the state, others sought it from outside them, and still others moved fluidly between these positions. In this chapter I explore print media representations surrounding those who struggled for the welfare and rights of Indigenous people, examining the lines along which framings of these prominent women fractured in a time of intense social and political change. I explore particularly the representation of these women as moderate voices or as radical activists, the gendered dimensions of such representations, the dubious distinction of receiving official honours for activist work, and the ambivalent relationships of these women with the feminist movement of the 1970s. Throughout, media representations of these women are interwoven with their own publicly articulated understandings of their lives and work. At the centre of the chapter is the figure of Cooper, who reached a level of fame far above that of most women involved in political activism or leadership roles.

Dame Whina Cooper and the Print Media

Born in the far north of New Zealand in the last years of the nineteenth century, Whina Cooper's first act of protest occurred when she was only eighteen. Mudflats important to local Māori were leased to a Pākehā farmer, who began to drain the land. Her father looked to the official channels of the courts and Parliament to overturn the lease, but Whina Te Wake, as she then was, gathered a group of Māori to follow behind those digging drains, filling them in again. Although they were charged with trespass, the lease was withdrawn, after action was taken on the issue by two Māori Members of Parliament (MPs). Becoming a leader in the Catholic church and in the community, Cooper (then Gilbert) was

---

1   M. King, *Whina: A Biography of Whina Cooper* (Auckland: Hodder and Stoughton, 1983), p. 237.
2   'A Matriarch's Passing', *Otago Daily Times*, 29 March 1994, p. 8.

an important supporter of Sir Apirana Ngata's schemes for the development of Māori land in the early 1930s. It was her efforts in support of these schemes that led to her first being 'noticed by the national press', with one report referring to her as 'the Amazon excavator'.[3] She reached national prominence shortly after leaving the Hokianga region for Auckland, having been elected as the first Dominion President of the Māori Women's Welfare League (MWWL) when it was founded in 1951. Following her resignation from this position in 1957, she continued to work as a leader in the community.

Figure 8: 'Photograph of Whina Cooper at Hamilton During the Māori Land March', 25 September 1975, Christian F. Heinegg.

Photograph. PA7-15-18. C. F. Heinegg Collection. Alexander Turnbull Library, Wellington, New Zealand.

---

3 M. King, 'Cooper, Whina 1895-1994', *Dictionary of New Zealand Biography*, updated 7 April 2006, accessed 7 May 2007, available from http://www.dnzb.govt.nz/dnzb/Find_Quick.asp?PersonEssay=5C32.

Her greatest act of leadership, however, was still to come. As Michael King argued, Cooper made an 'imprint ... on the national consciousness' during her leadership of the 1975 land march that 'persisted for the remainder of her life'.[4] She had become the leader of a group formed to halt the loss of Māori land, Te Rōpū o te Matakite (Those with Foresight). Aiming to draw Māori together and bring the alienation of Māori land to the attention of the Pākehā population, the group agreed on a march as the appropriate protest.[5] The march began from Te Hāpua in the far north in September 1975, led by Cooper and her granddaughter. Almost a month to the day after they had set off, the marchers reached Parliament on 13 October. Cooper presented a memorial of rights and a petition with 60,000 signatures. Moving back to the Hokianga in 1983, she 'reached her widest audience' in 1990, speaking at the opening of the Commonwealth Games in Auckland.[6] When she died at the age of ninety-eight in 1994, her tangihanga (funeral) was attended by 'many thousands' as well as being screened live on television.[7]

As a leader within Māoridom, Cooper's relationship with the media was complex and sometimes mutually beneficial. While those campaigning for Indigenous rights were generally not backed by a publicity machine to the extent that those famous in sports or the performing arts were, the media remained a crucial marketing tool – the commodity being the message rather than the person. Cooper's awareness of the importance of a working relationship with the media, and her ability to gain coverage for an issue or event, were noted by several of those who wrote about her life and work. Her biographer, King, considered that although her rise to national prominence while president of the MWWL was partly due to 'the general newsworthiness of league activities', it was 'in even greater measure a reflection of the flair with which she dealt with journalists'.[8] Denis Welch, writing in the *New Zealand Listener*, noted that journalists became accustomed to 'being summoned for interviews – monologues, rather – that might go on for hours'.[9] An obituary in the *Dominion* described her as 'seldom reluctant to use news media', as evidenced by the occasions when she 'threatened' to return the honours she received as a response to 'government inaction' on various concerns.[10] One moment at which her ability to achieve media coverage was clearly demonstrated occurred mere weeks before her death. Newspapers across the country reported that she had called Sir Graham Latimer, the chair of the New Zealand Māori Council, to visit her in hospital because she wished him

4   Ibid.
5   King, *Whina*, p. 207.
6   King, 'Cooper, Whina'.
7   Ibid.
8   King, *Whina*, p. 179.
9   D. Welch, 'Whina: Last of the Red-Hot Autocrats', *New Zealand Listener*, 4 June 1994, pp. 29-30.
10   '"Mother of Nation" a Battler From the Very Beginning', *Dominion*, 28 March 1994, p. 7. The same obituary also appeared in other newspapers around the country.

to 'inherit her place in Maoridom'.[11] In the original story, *New Zealand Herald* reporter Heather Ayrton wrote that Cooper had asked her to go to Middlemore Hospital 'to witness the passing of responsibility'.[12] Yet despite Cooper's media sense, her treatment in the media was not always helpful to her, at times arguably weakening her message through depicting her in racialised and gendered tropes.

The Mother of the Nation? Framing Whina Cooper

When Cooper died in 1994, the *New Zealand Herald* reported that an estimated 30,000 people had gone to her tangihanga, which lasted several days.[13] The Queen and Prince Philip sent condolences, and tributes from politicians and public figures were reported in all the major daily newspapers. The Prime Minister, Jim Bolger, was quoted describing Cooper as having 'persuaded and pursued' various Prime Ministers over the years 'for the advancement of New Zealand', and as having 'always talked about one people, calling for them to work together'.[14] Cooper's advocacy for Māori was thus subsumed under her vision for the country as a whole. Some letters to the editor which were published after her death displayed similar understandings of her life and work. One, which included a tribute from the Auckland Multicultural Society, exhorted readers to 'remember Dame Whina's goal for our future', quoting her statement that all 'should live in harmony'.[15] Another lamented that Cooper had 'passed on without seeing her vision become a reality of us all joining together as a united nation'.[16] A third referred to Cooper's 'dream' that Māori and Pākehā would 'live together as one people', urging readers not to let 'this great woman's dream die with her passing'.[17] In mourning for this universally loved figure, it seemed, Māori and Pākehā could come together as one, just as Cooper herself would have desired. Reading coverage of her death in New Zealand's major daily newspapers, it would be easy to assume that this understanding of her life and achievements was universally shared. Particularly in editorial material, where opinion predominated over biographical detail, Cooper was placed as an advocate of assimilation, harmony and tolerance.

In the political hub of Wellington, readers of the *Dominion* were assured that while Cooper had 'welcomed' the Māori 'cultural and political renaissance' of

---

11   H. Ayrton, 'Dame Whina Names Her Heir', *New Zealand Herald*, 3 March 1994, section 1, p. 1.

12   Ibid.

13   H. Ayrton and M. Roderick, 'Farewell Gift of Food and Lotto Ticket', *New Zealand Herald*, 2 April 1994, section 1, p. 22.

14   H. Ayrton, 'Thousands Journey to Mourn Matriarch', *New Zealand Herald*, 28 March 1994, section 1, p. 1.

15   J. Buckland, letter to the editor, *New Zealand Herald*, 2 April 1994, section 1, p. 8.

16   B. Appleby, letter to the editor, *New Zealand Herald*, 5 April 1994, section 1, p. 8.

17   A. A. Brooks, letter to the editor, *New Zealand Herald*, 5 April 1994, section 1, p. 8.

the 1970s and 1980s, she had 'never endorsed the rise in biculturalism that grew with it' and which brought 'the concept of one nation, two people'. Under the headline 'A Maori for all races', this editorial asserted that it was instead 'the earlier pursuit of assimilation, the notion of one nation, one people' that drove Cooper, and that her life had benefited all of New Zealand.[18] Although Cooper had often spoken of the need for unity between Māori and Pākehā, however, she was not an advocate of assimilation. In 1982, she was quoted in the *New Zealand Woman's Weekly* expressly stating that she 'was always against assimilation'.[19] In the south, the *Otago Daily Times'* editorial was similarly focused on Cooper's desire for Maori and Pakeha to live together in harmony. The editorial mourned the death of one who had 'represent[ed] for many New Zealanders hope for Maori and pakeha unity'. Cooper had 'refused to preach the separatist path', it declared, and thus, 'despite her role in the land march ... and her outspoken views' had 'earned the respect of many "middle" New Zealanders' through 'her concerns for unity and her vision of people working together'.[20] Wellington's *Evening Post* pursued similar themes. Cooper had 'eschewed confrontation', its editorial stated, 'her guiding vision' being one of 'a society in which the two major races lived in harmony'. She was praised for having been 'adept at vigorously advancing Maori interests without resorting to antagonism or animosity'. This editorial did also acknowledge that there had been disagreement within Māoridom over Cooper's approach. It was 'too passive' for 'contemporary activists', the editorial reflected, while being for Pākehā 'the non-threatening side of Maori advocacy'. Cooper, it suggested, had been someone who 'kept alive the hope that New Zealand could still be the bicultural showplace which, in more settled times, it genuinely seemed to be'.[21] The Christchurch *Press* likewise depicted Cooper as a figure of hope, observing that she 'lived [the] ideal' of 'racial tolerance' and that 'her example can continue to animate the nation'.[22] The common focus on Cooper's desire for Māori and Pākehā to live amicably together thus often worked to reinvigorate the myth of New Zealand as a place of racial harmony.

Not all coverage of Cooper's death depicted her as a voice for racial tolerance. Her forceful nature and leadership were also acknowledged, as was her contribution to drawing attention to land rights through the 1975 land march. In Auckland, where she had lived and worked for many years, and where multiculturalism was perhaps a political necessity, an editorial in the *New Zealand Herald* focused upon her achievements and her determination rather than upon her dream of

18   'A Maori For All Races', *Dominion*, 29 March 1994, p. 6.
19   J. Wheeler, 'Dame Whina Will Fight to the Last Breath', *New Zealand Woman's Weekly*, 12 July 1982, p. 5.
20   'A Matriarch's Passing', p. 8.
21   'Dame Whina: A Mighty Tree Fallen', *Evening Post*, 28 March 1994, p. 8.
22   'Dame Whina Cooper', *Press*, 29 March 1994, p. 11.

unity, describing her as 'a voice to be heard'.[23] Nonetheless, the reiteration of her belief in living together harmoniously often took the place of her other aspirations as lessons were drawn from her life. Exhortations to continue her work for Māori welfare or land rights were conspicuously absent from much of the coverage of her passing. Māori media pioneer Derek Fox suggested in an editorial in *Mana* magazine that the politicians who responded to Cooper's death by 'applauding in public someone whose work they have opposed and whose dreams they are destroying', and the 'mainstream media' who 'wallowed in the spectacle' of her tangihanga, had alike acted with 'a ... mixture of gall, ignorance and hypocrisy'. While Cooper had 'argued for unity between Maori and Pakeha', he wrote, she had seen 'the path to that harmony [as] one along which Maori rights were acknowledged and restored'.[24] Interestingly, at least one obituary for Oodgeroo in Australia had also praised her for working towards unity, stating that 'her dream was that everyone should live in harmony regardless of skin colour'.[25] Framing such forceful champions of Indigenous rights in this way potentially limited the challenge that they posed to mainstream social and political formations. Moreover, if women such as Cooper and Oodgeroo had seemed to test received notions of (white) femininity through their vigorous advocacy, framing them as promoters of peace and tolerance after their deaths potentially re-imagined them as womanly, naturally peaceful and nurturing.

Media representations of Cooper after her death also often presented her as a larger-than-life figure. The Christchurch *Press* portentously stated in its editorial that Cooper's death brought 'together great themes that are fundamental to New Zealand', such as 'the coexistence of the races; the impact that an individual can make in our society; [and] the creation of a tolerant culture that is not simply transplanted but that draws definition from a unique and living tradition'. These were, claimed the editorial, 'the things that this matriarch personified'. Much was made of her age, the writer stating that 'great age was entwined with great events in the person of Dame Whina', who had been 'raised among Maoris who had had personal contact with the founding of European settlement' in New Zealand.[26] In a number of stories published around the time of her death, reference was made to her as the 'Mother of the Nation', or 'Te Whāea o te Motu', a title which the MWWL had bestowed upon her.[27] This phrase was used to describe her in the press far more after her death than it had been during her life, and was part of a set of representations which developed around her particularly in the 1990s. During the Waitangi Day celebrations in 1990, New Zealand's sesquicentennial year, Cooper was interviewed on television by broadcaster Paul Holmes. He

23 'A Voice to be Heard', *New Zealand Herald*, 28 March 1994, section 1, p. 8.

24 D. T. Fox, editorial, *Mana*, no. 6, July-September 1994, p. 1.

25 'Farewell: May Her Dreaming Be Powerful', *Courier-Mail*, 21 September 1993, p. 8.

26 'Dame Whina Cooper', p. 11.

27 I. Byron, *Ngā Perehitini: The Presidents of the Māori Women's Welfare League, 1951-2001* (Auckland: Māori Women's Development, 2002), p. 20. The title held different connotations in this context.

introduced her as 'one of New Zealand's most respected people' and 'someone who could almost be the mother of us all', and the interview which followed had 'an almost reverential focus on Dame Whina herself'.[28] After her death, the *Sunday Star-Times* described her in a headline as 'the nation's matriarch'.[29] Depicted in these ways as an elderly woman cherished by the whole nation, a loved New Zealander, Cooper was no longer represented as an advocate of Māori rights so much as she was mobilised as a reassuring symbol that New Zealand race relations could still be the best in the world.

However, Cooper was a much more complex figure and during her lifetime was subject to considerable criticism, particularly from Māori. As King once observed, 'no Maori leader has attracted more public praise from Pakeha people and more public criticism from sectors of Maoridom'.[30] Writing in the *Sunday Star-Times* after Cooper's death, Brian Rudman contended that there had been two different views of her in previous years, a Pākehā view and a Māori view. Pākehā had begun to take notice of her following the land march, he suggested, leading to her 'near beatification', while she had had a number of opponents among Māori.[31] A common criticism had been that she was domineering as a leader. During her time as president of the MWWL, some members became unhappy with her 'autocratic leadership style and ... peremptory manner'.[32] King believed that there was some basis to suggestions that Cooper's 'dictatorial style of leadership' was a factor in the divisions which occurred at the end of the land march.[33] For Māori, Cooper was not a figure to be uncomplicatedly celebrated or acclaimed as 'the Mother of the Nation'.

Several authors suggested that the Pākehā celebration of Cooper occurred because she was a non-threatening figure. In 1980, she was quoted in the *New Zealand Herald* reflecting that 'all the work I have done all along has been for both Maori and Pakeha races'.[34] Eight years later, she was featured in the *New Zealand Woman's Weekly*'s 'Scene and Heard' page, a space more commonly reserved for social notes and gossip, making a similar statement. Beside a picture of her smiling beatifically, the small piece stated that 'Maori matriarch Dame Whina Cooper ... has a message for us all: "We are one people"'. She had 'spent a lifetime working for racial harmony in New Zealand', it continued, and 'at 93, still firmly believes Maori and Pakeha can live together happily and peacefully'.[35] Statements such as these may have endeared her to Pākehā unsettled by the

---

28   S. Abel, *Shaping the News: Waitangi Day on Television* (Auckland: Auckland University Press, 1997), pp. 123-124.
29   T. McRae, 'Dame Whina – the Nation's Matriarch', *Sunday Star-Times*, 27 March 1994, p. A9.
30   M. King, 'Whina – Te Whaea o te Motu', *Mana*, no. 1 (1993), p. 91.
31   B. Rudman, 'After Whina, Maori to Share the Mantle', *Sunday Star-Times*, 3 April 1994, p. C1.
32   Byron, p. 19.
33   King, *Whina*, p. 228.
34   'Dame Whina ... Her Job Not Over', *New Zealand Herald*, 31 December 1980, p. 1.
35   'Scene and Heard', *New Zealand Woman's Weekly*, 13 June 1988, p. 50.

upsurge in Māori protest activity since the 1970s. Ranginui Walker, professor of Māori Studies at Auckland University, was once quoted remarking that 'the pakeha perception of her is all that lovely 1990s stuff'. He continued:

> the pakeha has been feeling under siege for the past 15 years with the Waitangi Tribunal and all these land cases, and here is this apparent voice of reason, calling for calm and peace and reconciliation and for us all to love each other.[36]

Similarly, Rawiri Hoani suggested that Cooper had 'had more universal appeal among pakeha than among Maori' since 'pakeha wanted to see a united Maori controlled by one moderate leader'.[37] Indeed, in many portrayals Cooper the land rights campaigner was submerged under Whina the iconic mother of the nation. Without naming sources, Denis Welch observed in the *New Zealand Listener* that some people felt 'her frequent calls for universal love and national unity … must have been music to the ears of politicians who found other Maori too problematic to deal with'.[38] Perhaps there was some relief in depictions of Cooper as 'the Mother of the Nation' and a voice for unity.

Mothers, Matriarchs and Moderates

Rather than as a voice for tolerance and unity, Cooper was at various times during her life represented in the media as forceful and as a fighter. In a 1955 profile in *Te Ao Hou: The New World*, the magazine published by the Department of Māori Affairs, she was described as 'a tremendous personality with few, if any, inhibitions and an "afraid of no one" complex'. The author, Melvin Taylor, noted that 'the most conspicuous' of the 'qualities' that had 'brought her to the top' were 'those that single her out as a fighter – a fiery, hard hitting one too'.[39] Twenty years later, a profile published in the *Evening Post* during the land march ran under the headline 'Long-Time Fighter For Her People'. In the article, she was described as 'a relentless fighter, a woman of no compromise where the rights of the Maoris [are] concerned'.[40] Still later, when she received the Order of New Zealand in 1991, she was described by the *Dominion* not only as an 'opponent of separatism', but also as being 'known for fiery oratory' which had 'made her one of Maoridom's most visible and controversial leaders'.[41]

---

36 Rudman, p. C1.
37 R. Hoani, 'My View From Te Wai Pounamu', *Kia Hiwa Ra*, no. 19 (1994), p. 18.
38 Welch, p. 29.
39 M. Taylor, 'Whina Cooper', *Te Ao Hou: The New World*, no. 12 (1955), p. 17.
40 G. David, 'Leader of Maori March is Long-Time Fighter For Her People', *Evening Post*, 4 October 1975, p. 16.
41 'Dame Whina a Top Level Living Treasure', *Dominion*, 15 June 1991, p. 8.

Although not usually termed an 'activist', Cooper was sometimes referred to in terms which suggested that she was radical. At the time of the land march, Pauline Ray wrote in the *New Zealand Listener* that it might 'seem somewhat improbable' that 'an old lady, albeit a surprisingly sprightly old lady' had become the leader of 'what is probably the most militant Maori organisation formed this century', but observed that 'Mrs Cooper has never been a conformist'.[42] Even in the *New Zealand Woman's Weekly* snippet which presented her 'message' as one of unity, the writer stated that 'age has not doused the fire in Dame Whina' and that she remained 'as politically conscious as ever'.[43] When she was made a dame in 1980, she was quoted in the *Dominion* saying that:

> I have worked with every government ... If I see some good in their policies I follow it. But I fight too, oh yes, I'm a fighter. And I'm still fighting.
>
> If it should be law I'll obey the law. But I will fight the law if it's not justice.[44]

Such a statement portrayed a very different figure from the 'Mother of the Nation' who dreamed of peaceful co-existence, although the two were of course not incompatible. In an extended interview broadcast in 1978, Cooper commented upon newspaper descriptions of her as 'fiery, forceful and fearless', observing that 'you've got to be fiery' because 'you got to be true in what you're speaking about'. At the same time, she stated that her heart was 'all love', and that 'I love my people, and I only wish, you know, I can do something for them while I'm alive'.[45]

After her death, alongside the focus on her desire for unity, the *Dominion*'s editorial also hinted at this different view of Cooper, stating that in the past 'her political views were as radical as her style and tactics', although she later seemed 'conservative'.[46] As this suggests, such varying understandings of Cooper's life and work can in part be ascribed to the passage of time. Cooper's methods of seeking social justice sometimes seemed too conservative to a young, urban generation of protesters. Certainly a rift was evident at the time of the land march. Upon arrival at Parliament, a group of marchers remained camped outside, an action which Cooper strongly opposed. She sought to dissociate the campers from the rest of the march organisation, stating in telegrams sent to the Prime Minister and the Minister of Māori Affairs that the protest was the initiative of

---

42　P. Ray, 'Final Battle Ahead', *New Zealand Listener*, 23 August 1975, p. 18.

43　'Scene and Heard', p. 50.

44　'Whina Says Name Doesn't Stop Fight', *Dominion*, 2 January 1981, p. 5.

45　W. Cooper, interview with A. Owen, 'Herea te Tangata ki te Whenua (Bind the People to the Land)', in *Speaking For Ourselves: Echoes From New Zealand's Past From the Award-Winning "Spectrum" Radio Series*, eds. A. Owen and J. Perkins (Auckland: Penguin, 1986), pp. 58-60.

46　'A Maori For All Races', p. 6.

Ngā Tamatoa and that the campers were not approved to use the organisation's banner in their protest. On other occasions, too, she opposed the methods of protest adopted by the new generation of activists. She considered that physically pushing then Governor-General Sir Keith Holyoake at Waitangi was 'a stupid way of protesting' because it 'set everybody against them' and nothing was accomplished by 'pushing around elderly people'.[47] She was also, particularly at the time of the land march, occasionally represented in ways which framed her as being more moderate than other protesters, as was the case in much of the press coverage of her death and tangihanga. After the breakaway protesters set up camp in Parliament grounds, one article in the *Dominion* referred to 'Mrs Cooper and other moderates' involved in the march, in contrast to 'militant' members of the march.[48] Such shifts underline the impact which generational differences may play in shaping representations. While Cooper continued to be depicted as determined and a fighter, she also came to be implicitly contrasted with the new generation of activists who emerged in the 1970s.

A representational divide between so-called 'radicals' and 'moderates' has been a common feature of media treatment of Indigenous peoples. In New Zealand, Sue Abel observed that television coverage of Waitangi Day in 1990 and 1995 placed Māori as either 'tame' (those seen as 'supporting the status quo') or 'wild' (and thus 'marginalised and demonised in news coverage').[49] Outside the media, in submissions to the Human Rights Commission after the haka party incident at Auckland University in 1979, Raymond Nairn and Timothy McCreanor identified a mode of discourse in which Māori were divided 'into "good" and "bad" sub-groups using a range of criteria'.[50] Similar framings were evident in representations of Māori women who became well-known for their protest activity. One who was implicitly constructed as moderate in contrast to the new generation of activists was Te Arikinui Dame Te Ātairangikaahu, the Māori Queen. Dame Te Ata, as she was often known, was clearly depicted as a moderate and unifying figure in an article which appeared in the *New Zealand Woman's Weekly* in 1990, New Zealand's sesquicentennial year. It was reported that she had 'a stern message for Maori radicals' intending to 'disrupt' the celebrations, and she was quoted saying that those who did not wish to commemorate the year should 'stay home'.[51]

---

47 King, *Whina*, pp. 223-228, 236.

48 'Militant Marchers "Disgrace to Race"', *Dominion*, 15 October 1975, p. 3. Cooper was quoted in the article referring to the campers as 'a disgrace to their race'. 'Militant Marchers', p. 3.

49 S. Abel, '"Wild Māori" and "Tame Māori" in Television News', *New Zealand Journal of Media Studies* 3, no. 2 (1996), p. 33.

50 R. G. Nairn and T. N. McCreanor, 'Race Talk and Common Sense: Patterns in Pakeha Discourse on Maori/Pakeha Relations in New Zealand', *Journal of Language and Social Psychology* 10, no. 4 (1991), p. 249. What has come to be referred to as 'the haka party incident' occurred in 1979, when a group of engineering students from the University of Auckland performing a parody of a haka (traditional dance) were confronted by Māori and Pacific Island students.

51 S. Haggie, 'Te Arikinui: "If You Don't Agree – Stay Home!"', *New Zealand Woman's Weekly*, 5 February 1990, p. 22.

Another implicitly depicted as moderate in contrast to many younger activists was Dame Miraka (Mira) Szaszy. Like Cooper a president of the MWWL, Szaszy devoted her life to Māori struggles. In an interview with Virginia Myers published in 1986, she reflected that she had become aware that 'Maori were being put down' and that this realisation had ignited her 'determination to fight for the Maori people'.[52] In coverage of her from the 1970s onward, however, she appears to have been usually constructed as moderate. Where her struggles for Māori rights were mentioned, they might be framed in non-threatening terms. For example, an article in Air New Zealand's in-flight magazine, *Pacific Way*, described her in 1993 as a 'champion of civil rights' who 'remain[ed] dedicated to the cause of social justice'.[53] Yet Szaszy herself more than once observed that she supported the goals of the new wave of activists, if not their tactics. She recalled in the interview with Myers that 'some of our methods [in the MWWL] came under attack' in the 1970s, and that 'emerging radical groups' such as Ngā Tamatoa were 'very critical' of the organisation, 'which they saw as part of the system' since it aimed for 'gradual change in a peaceful way'. Of such groups, she reflected that she 'agreed with their principles but not their strategies'. In 'my own time', she commented, 'I think I was already a very radical person'.[54]

In Australia, a similar representational divide between moderate and radical was often invoked in media representations of prominent Aboriginal women who worked for social and political change. Lowitja O'Donoghue became well-known through working from within the bureaucracy despite the frustrations she experienced. She held positions within the Department of Aboriginal Affairs, as the first chair of the National Aboriginal Conference, within the Aboriginal Development Commission, and as the inaugural head of the Aboriginal and Torres Strait Islander Commission (ATSIC). In 1985, after being chosen as the winner of the Australian of the Year award, the Adelaide *Advertiser* reported that she 'shuns the description "activist" in favour of "moderate"'.[55] A decade earlier, Stewart Cockburn had observed in the same publication that 'in working towards Aboriginal objectives, Miss O'Donoghue's personal style is low key'. 'She finds it more effective', he stated, 'to work her way around obstacles than to try to topple them'.[56] O'Donoghue was sometimes represented as assimilated, and her life as demonstrating the success of official assimilation policies. Cockburn remarked that she had 'helped explode an old, convenient but false white prejudice', and had 'demonstrated that, given a fair go, tribal Aborigines can not only be fully assimilated or integrated into white society in one generation, but can assume

52   V. Myers, *Head and Shoulders* (Auckland: Penguin, 1986), p. 238.

53   I. Sharp, 'Mira Szaszy', *Pacific Way*, no. 58 (1993), p. 30.

54   Myers, p. 241.

55   B. Parsons, 'Why Tears Fell on Lois's Happy Day', *Advertiser*, 30 January 1985, p. 2.

56   S. Cockburn, 'The Saga of Lois O'Donoghue: An Aboriginal Leader in a White Society', *Advertiser*, 13 March 1975, p. 5.

comfortable and undisputed leadership roles in that society'.[57] Although media stories about O'Donoghue in the 1980s and 1990s sometimes depicted her as having fought for Aboriginal rights or fought her way to the top, she was also described in non-threatening terms. The *Advertiser* referred to her in 1988 as 'a tireless worker for Aborigines' in South Australia, and the Brisbane *Courier-Mail* observed in 1996 that 'long before she became one of the nation's most recognisable faces, she was already working to improve the lot of Aborigines'.[58]

Figure 9: 'Miss Lois O'Donoghue, Australian of the Year', Michael Jensen.

Photograph. nla.pic-an24188590. National Library of Australia, Canberra.

---

57   Ibid.
58   'Lois … a Tiny City Lane Which Means a Lot', *Advertiser*, 24 May 1988, p. 2; K. Sweetman and J. Sommerfield, 'War Weary', *Courier-Mail*, 6 December 1996, p. 17.

Such depictions also carried gender baggage, reflecting a (white) conception of femininity that valued selfless work on behalf of others without seeking the limelight or needing reward. The *Australian Women's Weekly* commented upon O'Donoghue's having long been 'a fighter for Aboriginal rights, but without publicity', implicitly contrasting her with more vocal and visible activists.[59] A similar perception of Cooper's activism was evident in the *Dominion* editorial after her death. She had 'led a turbulent life', it read, 'but her activism was born of selflessness'.[60] Throughout the nineteenth century, many middle-class women found an outlet for their energies in charitable work; such selfless, unpaid work for others being widely viewed as compatible with the powerful ideology of domesticity that otherwise circumscribed women's lives. Framing protest activity in this way thus potentially rehabilitated it as being compatible with such ideas of femininity.

At least once, O'Donoghue was explicitly compared to Pat O'Shane. Although O'Shane was also a prominent Indigenous woman working for Indigenous rights from within the bureaucratic and institutional structures of the state, she was often depicted as a more controversial figure than was O'Donoghue. O'Shane had begun her career as a teacher, studied law and become a barrister, worked within the public service and been appointed as a magistrate in New South Wales (NSW) in 1986. In an interview in 1991, she told of becoming involved in 'the Black Military' when she went to Sydney in the early 1970s, and of travelling to Canberra for the tent embassy protest.[61] She was quoted in 1983, while head of the NSW Department of Aboriginal Affairs, saying that 'I see myself as an activist within bureaucracy' and that she felt 'it is incumbent upon people like myself to effect some change in attitudes'.[62] Charles Perkins, a key figure in the 1965 Freedom Ride and a prominent public servant, had been quoted in the *Canberra Times* making a similar statement several years earlier, after his promotion to deputy secretary of the federal Department of Aboriginal Affairs. He would be, he had stated, 'no less an activist or no less militant'.[63]

---

59 G. Lyle, 'A Distinguished Australian Speaks Out: "We Have to Solve Our Differences and Live Together"', *Australian Women's Weekly*, April 1985, p. 27.
60 'A Maori For All Races', p. 6.
61 L. Behrendt and S. Walsh, 'From Cairns to the Courtroom', *Polemic* 2, no. 3 (1991), p. 161.
62 T. Krause, 'Tough Lady Who Can't Sit Pat', *Australian*, 6 June 1983, p. 8, biographical cutting files, National Library of Australia, Canberra.
63 'No Less an Activist, Says New Deputy Secretary', *Canberra Times*, 8 September 1979, p. 13.

Figure 10: 'Portrait of Pat O'Shane Taken at the Constitutional Convention, Canberra, 2-13 February 1998', Loui Seselja.

Photograph. nla.pic-an20168637. National Library of Australia, Canberra.

Media portrayals often depicted O'Shane as fierce and controversial, despite her position within the public service and the judiciary. Notwithstanding her position of power within the legal system, she was described in one article in the *Sydney Morning Herald* in 1993 as 'a champion of the vulnerable and a foe of the establishment'.[64] Throughout her career as a magistrate, many articles described her in terms such as 'outspoken magistrate' or 'controversial NSW magistrate'.[65] One story in the *Daily Mirror* in 1985 was headlined 'Freedom Fighter'.[66] In an extended profile published in the *Australian Magazine* in 1993, Kate Legge emphasised O'Shane's fiery nature, referring to her among other things as a 'fighter', a 'rabblerouser' and a 'stirrer', as well as describing her as 'full of fire' and someone that 'no-one wants to cross'. Legge compared O'Shane to 'other successful Aboriginal women' such as O'Donoghue, who was 'not nearly as smouldering, although she has good reason'. Rather, O'Donoghue was 'a quiet achiever' and a 'conformist who plays by the rules'.[67] Although both women worked for change from within the institutional system, a divide was thus drawn between them in terms of their approaches and strategies.

In many of these depictions, gender was clearly important. The image of the mother was a recurring one. Echoing portrayals of Cooper, O'Donoghue was profiled in the *Sunday Age* in 1994 under the headline 'Mother of the Nation'. Described as the 'elder stateswoman of Aboriginal politics', she was framed as having sacrificed (among other things) the chance to have her own children in order to work for Aboriginal people, and to have gained 'a much wider family in place of the ordinary, a sort of motherhood which embraces her entire people'.[68] Sydney-based Shirley Smith, an important figure in the Aboriginal community in Redfern, was better known as Mum Shirl. Occasionally depicted as a formidable woman or an activist, she was also often portrayed as caring, nurturing or motherly. One such description appeared in the *Daily Mirror* in 1984, where she was referred to as 'the tireless Aboriginal welfare worker with the big heart'.[69] Descriptions like this held far different connotations than did 'activist'. Even in an article in which she was described as 'swearing like a bullocky', 'yelling down the phone at bureaucrats' and feeling 'perpetual rage', she was portrayed as a mother in that she was 'fight[ing] for her oppressed "family" of Aborigines'.[70] Such matriarchal rage was perhaps more acceptable than was the rage of younger activist women.

In New Zealand, older Māori women were often referred to in the press as 'matriarch' or 'kuia' (elderly woman). Cooper and Szaszy were frequently

---

64 A. McGregor, 'Sweet Justice', *Sydney Morning Herald*, 20 March 1993, p. 39.

65 For example: P. Green, 'O'Shane Declares Her Hand For a Just Republic', *Australian*, 27 October 1997, p. 2; M. Gunn, 'Magistrate Blasts "Sexist Judiciary"', *Australian*, 30 August 1993, p. 4; E. Higgins, 'Sexist Judiciary Denies Equal Justice, Says Magistrate', *Australian*, 6 May 1993, p. 3.

66 S. Orr, 'Freedom Fighter', *Daily Mirror*, 13 March 1985, p. 61.

67 K. Legge, 'In the Case of Pat O'Shane', *Australian Magazine*, 31 July 1993, pp. 9, 11-12.

68 D. Stone, 'Mother of the Nation', *Sunday Age*, 15 May 1994, Agenda section, p. 5.

69 'Mum Shirl Refuses to Hang Up Her Apron!', *Daily Mirror*, 11 April 1984, p. 7, biographical cuttings, National Library of Australia, Canberra.

70 E. Brenchley, 'Black Saint', *People*, 27 April 1978, p. 14.

described in these terms later in life. As the image of the mother is generally a moderate one, so too is the image of the matriarch. Reference was often made to Cooper's age during the land march, and in many later articles about her. She was described by Gabriel David in the *Evening Post* in 1975 as a 'rather amazing old Maori woman', and as 'this remarkable woman of 82'.[71] The *Dominion* noted her 'frail and stooped' appearance as she led marchers to Parliament.[72] She was framed as a grandmotherly figure in the *New Zealand Woman's Weekly* in 1974, after she received the CBE (Commander of the Order of the British Empire), and she appeared in this light in a now-famous photograph which appeared in the *New Zealand Herald* in 1975, showing Cooper beginning the land march holding her granddaughter's hand.[73] Being framed as a mother, grandmother or matriarch often appeared to imply not merely family status or age, but also a moderate approach to seeking change. It was the very incongruity of an elderly woman leading a protest march which seemed to fascinate in many press reports of the land march.

Radicals, Riots and Reformed Revolutionaries

Evan Te Ahu Poata-Smith pointed out that the 'intensity and momentum of Maori political activism has never been consistent', with 'upturns in protest activity' being 'followed by downturns in struggle and vice versa'. During the 1970s, there was 'a dramatic upsurge in Maori activism'.[74] In Australia too, an intensification of Aboriginal activism occurred from the late 1960s. As I have begun to suggest, many representations of Indigenous women who became known for their struggles for social change in this period constructed a divide between moderate campaigners and radical activists, which often also meant between older and younger women. A similar observation might be made of depictions of Indigenous men who campaigned for change in Australia and New Zealand during these years. Graham Latimer, the chair of the New Zealand Māori Council and a member of the conservative National Party, was often implicitly portrayed as moderate, in contrast to men such as Tame Iti, Syd Jackson, Ken Mair and Hone Harawira, who were regularly depicted as radicals and extremists. Moreover, as Sue Abel observed in relation to television news reports about Waitangi Day in 1995, the acknowledgement that there were

---

71   David, p. 16; G. David, 'Maori March Might Arrive Too Soon: A Brake to Keep to Schedule', *Evening Post*, 1 October 1975, p. 7.
72   'Radicals Confront Elders: Young Marchers Debate Parliament Sit-In', *Dominion*, 14 October 1975, p. 1.
73   'The Long Road Ahead', *New Zealand Herald*, 20 September 1975, section 1, p. 16; 'The Educator Who "Came From Nothing"', *New Zealand Woman's Weekly*, 11 November 1974, p. 7.
74   E. S. T. A. Poata-Smith, 'He Pokeke Uenuku i Tu Ai: The Evolution of Contemporary Maori Protest', in *Nga Patai: Racism and Ethnic Relations in Aotearoa/New Zealand*, eds. P. Spoonley, D. Pearson and C. Macpherson (Palmerston North: Dunmore, 1996), p. 97.

justified grievances among Māori did not necessarily remove this rhetorical divide. She suggested that Māori were still constructed as 'tame' or 'wild' in terms of their 'tactics': those constructed as 'tame' might hold 'radical views' but nevertheless 'work[ed] within the system', while those constructed as 'wild' were those who 'ignore[d] this way of working and use[d] confrontation and disruption'.[75] Leonie Pihama has also identified 'the activist/radical/excessive Other' as one of the 'dominant discourses' about Māori 'which have constructed limited notions of who we are, derived from colonial representations of Maori'.[76] This representational divide meant that some prominent Aboriginal and Māori women who campaigned for change might more accurately be called notorious, at least in relation to representations of them in the media.

Women who were part of the new activist groups of the 1970s, in particular, were frequently represented as dangerous radicals. In New Zealand, one such woman was Titewhai Harawira, a prominent campaigner for Māori rights who was consistently depicted as radical and threatening, and who continues to be portrayed in such ways in the early twenty-first century. Another was Eva Rickard, who led the fight to have land at Raglan returned to Māori, and who later declared an independent state, Whāingaroa, in 1996. A profile of Rickard in the *New Zealander* magazine in 1981 described her as 'a direct descendant of the ravaging chief Te Rauparaha', one who had 'rebellion in her blood'.[77] Those seeking change through protest have often been marginalised and made to appear threatening both through the use of negative labels, and through media coverage focused upon their protest actions rather than upon their ideas.[78] Rickard was sometimes described in terms that carried such negative connotations. Two articles shortly before her death in 1997 referred to her respectively as a 'veteran activist' and a 'veteran Maori activist'.[79] Likewise, Harawira was, and is, persistently described in such ways. In a variety of New Zealand newspapers in 1998 and 1999, she was termed a 'Maori activist', 'Waitangi activist' or 'notorious activist'.[80]

Both Harawira and Rickard have commented upon these labels. In an article in *Te Kaea*, a magazine published by the Department of Māori Affairs, in 1979,

---

75   Abel, '"Wild Māori" and "Tame Māori"', p. 36.

76   L. Pihama, 'Repositioning Maori Representation: Contextualising *Once Were Warriors*', in *Film in Aotearoa New Zealand*, eds. J. Dennis and J. Bieringa (Wellington: Victoria University Press, 1996), p. 191.

77   M. Tully, 'Eva Rickard', *New Zealander*, 1981, p. 62.

78   See I. Stuart, 'Tauiwi and Maori Media: The Indigenous View', *Pacific Journalism Review* 3, no. 2 (1996), accessed 25 February 2009, available from http://www.asiapac.org.fj/cafepacific/resources/aspac/Maori.html.

79   C. Robertson, 'Plan to Crown Maori King Angers Rickard', *Evening Post*, 24 October 1997, p. 3; 'Maori to Blame For Their Own Problems, Says Veteran Activist', *Waikato Times*, 8 October 1997, accessed from Factiva, 4 June 2008.

80   See for instance: R. Berry, 'Waitangi Activist at PM's Side', *Sunday Star-Times*, 17 January 1999, p. A6; M. Hewitson, 'Cultural Crusader', *New Zealand Herald*, 14 February 1998, p. G3; R. Laugesen, 'Matriarch Games', *Sunday Star-Times*, 24 January 1999, p. C3; C. Robertson, 'Minder for PM at Waitangi', *Evening Post*, 18 January 1999, p. 1.

Rickard stated: 'We knew as children who we were and where we belonged'. 'But in the Pakeha world', she continued, 'it's Eva Rickard militant activist, stirrer, gang-member, trouble-maker and all the other names thrown at me since the battle began'.[81] In the *New Zealand Herald* in 1998, reporter Michele Hewitson observed that Harawira did not refer to herself as 'a nationalist, a radical or a separatist', and quoted her stating that she was simply 'a very strong Maori woman'.[82] Similarly, in the *Sunday Star-Times* in 1999, Harawira was quoted commenting 'I'm not an activist, that's a label', as well as that she was 'pro-Maori' rather than 'anti-white' and that she was 'a beautiful Maori woman with a very clear-headed political analysis who has been working tirelessly for constitutional change', rather than the scary extremist portrayed in the media.[83] In an interview with broadcaster Brian Edwards in the late 1990s, Harawira stated that the media had developed a certain image of her, and recalled once having been told by a reporter that her words would not be quoted because they did not match that image.[84] When deployed in media coverage of Rickard's struggle to regain lands wrongfully taken, or of Harawira's actions and opinions, such negative labels could have a potent de-legitimising effect.

Before she became involved in business ventures and sought election to Parliament, similar labels were applied to Donna Awatere Huata (then Awatere). A key figure in protests against the Springbok tour of New Zealand in 1981, she was arrested and charged multiple times during the tour. Huata was also the author of a powerful text on sovereignty published in 1984, *Maori Sovereignty*. She remembered that in the late 1970s, when Prime Minister Robert Muldoon 'announced a list of New Zealanders he considered dangerous subversives', she 'was at the top', and that she 'got seared into people's memories as one of the causes of the worst violence of the Springbok tour'.[85] She remembered being 'called a Cuban-trained urban revolutionary' after travelling to Cuba, although 'we never considered those kinds of violent acts' and she thought that the 'Maori radical movement has been extraordinarily peaceful'.[86] Throughout the rest of her career, allusions were continually made to her past involvement in activism. When she published her autobiography in 1996, when she joined the conservative ACT political party and entered Parliament the same year, and even when she appeared in the *New Zealand Woman's Weekly* in 2003 apologising for claiming that she had lost weight by dieting when she had instead had her stomach stapled,

---

81   E. Rickard, 'Te Karanga a Tainui Awhiro', *Te Kaea*, December 1979, p. 17.
82   Hewitson, p. G3.
83   Berry, p. A 6.
84   Brian Edwards, interview with Titewhai Harawira, Radio New Zealand, item C1337, Sound Archives/Ngā Taonga Kōrero, accessed 21 October 2008, available from http://www.radionz.co.nz/specialfeatures/treaty/events-1990s, at 37.01-38.56.
85   D. A. Huata, 'Walking on Eggs', in *Heading Nowhere in a Navy Blue Suit and Other Tales From the Feminist Revolution*, eds. S. Kedgley and M. Varnham (Wellington: Daphne Brasell, 1993), p. 127.
86   P. Panckhurst, 'Donna and Her Dad', *New Zealand Herald*, 3 December 1994, section 3, p. 5.

her radical past was often referenced rather than her work prior to seeking election, which included formulating a reading programme for children and providing consultation on bicultural management for organisations. Peter Calder referred to her in the *New Zealand Herald* in 1997 as 'the ACT list MP and one-time firebrand 1970s radical', Rudman wrote of her in the *New Zealand Listener* in 1996 as a 'former firebrand' who was 'once a scourge of the establishment', and Mere Mulu described her in 2003 in the *New Zealand Woman's Weekly* as a 'former Maori radical' as well as an MP.[87] In *Mana* magazine, on the other hand, Tahu Kukutai detailed her various careers and described her as a 'versatile achiever'.[88]

Huata herself has spoken publicly about her press image. In 1982 in the *Evening Standard*, she was quoted stating that she was 'not a Marxist, an activist, a radical' because these were 'simply labels which try to prove people to be isolates' whereas she was rather someone who 'articulates[s] the views of Maori people'.[89] More than a decade later, she was quoted in *Mana* commenting that, while 'proud' of her involvement in Ngā Tamatoa, 'it was at a cost' because:

> I took a lot of flak and on one occasion was passed over for a job I was guaranteed of getting, because of my activist involvement. Even now people see me as Donna Awatere the radical, and have all sorts of mindsets …[90]

Representations of her as a 'wild' Māori thus continued to have repercussions in her later life and career.

The transformation of erstwhile radicals into less threatening figures was made much of in media representations of some women as they grew older and their lives changed. Huata's shift from being a key figure in protest activity to entering Parliament as a member of a conservative party was described by Caroline Courtney in *Next* magazine as a 'stunning political conversion' from being 'a tigress of the 70s and 80s Maori activist movement, who railed against "white rule" and "white hatred"', to 'a right wing Act MP purring inside the parliament she once despised'.[91] Ripeka Evans was also portrayed as having undergone a vast shift, having been a member of Ngā Tamatoa and one of those who had travelled to Cuba. When appointed 'cultural and planning assistant' to Television New Zealand director-general Julian Mounter, her prior incarnation as an activist

---

87   P. Calder, 'Donna Ducks Down Memory Lane to St Mary's', *New Zealand Herald*, 30 August 1997, p. A24; M. Mulu, '"I'm Truly Sorry"', *New Zealand Woman's Weekly*, 3 March 2003, p. 13; B. Rudman, 'Rage Remembered', *New Zealand Listener*, 8 June 1996, p. 38.

88   T. Kukutai, 'Another Target For Donna', *Mana*, no. 9 (1995), p. 58.

89   'Radicals View Black and White', *Evening Standard*, 18 September 1983, clipping held in New Zealand Biographies Index, 1983 v2 p84, National Library of New Zealand, Wellington.

90   Kukutai, p. 58.

91   C. Courtney, 'Changes of Heart', *Next*, no. 83 (1998), p. 54.

was a major focus in a *New Zealand Woman's Weekly* profile. The article began by drawing a parallel between her past 'image', when she was 'portrayed in the media as a militant extremist', and 'the one [she] presents today'. The article noted that she had been included on a Security Intelligence Service list of 'subversives' and 'radicals' in 1981 and quoted another who was on the list, Don Carson, observing that his activist involvement did not generate the same level of 'suspicion' as that which surrounded Evans.[92] Yet although the tone of the article was that such treatment of Evans was unfair, it remained an article about how a former militant now held an important and respected position. Similar representations appeared as recently as 2007 in a piece in the *Sunday Star-Times*. Evans was said to have 'once ... advocated bloody dissent' and to 'sound just like a terrorist', but to have shifted to 'fight[ing] for Maori from within the system'.[93]

In Australia, although not always identified as Aboriginal, Roberta (Bobbi) Sykes was depicted as undergoing a similar transformation. In the early 1970s she was referred to as 'a shapely black militant from Queensland' and as a 'militant Aborigine' who was as 'controversial' in Australia as Angela Davis was in the United States.[94] In 1994, the *Australian* commented that she was in 1972 'Bobbi Sykes – branded a ratbag militant, trampled by police and arrested at the Aboriginal Tent Embassy' but had become 'author, poet and scholar Dr Roberta Sykes – 1994 winner of Australia's Human Rights Medal'.[95] This focus on the transformation of activists sometimes gave the impression that they had left behind their political convictions as they matured. In New Zealand, rehabilitation of those who had disturbed the myth that race relations were the best in the world had the potential to reinvigorate that myth.

If representations of reformed radicals could thus marginalise their former selves, other rhetorical formations could also act to marginalise those involved in protest activities. Representations in the media are shaped at least in part by dominant news values. Protest activity was clearly newsworthy. Besides being active and involving conflict, it was frequently also expected. Abel observed that protests which occurred at Waitangi during the celebrations in 1990, New Zealand's sesquicentennial year, 'fulfilled many of the criteria for newsworthiness', including being 'predictable'. Because such activities had been reported in the past, they were recognisable to audiences, and journalists 'had a ready-made format in which to tell the story'.[96] Similarly, Graeme Turner observed

---

92   R. Vincent, 'Ripeka Evans: Eight Years On ... A New Image', *New Zealand Woman's Weekly*, 12 January 1987, pp. 10-11.

93   A. Hubbard, 'The Reformed Revolutionary', *Sunday Star-Times*, 21 October 2007, accessed from Factiva, 4 June 2008.

94   G. Fisher, 'Bobbie Spreads the Word on Solidarity', *Advertiser*, 15 March 1972, p. 4; A. Trengove, 'Black, Beautiful and Angry', *Advertiser*, 19 August 1974, p. 4.

95   S. Horsburgh, 'Sweet Reward For a "Militant"', *Australian*, 14 November 1994, p. 2.

96   Abel, *Shaping the News*, p. 67.

that in relation to the Australian Bicentennial year in 1988, 'the international media were quoted as nominating the Aboriginal rights issue as the only really interesting angle they had'.[97] In both Australia and New Zealand, criticism of media depictions of protest activity has included the charge that reports of protest activity were 'sensationalist' and often provided little information about the social, economic or historical contexts of the protests.[98] While not necessarily deliberate, the continued deployment of familiar rhetorical frames in depictions of protest activity frequently led to the repetition of negative representations which had the potential effect of marginalising the protesters. Laura Ashley and Beth Olson have similarly observed rhetorical and structural ways in which women in the feminist movement in the United States between 1966 and 1986 were marginalised in the media.[99] One such depiction of Aboriginal protesters in the lead-up to Australia Day in 1988, as noted by Turner, was 'the construction of black groups as politically divided' and the suggestion that their protest would be weakened by those divisions. Yet after a protest march was held in Sydney, media stories about it were 'surprisingly positive'. Turner argued that the 'obvious success of the march allowed media reports to emphasise its joyfulness, thus ... limiting the extent to which it compromised the official celebrations'.[100] Representations of protesters as holding extreme opinions or behaving in extreme ways, like representations of protest groups as internally divided, could deflect attention from their grievances and marginalise their protests.

In their examination of media representations of Aboriginal women at the time of the Bicentenary, Cathy Greenfield and Peter Williams also observed that depictions in the media could marginalise activists. Irene Watson, who made criticisms of planned laws about Aboriginal heritage, was depicted as 'radically unrepresentative of the Aboriginal communities on whose behalf she [had] spoken'. Greenfield and Williams argued that the recurring depiction of Watson as 'a strident and radical activist' had 'set the conditions for [the] particular marginalisation and dismissal of the policy criticisms she put forward'.[101] Occasionally, prominent Indigenous women who were involved in protest activities were represented in similarly marginalising ways. Profiling Pat O'Shane in the *Australian Women's Weekly*, Rosemary Munday wrote not unsympathetically of O'Shane's views of the experiences and status of Aboriginal

---

97   G. Turner, *Making It National: Nationalism and Australian Popular Culture* (St Leonards: Allen and Unwin, 1994), p. 84.

98   See for instance: D. Hollinsworth, '"My Island Home": Riot and Resistance in Media Representations of Aboriginality', *Social Alternatives* 24, no. 1 (2005), p. 19; R. Walker, 'The Role of the Press in Defining Pakeha Perceptions of the Maori', in *Between the Lines: Racism and the New Zealand Media*, eds. P. Spoonley and W. Hirsh (Auckland: Heinemann Reed, 1990), p. 45.

99   L. Ashley and B. Olson, 'Constructing Reality: Print Media's Framing of the Women's Movement, 1966 to 1986', *Journalism and Mass Communication Quarterly* 75, no. 2 (1998), pp. 263-277.

100   Turner, pp. 85-86.

101   C. Greenfield and P. Williams, 'Bicentennial Preliminaries: Aboriginal Women, Newspapers and the Politics of Culture', *Hecate* 13, no. 2 (1987–1988), p. 85.

people. Discussing the impact of 'the Queensland Act' on Aborigines, Munday wrote that those 'placed "under the Act"' were subject to 'rules and regulations that touched almost every aspect of their lives and created *what Pat O'Shane regards as* offensive limitations'.[102] In this statement, what was perhaps an effort to write in a balanced way had the potential effect of marginalising O'Shane's opinion.

Rhetorical devices could also have the effect of taming a forceful woman. An article by Catherine Martin profiling Mum Shirl appeared in the *West Australian* when she visited Western Australia in 1973. Quoting Mum Shirl as saying that 'I am here to stir up the blacks', Martin then wrote that Mum Shirl was 'no trouble-shooter', and that if she had been educated 'beyond the age of 14', she 'might have preferred the word "inspire" to "stir"'.[103] After Rickard's death, an article published in the *New Zealand Herald* described major events in her life. Near the end of the piece, it mentioned that she had 'found time' to act in a Merata Mita film (*Mauri*) and to 'float the idea of setting up an independent Maori republic in Raglan'.[104] What was probably her most challenging act was thus depicted as an idea rather than an action, and as a matter of passing interest with little significance. Such a textual move did not make Rickard appear dangerous, but it glossed over uncomfortable aspects of her life's work, thus retaining the celebratory tone of the article.

These depictions of prominent Indigenous women involved in protest activity were inevitably also shaped in terms of gender. Identifying one common construction of Māori in the media as that of 'radical political activist', Melanie Wall commented on the gender implications of such a stereotype. Besides working to 'maintain the hegemonic status quo by delegitimising the political aspirations of Maori activists', the stereotype also operated to 'to further delimit and constrain Maori identity through masculine signifiers of a violent primitivism'.[105] Thus, although Indigenous men involved in protest activity were also often represented as dangerous radicals, there were different implications when such depictions were applied to women. One such implication was perhaps that women who stepped outside accepted limits of behaviour to protest were more threatening than men who did so. When Deirdre Macken wrote in the *Age* in 1986 that O'Shane's 'radical politics' had 'finally split her marriage', the image of activist women as unnatural was potentially underlined.[106] Such

---

102   R. Munday, '"If You Can Make It, Why Can't 160 Thousand Others?"', *Australian Women's Weekly*, 8 August 1979, p. 11, my emphasis.

103   C. Martin, 'She's Still Speaking Up For the Timid Ones', *West Australian*, 14 February 1973, p. 7.

104   C. Guy, 'A Maori Icon: How Eva Won Mana as a Battler', *New Zealand Herald*, 8 December 1997, p. A16.

105   M. Wall, 'Stereotypical Constructions of the Maori "Race" in the Media', *New Zealand Geographer* 53, no. 2 (1997), p. 43.

106   D. Macken, 'For Pat O'Shane, SM, Justice is More Than a Simple Matter of Black and White', *Age*, 16 August 1986, p. 2.

behaviour was not womanly. Indeed, being seen not to be an activist could draw praise for young women in the 1970s and 1980s. One profile of Tracey Moffatt in the *Advertiser* in 1988 stated that she was 'a young Aborigine with plenty to say' but 'no flag-waving activist'.[107] In other instances, being female could sometimes lessen the impact of an activist's words. In a profile of Sykes in the *Advertiser*, Alan Trengove quoted her discussing 'sexist' reactions to her which downplayed her ideas. He described her a 'militant Aborigine' and as 'black, beautiful, angry and articulate', and wrote that he was 'taking a lot of notice' of her although 'finding it impossible to overlook her gender'.[108] When Rickard died, a number of articles referred to her as a 'matriarch' or 'kuia', as articles about Cooper had done at the time of her death. One referred to her as 'one of the country's most respected Maori rights matriarchs'.[109] Another article noted that, as well as provoking Pākehā hostility, Rickard was 'criticised by radical Maori' for using the 'Pakeha court system' in the struggle to regain land at Raglan.[110] In old age and death, it seemed, her rehabilitation from radical to respected matriarch had begun.

Recognition: Honours From the Establishment

The representational divide between those seen as radical and those seen as moderate was also sometimes recalled in media depictions of disagreements between those campaigning for Indigenous rights. One aspect of the divide appeared to relate to the degree of involvement in official institutional structures which campaigners were considered to have. Several stories reported that prominent Māori and Aboriginal women working for change through parliamentary and bureaucratic structures had been criticised as having sold out the cause by entering those institutions. Pat O'Shane was reported to be the target of such criticism on a number of occasions. While she was head of the NSW Department of Aboriginal Affairs, the *National Times* quoted Paul Coe, who was described as 'one of the country's more radical black leaders', commenting that she had 'become aloof' and that she 'claims she's the conscience of the Aboriginal people, when really she has lost contact with what Aborigines are thinking'.[111] The *Sunday Telegraph* reported in 1983 that 'her critics have claimed success has put her "out of touch" with aboriginal people, [and] that

---

107 P. Hackett, 'Tracey Wants to Picture Blacks in Right Light', *Advertiser*, 22 March 1988, p. 16.

108 Trengove, p. 4.

109 R. Knight and S. McCabe, 'Maoridom Weeps For Eva Rickard, Matriarch', *New Zealand Herald*, 8 December 1997, p. A1.

110 Guy, p. A16.

111 R. Milliken, 'The Pat O'Shane Path to Power', *National Times*, 26 December 1982–1 January 1983, p. 22.

she has failed to protect their interests'.[112] O'Shane was reportedly 'slated ... as an Aunty Tom' when she became a magistrate, being 'accused of becoming part of the system'.[113] Similarly, Huata 'was branded as having sold out' when she began a consulting company with another woman which advised government departments and 'offered bicultural training' to companies and organisations.

Huata herself was quoted in *Mana* saying that 'in many ways I believe I'm still an activist because IHI [the company] is reinforcing my notions of tino rangatiratanga [self-determination or sovereignty]', as well as because the company was helping to bring about 'a real change of attitudes among the people who hold the power, the decision makers'.[114] Joining the conservative ACT party was, as already observed, a further step from her earlier image as a radical activist. She was quoted at the time saying that 'I believe we've made enormous strides', which the reporter noted was 'why she no longer believes in activist action'.[115] Earlier, in 1994, she was quoted commenting that 'I am very much committed to the idea of giving people back the responsibility for managing their own future'.[116] Representing oneself as continuing to be an activist within the context of the institution was not only a contrast to depictions that suggested a transformation had occurred. It was also a response to criticisms of having sold out.

Similar debates were evident in the many stories about prominent Indigenous women who received state honours for their work campaigning for Indigenous welfare or rights. A number of these women received or were offered honours, and their reasons for accepting, declining or returning them were sometimes featured in the media. Particularly for those who had for many years challenged the settler state's usurpation of land and sovereignty, the decision to accept or decline an honour could be fraught. Reasons for accepting honours were often reported to be related to ideas that the award would be an important recognition of an Indigenous woman, that it would be accepted on behalf of all Aboriginal or Māori people, or that it might increase the influence of the recipient in the future. O'Donoghue received the AM (Member of the Order of Australia) in 1976 and the CBE (Commander of the Order of the British Empire) in 1982 for service to the 'Aboriginal community', and the AC (Companion of the Order of Australia) in 1999 for 'public service through leadership to Indigenous and non-Indigenous Australians in the areas of human rights and social justice', especially as ATSIC chairperson.[117] She was quoted in the *Advertiser* in 1977 saying that she was

---

112   G. Reilly, 'A Giant Step', *Sunday Telegraph*, 27 March 1983, p. 33.
113   McGregor, p. 39.
114   Kukutai, p. 59.
115   S. Gregg, 'Donna's Been Thinking, Too', *Sunday Star-Times*, 9 June 1996, p. C3.
116   Panckhurst, section 3, p. 5.
117   For details of these awards, see: Australian Government, 'It's an Honour: Australia Celebrating Australians', updated 12 December 2006, accessed 26 February 2009, available from http://www.itsanhonour. gov.au/honours/honour_roll/search.cfm?aus_award_id=872333&search_type=advanced&showInd=true.

'proud to receive' the AM, 'not only for myself but for the Aboriginal people' and that 'I have accepted the award on their behalf'.[118] When Mum Shirl received the MBE (Member of the Order of the British Empire), the Melbourne *Herald* quoted her saying that she considered refusing it, and that the award was not as significant a 'thrill' as she gained from providing help to those in need. The article reported that she was convinced to accept the award by 'her 12-year-old granddaughter, Dianne, who told her it would be a great thing for Aboriginals and would "Give us some incentive to lift ourselves out of oppression"'.[119] Szaszy was reported to have 'done much soul-searching' before accepting her damehood in 1989, because 'her dedication to working for the honouring of the Treaty of Waitangi, and her belief that there is nothing to celebrate in New Zealand until that happens, left her in a dilemma' about whether or not to accept. She was reported to have said that the 'decision to accept … was, in the main, a tribute to the many people who earned it with her'.[120] Gladys Elphick, whose achievements included being a founder of the Aboriginal Women's Council, received the MBE for service to the Aboriginal community. Although she accepted the award, however, she was quoted in the Adelaide *Advertiser* commenting that the award of South Australia's Aborigine of the Year in 1984 was 'the one I wanted because it comes from my own people, and that makes it special'.[121]

Rickard, on the other hand, reportedly declined awards. She had, as mentioned above, declared an independent state, Whāingaroa, in 1996. The declaration stated that it was 'time' for 'the people of Whaingaroa' to reclaim the 'independence taken from them', and that they 'accordingly declare their independence as a sovereign state'.[122] Rickard also sent a letter to Queen Elizabeth informing her of the impending declaration. A year later, after her death, a piece in the *Waikato Times* reported that her husband had revealed that she had declined offers of the QSM (Queen's Service Medal), because she 'didn't want the gongs and titles of the British, whose troops stripped her tribe of their land'.[123] While Whāingaroa's declaration of independence was made only shortly before her death, it asserted tino rangatiratanga, and suggests that Rickard would not accept a medal from the state which had usurped that. Similar reference to history was reportedly behind Faith Bandler's refusal to accept the MBE in 1976. Although not Aboriginal,

---

118 'Aboriginal Woman Gets Aust. Award', *Advertiser*, 28 July 1977, p. 12.
119 A. Pinches, 'I Almost Said No – MBE Shirl', *Herald*, 11 June 1977, p. 3. Various stories appeared about Mum Shirl's acceptance of the MBE. Another was that she 'said she had refused to accept honours from the Queen some five times, but finally, a grand-daughter accepted an MBE on her behalf'. M. Heary, 'The Enigma Called Mum Shirl', *Woman's Day*, 21 July 1986, p. 19. Still another was that she 'refused to accept the equivalent of a knighthood but she accepted an MBE from the Queen'. Brenchley, p. 14.
120 'Szaszy Made Dame, 5 Knighted', *Evening Post*, 30 December 1989, p. 1.
121 C. Hirst, 'Aboriginal Honour For Aunty Glad', *Advertiser*, 7 September 1984, p. 3.
122 The Declaration of Independence of Whaingaroa', accessed 13 May 2008, available from http://aotearoa .wellington.net.nz/imp/whai.htm.
123 'Spark That Ignited Eva's Spirit', *Waikato Times*, 12 December 1997, accessed from Factiva, 4 June 2008.

Bandler was active in Aboriginal rights organisations and a key figure in the campaign for the 1967 referendum. Her father, as a boy, had been forcibly taken from Ambrym in Vanuatu to work on sugar cane fields in Queensland. Bandler was quoted in the *Sydney Morning Herald* in 1976 saying that: 'I can't possibly accept an award from an empire that kidnapped my father … and enslaved him as a cane worker'.[124] Almost a decade later, in 1984, Bandler accepted an AM, perhaps feeling differently about a uniquely Australian award than she did about an imperial one. Whatever the motives of those who had nominated these women for honours, they considered it impossible to accept an award from the state or empire against whose policies they had struggled for years.

Other women accepted honours at the time, and later chose to return them. One such was Oodgeroo Noonuccal, whose decision to return her MBE and change her name was discussed in Chapter Four. Another was prominent actress Justine Saunders, who returned her OAM (Medal of the Order of Australia) in 2000. Newspapers across Australia carried the story, reporting that she was returning the award in protest against claims by the Howard government that there had been no 'stolen generation'. The *Sydney Morning Herald* quoted her saying that she would return the award 'to the Government that has told me my past was a lie'.[125] The return of honours could thus be mobilised by recipients in their challenge to state policies and actions. Declining or returning honours was more powerful when publicised, a point which displays the complexity of activists' relationships with the media. Sometimes marginalised by it, they nonetheless continued to need it.

During her lifetime, Cooper received several royal honours, beginning with an MBE in 1953. This was followed by a CBE in 1974, and she then received the DBE (Dame Commander of the Order of the British Empire) in 1980 for her services to the Māori people. In 1991, she received New Zealand's highest honour, the Order of New Zealand (ONZ). After her death, the *Dominion* reported that she had 'delighted in the honours bestowed on her but regarded herself as a symbolic recipient only, on behalf of her people'.[126] An editorial in the *Auckland Star* at the time she received the damehood represented her in terms of her work toward racial harmony, the theme that was repeated so often after her death. The writer observed that 'the title acknowledges life-long work for both Maori and Pakeha races' and that 'all New Zealanders will take pleasure from this'.[127] At the same time, the *Evening Post* reported the award under the headline 'Dame Whina irked fellow marchers in land protest'. The story began with a description of her as having 'plummeted from the Maori popularity stakes' after

---

124 G. Williams, 'Black Author Rejects MBE', *Sydney Morning Herald*, 4 December 1976, p. 1.
125 M. Grattan, M. Metherell and M. Seccombe, 'Black Backlash Grows', *Sydney Morning Herald*, 4 April 2000, p. 1.
126 '"Mother of Nation"', p. 7.
127 'Honoured', *Auckland Star*, 31 December 1980, p. 6.

her break with those who wished to remain camping at Parliament following the march, and the article quoted negative responses to her damehood from two men involved in the march. One, Barney Pikari, was quoted saying that Cooper had 'become a yes person for the government' and that had she 'gone further than a land march and become radical she wouldn't have got the award', while the other, Tom Poata, was quoted saying that the award was 'a reward for doing a job for the system'.[128] Cooper was to be invested with her honour at Waitangi marae (meeting place), along with Latimer, who had been granted a knighthood. As King noted, the decision that the investitures be held at Waitangi marae, on Waitangi Day, was 'more controversial' than the honours alone would have been.[129] Since its establishment as a public holiday in 1973, Waitangi Day had been 'a symbolically contested event'. As elaborate official celebrations were held at Waitangi, some sectors of Māori opinion viewed the day as a moment for 'reaffirm[ing] the sacredness' of the Treaty, and others considered celebration inappropriate until the Treaty was honoured.[130]

The investitures held at Waitangi in 1981 were attended by a group of protesters who intended to 'peacefully disrupt' them.[131] Cooper later recalled that:

> I heard the protesters shouting at me, but I didn't look. Then one of them ran out and tried to knock my son over … I could hear the commotion. I just kept going and the Governor-General pinned my medal on me …[132]

The incident was widely reported in the press, and the protest was depicted as a 'full-scale riot'.[133] In the *Auckland Star*, the headline screamed: 'Police, activists brawl on marae'.[134] In much of the coverage, the protesters were depicted as a fringe element, and their views marginalised. The *Auckland Star* story emphasised that they had attacked an elderly woman, observing that 'frail Maori elder Dame Whina Cooper and her son' were 'almost knocked to the ground'.[135] Another stressed Cooper's status as 'a fighter for Maori land rights', potentially implying that the protesters' disapproval of her actions was unreasonable.[136] Nairn and McCreanor argued that in submissions to the Human Rights Commission on the haka party incident, Māori 'dissent' was 'cast as the work of a tiny minority of congenital troublemakers who [sought] to arouse a wider Maori discontent

---

128   'Dame Whina Irked Fellow Marchers in Land Protest', *Evening Post*, 31 December 1980, p. 1.
129   King, *Whina*, pp. 235-236.
130   K. M. Hazlehurst, 'Ethnicity, Ideology and Social Drama: The Waitangi Day Incident 1991', in *The Urban Context: Ethnicity, Social Networks, and Situational Analysis*, eds. Alisdair Rogers and Steven Vertovec (Oxford: Berg, 1995), pp. 81-83.
131   Quote from Ben Tamatoa, in Staff Reporter, 'Waitangi Protesters on Disruption Course', *Auckland Star*, 5 February 1981, p. 2.
132   King, *Whina*, p. 236.
133   J. Cochrane, 'Media Treatment of Maori Issues', *Sites*, no. 21 (1990), p. 8.
134   'Police, Activists Brawl on Marae', *Auckland Star*, 6 February 1981, p. 1.
135   Ibid.
136   'Treaty Protest Cuts Little Ice', *Evening Post*, 7 February 1981, p. 4.

to further their own political ends'.[137] After the disruption of Cooper's and Latimer's investitures, several newspapers reported Prime Minister Robert Muldoon's view that the protesters were 'pakeha-led and trained and a disgrace to Maoridom'. He was quoted in one such article saying that they were 'given the customary and traditional privilege[s] of the marae' and had 'abused them in a pakeha-style protest'.[138] Such statements not only claimed to define Māori-ness, but presented the protesters as not being properly Māori, which had the effect of de-legitimising their protest.

In the weeks before the investitures took place, several press stories discussed Māori opinions of the honours and the possibility of protest on the day. The *Auckland Star* reported that a group of protesters intended to 'peacefully disrupt' the investitures, as they considered it 'wrong' for Cooper and Latimer 'to accept the honours'. The reporter observed that 'many' Māori did support Cooper and Latimer, seeing the awards as 'genuine honours'.[139] It thus presented Māori as divided (over the honours) rather than agreed (over issues such as land rights or the failure to honour the Treaty). Stories reporting the protests at Waitangi likewise often stressed the conflict between Māori. In its report, the *Auckland Star* quoted one of the protesters calling out to Cooper: 'once you accept that declaration you become part of the State'.[140] Rickard was later quoted recalling that protesters at the investiture 'chanted "sell-out"'.[141] Harawira, who had been part of the land march in 1975, also considered that the failure of leaders such as Cooper to support the campers after the march was a sell-out. She was quoted in 1982 saying: 'Hah! They both got knighthoods last year … The ones that get too close to the pakeha, they're the ones that turn on us'.[142] Cooper herself, however, saw the damehood in a different light. As she explained:

> They should have just stayed with what they were originally protesting about, the treaty. They didn't understand that I'd have more power when I'd been invested, more power to fight for them and for all the Maori people against the Government.[143]

Cooper thus saw no contradiction between accepting the honour for her past efforts, and continuing to say what she thought about government actions in the future. Indeed, she considered that the honour would increase her influence in future campaigns for Māori rights. She had, in fact, reportedly threatened during the land march to return her honours if the group's 'demands [were] not met'.[144]

---

137 Nairn and McCreanor, pp. 248-249.
138 'Pakeha-Led Hooligans a Disgrace to Maoridom', *Evening Post*, 7 February 1981, p. 4.
139 Staff Reporter, p. 2.
140 'Police, Activists Brawl on Marae', p. 1.
141 Welch, p. 29.
142 D. Awatere, 'Wāhine Ma Kōrerotia', *Broadsheet*, no. 101 (1982), p. 27.
143 King, *Whina*, p. 236.
144 S. Gray, 'If March Fails, Medals Returned', *New Zealand Herald*, 27 September 1975, section 1, p. 3.

Press reports which focused on the divide among Māori about the honours, rather than on the wide agreement about land rights or the Treaty, failed to see that the contest over honours was in some ways merely a contest about what might be the best way to achieve widely desired goals.

O'Donoghue was also subject to criticisms for accepting an award. When she accepted the Australian of the Year award in 1984, another Aboriginal woman, Mary Cooper, was quoted in the *Advertiser* referring to O'Donoghue as 'a Judas' and 'a traitor' because she had accepted 'a tin medal' and with it the 'bloodshed' that followed the arrival of white people in Australia. O'Donoghue was quoted in the article responding to these criticisms by saying that she had foreseen some criticism, but that 'I believe as a responsible citizen and a responsible Aboriginal I have a responsibility to bridge the gap between black and white in this country'. She was reported to have stated that 'she was confident her decision to accept was right because she was deemed to have earned it as an Aborigine and a woman'.[145] She was quoted in the *Australian Women's Weekly* saying:

> When I was asked to accept the award, I thought about Australia Day and its connotations but I also thought it would be a recognition of an Aboriginal and of a woman.

She added that 'I don't condone what has happened since 1788 but we are all here now and we have to solve our differences and live together as Australians'.[146] In a report in the *Advertiser* which commented that there was a 'danger of being perceived to have lost touch with the people back in the bush' for those who were recognised in the white world, O'Donoghue was quoted commenting that such 'criticism comes on occasions', but that 'if I wasn't working at the local, State and national level in the way I have done all these years, they (the communities) may not be in the position that they are in now'. The headline of the report was 'Why tears fell on Lois's happy day', and it presented Mary Cooper as having 'tarnished' the shine of the honour for O'Donoghue.[147] In press reports which focused on criticisms made of those who accepted honours, the representational divide between 'tame' and 'wild' was thus sometimes reinforced.

Feminism, Gender and Indigenous Activism

While Indigenous men involved in protest activity were often depicted in similar ways to those outlined above, particularly in relation to the divide between radical and moderate, there were clearly also ways in which representations of

---

145   B. Parsons, 'Lois Called "Judas" Over "White Award"', *Advertiser*, 29 January 1985, p. 18.
146   Lyle, p. 27.
147   Parsons, 'Why Tears Fell', p. 2.

Indigenous women known for their activism were shaped by ideas about (white) femininity. Moreover, although many activist women appeared to consider issues of Indigenous rights to have primacy over issues of gender, they were nonetheless aware of the social and political positions of women. Much of Cooper's most significant work before 1975 was done through a women's organisation, the MWWL, and her position as a former president of the organisation was often referenced in articles about her in the press later in her life. In its early years, as Szaszy suggested in an interview, the centre of the league's attention was 'the home – the children and mothers'.[148]

Cooper's work was never restricted to the concerns of women, however. Because there was 'no other national organisation' to advocate for Māori, the MWWL 'took up all issues to do with the Maori world' and thus 'went far beyond the original intention of the organisation'.[149] Ray, writing in the *New Zealand Listener* in 1975, asserted that Cooper 'typically, ... discouraged the league from becoming a gossip ground for women' and 'fashioned it into a powerful pressure group', thus implying that women's groups had a tendency to become tea-and-biscuits groups.[150] In *Te Ao Hou* in 1955, Cooper was described as having 'dominated many positions where one would expect to find a man at the helm'.[151] The *Evening Post* noted that she had, before her move to Auckland, 'never hesitated to trespass into recreations and sports normally preserved for males', citing as an example her presidency of a rugby union branch and her development of 'tactical plans' for matches.[152] Cooper herself reportedly once said that her father 'wanted me to be a boy so in a sense I became one; strong, a warrior, a soldier for God and for my people, our people'.[153] Thus she appeared to represent herself in masculine terms, as outside her gender. After her death it was reported that among other controversial views, she had 'called for women to stay home and look after their children rather than join protest marches'.[154] Representations of Cooper as mother and matriarch were interwoven with representations of her as taking the place of a man, leading from the front with unusual strength and determination.

In itself, Cooper's position of leadership had important gendered dimensions. As the *Dominion* phrased it after her death, perhaps recasting her as a champion of women's rights: 'on the marae she did not hesitate to break with tradition in speaking and taking the leadership role in tribal and racial affairs'.[155] In

---

148   S. Hawke, 'Mira Szaszy', *Broadsheet*, no. 114 (1983), p. 12.
149   Ibid.
150   Ray, p. 18.
151   Taylor, 'Whina Cooper', p. 17.
152   David, 'Leader of Maori March', p. 16.
153   McRae, 'Dame Whina', p. A9.
154   'Young Whina Swept Up in Maoridom', *New Zealand Herald*, 28 March 1994, p. 9.
155   '"Mother of Nation"', p. 7.

its editorial after her death, the *Evening Post* similarly observed that through 'sheer force of personality' she 'rose above the customary limitations faced by Maori women seeking to assert themselves on the marae' and along with Te Puea 'established beyond all doubt the right of women to take a leadership role in Maori society'.[156] Indeed, Cooper sometimes attracted criticism for being 'a woman taking what many Maoris regarded as a man's role, by standing up and speaking in public, and by taking the initiative on matters of Maori protocol'.[157] Her response to these criticisms, quoted by King in his biography of her, was that:

> I knew some people were wild at me. They said things like, "Oh that woman. She's taking the part of a man".

However, she said:

> I've never stopped the men doing anything. I've been waiting for years for men to put the world to rights, and they hadn't. Well – God gave me eyes to see, a head to think, a tongue to talk. Why not use them, why not share what I know?[158]

In the *New Zealand Listener* after Cooper's death, Welch suggested that 'at least some of the hostility towards her arose out of wounded male Maori pride, unused to such female effrontery'. He quoted a younger woman, Kathie Irwin, stating that 'the legacy she left young Maori women is absolutely tremendous' since 'she saw no barriers and just went for it, and her sex and her race were no reason for her not to be successful'.[159] Age may have assisted Cooper in taking a leadership position. Szaszy once observed that 'only when Maori women reached old age and were seen as no longer a threat to male domination, were they generally free from discrimination within Maori society, at least outside the marae forum', and that 'their age allows them to say things that really are listened to, even if they are not accepted'.[160] Ironically, age also played a part in representations that placed Cooper as a non-threatening matriarchal figure who did not speak in challenging ways.

For some women who became known for their campaigns for change, struggling for social justice for Māori or Aboriginal people sat easily alongside supporting feminist concerns, as mentioned in Chapter One. Interviewed by Virginia Myers for *Head and Shoulders*, a book about successful women, Szaszy recalled having become aware of the oppression of women as well as of Māori when she began

---

156 'Dame Whina', p. 8.

157 King, *Whina*, p. 180.

158 Ibid.

159 Welch, p. 32.

160 M. Szaszy, 'Opening My Mouth', in *Heading Nowhere in a Navy Blue Suit and Other Tales From the Feminist Revolution*, eds. S. Kedgley and M. Varnham (Wellington: Daphne Brasell, 1993), p. 83.

working in a government department, and having observed 'job discrimination' within the department.[161] Similarly, O'Shane told Susan Mitchell in an interview for *Tall Poppies* that she 'could never accept the secondary status of women' and that her parents 'used to tell me that I was just as capable of achieving as the boys'. A strong supporter of both Indigenous and women's rights, she observed that 'amongst Aboriginal women I do my best to raise their consciousness both as women and as Aboriginals. Within the Aboriginal movement, she stated, she had experienced issues similar to those that white women experienced: 'It was the same old line, "You can make the coffee but we'll make the decisions and speak to the media".[162] O'Shane received much publicity for her judgement in what became known as the Berlei case. Five women were charged with having defaced an advertising billboard which they considered sexist. Although O'Shane found the charges proved, she decided that convictions would not be recorded against the women. After giving the verdict, she made a statement about violence against women in society, which was *obiter dictum* (that is, it did not form part of the *ratio decidendi*, or reason for deciding). A number of commentators appeared to miss this critical point. O'Shane was severely criticised by some observers, and it was reported in the media that the Director of Public Prosecutions in NSW wanted the decision overturned. Although she had not overstepped her legal powers in making the decision, an article in the *Daily Telegraph Mirror* at the time of the case referred to her as a 'crusading magistrate' who 'looks beyond the law', implying that she had done so in this case.[163] O'Shane was thus represented as a radical and controversial figure in terms of feminist issues as well as in terms of Aboriginal issues.

Some prominent Indigenous women also spoke against sexism among Indigenous men or within cultural practices, although this was often a problematic issue given that Indigenous cultures were historically criticised by Europeans as being oppressive of women. Szaszy was a strong advocate of Māori women's concerns, as mentioned above, speaking in particular against the practice followed by some iwi (tribes) of not allowing women to speak upon the marae ātea (the courtyard in front of the wharenui, or meeting house, on the marae, on which visitors are welcomed and issues debated). In the interview with Myers, she noted that she thought 'the marae has become a symbol of the oppression of Maori women, because they are not allowed to speak on it', and remembered that she had 'experienced that I was not equal to men' on the marae, although her ability to speak in Māori was 'as good as if not better than that of the men I listened to'. Sensitive to the possible impact of making such concerns public, she recalled that for the most part she did not speak about these matters for twenty

---

161   Myers, pp. 238, 243.
162   S. Mitchell, *Tall Poppies: Nine Successful Australian Women Talk to Susan Mitchell* (Ringwood: Penguin, 1984), pp. 149, 153-154.
163   S. Williams, 'Pat Fights For Justice', *Daily Telegraph Mirror*, 17 February 1993, p. 11.

years, since 'with the resurgence of Maoritanga' she wished 'to give the culture a chance of survival without undermining it'. In 1982, she spoke on the position of Māori women at the MWWL conference. The speech did not receive much support, being criticised strongly by both men and women.[164]

Prominent non-Indigenous women who campaigned on feminist issues, like both male and female Indigenous activists, were often subject to stereotypical depictions and labelling in the media. This was particularly the case for those involved in the women's liberation movement, or those who were perceived as the radical fringe of the women's movement. Leading New Zealand feminist campaigner and author Sandra Coney once observed that 'male journalists' in the 1970s 'had a field day with women's liberation, lampooning, misreporting and showing such deliberate bias that there came a time when they were banned from reporting some women's events'.[165] Yet Szaszy appears not to have been represented as radical, as discussed above, despite being occasionally depicted as a determined fighter. Such a depiction often seemed to occur in relation to her advocacy of Māori women's rights, particularly speaking rights on the marae. After her death in 2001, a *Sunday Star-Times* obituary was headlined 'Champion for Rights of Maori Women'. The author, Tony Potter, wrote that Szaszy had had an 'often feisty career', giving as an example that she was 'regularly outspoken ... about the practice of not allowing women to speak on the marae'.[166] Her struggle for Māori women's rights, however, could be considered non-threatening because it was a struggle against Māori men, rather than against Pākehā men or Pākehā institutions. Thus, although her campaign for speaking rights for Māori women on the marae was in some ways a radical one, it was not usually portrayed as such in the mainstream media, which tended to treat Māori society as backward in this respect and Szaszy's views on the matter as simply common sense.

While some women were equally concerned with the causes of the feminist movement and those of Indigenous movements, others prioritised the latter. The women's liberation movement, Szaszy thought, 'seemed somewhat alien to most Maori women'.[167] Te Awekotuku suggested that 'so few Maori women join[ed] women's liberation in its earliest days' due to there being 'so many other consuming struggles', such as retaining land, language and culture.[168] Huata became involved in the feminist movement through 'a personal issue', her mother's 'right to equal pay'. She recalled:

164　Myers, pp. 242-243.

165　S. Coney, *Out of the Frying Pan: Inflammatory Writings 1972-89* (Auckland: Penguin, 1990), p. 66.

166　T. Potter, 'Champion for Rights of Maori Women', *Sunday Star-Times*, 23 December 2001, p. C5.

167　Szaszy, p. 80.

168　N. Te Awekōtuku, *Mana Wahine Maori: Selected Writings on Maori Women's Art, Culture and Politics* (Auckland: New Women's Press, 1991), pp. 10-11.

> I didn't see any conflict between the Maori and women's movements at first but as time went by this changed. I expected the feminist movement to be more understanding and supportive of Maori issues.

She added:

> I also felt that the conflict with men within the Maori movement was an issue Maori women had to sort out for themselves, and was not the business of Pakeha feminism.

For Huata personally, 'the Treaty was and still is the number one issue', and the right of women to speak on marae was not an issue she 'felt strongly about' since it was 'one of our rituals' and she felt 'sentimental about' these since they had been 'shovelled about enough'.[169] Depictions of Indigenous women involved in protest activity which focused upon their so-called radicalism could thus elide the ways in which they supported the upholding of traditional practices.

Tent Embassies Across the Tasman

Despite the persistent myth that New Zealand race relations were the best in any settler colony, and particularly better than in Australia, considerable parallels were evident across the Tasman both in relation to the surge in protest activity from the 1970s and in relation to the ways in which protesters were frequently represented in the media. At least one suggestion was made in the New Zealand press that those who camped outside Parliament following the land march were deliberately paralleling the Aboriginal tent embassy in Australia three years earlier. An editorial in the *New Zealand Herald* in 1975 commented that the protesters apparently thought that they were 'following the example of the Australian Aborigines who set up a tent at Parliament in Canberra', as well as of 'the American Indians who seized various points in the United States'. However, it continued, 'such actions have won little, if any, respect' and 'it would be far-fetched to claim that the position of these races closely resembles that of the Maoris', who have 'their own direct representatives in the Parliament they are picketing'.[170] In order to uphold the myth of superior race relations, the vocal and increasing protests of the 1970s and 1980s had to be downplayed or marginalised and could only be understood as the work of a few troublemakers. To acknowledge the grievances of the protesters would have been to disrupt the myth.

---

169 Huata, pp. 120-123.
170 'Harming Their Own Cause', *New Zealand Herald*, 16 October 1975, section 1, p. 6.

Creating a representational divide between radical and moderate allowed the appearance of liberalism in support of the grievances of the moderates, while denigrating the radicals as extreme. A focus on protest actions, personalities and divisions within the movement, deliberately or not, elided the ideas of protesters and masked the wide agreement which existed among many Māori people on issues surrounding the Treaty. Indeed, Nairn and McCreanor have suggested that blaming a small number of 'stirrers' in the late 1970s for the increase in protest activity implied that such 'unrest' was 'an unpleasant aberration in an otherwise harmonious history', and thus easily solved if the 'stirrers' would cease their disruptive behaviour. Depicting 'stirrers' as 'a minority that [was] extreme in its views and of questionable mental status' meant that 'their actions and arguments [could] be dismissed from serious consideration in any reasonable discussion of social issues', as well as allocating 'blame for the deteriorating state of race relations to stirrers' meaning that a solution to this could be suggested 'without considering the possibility that many Maori are genuinely disadvantaged'.[171]

If there was no myth of superior race relations to uphold in Australia, there was nevertheless an important myth holding that all could have a 'fair go', and protest was an uncomfortable reminder that it had not been so for some within the population. Whether a deliberate strategy or not, representing protesters as extreme and dangerous radicals who could therefore be dismissed rather than listened to, or as moderate voices who could be praised for their desire to live in unity, allowed an avoidance of issues and perhaps of guilt. If race relations were different across the Tasman, even if they were better, there was nevertheless a similar resistance to acknowledging the grievances of protesters and similar representations with similar effects of marginalisation. Much of this chapter has focused on the period from 1970-2000. Prior to that, few ripples were allowed to disturb the calm pools of the myth of superior race relations in New Zealand, or of the country of the fair go, in which Aboriginal people were to be assimilated into white Australian ways of life.

Conclusion

This chapter has explored representations of those Māori and Aboriginal women whose fame, or sometimes notoriety, stemmed from their political activism or leadership in struggles for social and political change. Unlike those famous for their sporting achievements or their work in the performing arts, these women were generally featured in the media in relation to political issues, and media profiles of them focused on political issues. Representations often split along a line between those constructed as moderate and those constructed as radical, and

---

171   Nairn and McCreanor, p. 254.

although such a representational divide was not limited to portrayals of women, gendered depictions were deeply implicated in the particular forms which it took. If radical activists were scary, radical women who also metaphorically transgressed gender boundaries were perhaps still more scary. Political movements, especially those seeking change, are never unanimous about either strategies or goals. As is evident in debates over honours, one critical but contested strategy for colonised peoples has been the creation of alliances with colonial authority. Media coverage which focused on divisions between Māori, as in relation to Cooper's becoming a dame, rather than on the wide agreement about land rights or the Treaty, failed to see that the divisions were largely about what might be the best way to achieve widely desired goals regarding Indigenous rights. In Australia, too, the construction of a divide between so-called radicals and moderates obscured the wide agreement among Aboriginal people over goals, if not over the means for achieving them. In some way, all protest may be considered a radical activity and, to this extent, all these women were represented as unusual in outspokenness and determination. The women whose representations were explored in this chapter were rarely represented as being assimilated. Yet the tendency for those constructed as moderates who worked through institutional structures to be contrasted with those whose methods of protest were more unorthodox and challenging, and the wave of celebration for Cooper as 'the Mother of the Nation', suggests that the nation's famous people were more easily celebrated if not threatening to that nation's conception of itself.

Chapter Six

Sandra Lee (later Lee-Vercoe), who was first elected to the New Zealand House of Representatives in 1993 as the member for Auckland Central, was once quoted stating that 'when you're a woman and you're a Maori and you're a conservationist you can sort of get the feeling that you're a three-time loser'. She sometimes felt, she said, as though she 'belong[ed] to every minority group which was ever invented'.[1] This chapter explores the experiences and print media representations of Māori and Aboriginal women who have entered the political system as Members of Parliament (MPs). The history of the participation of Māori and Aboriginal people in the parliamentary system in New Zealand and Australia highlights divergences between experiences of colonisation across the Tasman. Although colonisation differed only in degree, the legislative provision of separate representation for Māori within the parliamentary system was a substantial point of difference. Far fewer Aboriginal people have become MPs than have Māori people, and only much more recently, and hence this chapter is largely focused upon New Zealand. I focus particularly on Iriaka Rātana and Whetū Tirikātene-Sullivan, the first Māori women to occupy parliamentary seats in New Zealand, while also discussing the experiences and representations of the Māori women who followed them into the House. I explore both the ways in which these women were represented in the print media, and the ways in which they articulated their own roles within the Parliamentary system. Within parliamentary systems historically dominated by white men, Māori and Aboriginal women are only now beginning to become prominent figures in the decision-making bodies of the New Zealand and Australian nations.

Race, Gender and Parliamentary Representation

Indigenous engagements with the parliamentary system of government were in many ways vastly different across the Tasman during the nineteenth and twentieth centuries. Perhaps the most critical structural factor shaping these different histories was the creation and retention of separate Māori representation in the New Zealand House of Representatives. Although originally intended as a temporary measure, dedicated seats for Māori have existed within the New Zealand Parliament since 1867. A separate Māori electoral roll was established in 1949, and from 1975 Māori were able to choose to enrol on either the general or the Māori roll. When dedicated Māori seats were introduced, however, the

---

1 S. Nealon, 'Sandra Lee Under Scrutiny', *New Zealand Woman's Weekly*, 23 July 2001, p. 22.

measure was not an unambiguously enlightened and liberal one. Catherine Iorns Magallanes has argued that 'the system of separate Maori seats ... effectively began as a means to disenfranchise Maori'.[2] Ranginui Walker similarly contended that the measure 'was only a token gesture with deceptively manipulative purposes underlying it', pointing out that had the number of Maori seats been calculated in relation to population figures, Māori would have received many more seats than were established in 1867.[3] Instead, the *Māori Representation Act 1867* restricted the number of Māori seats to four, and this number was not increased for over a century. Until 1967 Māori (excepting so-called 'half-castes') were only able to stand for election in Māori seats, not in general ones.[4] Māori influence in Parliament was thus limited by the small number of Māori representatives. Further, since the number of general seats was revised upwards as the population grew while the number of Māori seats was not, and since the number of people opting for the Māori electoral roll had no impact on the number of Māori seats, this imbalance became greater over time.

During the twentieth century, the continued existence of the Māori seats was at times the subject of debate, and it remains so in the twenty-first century. Recently, the need for separate Māori seats was questioned because Māori were being elected to general seats in increasing numbers, particularly after New Zealand's switch to a Mixed Member Proportional (MMP) electoral system in 1996. New Zealand professor of law Philip Joseph argued that having dedicated seats, the number of which itself increased, as well as having Māori people getting elected to general seats 'amount[s] to reverse or indirect discrimination', which was contrary to human rights legislation prescribing a 'non-discrimination standard'.[5] The Royal Commission on the Electoral System (RCES) which reported in 1986 had supported the abolition of the Māori seats and the creation of a common electoral roll if MMP were adopted, but such a step was opposed by many Māori and the seats were preserved when the change to MMP occurred.[6] This shift in the electoral system nevertheless played an important part in increasing Māori representation in Parliament. The number of Māori seats was henceforth to be determined in relation to the number of voters on the Māori roll, which meant that the number of seats increased to five in 1996, six in 1999 and seven in 2002.

---

2   C. J. Iorns Magallanes, 'Indigenous Political Representation: Identified Parliamentary Seats as a Form of Indigenous Self-Determination', in *Unfinished Constitutional Business? Rethinking Indigenous Self-Determination*, ed. B. A. Hocking (Canberra: Aboriginal Studies Press, 2005), p. 110.

3   R. Walker, 'The Maori People: Their Political Development', in *New Zealand Politics in Perspective*, ed. H. Gold (Auckland: Longman Paul, 1992), p. 382.

4   Electoral Commission, 'Maori and the Vote', *Elections New Zealand*, updated 9 April 2005, accessed 19 January 2009, available from http://www.elections.org.nz/democracy/history/Maori-vote.html.

5   P. A. Joseph, 'The Maori Seats in Parliament', in *Te Oranga o te Iwi Maori: A Study of Maori Economic and Social Progress*, Working Paper 2 (Wellington: New Zealand Business Roundtable, 2008), p. 15.

6   B. Easton, *The Whimpering of the State: Policy After MMP* (Auckland: Auckland University Press, 1999), p. 36; Royal Commission on the Electoral System, *Report of the Royal Commission on the Electoral System: Towards a Better Democracy* (Wellington: V. R. Ward, 1986), pp. 81-113.

The proportional voting system of MMP created a more favourable environment for smaller parties, thus making specifically Māori parties more viable, and the inclusion of list MPs in Parliament meant that parties felt it increasingly necessary to put forward a list of candidates which was inclusive of women, Māori and other groups.[7] Moreover, since the MMP system gives each voter both a vote for a candidate in their electorate and a vote for the party that they wish to hold power, all parties have an increased need to attract Māori voters, who had been paid scant attention for much of the twentieth century, while the four Māori seats were safe Labour seats.[8] Following the shift to MMP, the number of Māori in Parliament did show a substantial increase, from six percent prior to the 1996 election to thirteen percent afterwards.[9]

At the same time, Māori have frequently sought political autonomy outside Pākehā institutions such as the parliamentary system. After the introduction of the Māori seats, as Walker has observed, Māori 'continued to pursue their own models of political development', two of the most important institutions being the Kīngitanga and the Kotahitanga (see Chapter One).[10] In 1886, King Tāwhiao sought government approval to institute a Māori council through which chiefs would 'administer Maori rights under the Treaty of Waitangi', and when denied this approval founded a council based in the Waikato, the Kauhanganui.[11] In the second half of the nineteenth century, Kotahitanga mo Te Tiriti o Waitangi (Unity under the Treaty of Waitangi), also referred to as the Māori Parliament (Pāremata Māori), was similarly an attempt to establish a chiefs' council in parallel to the Pākehā parliament which would administer Māori affairs.[12] Although not including Waikato, where the Kauhanganui had been instituted, the Kotahitanga was pan-tribal and represented more iwi (tribes) than earlier organisations had done.[13] Through this body, a Native Rights Bill was introduced into the House of Representatives in 1884. Rather than debating the bill, which would have given the Māori Parliament jurisdiction over Māori and the right to examine land issues, the Pākehā MPs 'simply walked out', meaning that there was no quorum.[14]

---

7 R. Mulgan, *Politics in New Zealand*, 2nd ed. (Auckland: Auckland University Press, 1997), pp. 64-65, 133-134. Under MMP, MPs are elected both through an electorate vote, thus entering parliament representing an electorate, and through a party vote whereby the proportion of the vote received by a party determines the number of seats that party receives, with seats not filled by electorate MPs being filled by those on a pre-announced party list.

8 Ibid., p. 133.

9 J. Karp, 'Members of Parliament and Representation', in *Proportional Representation on Trial: The 1999 New Zealand General Election and the Fate of MMP*, eds. J. Vowles et al. (Auckland: Auckland University Press, 2002), p. 131.

10 Walker, p. 383.

11 Ibid.; J. A. Williams, *Politics of the New Zealand Maori: Protest and Cooperation, 1891-1909* (Seattle and London: University of Washington Press, 1969), pp. 43-44.

12 Walker, p. 384.

13 M. H. Durie, 'Mana Maori Motuhake: The State of the Maori Nation', in *New Zealand Politics in Transition*, ed. R. Miller (Auckland: Oxford University Press, 1997), p. 373.

14 Ibid., pp. 373-374.

In the early twentieth century, the lead in Māori political activity shifted to a group of young, educated men, known as the Young Māori Party, who worked within the parliamentary system to achieve their goals.[15] These men were followed by a group of MPs linked to the Rātana movement, aligned with the Labour Party.[16] A national Māori Council was eventually established in 1962 under the National Government, but was simply to perform an advisory role in relation to Māori policy (see Chapter One).[17] The Māori Women's Welfare League (MWWL), in which Whina Cooper played such a prominent part, was also a national forum for Māori. In the late twentieth century, a group of young, urban activists re-ignited the focus on Māori autonomy, calling for the recognition of tino rangatiratanga (self-determination or sovereignty), which according to the Māori text of the Treaty had never been ceded.

In Australia, in both federal and state governments, far fewer Aboriginal people have held parliamentary office than have Māori people in New Zealand. By the end of the twentieth century, a mere two Aboriginal men had been elected to parliament at the federal level, Neville Bonner and Aden Ridgeway. Both men were senators, Bonner representing Queensland between 1971 and 1983, and Ridgeway representing New South Wales between 1999 and 2005. No Aboriginal women had been elected to either house of the Federal Parliament. At the state level, only eight Aboriginal men, and no women, were elected before the end of the twentieth century. Of these eight men, six were elected to the Northern Territory Legislative Assembly (reflecting the larger proportion of the population who identified as Aboriginal in the Territory), one to the Queensland Legislative Assembly and one to the Western Australian Legislative Assembly.[18]

In many parts of Australia, Aboriginal people were also denied the vote for considerably longer than were Māori. At Federation, the *Commonwealth Franchise Act* of 1902 denied Aboriginal people the vote unless they had been on the electoral roll before 1901, meaning that even in states which had previously granted Aboriginal people the right to vote, that right would not apply to those from such states who reached voting age after 1901.[19] Although such stark denial of the vote was later relaxed in some states, as well as for those who

---

15 Walker, pp. 385-386. Although it is widely used, however, such a description is erroneous, as these men did not form a political party. Walker, p. 386.

16 The prophet and leader Tahupōtiki Wiremu Rātana sought to control the four Māori seats in order to unify the Māori voice in Parliament, and after winning the first two seats in 1935 he allied the Rātana movement with the Labour Party, which had won that election. The other two Māori seats were won by Rātana candidates in 1938 and 1943, and the alliance between the movement and the Labour Party continued for several decades. Walker, p. 387.

17 Ibid., p. 388.

18 A booklet produced by the Australian Electoral Commission lists these men: Eric Deeral in Queensland, Ernie Bridge in Western Australia and John Ah Kit, Wesley Lanhupuy, Neville Perkins, Maurice Rioli, Stanley Tipiloura and Hyacinth Tungutalum in the Northern Territory. Australian Electoral Commission, *History of the Indigenous Vote* (Kingston: Australian Electoral Commission, 2006), pp. iv-1.

19 Ibid., p. 5.

had served in the military, it was not until the passage of amendments to the *Commonwealth Electoral Act* in 1962 that all Aboriginal people could vote in federal elections. Queensland was the last state to allow Aboriginal people to vote in state elections, in 1965.[20] In New Zealand, on the other hand, Māori men were never explicitly denied the franchise although many were in practice initially excluded from it as they did not meet individual property rights qualifications, and Māori women received the vote along with Pākehā women in 1893.[21] In debates on the possibility of federating with the Australian colonies at the turn of the nineteenth century, some opponents cited concerns that Māori would suffer disenfranchisement or that New Zealand's 'enlightened record' of race relations would be harmed through federation.[22] Regardless of the relative impact that such concerns had on the final decision over federation, the early inclusion of Māori into the political system appeared to play an important part in the widely held belief that New Zealand race relations were superior to those in other settler societies.

Given the small numbers of Aboriginal people elected to state and federal parliaments, the existence of dedicated Māori seats within the New Zealand Parliament was at times considered a model to follow in Australia. Doug Nicholls sent a request to the Prime Minister and other party leaders in Federal Parliament in 1949 that an Aboriginal person should be elected to the federal House of Representatives by an Aboriginal vote. In the federal Senate, Ridgeway was a supporter of the establishment of dedicated seats for Aboriginal people.[23] In the late twentieth century, several proposals were made for dedicated Aboriginal seats in the Commonwealth Parliament, and an inquiry was also held into the possibility of establishing dedicated seats for Aboriginal people in the Parliament of New South Wales (NSW).[24] Franca Arena gave a speech in the NSW Legislative Council in 1995 asking that the State Government 'consider legislation to ensure that a number of dedicated Aboriginal seats be set aside so that the voice of the first Australians can be heard in this Parliament'.[25] She commented upon the existence of dedicated seats for Māori in New Zealand, observing (wrongly) that Australia only gave Aboriginal people the vote in 1967 while Māori were able to

---

20 Ibid., pp. 5-8.

21 A. Sullivan, 'Maori Politics and Government Policies', in *New Zealand Politics in Transition*, ed. R. Miller (Auckland: Oxford University Press, 1997), p. 367.

22 J. Bennett, 'Redeeming the Imagination: A Trans-National History of Australia and Aotearoa/New Zealand, 1890-1944' (PhD thesis, University of Melbourne, 1997), p. 313.

23 A. Reilly, 'Dedicated Seats in the Federal Parliament for Indigenous Australians: The Theoretical Case and its Practical Possibility', *Balayi* 2, no. 1 (2001), pp. 82-83.

24 Ibid., p. 83. A report in Queensland in 2003 also considered the possibility of establishing dedicated Aboriginal seats in that state. K. Struthers, 'Hands on Parliament: Indigenous Peoples' Participation in Queensland's Democratic Processes', *Indigenous Law Bulletin* 5, no. 27 (2003), p. 4.

25 'Aboriginal Representation in Parliament', *Hansard and Papers*, Legislative Council, Parliament of New South Wales, updated 5 December 2007, accessed 16 July 2008, available from http://www.parliament.nsw. gov.au/prod/parlment/ hansart.nsf/V3Key/LC19950920009, p. 1131 (20 September 1995).

vote much earlier, and stating that 'the New Zealand example is in stark and vivid contrast to the way in which Australia has treated its Indigenous people'.[26] Such seats would, if tied to Aboriginal population figures, be fewer than is the case in New Zealand. As Alexander Reilly observed, for representation in Federal Parliament to 'mirror the population of Aboriginal people', the 148-member House of Representatives would include three Aboriginal members, given that Aboriginal people formed just over two percent of the Australian population in 1996. As there was one Aboriginal senator between 1971 and 1983 and one between 1999 and 2005 in a 76-member House, he noted that representation in the Senate was closer to proportional.[27] The issue of including dedicated seats in a parliamentary system is a complex one. While many Māori have argued strongly for the retention of the seats as providing guaranteed representation and as a symbolic recognition of the status of Māori as Treaty partners, others have supported their abolition as a flawed model that can sideline Māori concerns. Yet however the seats are viewed, their existence plays a large part in explaining the greater numerical representation of Māori in Parliament than of Aboriginal people in Australia.

Divergent histories are also evident across the Tasman in relation to women's inclusion in the parliamentary system. As previously mentioned, women became eligible to vote in New Zealand in 1893, and in Australia (white) women received the Commonwealth franchise in 1902, having already become eligible to vote in South Australia and Western Australia. As Patricia Grimshaw has shown, 'the politics of race' were ever present in debates surrounding the passage of women's suffrage in both Australia and New Zealand, as was also the case in Hawai'i.[28] Women were not eligible to stand for election to Parliament in New Zealand until 1919, following the passage of the *Women's Parliamentary Rights Act*, while in Australia women were granted the right to stand for election in the Commonwealth Parliament at the same time as the vote was achieved, as was also the case in South Australia. It took considerably longer in both countries, however, for women to be elected to office. New Zealand's first female MP was Elizabeth McCombs, elected for Lyttelton in 1933 through a by-election after the death of her husband James McCombs, who had held that seat until his death. At a federal level in Australia, the first women elected were (Dame) Enid Lyons in the House of Representatives and Dorothy Tangney in the Senate, both in 1943, although some few women had been elected to state parliaments before this. The numbers of women elected remained small in both Australia and New Zealand for much of the century, and were still well below what was proportionate to population figures at the turn of the twenty-first century.

---

26   Ibid., p. 1133.
27   Reilly, pp. 85-86.
28   P. Grimshaw, 'Settler Anxieties, Indigenous Peoples, and Women's Suffrage in the Colonies of Australia, New Zealand, and Hawai'i, 1888 to 1902', *Pacific Historical Review* 69, no. 4 (2000), p. 572.

Prevailing ideological constructions of gender, the pressures of family responsibilities, the nature of particular electoral systems, the aggressive atmosphere inside the debating chamber and difficulties in gaining selection, particularly in safe seats, have been among the obstacles to women's parliamentary representation identified by scholars, although many of these factors have decreased in importance over the course of the twentieth century.[29] Christine Fletcher, who was first elected in New Zealand in 1990, recalled those voting on the selection of a candidate asking her who would take care of her family, while Sonja Davies, who was first elected in 1987, remembered being referred to in derogatory terms such as 'granny', 'Auntie' and 'girlie' when she spoke in the House.[30] As in the case of Māori representation, MMP has arguably increased the number of women in Parliament in New Zealand, although it has not removed the 'underlying conditions creating the lack of political power'.[31] The Royal Commission on the Electoral System (RCES) considered that a shift to MMP would facilitate a rise in the number of women MPs, and indeed, in the first election held under MMP in 1996 the percentage of MPs who were women did rise, from twenty-one percent to twenty-nine percent.[32] In 1992, Rae Julian noted that New Zealand was ranked eleventh worldwide in relation to the 'representation of women in national legislative bodies', while Australia was twentieth, both being well ahead of the United States and the United Kingdom.[33] Since then, New Zealand has had two female Prime Ministers, and Australia its first female Prime Minister.

As might be expected, Australia and New Zealand differed regarding the representation of Indigenous women in parliament. The first Māori woman to become an MP was Iriaka Rātana, who entered Parliament in 1949 and served until 1969 in the seat for Western Māori. The second was Whetū Tirikātene-Sullivan, elected in a by-election in 1967 for the seat of Southern Māori. No Aboriginal woman entered either state or federal parliaments in Australia until Carol Martin was elected to the Western Australian Legislative Assembly in 2001. At the time of writing, no Aboriginal women have been elected to Federal Parliament in either house.

29 See for instance: R. Julian, 'Women: How Significant a Force?', in *New Zealand Politics in Perspective*, ed. H. Gold (Auckland: Longman Paul, 1992), pp. 403-405; E. McLeay, 'Rules, Values and Women's Representation in the New Zealand Parliament', in *Representing Women in Parliament: A Comparative Study*, eds. M. Sawer, M. Tremblay and L. Trimble (Abingdon: Routledge, 2006), p. 71-76; M. Wilson, 'Women and Politics', in *New Zealand Politics in Transition*, ed. R. Miller (Auckland: Oxford University Press, 1997), pp. 418-427.
30 A. Baysting, D. Campbell and M. Dagg, eds., *Making Policy Not Tea: Women in Parliament* (Auckland: Oxford University Press, 1993), pp. 18, 137-138.
31 Wilson, p. 426.
32 Ibid., pp. 423-424.
33 Julian, p. 401.

Māori women, particularly those of high birth, have always been able to play a significant part in leadership, although in some iwi women are only rarely recognised as leaders in their own right. Several women are known to have signed the Treaty of Waitangi, including Rangi Topeora and Kahe Te Rau o Te Rangi. Nonetheless, Māori women faced greater difficulties in being elected than did either Māori men or Pākehā women, and a similar situation appears to have faced Aboriginal women in Australia. Sandra Wallace argued that although 'most' women standing for election in New Zealand prior to the 1990s 'faced a certain degree of prejudice' due to their being female, the position of Māori women was 'very much worse' for they also met with 'a lot of traditional cultural opposition', at least among some iwi. Both Rehutai Maihi, who in 1935 was the first Māori woman to seek election, and Katariana Nutana, who stood in 1949, confronted 'the aversion of tribal elders who objected to women entering politics', as did Rātana in her successful bid in 1949.[34] Māori and Aboriginal women were also less likely to stand for election. Between 1919 and 1969 six Māori women stood for election to Parliament in the four Māori seats. Wallace pointed out that, if Rātana were not included (since she stood many times), a count of the number of campaigns in which Māori women sought election showed that Māori women 'were less likely than Pakeha women to seek election to Parliament, even in a Maori seat'.[35]

A number of the women whose experiences and media representations have been discussed in this book ran unsuccessfully for election during their lives. Standing as an independent, Whina Cooper placed sixth in the race for the seat of Northern Māori in 1963. Oodgeroo stood for election in Queensland twice, in the Greenslopes electorate in 1969 and for the seat of Redlands in 1983. In 1977, the *Sydney Morning Herald* reported that Shirley Smith (known as Mum Shirl) was 'the No 1 candidate on the NSW ticket of the new Uniting Party, representing Aborigines and migrants'. She was quoted stating that 'we ain't got no money to fight an election campaign and I don't stand a chance', but that 'someone has to show the young blacks and migrants how to do it, how to become leaders, because they haven't got much confidence'. She expressed her hope that 'if I show the way maybe a black will get into Parliament the next time'.[36]

What, then, enabled Rātana and Tirikātene-Sullivan to be successful in their bids for election? Mira Szaszy pointed to several important factors in an interview in 1986 when she said that:

---

34   S. Wallace, 'Powder-Power Politicians: New Zealand Women Parliamentary Candidates' (PhD thesis, University of Otago, 1992), pp. 310-312.
35   Ibid., pp. 79-80.
36   G. Williams, 'Redfern's "Mum" Shirl Takes Her People's Fight All the Way', *Sydney Morning Herald*, 5 December 1977, p. 7.

It was suggested I stand for Parliament, but it was difficult to get into the Maori seats which rarely changed hands. I also faced the problems of being a woman and having to oust a Ratana.[37]

As well as her position as a woman, she observed the strength of the alliance between the Rātana movement and the Labour Party, which made the four Māori seats safe Labour seats for a considerable period of time. Both Rātana and Tirikātene-Sullivan entered Parliament through this alliance, and it was not until Sandra Lee was elected in 1993 that another Māori woman was elected. Tirikātene-Sullivan herself was quoted in a documentary about women in politics commenting that it was 'interesting' that she and Rātana, the only two Māori women to have been elected at the time, 'came on the background of [the] Rātana movement, where women are accepted in every way'.[38] Unlike many women candidates, Māori or Pākehā, Rātana and Tirikātene-Sullivan thus gained selection in safe seats.

The Forerunners: Iriaka Rātana and Whetū Tirikātene-Sullivan

Born Iriaka Te Rio in 1905 at Hiruhārama, or Jerusalem, Iriaka Rātana moved to the Rātana pā (fortified village) in her teenage years and became part of the performing groups which travelled through New Zealand with the prophet and leader Tahupōtiki Wiremu Rātana. She was part of the concert party which travelled overseas with him in 1924. During this trip an attempt was made to place Māori grievances over breaches of the Treaty before King George V, who denied the group an audience. Becoming a second wife to Rātana, she was by 1939 'one of the most influential women leading the Ratana movement'.[39] After his death, she married again, to one of his younger sons, Matiu Rātana. He was elected as the MP for Western Māori in 1945, and became tumuaki (head or leader) of the Rātana church in 1946. Pregnant with her seventh child when her second husband died in 1949, she sought nomination as a candidate for his parliamentary seat. Although the Labour Party initially preferred a non-Rātana candidate rather than a woman with many children, she was endorsed as the Labour candidate after having already begun campaigning and having stated that she would otherwise stand as an independent, potentially taking with her the Rātana votes on which

---

37   V. Myers, *Head and Shoulders* (Auckland: Penguin, 1986), p. 248.
38   J. Rymer, dir., *Standing in the Sunshine: Power* (New Zealand: Isambard Productions, 1993).
39   A. Ballara, 'Ratana, Iriaka Matiu 1905-1981', *Dictionary of New Zealand Biography*, updated 7 April 2006, accessed 1 December 2006, available from http://www.dnzb.govt.nz/dnzb/default.asp?Find_Quick. asp?PersonEssay=5R7.

the Labour Party relied.[40] On 29 November 1949, she was elected with 6,317 more votes than her closest opponent.[41] In the 1957 election, she won her seat with the highest majority of any candidate, but did not seek a Cabinet position.[42] A foundation member of the MWWL, she received the OBE (Officer of the Order of the British Empire) in 1971, following her retirement from Parliament in 1969. She died at the age of seventy-six in 1981.

Figure 11: 'Iriaka Matiu Rātana', c. 1949. Tesla Studios. Mitchell-Anyon.

Photograph. F-55126-1/2. Alexander Turnbull Library, Wellington.

---

40   T. MacDonald, 'Iriaka Ratana', in *The Book of New Zealand Women/Ko Kui Ma Te Kaupapa*, eds. C. Macdonald, M. Penfold and B. Williams (Wellington: Bridget Williams, 1991), p. 548; J. McCallum, *Women in the House: Members of Parliament in New Zealand* ([Picton]: Cape Catley, 1993), pp. 59-60.
41   Ballara, 'Ratana, Iriaka'.
42   McCallum, p. 63; K. Sinclair, *Walter Nash* (Auckland: Auckland University Press, 1976), p. 304.

Rātana was elected during an era in which assimilation was a central framework for approaching Māori affairs. During her time in the House, she argued that Māori must reach a position of socio-economic equality with Pākehā, often urging that the Government assist Māori in this process of advancement. She stated in 1961 that 'no Maori would want to live in the old way we used to live when the Maori was uneducated'. Speaking about the migration of Māori to urban areas, she exhorted Māori to 'show even greater willingness to face up to this great challenge of adjustment', while also asking Pākehā for 'tolerance and understanding' and 'a continuing and increased readiness to extend the helping hand of friendliness and brotherhood'.[43] Although she sometimes spoke of there being unity between Māori and Pākehā, she also argued that Māori should be able to retain their cultural identity. In 1962 she told the House that 'as a Maori, I must preserve my identity'.[44] The Treaty of Waitangi remained a sacred document to Rātana. In addressing the Budget in 1956, she remarked briefly upon previous speakers' thoughts, before turning to 'a subject not mentioned in the Budget'. That subject, which she was 'sure the whole House will agree is important', was the Treaty of Waitangi. Rātana pointed out that 'had that treaty not been signed by representatives of our two peoples it is probable that we would not be meeting here in Parliament today, and there would be no such thing as the presentation of Budgets'.[45] Nearing the end of her career in Parliament in the 1960s, she began to speak more strongly of her disapproval of Government actions.[46] In 1961, she remarked in the House that New Zealand 'leads the world in telling other countries, and especially coloured peoples, how they should look after their people who need help and assistance within their own boundaries', and asked if 'our own house' was 'in order'. She answered that 'it is not', and stated that 'we should spend more time actively helping to clean up the factors which keep the Maori race in the position it is in today'.[47]

Whetū Tirikātene-Sullivan, as mentioned above, also had close ties to the Rātana movement. She was born at the Rātana pā in 1932, the daughter of (Sir) Eruera Tirikātene, who was elected as the MP for Southern Māori that same year. Narratives of her life sometimes tell that Tahupōtiki Wiremu Rātana prophesied before her birth that she would become a leader.[48] After finishing school, she worked in the public service in several secretarial posts before studying for a Bachelor of Arts at Victoria University of Wellington, which she finished in 1964. While at the Australian National University in Canberra writing a doctoral thesis on contemporary Māori politics, her father died and she was asked to stand

---

43   *New Zealand Parliamentary Debates*, House of Representatives, vol. 327, pp. 1701, 1703 (24 August 1961).
44   *New Zealand Parliamentary Debates*, House of Representatives, vol. 330, p. 274 (20 June 1962).
45   *New Zealand Parliamentary Debates*, House of Representatives, vol. 309, p. 1760 (12 September 1956).
46   Ballara, 'Ratana, Iriaka'.
47   *New Zealand Parliamentary Debates*, House of Representatives vol. 327, p. 1700 (24 August 1961).
48   For instance: K. Boon, *Whetu Tirikatene-Sullivan* (Wellington: Kotuku, 2006), p. 5; McCallum, p. 93.

for election in his seat. She was elected in 1967, then the youngest woman ever elected as an MP.[49] When the Labour Party came to power in 1972 she became the first Māori woman to hold Cabinet rank, holding the portfolios of Tourism and the Environment, as well as being Associate Minister of Social Welfare. Tirikātene-Sullivan was appointed to New Zealand's highest honour, the Order of New Zealand, in 1993, shortly before losing her seat in the 1996 election.

Figure 12: 'Whetū Tirikātene-Sullivan, 1984'.

Photograph. EP-Portraits of New Zealanders-Tirikātene-Sullivan, Whetū-02. Dominion Post Collection. Alexander Turnbull Library, Wellington, New Zealand.

---

49   McCallum, pp. 93, 95.

A Dubious Distinction? Being First

Like Rātana and Tirikātene-Sullivan, many of the famous Māori and Aboriginal women mentioned in this book were acclaimed as having achieved a 'first' at some point during their lives, or as being pathbreakers (see also Chapter Four). In some cases, the women were hailed as the first Indigenous woman, in others as the first Indigenous person and in still others as the first woman to reach a particular position or to achieve a particular success. As well as being the first Māori woman to hold a Cabinet post, Tirikātene-Sullivan was the first woman to give birth while a sitting MP when she had her first child in 1971, and her experiences in this 'unique position' were the main subject of a *New Zealand Woman's Weekly* article that year.[50] When she won election in 1993, Sandra Lee became the 'first woman Maori elected to a general seat' rather than a Māori one, as well as having been earlier in her career the 'first Maori woman to head a county council' in New Zealand.[51] National Party MP Georgina Te Heuheu was reportedly 'the first Māori woman to gain a law degree and [to] achieve admission to the High Court'.[52] In Australia, Linda Burney became the first Aboriginal person elected to the Parliament of New South Wales in 2003, and Marion Scrymgour became the first Aboriginal person to lead a government in Australia when she was made Acting Chief Minister of the Northern Territory in January 2008, having earlier become the first Aboriginal woman to hold Cabinet office. Prominent Māori and Aboriginal men might likewise be acclaimed for having broken barriers in this way. When Bonner was selected for the Senate in Queensland, the *Australian Women's Weekly* reported this under the headline 'Warm-hearted Mr. Bonner makes history', and the reporter observed that 'as an Aboriginal, Mr. Bonner made a historic breakthrough in Australian politics when he was selected' as he would be 'the first Aboriginal Member of any Australian Parliament'.[53] Many press reports throughout his career repeated this refrain, describing him as the 'first' or the 'only' Aboriginal parliamentarian.[54] Being acclaimed as having achieved a first in this way appeared to make a person more newsworthy, and those writing about well-known Māori or Aboriginal women in

50   C. Mackenzie, 'A Breath of Fresh Air in a World of Middle-Aged Men?', *New Zealand Woman's Weekly*, 8 February 1982, p. 4; C. Raymond, 'Baby Daughter Gives MP Unique Position in House', *New Zealand Woman's Weekly*, 13 September 1971, pp. 24-26.

51   'Lee's Magnetism Attracts a Fierce Loyalty', *Sunday Star-Times*, 13 November 1994, p. A4; L. Patrick and D. Heka, 'Post Parliament But Not Post Politics', *Tū Mai*, no. 36 (2002), p. 16.

52   'Meet the Country's 17 Māori MPs', *Kōkiri Paetae*, no. 25 (1999), p. 3.

53   M. Millar, 'Warm-Hearted Mr. Bonner Makes History', *Australian Women's Weekly*, 9 June 1971, p. 7.

54   See for example: 'Bonner Upset by Uncle Tom Label', *Australian*, 9 February 1972, p. 5; J. Cunningham, 'For Neville Bonner Life Wasn't Always Easy', *Sydney Morning Herald*, 14 July 1979, p. 10; T. Gilmour, 'Historic Start to New Thrust For Aborigines', *West Australian*, 10 December 1979, p. 7; '"Rebel" Bonner Back on a Familiar Trail', *Australian*, 30 December 1977, p. 2.

the media often listed any such claim to fame that a woman might have. A number of newspaper articles about Rātana's death in 1981, for instance, observed in the headline or first paragraph that she was the first Māori woman elected as an MP.[55]

For some women, achieving firsts was almost a way of life, with each new position breaking further barriers. A string of firsts was often attached to media narratives about Pat O'Shane. As Kate Legge wrote in the *Australian Magazine* in 1993, 'if she wasn't the first woman, she was the first Aborigine, and if she wasn't the first Aborigine, she was the first Aboriginal woman'.[56] Profiles of O'Shane frequently noted that she was the first Aboriginal woman to become a teacher in Queensland, the first Aboriginal person to gain a law degree and to gain a Master of Law degree, the first Aboriginal person to become a barrister, the first Aboriginal person and the first woman to head a government department at the state level, the first Aboriginal person or first Aboriginal woman to become a magistrate or the first Aboriginal person to be appointed the chancellor of a university.[57] Sometimes, fine-grained distinctions were required to make a claim that a woman had achieved a first. When Lorraine Liddle was admitted to the Bar, several newspapers considered her achievement newsworthy in large part because she was the 'Northern Territory's first Aboriginal barrister', the 'first Aboriginal barrister of the Northern Territory' or, as the *Sydney Morning Herald* carefully put it, 'understood to be the first Aborigine born in the Territory to practice law there'.[58] In the *New Zealand Woman's Weekly* in 1990, Sonya Haggie asserted that, unsurprisingly, Te Arikinui Dame Te Ātairangikaahu was 'the first New Zealand woman to become a monarch'.[59]

Continual repetition of the achievement of one or more firsts might have underlined the newsworthiness of the women being written about, but it was a distinction which could have potentially negative discursive effects (as demonstrated in the literary context in Chapter Four). A status as first made these women appear exceptional, and thus could also set them apart as difficult to emulate. Further, it could place them as having been successfully assimilated

55 For example: 'First Maori Woman MP Dies at 76', *Evening Post*, 22 December 1981, p. 30; 'Death of Mrs Ratana: Maoridom Loses One of its Greatest Figures', *Wanganui Chronicle*, 23 December 1981, p. 3.
56 K. Legge, 'In the Case of Pat O'Shane', *Australian Magazine*, 31 July 1993, p. 8.
57 See: S. Kirk, 'Women of the Eighties', *Sydney Morning Herald*, 19 December 1989, p. 16; B. Lagan, 'O'Shane Retires, Leaving Her Mark on Bench', *Sydney Morning Herald*, 30 April 1997, p. 3; 'Magistrate O'Shane "Couldn't Go On"', *Canberra Times*, 13 May 1997, p. 4; L. Nicholson, 'Pat Says Goodbye to "Bureaucracy of Suspicion"', *Daily Telegraph*, 23 July 1986, p. 3; M. Scott, 'O'Shane Savages "Elite Uni" Reforms', *Sydney Morning Herald*, 6 April 1995, p. 7; S. Williams, 'Pat Fights For Justice', *Daily Telegraph Mirror*, 17 February 1993, p. 11.
58 'Aboriginal Barrister For NT', *West Australian*, 15 February 1986, p. 25; P. Broekhuisje, 'Aboriginal Barrister Sets Out to Beat the Barriers of Prejudice', *Daily Telegraph*, 19 February 1986, p. 18; J. Friedlander, 'Taking the Rule of Law to Her People', *Australian*, 14 February 1986, p. 3; G. McManus, 'Lorraine – the Territory's First Black Barrister', *Australasian Post*, 14 August 1986, p. 14; 'NT Aboriginal First', *Sydney Morning Herald*, 16 April 1986, p. 6.
59 S. Haggie, 'Te Arikinui: "If You Don't Agree – Stay Home!"', *New Zealand Woman's Weekly*, 5 February 1990, p. 23.

into non-Indigenous institutions and systems of power, potentially serving to confirm that such assimilation was possible. If these women, or men, were first, others could be expected to follow. These figures could thus be read as implying that assimilation was occurring inevitably and successfully. The celebration of such achievements could also potentially mask the difficulties faced in reaching the positions in question, and could obscure how far out of the reach of many Indigenous people such successes lay. Lee was quoted in *Tū Mai* in 2002 saying that 'a lot of mainstream media thought that a Maori woman winning a general seat was just great', but she told them that 'far from being an achievement it was an indictment on the electoral system, that it kept Maori women out of parliament in that area of general seats for so long'.[60] Some months after being admitted to the Bar in 1986, Liddle was quoted in the *Age* observing that:

> I do not want to become an Aboriginal success story. That simply shifts attention away from the majority of Aboriginal people who, in a place like Alice Springs, lead desperate lives …

It would only be when there were 'hundreds of Aboriginal lawyers and doctors and other professionals' that 'things [would] really be different', she said.[61] Echoing the narratives of Indigenous women's success in sports and the performing arts discussed in Chapters Two and Three, media framings that represented a woman as a first could thus imply that barriers to success had been removed, and that similar achievement was open to all Indigenous people if they had the determination to succeed. Ironically, these narratives could place the women both as exceptional, and therefore newsworthy, and as representatives of their people's successful assimilation.

At the same time, the achievements of some of the first women to enter Parliament were potentially diminished by the assertion that they followed their male relatives into the position. Academics and other commentators have observed in many countries that a number of women entering parliamentary office were related to former male MPs who had usually died, particularly among the first women elected. The phenomenon is sometimes referred to as 'male equivalence', 'widow's succession' or 'the substitution factor'. In this analysis, 'the relationship between the woman and her husband or father is assumed to account for her entry into Parliament', and she was often presumed to be less than efficacious as an MP.[62] Both Rātana and Tirikātene-Sullivan succeeded male relatives in the

---

60   Patrick and Heka, p. 16.

61   M. Gawenda, 'Back Home to do Her Bit For Her People at Last', *Age*, 1 November 1986, Saturday Extra section, p. 4.

62   S. Wallace, '"Like Father, Like Daughter"? A Reassessment of the Concept of Male Equivalence in New Zealand', *Women's Studies Journal* 7, no. 1 (1991), p. 17.

seats they held, Rātana following her husband and Tirikātene-Sullivan following her father. Tirikātene-Sullivan was at times described as having taken over the seat of Southern Māori from her father.[63]

Wallace has challenged this understanding of the electoral success of women in Parliament in New Zealand. As she shows, while thirty-six women were elected in New Zealand prior to the 1993 election, only five were related to the person who had held the seat immediately prior to their election and two were 'closely related to former MPs'. While the potential public perception of these women as simply dutiful wives and daughters who were continuing their male relative's work might have assisted them in reaching the House, Wallace observed that they often had considerable political experience in their own right and were active and capable as MPs. As well, a number of male MPs in New Zealand had also been related to former MPs. Rātana's husband, for example, had himself followed his brother into the Western Māori seat.[64] Reiteration of the relationship a woman had with a previous MP could thus unfairly imply that she was less capable than were other MPs.

Representing Gender and Race in the Print Media

Like many non-Indigenous women who were elected to parliament, Rātana and Tirikātene-Sullivan sometimes faced obstacles because they were female, both before and after their election. In Rātana's case, the intense opposition to her decision to stand for election was reported in the press, and explicitly linked to her being Māori. When she began campaigning in 1949, several articles in Wellington's *Evening Post* reported criticism of her decision by Māori leaders. One story reported that Māori leaders from Waikato and Maniapoto iwi had opposed the selection of women as parliamentary candidates at a recent hui (meeting). Among those reported to have expressed such opposition was Te Puea Hērangi, who with other leaders was reported to have stated that it was against tradition for a woman to 'be at the prow of a canoe' and that it was not 'fitting for a woman to lead a war party'. Te Puea had reportedly been asked to stand herself for the Western Māori seat in 1946, and had 'declined the invitation on principle'.[65] Speaking at a meeting held by Rātana, Tohuroa Parata, who was identified as 'one of the leading chiefs', reportedly said that 'in standing [Rātana] had broken the custom of her ancestors, and that he would not vote for a woman',

63   See for instance: S. Kilroy, 'Political Dynasty Ends After 64 Years', *Dominion*, 25 October 1996, p. 1; K. Scherer, 'Leaving with "Grace, Serenity"', *Evening Post*, 25 October 1996, p. 1.
64   Wallace, '"Like Father, Like Daughter"?', pp. 18-26.
65   'Maori Leaders … Unwilling to Follow a Woman', *Evening Post*, 26 November 1949, p. 8.

as well as that her 'place was in the home'.[66] Another article observed that the National Party candidate for the seat, Hoeroa Marumaru, had been reminded by Māori leaders of a saying recommending that 'if the hen crows, screw its neck!'[67]

Rātana herself seems to have responded spiritedly to these criticisms. At the meeting at which Parata censured her, she reportedly noted that she had been criticised for seeking election when she had six children, and was quoted saying that she wished she had more. She was also quoted as having said that she had been asked whether she 'would be able to stand up to all the clever, well-educated men' in Parliament, to which she responded that 'there is a saying that women have long and broad tongues', and that 'the Speaker will find it very difficult to keep me in order when my tongue gets under way!'[68] In focusing upon opposition to Rātana's election that stemmed from Māori custom, press reports elided the difficulties Pākehā women also faced in being selected as candidates.

At the time of Rātana's death in 1981, media coverage displayed a more explicit focus on Māori custom as backward in its approach to gender relations. Koro Wetere, then MP for Western Māori, was quoted in the *Evening Post* stating that Rātana had 'effectively broke[n] down the barriers in Māori circles to having a woman in power', which he described as having been 'truly against the customs and traditions of the time'.[69] The path-breaking nature of her achievement was thus recognised by Māori leaders as well as by those writing of her in the press. However, some representations of her as a path-breaker presented her in ways which reflected the social and political context of the late 1970s and early 1980s. In a particularly striking example, an article in the *Wanganui Chronicle* observed that in following her husband into office and holding the seat for twenty years, Rātana 'inadvertently became an early "women's libber"' because she 'was forced to overcome cultural and traditional barriers against a woman holding a position of power and authority above men in Maori circles'.[70] This depiction re-imagined her as a feminist activist, transforming the epithet of 'women's libber' into a positive description by emphasising that she was 'forced' to be so in order to surmount the obstacles posed by Māori custom. Rātana would almost certainly have never considered herself in this way, and nor would she have placed herself in opposition to Māori tikanga (custom). Indeed, the writer of the article noted that it was through 'her thorough grounding in all aspects of Maoritanga [culture and beliefs]', as well as her work habits and her 'genuine concern for the welfare of all people', that she eventually 'won the respect of those who initially opposed her place in the House'.[71] Such reference to her as having broken barriers relating

---

66 'Chief Says … Maori Custom Broken', *Evening Post*, 28 November 1949, p. 8.
67 '"If the Hen Crows, Screw Its Neck!"', *Evening Post*, 28 November 1949, p. 8.
68 'Chief Says', p. 8.
69 'First Maori Woman MP Dies', p. 30.
70 'Last Respects Paid to Mrs Iriaka Ratana', *Wanganui Chronicle*, 29 December 1981, p. 2.
71 Ibid.

to Māori tradition failed to acknowledge the obstacles which also faced Pākehā women seeking to become MPs, or the small number who had achieved that goal. These representations could thus imply that Māori culture was the problem, obscuring Pākehā cultural opposition to women in power.

In common with Pākehā women who entered Parliament as MPs, Māori women MPs were often represented in gendered frames in the media. Many scholars have examined media depictions of women in politics or as world leaders, identifying gendered patterns of representation such as a greater emphasis upon their domestic lives than upon those of men in similar positions, a focus upon their physical appearance, or the use of 'common gendered frames' in stories about them.[72] Māori women might be represented in these ways as well, particularly in women's magazines. Shortly after Tirikātene-Sullivan was elected to Parliament, the *New Zealand Woman's Weekly* profiled her in 1968 under the headline 'A "Shining Star" of Maori Womanhood'. She was described as appearing 'fragile', having 'a slight figure and finely-boned, aristocratic Maori features' and wearing her 'thick dark hair … girlishly long'.[73] A 1973 article after she became the Minister of Tourism described her as 'this woman with the flowing black hair and colourful clothes, Polynesian-patterned', who might 'become a striking ambassador for New Zealand tourism'.[74] Reminiscent of the way in which Maureen Kingi was represented as an ambassador for New Zealand in her role as Miss New Zealand (see Chapter Three), this comment implied that Tirikātene-Sullivan would be a passive figure whose looks were at least as crucial to her job as her deeds. Some years later, Alliance MP Sandra Lee's physical appearance was mentioned a number of times in articles about her. In 1994, when she replaced Jim Anderton as leader of the Alliance party, Karyn Scherer described her in the *Evening Post* as 'a glamorous 42-year-old Maori grandmother with a trademark whisper and a lot of hair'.[75] Ruth Laugesen wrote in the *Sunday Star-Times* in 2000 that Lee was '48, a grandmother and one of parliament's most glamorous women'.[76] As was noted in *Mana* in 1996, Lee thus had 'a consistently high profile because of her glamorous grandma image' as well as because of 'her advocacy of issues … and her prominent role in the Alliance'.[77]

Profiles of Māori women MPs in newspapers and magazines were often clearly shaped by gendered frameworks, frequently placing a greater emphasis on

---

72 See for example: C. Jenkins, 'The More Things Change: Women, Politics and the Press in Australia', *Ejournalist* 2, no. 1 (2002), accessed 27 February 2009, available from http://ejournalist.com.au/v2n1/cathy. pdf; P. Norris, 'Women Leaders Worldwide: A Splash of Color in the Photo Op', in *Women, Media, and Politics*, ed. P. Norris (New York: Oxford University Press, 1997), p. 164.

73 L. Newick, 'A "Shining Star" of Maori Womanhood', *New Zealand Woman's Weekly*, 22 April 1968, p. 8. The article translated her name, Whetū Mārama, as 'Shining Star'. Newick, p. 8.

74 J. Leigh, 'Minister as Salesman of New Zealand', *Auckland Star*, 17 February 1973, p. 5.

75 K. Scherer, 'Party on a Platter: A Big Challenge for Sandra Lee', *Evening Post*, 12 November 1994, p. 13.

76 R. Laugesen, 'Alliance MP Gives Rivals No Lee-Way', *Sunday Star-Times*, 13 August 2000, p. A11.

77 P. Bensemann, W. Harawira and D. Fox, 'Rambo or Rangatira?', *Mana*, no. 13 (1996), p. 24.

domestic details and personality traits than might be expected in similar pieces about male MPs, whether Māori or Pākehā. This was particularly the case in profiles published in women's magazines, a genre of publication within which male MPs were in any case less likely to be profiled. In articles collected from women's magazines, most published during the 1960s and 1970s, nearly two-thirds of the accompanying images depicted Tirikātene-Sullivan with her husband or children, or in a domestic setting. One article which appeared in the *New Zealand Woman's Weekly* in 1972 described Tirikātene-Sullivan as a 'busy Maori MP and mother', and focused upon her efforts in fashion design rather than upon her work as an MP.[78] In such profiles, Tirikātene-Sullivan was sometimes asked about how she would or did combine motherhood with her parliamentary role. In the *New Zealand Woman's Weekly* in 1968, she was asked whether or not her work in Parliament might 'mean postponing parenthood', to which she was quoted responding practically that she and her husband would simply 'need a nanny to help with [the] care' of any children she had while an MP.[79] After her first child was born, an article in the *New Zealand Woman's Weekly* reported in detail on the organisation of her domestic routine. Tirikātene-Sullivan's new daughter had travelled with her mother and been taken along to Parliament, and was later 'cared for within the ages-old Polynesian concept of the extended family'.[80] It is difficult to imagine such emphasis being placed on a male MP's role as a father and domestic arrangements.

Māori women who became MPs were also sometimes described in terms of their supposedly feminine personality traits. Profiling Tirikātene-Sullivan in the *Auckland Star* in 1973, after she had become Minister of Tourism, Jack Leigh placed considerable emphasis on her femininity. Although she had 'not yet made her impact as Minister of Tourism', he wrote, her 'style' was becoming evident, and that style was 'something feminine and artistic – a feat of personality rather than performance, so far'. Her intention to 'redecorate' in the hotels owned by the Tourist Hotel Corporation was described as 'the woman's touch' on the portfolio. A visit she had made to Fiji was said to have 'revealed … the main axis of her personality', and she was described as 'sensitive', 'soft-spoken' and 'carr[ying] her love for her family around as part of her whole aura, her personality'. Such traits were, Leigh wrote, 'splendid qualities in a woman, you may think, but hardly essential to one of Cabinet rank'.[81]

A profile of Lee by Laugesen over twenty years later, in 1995, also made reference to femininity in this way. Although Laugesen appeared supportive of Lee, and recognised that she would be 'battling to create a new female archetype

---

78 S. Cornwell, 'MP Finds Empathy With Fashion-Art', *New Zealand Woman's Weekly*, 11 December 1972, p. 8.
79 Newick, p. 10.
80 Raymond, p. 24.
81 Leigh, p. 5.

of leadership in the minds of the public', she argued that Lee might have more success because she was seen to be different from fellow MPs Helen Clark, Ruth Richardson and Jenny Shipley, all of whom were 'seen by many as cold, hard and without emotion'. Laugesen suggested that Lee's 'occasionally tremulous voice, waves of long black hair and classical features' made her 'a very feminine politician', and that she might therefore not provoke the 'hostility in male voters' that other political women had done.[82] Despite the significant shifts in social and political context which had occurred between Tirikātene-Sullivan's appointment as a Minister and Lee's accession to the leadership of the Alliance, similar discourses about what constituted femininity continued to be echoed in representations of these women in the media.

Even in articles which supported the election of larger numbers of women to Parliament, such gendered frameworks of representation could reappear. In her profile of Tirikātene-Sullivan in the *New Zealand Woman's Weekly* in 1968, Leah Newick wrote that 'youthful Mrs Whetu Tirikatene-Sullivan' spoke 'sound sense in a soft voice' and was 'herself a refutation of the rather tedious notion that a pretty head shouldn't bother itself about politics'.[83] Most of the pictures accompanying the article showed Tirikātene-Sullivan in situations outside her parliamentary role, including one in which she appeared to be in her kitchen cooking while her husband sat at the table and one in which she was shown dressed in a glamorous dress and applying perfume before a mirror. One picture which showed her in her parliamentary role depicted her standing beside a desk with a basket of papers, appearing a secretary as much as an MP. On the cover of the magazine, she was pictured sitting in a subordinate position on the floor beside her husband, who sat above her in a chair. In another article in the *New Zealand Woman's Weekly* in 1982, Catharine Mackenzie profiled the eight women then in Parliament. A significant proportion of the piece focused on how the women managed their lives and parenthood without being supported by a wife at home. For Tirikātene-Sullivan and her husband, Mackenzie stated, 'family life is paramount', and she described how Tirikātene-Sullivan dealt with the challenge of trying to be both mother and MP.[84] Although the article appeared to consider the women MPs as able to be advocates on women's issues in Parliament, little attention was paid to their ideas on particular issues. In women's magazines in particular, Māori women MPs were thus portrayed in similarly domestic ways to those in which Pākehā women MPs were frequently depicted.

At other times, however, gender was largely irrelevant to representations of Māori women in Parliament, their position as women MPs giving way to their position as Māori MPs. One permutation of such representations was the depiction of the

---

82   R. Laugesen, 'On a Lee Shore', *Dominion*, 2 February 1995, p. 9.
83   Newick, p. 8.
84   Mackenzie, p. 4.

women as, like male Māori MPs, advocates for Māori people in Parliament (see below). Representations of Māori women MPs in the media, like those of men, could also fall into similar binaries as those of activist women (see Chapter Five), a distinction being drawn between those depicted as assimilated or moderate and those depicted as radical. In the late 1960s and early 1970s, Tirikātene-Sullivan was occasionally represented as an exemplar of integration. A 1967 profile of her in *University Focus* magazine, the magazine of the New Zealand University Students' Association, took this approach. Titled 'the "new" Maori', it began by asserting that 'physically, culturally, and educationally, the 32 year old new member for Southern Maori represents this generation's most triumphant synthesis of Maori and European societies'. Describing Tirikātene-Sullivan as having been 'immersed in Maori culture from childhood' and as fluent in the Māori language, the author[s] claimed that her 'ascendancy in politics represents a unique blending of Maoridom, youth, femininity and intellectual attainment'. She was described as 'a vital, intelligent woman of stature' and as 'a repository of the highest attainment of two races'. Tirikātene-Sullivan was reported to believe that the integration of Māori and Pākehā was achieved through intermarriage, and the article was accompanied by small pictures of her and her Australian husband captioned 'Intermarriage ...' and '...brings integration'.[85] An article in 1974 in the *New Zealand Woman's Weekly* also represented Tirikātene-Sullivan as an exemplar of integration. Reminiscing about the Royal Tour of 1953-1954, Dorothy Moses wrote that when Tirikātene-Sullivan performed Māori song with a group at the end of the tour, 'it seemed ... a fitting climax to Her Majesty's visit that, in her last few moments in New Zealand, she should see combined in one slim girl capable, modern secretaryship and traditional Maori symbolism'.[86] Such a combination of beauty, exoticism and modernity had been similarly applauded in Maureen Kingi and Kiri Te Kanawa in the 1960s (see Chapter Three). It was a racialised and gendered depiction which emphasised that New Zealand was a place of harmony, where Māori and Pākehā were one people.

By the end of the twentieth century, following the upsurge in Māori activism of the 1970s and 1980s, such portrayals had been replaced by oppositional representations of Māori women MPs as conservatives or radicals. Occasionally, Tirikātene-Sullivan had been depicted as holding radical views in the 1970s. Leigh described her in the *Auckland Star* in 1973 as 'a woman with a social conscience who is outspoken on racial matters'. In the interview which followed, Leigh asked her about her 'standpoint on the subject of race – for which she has reserved some of her strongest public statements'. Tirikātene-Sullivan responded that she believed 'in the priority of the individual as an individual, irrespective of race, sex, creed and class' and had therefore 'expressed myself

---

85 'The "New" Maori', *University Focus*, June-July 1967, pp. 3-4.
86 D. Moses, 'Unique Meeting of Families in Government House', *New Zealand Woman's Weekly*, 21 January 1974, p. 4.

because of my strong convictions' when someone was 'discriminated against purely on the grounds of their ethnic origin'. The media had depicted her as 'a bit of a radical', she continued, but such a depiction did not 'represent me as I believe I am'; she preferred to 'hope' that she could be an 'interpreter between Maori and Pakeha'.[87] By the mid-1980s, Tirikātene-Sullivan was sometimes portrayed as holding moderate views in contrast to those of younger, urban activists. An article in the *New Zealand Herald* in 1986 about her efforts to gain greater official recognition for the Māori language stated that 'hers has not been a high-profile campaign', implicitly contrasting it with the campaigns of others. Instead, she was credited with 'spirited behind-the-scenes lobbying' which had 'laid much of the groundwork for the introduction of legislation to make Maori an official language of New Zealand'. Tirikātene-Sullivan was quoted saying that she had not been 'a high-profile person' and that much of her work had been 'behind the scenes'.[88] In another article, she was quoted explaining that this low profile was because she led a busy life and there was 'simply no spare time to devote to public relations'.[89] Shortly before she lost her seat in 1996, an article in the Christchurch *Press* in 1994 referred to Tirikātene-Sullivan and the three other Māori MPs as 'aging MPs who [had] increasingly lost touch with the emerging forces in Maoridom'. Tirikātene-Sullivan was described as one of the 'older, conservative and tribally loyal' Māori MPs, and as 'a dignified elderly woman with longstanding and deep links among Maoridom's traditional, tribal leaders'.[90]

Following the 1996 election, a number of new Māori MPs entered the House, both in the Māori seats and in general electorate seats. The familiar binary opposition between moderate and radical continued to be played out in some representations of these new MPs in the media. To some degree, this binary was evident in the brief labels that were applied to the new MPs in articles surveying the election results in 1996. While the *Evening Post* described National Party MP Georgina Te Heuheu as a 'Waitangi Tribunal member' and Labour MP Nanaia Mahuta as a 'Tainui Trust Board researcher', Donna Awatere Huata was termed among other things 'a former Maori radical', and Tariana Turia, who had been part of the occupation of the Moutoa Gardens (Pākaitore) in 1995, was referred to as a 'young radical'.[91] Male Māori MPs were also subject to such labelling, with new Labour MP Joe Hawke, who had been a leader in the Bastion Point protest,

---

87 Leigh, p. 5.
88 D. Millar, 'Long Crusade to Revive Maori Tongue', *New Zealand Herald*, 4 June 1986, section 2, p. 1.
89 S. Scott, 'A Challenge for Southern Maori', *Evening Post*, 7 March 1990, p. 7.
90 O. Riddell, 'Labour Row With Maori MP Looks Like a Sign of a Dying Relationship', *Press*, 15 February 1994, p. 11.
91 The Moutoa Gardens in Wanganui were occupied by protesters for seventy-nine days in 1995. The land, which was the subject of a Treaty claim, was said to have been the site of a pā and place of trade which had been reserved for Māori from the purchase of Wanganui.

described as a 'veteran activist'.[92] The *Dominion* referred to these women in similar terms, although providing more detail. Te Heuheu was described as 'the first Māori woman to get a law degree', and also as a member of the Waitangi Tribunal and Waikato University Council, while Mahuta was labelled a 'niece of Tainui negotiator Sir Robert Mahuta, and a Maori studies researcher'. Huata was termed a 'former Maori radical' who had begun a 'consultancy business offering executives bicultural skills programmes', and Turia was described as a 'Maori radical' who had been 'one of the leaders of the Moutua Gardens occupation'.[93]

Some press articles also displayed a significant level of discomfort with the presence of so-called radicals in Parliament. Press coverage about Turia, in particular, often appeared to consider her a dangerous radical, especially when she became involved in controversial incidents. One *New Zealand Herald* article in 1997 referred to her as 'the controversial Labour Maori MP', while another in 2000 termed her a 'radical minister' and stated that she was 'now beating her anti-colonialist drum from the Beehive'.[94] Writing in the *Sunday Star-Times* in 2000, Anthony Hubbard described her as 'a doting grandmother with a gift for causing offence' and stated that since she was 'a genuine radical in a mainstream party' she was 'doomed to dwell in hot water'.[95] Such a concern was also occasionally evident in relation to Lee, both in relation to her affiliation with a specifically Māori party and her environmentalist stance.[96] She was described in the *Evening Post* in 1994 as having a 'fiesty and uncompromising stance on a wide range of issues', and was herself said to be 'wary of those who use her Mana Motuhake affiliations to label her as a Maori extremist'.[97]

Representing Gender and Race in the House

As is implied in these media depictions, both male and female Māori MPs were often understood as being advocates for Māoridom as a whole in their parliamentary position. This point illustrates once again the multivalent nature of the concept of representation. The preceding section of the chapter emphasised the ways in which Māori women MPs were represented by others in the media; this section focuses upon the ways in which they acted as and understood themselves to be representatives of Māori within Parliament. Many Māori

---

92 K. Scherer, 'MMP Delivers at Least 15 Maori MPs', *Evening Post*, 14 October 1996, p. 12.

93 '45 First-Timers in Parliament', *Dominion*, 14 October 1996, p. 2.

94 P. Herbert, 'Turia Free to Speak Out: Labour's Maori MPs to Ensure "Co-Ordination"', *New Zealand Herald*, 11 June 1997, p. A5; A. Young, 'Radical Minister Turia Has Space to Beat Her Drum', *New Zealand Herald*, 26 August 2000, p. A5. The Beehive is a popular name for the executive wing of the New Zealand parliamentary buildings.

95 A. Hubbard, 'Turia Never Far From Trouble', *Sunday Star-Times*, 27 August 2000, p. C5.

96 Lee was a member of Mana Māori Motuhake, one of the small parties which formed the Alliance.

97 Scherer, 'Party on a Platter', p. 14.

women did articulate their own view of their parliamentary role in this way, frequently considering themselves to be advocates for Māori in the House, and sometimes focusing upon Māori issues in their work as MPs.

While MP for Western Māori, Rātana worked hard on issues of concern to Māori. A member of the Māori Affairs Committee, she also worked with others to achieve the *Māori Vested Lands Administration Act 1954*, to protect ancestral land, and to improve living conditions at the Rātana pa.[98] Rātana did not speak often in the House, and when she did, she often focused upon issues of Māori welfare. In her maiden speech, given in 1950, she concentrated upon matters such as housing, health and land.[99] In focusing on the needs of Māori throughout New Zealand rather than on the specificities of her electorate or the state of the entire country, hers was a somewhat unusual maiden speech.[100] For Rātana, giving this first speech was 'an ordeal'. She told the House in 1961 that it was 'not easy to come here with a Maori mind and a Maori understanding, and try to express one's views, as a Maori, in your language'.[101] Three years later, during the Budget debate, Rātana observed that she would 'not make any attempt to go far afield in … money matters and other subjects', but would instead discuss 'matters that are bound more closely to the well-being of the Maori people'.[102]

Tirikātene-Sullivan, who also held a Māori seat, likewise often focused upon matters of concern to Māori. Like Rātana's, her maiden speech in 1967 dealt with the situation of Māori throughout New Zealand. She expressed her intention to 'address my first remarks in this House' to 'the disparity in the socio-economic levels … between Maori and pakeha New Zealanders'. Nearing the end of the speech, she stated that there existed 'a glaring disparity between the apparently harmonious situation in New Zealand's race relations and the real socio-economic levels', warning that if New Zealanders 'continue to rest on the laurels of past achievements' the country's 'hard-won reputation' for racial harmony would be lost.[103] She was quoted in a 1993 publication saying that 'I am here in Parliament as a Māori advocate', and would act as such for 'all the Māori people, irrespective of tribe'.[104]

Many Māori MPs who did not hold specifically Māori seats, both men and women, nonetheless also considered themselves to have a role within Parliament as advocates for Māori. Te Heuheu was quoted in *Mana* in 2004 explaining that she had entered Parliament as a member of the conservative National

---

98   Ballara, 'Ratana, Iriaka'; McCallum, pp. 62, 66.

99   *New Zealand Parliamentary Debates*, House of Representatives, vol. 289, pp. 335-337 (12 July 1950).

100 P. Horn, M. Leniston and P. Lewis, 'The Maiden Speeches of New Zealand Women Members of Parliament', *Political Science* 35, no. 2 (1983), p. 256.

101 *New Zealand Parliamentary Debates*, House of Representatives, vol. 326, p. 406 (11 July 1961).

102 *New Zealand Parliamentary Debates*, House of Representatives, vol. 300, p. 1386 (22 September 1953).

103 *New Zealand Parliamentary Debates*, House of Representatives, vol. 350, pp. 548, 551 (16 May 1967).

104 Baysting, Campbell and Dagg, eds., p. 9.

Party because she thought it 'important that Maori perspectives are present in every party that aspires to wield power in Parliament'. It was, she said, 'just not acceptable in Aotearoa New Zealand today that a main political party should not have immediate access to Maori perspectives'.[105] She thus placed herself as a mouthpiece for Māori concerns and viewpoints within the National Party.

However, Tirikātene-Sullivan voiced her doubts after her retirement about the possibility of Māori MPs being able to advocate for Māori concerns if elected to general electorates. Commenting on the formation of the Māori Party in 2004, she observed that the pressure on Georgina Beyer as an MP for a general electorate to support the Government over the foreshore and seabed issue rather than to 'vote as she wanted to, as a Maori' had 'refuted my hopes ... that a Maori could speak for Maori as an MP for a general electorate'.[106] Perhaps because of the tendency for Māori MPs to place themselves as advocates for Māori interests, Lee told *Tū Mai* in 2002 that it was 'very difficult being a Maori politician' since 'opposition politicians can accuse Maori politicians more easily of some kind of bias or advocacy'.[107] In Australia, after his parliamentary career was over, Bonner similarly spoke of being an advocate for Aboriginal concerns while in the Senate, though also hinting at the difficulties of doing so from within a conservative party. A Liberal Senator for Queensland, he detailed how he had sought to 'consolidate' his position and 'present my bonafides as a senator representing all people' before beginning to promote Aboriginal interests.[108]

At the same time, Indigenous women MPs sometimes expressed a desire that they not be confined to working on specifically Indigenous matters, or representing Indigenous people. Just as Māori and Aboriginal writers and filmmakers did not always wish to be understood as 'Indigenous writers', but simply as 'writers', Indigenous women and men elected to Parliament did not want to be confined solely to a position in which they represented Indigenous concerns. Tirikātene-Sullivan was quoted in the *New Zealand Woman's Weekly* in 1968 saying that she saw her parliamentary position as 'a two-fold role', in that she sought both to 'interpret one culture ... to another' and to 'make the greatest possible contribution' while in office. In relation to the latter aspect of her job, she remarked upon a 'popular misconception that a Maori member deals only with Maori matters'.[109] For Lee too, Māori issues were only part of her political agenda. An ardent conservationist, she was quoted in the *Sunday Star-*

---

105   C. Archie, 'Pushing the Boundaries – Providing the Voice', *Mana*, no. 59 (2004), p. 40.

106   Ibid., p. 42. The controversy related to ownership of the foreshore and seabed, a right which many Māori claimed through the Treaty.

107   Patrick and Heka, p. 16.

108   N. Bonner, interview with R. Hughes, conducted 13 January 1992, in *Australian Biography*, accessed 9 March 2009, transcript available from http://www.australianbiography.gov.au/subjects/bonner/ interview3. html, tape 3; see also T. Rowse, '"Out of Hand" – The Battles of Neville Bonner', *Journal of Australian Studies*, no. 54-55 (1997), p. 104.

109   Newick, p. 8.

Times in 2002 saying that she had 'particularly enjoyed being the minister of conservation' because she had 'been an activist for a long time and getting to be the minister was like being let loose in the lolly shop'.[110]

Likewise in Australia, Linda Burney, who was elected to the Legislative Assembly in New South Wales in 2003, made it clear that she did not wish to be considered as a voice only on Aboriginal affairs. While she stated in one interview that her Aboriginality was 'what guides and directs me' and that she would therefore be involved in 'Indigenous issues', she also thought that it was 'about time that people recognised that Indigenous people have views about our health, the roads we travel on, the environment we live in, infrastructure and development'.[111] Asked in another interview if she felt 'a special responsibility to act as a bridge between the cultures', she responded that while she did feel such a duty, she was also 'well aware that there is a Minister for Aboriginal Affairs' and therefore would 'offer advice when I'm asked'.[112] Being restricted to Indigenous issues could potentially be as frustrating as being unable to address them.

Māori women MPs sometimes felt a common connection with each other, and with the Māori men who were in Parliament, in their desire to advance the interests of Māori. Te Heuheu was quoted in *Mana* in 1999 recollecting that when giving her maiden speech she was 'truly mindful of all the other Maori MPs who had come through this place before me'. In the same article, Lee was quoted suggesting that there was a 'basic grace' in relationships between Māori MPs, since 'they have a greater imperative because, no matter how much they argue ideologically about what they're doing, they're all tangata whenua [people of the land] and have a greater obligation to Maori first and foremost'.[113] Turia, who was elected for Labour in 1996 and resigned the party to establish the Māori Party in 2004, similarly felt that there was a common bond among the Māori members of the House. She was quoted observing that it was 'different being a Maori MP ... to being a mainstream MP' because 'we come here with a lot of common purpose ... and so we have points of commonality, points of agreement', which might be articulated differently but which meant that 'we know that it's highly likely our Maori colleagues, no matter what party, will be supportive'. Labour MP Nanaia Mahuta also saw herself as 'another voice around the table advocating on behalf of Maori in particular areas'. She pointed out that 'Maori MPs have come together with a common purpose on a few issues', as had women MPs.[114] Such a connection was not shared by all Māori MPs, however. New Zealand First's Rana

---

110 S. Catherall, 'Sanctuary in the Lee of Politics', *Sunday Star-Times*, 28 July 2002, p. A11.
111 'Representing Diversity: Linda Burney MP', *ATSIC News*, Winter 2003, p. 19.
112 C. Boaden, 'Interview with Linda Burney', *Public Administration Today*, no. 6 (2006), p. 6.
113 W. Harawira, C. Archie and C. Robertson, 'Our Women MPs ... United They Stand?', *Mana*, no. 29 (1999), pp. 24, 27.
114 Ibid., pp. 28, 32-33.

Waitai was quoted in the *Dominion* in 1996 emphasising the party divisions that existed between Māori MPs. There was, he thought, 'no commonality between a Maori in ACT and a Maori in NZ First'.[115]

Among the women, some felt a particular connection through their position as Māori women. Asked about her relationship with other Māori women in Parliament, Te Heuheu observed that she had familial ties to some, meaning that 'first and foremost there's something far more important than what political party I belong to as a Maori'. Turia thought that the Māori women MPs had a bond as Māori women, commenting in *Mana* that they had 'a mutual respect for one another' and that 'Maori women are a lot more focused on the issues, in that they are more collaborative in their approach and we do have a closer bond than with the men'.[116] In a speech at the School of Māori Business Studies at Canterbury University in 2006, Turia suggested that 'the connections we have transcend party boundaries'. At the same time, she thought that Māori women in parties other than the Māori Party faced 'difficulty' in that 'the operating instructions come under the party banner … more than the exceptional qualities and values we practice as tangata whenua'.[117]

Such connections between women were not always evident, however. A rift was clear between Lee and Alamein Kopu, an MP for the Alliance until she resigned to become an independent and formed the short-lived Mana Wāhine Te Ira Tangata Party. Kopu felt that there was 'no collaboration among the Maori women MPs or a Maori caucus, because they all go back to their parties', and she felt that she received 'more support' from the Māori men in Parliament. She stated that 'Maori women's issues' did not 'get a fair hearing or come to the fore' because people were 'too busy playing party politics', and that while 'we all talk about the Treaty and tino rangatiratanga', it was 'almost impossible to get a strong point across or accepted in Parliament because too many other Maori from the other parties are counteracting you'. Lee also criticised other Māori MPs, both men who 'talk[ed] tough on the marae and then vote[d] soft with the National Party', and women in the Government who failed to veto policies which would impact negatively upon Māori.[118] While generally regarding themselves as being in Parliament to advance the interests of Māori, the women thus did not always agree on how that ought to be done, sometimes being divided across party lines.

---

115   A. Kominik, 'MPs Claim Territorial Rights Over Homeless Newcomers', *Dominion*, 19 October 1996, p. 1. The ACT Party is a right wing party which espouses free market principles and tax cuts, while New Zealand First is a populist and nationalist party.

116   Harawira, Archie and Robertson, pp. 25, 28.

117   T. Turia, 'Being a Maori Woman in Politics', updated 23 September 2006, accessed 22 July 2008, available from http://www.scoop.co.nz/stories/PA0609/S00509.htm.

118   Harawira, Archie and Robertson, pp. 27, 35.

If Māori women MPs often considered themselves to be advocates for Māori, whether they held Māori or general seats or were list MPs, their position as women in Parliament was more complicated. Many of the first Pākehā women to stand for election sought to justify their campaigns through arguments which emphasised their difference as women, and therefore their special ability to represent the interests of women and children. Many women who stood for election in New Zealand between 1919 and 1969 were supportive of the goals of women's organisations, explained their views on particular issues of policy in terms of their being women and discussed women's issues in their campaign speeches far more frequently than did men who stood for election.[119] In the House, Sandra Grey has demonstrated that women MPs in New Zealand were more likely to make explicit reference to their gender in speeches than were men, saying for instance that they spoke on an issue 'as a woman'.[120] Women in Parliament were sometimes also represented in the media as advocates for women's issues. Writing in the *New Zealand Woman's Weekly* in early 1982, Mackenzie considered that the eight women then in Parliament would seek to advance women's status and prevent women's issues from being ignored.[121] Many Māori women MPs, however, seemed to consider their position as advocates for Māori to be more central than any role they might have had as advocates for women, as was evident from the emphasis placed on Māori issues in their speeches and in interviews which they gave. Speaking about being a Māori woman in Parliament, Turia observed that 'being a Maori woman in politics to me, is essentially about being Maori', thus emphasising her position as Māori rather than her position as a woman.[122]

Yet Māori women MPs did promote issues affecting Pākehā women as well. Rātana commented in the House in 1961 that she was looking forward to hearing the maiden speeches of the new MPs, and in particular, to that of 'the lady member for Gisborne', Esme Tombleson. Rātana expressed her 'full confidence' that 'she as a woman and I as a woman, with others on this side, will fully understand the needs of all our womenfolk in this country'.[123] Rātana was once described by Tirikātene-Sullivan as 'the first Māori feminist'.[124] Tirikātene-Sullivan herself sometimes took a feminist approach to women's issues, at least in the early part of her parliamentary career. Debating the *Contraception, Sterilisation and Abortion Bill* in 1977, she asked if women should 'be compelled to accept that we are carriers of life, despite our private will and all our intellectual

---

119 Wallace, 'Powder-Power Politicians', pp. 180-182.
120 S. Grey, 'The New World? The Substantive Representation of Women in New Zealand', in *Representing Women in Parliament: A Comparative Study*, eds. M. Sawer, M. Tremblay and L. Trimble (Abingdon: Routledge, 2006), pp. 140-141.
121 Mackenzie, p. 4.
122 Turia, 'Being a Maori Woman in Politics'.
123 *New Zealand Parliamentary Debates*, House of Representatives, vol. 326, p. 406 (11 July 1961).
124 Rymer, dir., *Standing in the Sunshine: Power*.

comprehension that we do not wish at a given time of our lives to accept this role?' Abortion was 'a fact of life practised in all cultures and civilisations from time immemorial', she said, including in Māori society. Further, she stated that 'freedom from unwanted reproduction is the very essence of women's equality', and that abortion was 'fundamental to a woman's ability to participate equally in society'. Women in New Zealand, she argued, 'must have the right to choose'. In addressing the issue, she observed that 'I speak as a woman, as a mother, and as one who subjectively experienced soul-searching anxiety about my third pregnancy'.[125] Twenty years later, while the National Party was in Government, Te Heuheu held the portfolio of Women's Affairs as well as chairing the Māori Affairs Select Committee and being appointed Associate Minister for Treaty of Waitangi Negotiations. In an article in the Christchurch *Press* in 1998, she was quoted remarking that she felt 'passionate' about proportional representation 'because it empowers more women to participate in the most powerful decision-making body we have – Parliament'. New Zealand, she said, must 'live up to [its] reputation' as being in the international vanguard in terms of gender equality 'by delivering policies that improve the position of women'.[126]

For many of the Māori women in Parliament, however, it was important to consider women's issues within a Māori framework. Like many activist women, they were asked about or commented upon the issue of Māori women's speaking rights on the marae. Rātana is said to have 'pushed for the boundaries of what was customary for women' by asking to speak, and an 'exception was often made ... because of the esteem in which she was held'.[127] She was reportedly once told that local practice meant that she could not speak, and replied that she would 'respect [that practice] right onto the floor of the House and if they need my vote I will remain silent'.[128] Tirikātene-Sullivan was quoted in the *New Zealand Woman's Weekly* in 1983 making a similar point, stating that there were 'some of my male Maori peers who do not accept that a Maori woman may speak on a marae ... yet who come to me as an advocate, sometimes even in their own case'.[129]

Māori women MPs often distinguished their approach to women's issues from that of Pākehā feminists, as did other Māori women. In a 1994 publication, Lee explained that 'Maori women tend not to describe themselves as feminists', preferring to speak about 'mana wahine [the dignity of women] as a philosophy

---

125 *New Zealand Parliamentary Debates*, House of Representatives, vol. 412, pp. 2367-2369 (19 August 1977).

126 'Minister Extols MMP', *Press*, 19 September 1998, p. 9.

127 S. Coney, *Standing in the Sunshine: A History of New Zealand Women Since They Won the Vote* (Auckland: Penguin, 1993), p. 44.

128 'Gagged on the Marae, Silent in the House?', *Evening Post*, 26 March 1969, p. 16.

129 M. McNicholas, 'Women on the Hill Carry Double Load', *New Zealand Woman's Weekly*, 14 November 1983, p. 6.

and a way of life, rather than feminism in a Pakeha sense'. She observed that although 'there are some things our women can't do in terms of protocol', there was 'always … work for Maori women, always an important role to play'. Moreover, she stated, 'the reality is that today Maori women are running almost everything', and doing so 'very well', and there were also things that men were unable to do on the marae.[130] At the same time, she found it 'sad' that in the late twentieth century 'so-called protocol arguments [were] being used to try and marginalise Maori women, or [to] minimalise their say over matters that affect their iwi or hapu [sub-tribe]'.[131] Turia similarly commented that 'if we recognise, and indeed we should, te mana o te wahine, that does not mean we elevate the status of women above men', emphasising the need for 'complementary, co-operative [and] respectful relationships'.[132] While Māori and Pākehā women who entered Parliament did occasionally share goals and perspectives across the House, Māori women MPs often rejected a Western feminist approach to issues.

Indigenous Women in Parliament Across the Tasman

Throughout this book, I have discussed differences and similarities in experiences and media representations of famous Māori and Aboriginal women. Perhaps more than in any other field of endeavour, there have been stark differences between Māori and Aboriginal engagements with the parliamentary system. Clearly, the early incorporation of Māori into the political system was one of a number of ways in which the Māori experience of colonisation differed from that of Aboriginal peoples. Although the suffering and loss experienced by Māori under colonisation is undeniable, and despite the less than enlightened reasons for which the Māori seats were first introduced, it may be said that on the whole Aboriginal people have historically been farther removed from the centre of political power than have Māori. It is difficult to speculate upon the reasons for this difference, although they undoubtedly lie in the divergent histories of these two white settler societies. It may be that Māori leaders who emerged through traditional hereditary structures of authority within iwi were recognised as leaders within the Pākehā world more readily than were the elders of Aboriginal nations. This point is perhaps particularly important in relation to women's status, since Aboriginal women have long exercised significant influence as elders within families and communities which has often not been recognised by non-Indigenous observers. Fay Gale noted in 1990 that non-Indigenous men

---

130   S. Lee, 'Tupuna on Our Shoulders', in *Vision Aotearoa/Kaupapa New Zealand*, eds. W. Ihimaera, R. Capper, and A. Brown (Wellington: Bridget Williams, 1994), p. 222.
131   A. Brown, ed., *Mana Wahine: Women Who Show the Way* (Auckland: Reed, 1994), p. 38.
132   Turia, 'Being a Maori Woman in Politics'.

tended to seek Aboriginal men 'to take leading roles in Aboriginal affairs rather than accept the reality of the position of women in their communities'.[133] A long line of strong Māori women in leadership roles is also evident throughout Māori history, from the female figures of mythology, to the women who signed the Treaty, to women in organisations such as the MWWL. Te Puea Hērangi was a nationally prominent woman of great mana (prestige or authority) and influence, and the Māori Queen, Te Ātairangikaahu, was also widely respected and loved. Lee once commented that 'I face an arduous task following in the footsteps of Maori women who have become a symbol for change, like Te Puea and those who later followed her path'.[134]

Despite the differences evident across the Tasman in the political experiences of Indigenous peoples, however, Māori and Aboriginal men and women who entered legislative assemblies in Australia and New Zealand sometimes faced similar problems, such as a lack of influence or difficulty reconciling party principles and personal standpoints as Indigenous people. Māori and Aboriginal men and women who became MPs also often viewed their role as parliamentarians similarly, as that of an advocate for Indigenous interests or a voice for Indigenous perspectives. This chapter thus highlights the multiple and complex meanings of the term 'representation'. Besides referring to the narratives and images constructed of these women in the press, the term refers to their own positions putting forward the views of a group or an individual, and this aspect of the concept has been central to the present chapter. In this sense of the concept, both Indigenous MPs and women MPs were and are frequently understood as representing a constituency not merely through their role as representatives for an electorate, but also by virtue of sharing a group identity, which itself is often implicitly understood as being biologically determined. It is this understanding of political representation as occurring through the presence of a person with a particular group identity that has often motivated calls to increase the numbers of women or the numbers of Indigenous people in Parliament.

Conclusion

Until the late twentieth century, only two Māori women had entered the New Zealand House of Representatives. Yet those who entered it then sometimes faced similar obstacles to those faced by Rātana and Tirikātene-Sullivan decades before, and were often represented in the media in similar ways. As Māori holding seats in the nation's decision-making body, these women were sometimes

---

133   F. Gale, 'The Participation of Australian Aboriginal Women in a Changing Political Environment', *Political Geography Quarterly* 9, no. 4 (1990), p. 391.
134   Brown, ed., *Mana Wahine*, p. 32.

depicted in oppositional ways which echoed representations of activists and social reformers, as conservatives and moderates or as separatists and radicals. As women in positions of power, they were often represented in gendered frameworks common to media coverage of many women in parliamentary office, both in New Zealand and internationally. In their own articulations of their parliamentary role, their position as Māori members of the House was often more central than was their position as women members. While Māori women MPs sometimes spoke about or promoted issues perceived as women's issues within Parliament, they more often concentrated upon Māori concerns and understood their role as being advocates for Māori within the House. If representations in the print media reflected highly mediated images of them to the media-consuming public, their efforts to represent Māori people in the House often reflected their own understandings of themselves and their work. The multivalent nature of the concept of 'representation' has been evident throughout this book, as famous Māori and Aboriginal women have been represented in the media by others through particular narrative frameworks, have represented themselves in various ways and have navigated multiple positions as representatives of their people. Like other famous Indigenous women in Australia and New Zealand, Indigenous women who held parliamentary office occupied an ambiguous position in relation to the settler nation. Often celebrated for their path-breaking achievement in reaching office, they joined representative bodies which had often failed to be representative of either women or Indigenous peoples, and through their determined advocacy challenged these settler nations to reshape their futures.

Conclusion

When Cathy Freeman ran for Olympic gold in Sydney in 2000, it was in a vastly different Australia from that in which a young Evonne Goolagong first picked up a tennis racket in the 1950s. While Aboriginal people had protested the injustices of colonisation since European settlement began, protest accelerated across the country from the 1960s, and became more broadly based. For many non-Aboriginal people, the intensification of demands for specifically Indigenous rights during the 1970s and 1980s, particularly for land rights, seemed radical and potentially threatening. Likewise in New Zealand, Māori had sought to have the Treaty of Waitangi honoured, and protested when it was not, almost from the day it was first signed. Protest intensified from the late 1960s, and many Pākehā responded to calls for self-determination and the righting of land-related grievances with alarm and uncertainty. A second wave of feminist activism also developed in the late 1960s and early 1970s, following the first wave in the late nineteenth and early twentieth centuries, and seeking more far-reaching change than simple equality in legal terms. Rather, the goal was to transform social and political structures to provide equality of opportunity, and to tear down the structures of male dominance, theorised as the patriarchy. For many outside the movement, this too was an unsettling prospect.

Part of a broader counter-cultural movement, the Aboriginal and Māori rights movements and the second wave feminist movement both contributed to reshaping social and political fabrics in Australia and New Zealand during the second half of the twentieth century. A drive toward assimilation was replaced by official, if limited, acceptance of the idea of self-determination, although this was largely reversed in Australia under the Howard government in the late 1990s. Women's social and political statuses also changed significantly on both sides of the Tasman. These dramatic transformations significantly altered the representational terrain, the contexts in which media depictions of prominent Māori and Aboriginal women were produced.

A number of Aboriginal and Māori women became nationally or internationally prominent during these years of change. Some became well-known for their sporting achievements, some for their work in the performing arts, some for their literary or artistic efforts, some for their labours within political institutions or activist organisations, and some for accomplishments in arenas not addressed in this book for reasons of space. Many of these famous women had complicated relationships with the protest movements that emerged from the late 1960s, relationships which sometimes changed significantly during their lives. Some were particularly involved in one movement, others shared the concerns of more than one, and still others were reluctant to become politically involved at all.

Frequently acclaimed as the first Indigenous person, the first woman or the first Indigenous woman to reach a certain level of success or to attain a particular position, these women's lives, achievements and opinions were often featured in the media, both within their own countries and overseas. Few reached the heights of international fame accorded Dame Kiri Te Kanawa, and few remained household names for any length of time. For some, fame was a fleeting thing. Nevertheless, the increasing numbers of Aboriginal and Māori women becoming widely known in the second half of the twentieth century reflected and to an extent inspired the dramatic social, cultural and political changes of the era.

In these pages, I have explored print media representations of many prominent Māori and Aboriginal women during this period, arguing that these often invoked recurring racialised and gendered tropes, as well as exhibiting common imaginings about an Australian or New Zealand nation, particularly when the woman in question might be understood as representing that nation on an international stage. As I have shown, these prominent women frequently challenged portrayals of themselves in the media, through their own public articulations of their lives and achievements. Further, I have attempted to highlight the shifts and continuities in patterns of representation which occurred over the half century covered by this study. During periods of intense change, particular discursive formations which were previously dominant may become subordinated to others. In print media depictions of famous Indigenous women, several competing and interacting discourses about assimilation, self-determination, Indigeneity, gender and feminism appeared, re-appeared and were transformed.

These shifting discourses often intersected with and were implicated in discourses about the nation. Two settler societies which have shared many historical experiences, Australia and New Zealand have also shared a number of threads in popular and academic conceptualisations of nation and national identity. In relation to the experiences of Indigenous peoples, however, widely-held notions of the nation have been markedly different across the Tasman. New Zealanders have often celebrated relations between Māori and Pākehā as harmonious, a model to the rest of the world. Australians have not been able to do the same regarding the situations of Aboriginal people. Running through this book has thus been an ongoing discussion about differences evident in imaginings of the nation in New Zealand and Australia, as inscribed in the print media on the raced and gendered figures of famous Indigenous women. Although I have had many discussions about trans-Tasman differences in relation to the experiences of Māori and Aboriginal people as I researched and wrote this work, I have become increasingly aware also of parallels in those experiences, and in media representations. There were, it seems to me, frequently only differences of degree, or differences of inflection based upon distinct experiences of colonisation on either side of the Tasman. Through examining portrayals of famous women, I have therefore also attempted to illuminate the parallel but divergent experiences and ideologies of assimilation, and its waxing and waning, in Australia and New Zealand.

I began this study with a consideration of depictions of Aboriginal and Māori sportswomen, focusing particularly upon Evonne Goolagong. Portrayals of Goolagong displayed an intricate web of popular beliefs about femininity, Indigeneity and nation. Ideas of racial difference, such as the trope of natural physical endowment, were deeply embedded in many depictions of her life and achievements, but she was also represented as a player who embodied particular white norms of femininity in the context of feminist pressure for change in the organisation of tennis as an international sport. Gendered depictions were less common in portrayals of Indigenous sportswomen that mobilised ideas of nation, perhaps reflecting a continuing reluctance to allow that women might represent the nation. At the same time, Goolagong was a comfortable figure to celebrate in mainstream media representations which exhibited an Australian nation, since she was not involved in the Aboriginal rights movement and could be perceived as successfully assimilated. In the last years of the century, media representations of Cathy Freeman that celebrated her as a symbol of reconciliation seemed to reflect a continuing desire to celebrate only those who could be perceived as non-threatening or assimilated. Freeman's success, like that of other well-known Aboriginal achievers, could suggest that hard work and determination were all that was required to succeed, thus upholding an image of Australia as an egalitarian, 'sporting' nation and denying entrenched disadvantage.

In the performing arts too, well-known Māori and Aboriginal women in the 1950s and 1960s were sometimes presented as exemplars of assimilation or integration, or as embodying the harmonious race relations in which New Zealand took pride. These depictions elided the continuing problems of disadvantage and discrimination which faced Aboriginal and Māori people, instead mobilising the racialised bodies of famous women as symbols of successful race relations that might hide potential stains on the national image. Such representations were clearly evident in writing about Dame Kiri Te Kanawa in the early years of her career. While successful Māori and Aboriginal men could also be depicted in such ways, many representations of women active in the performing arts were also heavily gendered. Portrayals of these women as glamorous and exotic beauties combined ideas about race, femininity and modernity in ways which could suggest a link between assimilation and modernity. As a new generation of performing artists appeared from the 1970s who were willing and able to speak out about the situations of Indigenous people both through their work and outside of it, many of these representations began to fade.

In the second half of the book, the focus shifted to women whose public image was more overtly political. In Chapter Four I examined representations of

Māori and Aboriginal women known for their creative work in literature and filmmaking. Literary works, artworks and films are commonly analysed for the messages which they might convey to readers, viewers or listeners, and political issues were often closely intertwined with ideas about the proper nature of art in narratives about these women. Depictions of writers and filmmakers could not easily mobilise them as non-political or as exemplars of assimilation. Unlike in representations of those who were known for their achievements in sport or the performing arts, discourses about the nation were frequently overtaken by discourses about Indigeneity. Gendered depictions were similarly subsumed by racialised depictions, as journalists and critics on both sides of the Tasman read the women and their work in terms of their Indigeneity. For the women themselves likewise, considerations of gender were often less important than issues of oppression based on race.

Many women who became prominent for their leadership activity, activism or work within the institutions of government also focused upon issues affecting Indigenous people rather than upon feminist concerns. To a large extent, portrayals of such women in the media reflected these priorities. In many depictions, the key representational trope was that of the activist. Representations often split along a line between those perceived as moderate and those perceived as radical. In this sense, these women might sometimes be represented as outsiders, threatening to a nation otherwise imagined either as racially harmonious or as racially homogenous. Patterns of representation in the media suggest that it was women such as Whina Cooper, who sought change whilst speaking of unity between Indigenous and non-Indigenous people, who were likely to be celebrated, while those who spoke more of self-determination and sovereignty were likely to be labelled in extremist terms.

In the final chapter, the divergences between the histories of Indigenous affairs in Australia and New Zealand became more evident. The long history of Māori participation in the parliamentary system stands in stark contrast to the largely recent inclusion of Aboriginal people within the parliaments of Australia. On both sides of the Tasman, however, ideas about gender intersected with ideas about race to disadvantage Indigenous women in terms of parliamentary representation. In the print media, portrayals of Māori women who became MPs again often subsumed gendered images under racialised images, although these women were also represented in gendered frames similar to those evident in representations of other women MPs, particularly in women's magazines such as the *New Zealand Woman's Weekly*. Māori women MPs themselves understood their positions as being more to advocate for Māori concerns than to advocate for women's concerns. Depictions also appeared to split along similar lines as did those of women who became known for their leadership, activism or work within the bureaucracy or judiciary: those who were considered radical placed in contrast to those viewed as moderate. If men and women depicted as extremist activists could be understood as being outside the nation, MPs who were depicted in such ways were implicitly more threatening, placed as they were within the decision-making bodies of the nation.

It is important to acknowledge that none of these depictions were ever hegemonic, for any representation exists alongside other competing representations. There was always a variety of voices, narratives and framings, including those articulated by the women themselves. Media portrayals of famous Māori and Aboriginal women were never fixed or uniform, being shaped by diverse factors and changing in uneven ways. Throughout, I have sought to take into account the historical specificities that may have shaped the representations under discussion, including the changing political and social contexts in which they were produced, their authorship, the divergent genres of publication they appeared within and the distinct fields of endeavour in which particular women became known. In different genres, for instance, different aspects of a woman's career or identity might be given primacy. In an industry publication such as *Opera News*, Te Kanawa might be primarily famous as a fine opera singer, while in the Māori Affairs Department's *Te Ao Hou: The New World*, her status as a successful Māori person might be considered equally significant. Relationships between famous people and the media are, moreover, carefully managed. The careers of many famous Indigenous women display just such efforts at media management, albeit with varying degrees of success. Finally, in any study of representations, it must be remembered that audiences read representations in multiple and conflicting ways, the variety of which is not easily accessible to the historian. The meaning of any particular representation must thus be understood as being inherently unstable.

Given these considerations, a popular approach to the study of representations has been to focus upon highly contextualised case studies. Susan Sheridan, Susan Magarey and Sandra Lilburn adopted such an approach in their study of representations of feminism in the Australian print media, commenting upon both the nature of newspaper research and the 'complexity of the relationship between feminism and the press'.[1] Though not strictly applying a case study method, I have focused upon depictions of several Māori and Aboriginal women whom I identified as among the most well-known and most frequently featured in the media. As well as foregrounding those women who were best known, this approach allowed the complexity of portrayals to be illuminated. Such rich and intricate stories reveal the ways in which human lives and circumstances may shape and transform representations, and acknowledge the women as not just the objects of those representations, but also as individual subjects who both

---

1   S. Sheridan, S. Magarey and S. Lilburn, 'Feminism in the News', in *Feminism in Popular Culture*, eds. J. Hollows and R. Moseley (Oxford and New York: Berg, 2006), p. 26.

participated in and grappled with their own media representation. Moreover, it is perhaps in multifaceted stories of representation, like these, that the challenge of bringing history and cultural studies closer together can best be met, as they provide an avenue both for the exploration of cultural processes and for the telling of human stories in all their tangled messiness. While it has not been possible within the bounds of this work to incorporate stories of the making of representations, both inside and outside of the newsroom, studying these would likewise allow this drawing together of the theoretical and the humanistic.

Notwithstanding such complexities and challenges in studying representations, recurring patterns and tropes were clearly evident in many depictions of prominent Māori and Aboriginal women, as I have demonstrated. Further, I have begun to chart the extent to which these patterns and themes were unique to representations of famous Indigenous women, or were replicated in portrayals of other Indigenous women, Indigenous men or non-Indigenous women well-known in the same fields, identifying a number of uneven but clear parallels. The persistence of tropes in relation to ideas of race, gender and nation is suggestive of a continuing ambiguity in the representation of those perceived as different within settler societies, in this case from a white male norm.

Media representations of prominent Indigenous women could contribute to the construction and maintenance of a binary opposition that has often been identified in representations of Indigenous peoples by non-Indigenous peoples: good versus bad. In many of the recurring representational tropes discussed, a line was implicitly constructed or upheld between those who might be considered acceptable models of Indigeneity by non-Indigenous readers and viewers, and those whose version of Indigeneity appeared too challenging. In the description of Cooper as 'a Maori for all races' after her death in 1994, for instance, the potential implication was that it was moderate and unifying figures who could be embraced by Pākehā New Zealanders as well as by Māori.[2] The preferred image of the nation thus continued to be one of harmony and integration. A similar point may be made about ideas of femininity as expressed in many depictions of these famous women. If Te Kanawa and Goolagong might be perceived as embodying acceptable versions of Indigeneity, they might also be perceived as embodying acceptable ideals of (white) femininity. Women portrayed as radical or dangerous activists, on the other hand, could rarely be perceived as embodying either.

A number of authors and scholars have argued that Indigenous people tend to be accepted by non-Indigenous people only when they conform to particular incarnations, those seen as naturally talented entertainers being embraced in contrast to those whose words and actions might appear challenging. In an interview given in 1998, Patricia Grace suggested that while Māori were 'thought

---

2   'A Maori For All Races', *Dominion*, 29 March 1994, p. 6.

of only in terms of our myths and legends, arts and crafts, singing and dancing that's acceptable and fine', but if 'seen to move outside those boundaries, we come up against suspicion and barriers'.[3] Academic and author Eve Fesl once asserted that Oodgeroo was expected by non-Indigenous Australia only to 'entertain', and to avoid political activism. 'Little has changed', she wrote in 1994, 'for while we "entertain" we are accepted and applauded, but mention "land rights" and the room empties but for a few'.[4] In the United States, Christopher Campbell similarly identified a supposedly 'positive' portrayal of African-American people in television news broadcasts, according to which success was only acceptable in 'entertainment' (including sport).[5] Although some Māori and Aboriginal women involved in politically-directed creative endeavour, leadership positions, activism or work in the institutions of government were celebrated, I suggest that those who could be perceived as challenging remained largely excluded from such celebration. Oodgeroo and Cooper, for instance, were celebrated more unequivocally after their deaths than during their lifetimes, and both were implicitly celebrated in contrast to a younger generation of activists who seemed to speak more about self-determination than about achieving unity between Indigenous and non-Indigenous peoples. A continuing tension thus existed in representations of well-known Aboriginal and Māori women, between depictions of them as successful, assimilated or modern in which their Indigeneity provided exoticism and newsworthiness, and depictions of them as fiery and outspoken women who were placed as the potentially threatening Other to an invisible but powerful white male norm.

This book, however, has been about more than simply the depiction by others of famous Indigenous women. It has also been about 'representing difference' in a broader sense, and an important theme has been the multivalent nature of the concept of 'representation'. Famous women were not only represented in the media by others. On the contrary, they represented themselves publicly in a variety of ways and navigated multiple positions as representatives of Māori or Aboriginal people. Penny Van Toorn has suggested that Aboriginal authors have found 'that Australia's structures of race impose a representative role, and that to decline such a role is in many ways to risk being perceived as culturally inauthentic'.[6] It was not only writers who were placed in such a role. Moreover, representation could play a part in the work and achievements of these women through the very nature of their field of endeavour. Sports stars represented their nations when competing in international competitions, but they might also, as women like Goolagong and Freeman demonstrated, mobilise that role for other

---

3   A. Sarti, *Spiritcarvers: Interviews With Eighteen Writers From New Zealand* (Amsterdam: Rodopi, 1998), pp. 54-55.
4   E. M. D. Fesl, 'The Road Ahead', *Australian Literary Studies* 16, no. 4 (1994), p. 144.
5   C. P. Campbell, *Race, Myth and the News* (Thousand Oaks: Sage, 1995), p. 62.
6   P. Van Toorn, 'Aboriginal Writing', in *The Oxford Companion to Aboriginal Art and Culture*, eds. S. Kleinert and M. Neale (Melbourne: Oxford University Press, 2000), p. 314.

representative purposes. Writers and filmmakers not only represented a particular view of the world to their readers and viewers through their work, they were also able to speak to political issues, and hence to make representations for a group or cause. In a similar way, musicians, actors and other performing artists could use their art, or their position as famous people, to speak politically. Those involved in leadership or activism clearly acted as advocates for a cause, while those who became MPs entered houses of representatives not solely as representatives for their electorate or party, being also perceived as representatives of all Māori or Aboriginal people by virtue of their participation in a group identity. As is evident from this discussion, many such representative statuses revolved around Indigeneity rather than around gender, although not exclusively so. Prominent Aboriginal and Māori women were often ambiguously placed in relation to being able to act as representatives of an Australian or New Zealand nation, an ambiguity perhaps intensified by the dominant social and cultural positioning of women.[7] Some of the famous women in this study were imagined as representing the nation in depictions in the press, especially when performing or competing overseas, while others were metaphorically denied such a status through depictions which placed them as radical, part of an unrepresentative minority.

Underlying this book has been an understanding that representations of the lives, achievements and actions of prominent people, in the media or in other forums of communication, are part of a wider cultural process of ascribing meanings to those lives, achievements and actions, as well as to other entities or abstract concepts such as race, gender or the nation. I have not sought to replace the multiple, conflicting and shifting meanings ascribed in the media to the lives of prominent Māori and Aboriginal women with my own, nor even with theirs. Rather, I have critically explored those meanings and the ways in which they intersected with popular understandings of race, gender and nation. At the beginning of the twenty-first century, some of the portrayals of Indigenous women discussed in this book appear strange, belonging to a more racist, more sexist past. Others seem quite familiar, descriptions that can still be found in the popular media and elsewhere. As I have demonstrated, they were part of a web of gendered and racialised representations, the echoes of which still resonate. The places these women, and those who follow them, will hold in national memories in the future remains to be seen. It is certain, however, that the media in all its forms – written, spoken, visual and digital – will play a central role in shaping those memories, and in representing to us our differences.

---

7   Women have often occupied a complicated and ambiguous position in relation to ideas of nation, and to related concepts of representation. See for instance: M. Lake, 'Women and Nation in Australia: The Politics of Representation', *Australian Journal of Politics and History* 43, no. 1 (1997), pp. 41-52.

Select Bibliography

Manuscript and Archival Collections

Biographical cuttings files, National Library of Australia, Canberra.

Celebrating Women Trust, Landmarks project, reference number 2004-284, Alexander Turnbull Library, Wellington.

Clippings about Whina Cooper, reference number MS-Papers-4285-5, and newspaper clippings, reference number MS-Papers-4285-7, Alexander Turnbull Library, Wellington.

Newspaper cutting books, SF 07.12, Australian Institute of Aboriginal and Torres Strait Islander Studies, Canberra.

New Zealand Biographies Index, National Library of New Zealand, Wellington.

Jedda: Documentation, Title No. 340233, National Film and Sound Archive, Canberra.

Kiri Te Kanawa, programmes and related material collected by the National Library of Australia, ephemera collection, National Library of Australia, Canberra.

Oodgeroo Noonuccal (Kath Walker) Clippings, 1960s-1990s, reference code 2991/1, Box 7177, Heritage Collections, State Library of Queensland, Brisbane.

Oral Histories

Essie Coffey interviewed by Hazel de Berg, 1980, DeB 1154, ORAL TRC 1/1154, Hazel de Berg collection, National Library of Australia, Canberra.

Brian Edwards, interview with Titewhai Harawira, Radio New Zealand, item C1337, Sound Archives/Ngā Taonga Kōrero, accessed 21 October 2008, available from http://www.radionz.co.nz/specialfeatures/treaty/events-1990s, at 37.01-38.56.

Newspapers and Magazines Sampled

Aboriginal and Islander Identity, sampled 1975-1979.

Advertiser, sampled 1950-2009.

Age, sampled 1950-2009.

Auckland Star, sampled 1950-1977.

Australian, sampled 1964-2009.

Australian Women's Weekly, sampled 1946-2009.

Broadsheet, sampled 1972-1997.

Bulletin, sampled 1950-2008.

Canberra Times, sampled 1950-2009.

Courier-Mail, sampled 1950-2009.

Dawn, sampled 1952-1969.

Daily Telegraph, sampled 1950-1990, 1996-2009.

Daily Telegraph Mirror, sampled 1990-1996.

Dominion, sampled 1950-2002.

Evening Post, sampled 1949-2002.

Herald, sampled 1950-1990.

Herald Sun, sampled 1990-2009.

Kia Hiwa Ra, sampled 1991-1998.

Kōkiri Paetae, sampled 1996-2006.

Mana, sampled 1993-2009.

Mercury, sampled 1950-2009.

New Dawn, sampled 1970-1975.

New Zealand Herald, sampled 1950-2009.

New Zealand Listener, sampled 1940-2009.

New Zealand Woman's Weekly, sampled 1950-2009.

Press, sampled 1950-2009.

Sunday Star-Times, sampled 1994-2009.

Sun-Herald, sampled 1953-2009.

Sun News-Pictorial, sampled 1950-1990.

Sydney Morning Herald, sampled 1950-2009.

Te Ao Hou: The New World, sampled 1952-1975.

Te Maori News, sampled 1992-1996.

Thursday, sampled 1968-1976.

Tu Tangata, sampled 1981-1987.

West Australian, sampled 1950-2009.

Note: weekend and Sunday editions of newspapers were included where such were published, and items from a range of other newspapers and magazines were accessed through search engines and other methods.

Official Publications

Australian Electoral Commission, *History of the Indigenous Vote* (Kingston: Australian Electoral Commission, 2006).

Booth, J. M. and Hunn, J. K., *Integration of Maori and Pakeha* (Wellington: Department of Māori Affairs, 1962).

Hunn, J. K., *Report on Department of Maori Affairs: With Statistical Supplement* (Wellington: R. E. Owen, 1961).

New Zealand Parliamentary Debates, House of Representatives.

Royal Commission on the Electoral System, *Report of the Royal Commission on the Electoral System: Towards a Better Democracy* (Wellington: V. R. Ward, 1986).

Books and Pamphlets

Abel, Sue, *Shaping the News: Waitangi Day on Television* (Auckland: Auckland University Press, 1997).

Anderson, Warwick, *The Cultivation of Whiteness: Science, Health and Racial Destiny in Australia*, 2nd ed. (Carlton: Melbourne University Press, 2005).

Andrews, Malcolm, *101 Australian Sporting Heroes* (Frenchs Forest: Child and Associates, 1990).

Attwood, Bain, *Rights for Aborigines* (Crows Nest: Allen and Unwin, 2003).

Attwood, Bain and Markus, Andrew, *The Struggle for Aboriginal Rights: A Documentary History* (St Leonards: Allen and Unwin, 1999).

Baird, Julia, *Media Tarts: How the Australian Press Frames Female Politicians* (Carlton North: Scribe, 2004).

Baker, Candida, ed., *Yacker 2: Australian Writers Talk About Their Work* (Sydney: Pan, 1987).

Ballantyne, Tony, *Orientalism and Race: Aryanism in the British Empire* (Houndmills: Palgrave, 2002).

Bandler, Faith, *Turning the Tide: A Personal History of the Federal Council for the Advancement of Aborigines and Torres Strait Islanders* (Canberra: Aboriginal Studies Press, 1989).

Barnett, Stephen and Sullivan, Jim, eds., *In Their Own Words: From the Sound Archives of Radio New Zealand* (Wellington: GP Books in association with Radio New Zealand Sound Archives, 1988).

Baysting, Arthur; Campbell, Dyan and Dagg, Margaret, eds., *Making Policy Not Tea: Women in Parliament* (Auckland: Oxford University Press, 1993).

Bell, Leonard, *Colonial Constructs: European Images of Maori 1840-1914* (Carlton: Melbourne University Press, 1992).

Bodo, Peter, *The Courts of Babylon: Tales of Greed and Glory in a Harsh New World of Professional Tennis* (New York: Scribner, 1995).

Bolton, Geoffrey, *The Oxford History of Australia: 1942-1988 The Middle Way*, vol. 5 (Melbourne: Oxford University Press, 1990).

Bonney, Bill and Wilson, Helen, *Australia's Commercial Media* (South Melbourne: Macmillan, 1983).

Bonwick, James, *The Last of the Tasmanians, or, the Black War of Van Diemen's Land* (London: Sampson Low, Son and Marston, 1870).

Boon, Kevin, *Whetu Tirikatene-Sullivan* (Wellington: Kotuku, 2006).

Booth, Douglas and Tatz, Colin, *One-Eyed: A View of Australian Sport* (St Leonards: Allen and Unwin, 2000).

Braden, Maria, *Women Politicians and the Media* (Lexington: University Press of Kentucky, 1996).

Brookes, Rod, *Representing Sport* (London: Arnold, 2002).

Broome, Richard, *Aboriginal Australians: Black Responses to White Dominance, 1788-2001*, 3rd ed. (Crows Nest: Allen and Unwin, 2002).

Brown, Amy, ed., *Mana Wahine: Women Who Show the Way* (Auckland: Reed, 1994).

Burgmann, Verity, *Power and Protest: Movements for Change in Australian Society* (St Leonards: Allen and Unwin, 1993).

Byron, Isolde, *Ngā Perehitini: The Presidents of the Māori Women's Welfare League, 1951-2001* (Auckland: Māori Women's Development, 2002).

Campbell, Christopher P., *Race, Myth and the News* (Thousand Oaks: Sage, 1995).

Cashman, Richard, *Paradise of Sport: The Rise of Organised Sport in Australia* (Melbourne: Oxford University Press, 1995).

Cawley, Evonne Goolagong and Jarratt, Phil, *Home! The Evonne Goolagong Story* (East Roseville: Simon and Schuster, 1993).

Chauvel, Elsa, *My Life with Charles Chauvel* (Sydney: Shakespeare Head, 1973).

Chesterman, John, *Civil Rights: How Indigenous Australians Won Formal Equality* (St Lucia: University of Queensland Press, 2005).

Chryssides, Helen, *Local Heroes* (North Blackburn: Collins Dove, 1993).

Cochrane, Kathie, *Oodgeroo* (St Lucia: University of Queensland Press, 1994).

Collins, Patricia Hill, *Black Feminist Thought: Knowledge, Consciousness, and the Politics of Empowerment* (New York and London: Routledge, 1991).

Coney, Sandra, *Out of the Frying Pan: Inflammatory Writings 1972-89* (Auckland: Penguin, 1990).

– – –, *Standing in the Sunshine: A History of New Zealand Women Since They Won the Vote* (Auckland: Penguin, 1993).

Conor, Liz, *The Spectacular Modern Woman: Feminine Visibility in the 1920s* (Bloomington: Indiana University Press, 2004).

Coram, Stella, *The Real and the Unreal: Hyper Narratives of Indigenous Athletes and the Changing Significance of Race* (Altona: Common Ground, 2007).

Curnow, Jenifer, Hopa, Ngapare and McRae, Jane, eds., *Rere Atu, Taku Manu! Discovering History, Language and Politics in the Maori-Language Newspapers* (Auckland: Auckland University Press, 2002).

Dann, Christine, *Up From Under: Women and Liberation in New Zealand 1970-1984* (Wellington: Allen and Unwin in association with Port Nicholson, 1985).

Dennan, Rangitīaria and Annabell, Ross, *Guide Rangi of Rotorua* (Christchurch: Whitcombe and Tombs, 1968).

Douglas, Kay, *Living Life Out Loud: 22 Inspiring New Zealand Women Share Their Wisdom* (Auckland: HarperCollins, 2001).

Downes, Peter, *Top of the Bill: Entertainers Through the Years* (Wellington: A. H. and A. W. Reed, 1979).

Easton, Brian, *The Whimpering of the State: Policy After MMP* (Auckland: Auckland University Press, 1999).

Eve in Ebony: The Story of "Jedda" ([Sydney]: [Columbia Pictures Proprietary], [1954]).

Fingleton, David, *Kiri Te Kanawa: A Biography* (Clio: Oxford, 1982).

Freeman, Cathy and Gullan, Scott, *Cathy: Her Own Story* (Camberwell: Penguin, 2004).

Goolagong, Evonne and Collins, Bud, *Evonne! On the Move* (New York: E. P. Dutton, 1975).

Grayland, Eugene, *Famous New Zealanders* (Christchurch: Whitcombe and Tombs, 1967).

Haebich, Anna, *Spinning the Dream: Assimilation in Australia 1950-1970* (North Fremantle: Fremantle, 2008).

Hargreaves, Jennifer, *Sporting Females: Critical Issues in the History and Sociology of Women's Sports* (London and New York: Routledge, 1994).

———, *Heroines of Sport: The Politics of Difference and Identity* (London and New York: Routledge, 2000).

Harris, Bret, *The Proud Champions: Australia's Aboriginal Sporting Heroes* (Crows Nest: Little Hills, 1989).

Harris, Norman, *Kiri: Music and a Maori Girl* (Wellington: A. H. and A. W. Reed, 1966).

Hartley, John and McKee, Alan, *The Indigenous Public Sphere: The Reporting and Reception of Aboriginal Issues in the Australian Media* (Oxford: Oxford University Press, 2000).

Hodge, Bob and Mishra, Vijay, *Dark Side of the Dream: Australian Literature and the Postcolonial Mind* (North Sydney: Allen and Unwin, 1991).

Huata, Donna Awatere, *My Journey* ([Auckland]: Seaview, 1996).

Jacobs, Linda, *Evonne Goolagong: Smiles and Smashes* (St Paul: EMC, 1975).

Jhally, Sut and Lewis, Justin, *Enlightened Racism: The Cosby Show, Audiences, and the Myth of the American Dream* (Boulder: Westview, 1992).

Jolly, Spencer, *The Miss Parade* ([n.p.]: Southern Press, 1974).

Joseph, Philip A., 'The Maori Seats in Parliament', *Te Oranga o te Iwi Maori: A Study of Māori Economic and Social Progress*, Working Paper 2 (Wellington: New Zealand Business Roundtable, 2008).

Karttunen, Frances, *Between Worlds: Interpreters, Guides, and Survivors* (New Brunswick: Rutgers University Press, 1994).

Kedgley, Sue, *Our Own Country: Leading New Zealand Women Writers Talk About Their Writing and Their Lives* (Auckland: Penguin, 1989).

Kell, Peter, *Good Sports: Australian Sport and the Myth of the Fair Go* (Annandale: Pluto, 2000).

Kendall, Allan, *Australia's Wimbledon Champions* (Sydney: ABC, 1995).

King, Michael, *Te Puea: A Biography* (Auckland: Hodder and Stoughton, 1977).

———, *Whina: A Biography of Whina Cooper* (Auckland: Hodder and Stoughton, 1983).

———, *The Penguin History of New Zealand* (North Shore: Penguin, 2003).

Lake, Marilyn, *Getting Equal: The History of Australian Feminism* (St Leonards: Allen and Unwin, 1999).

Lange, Raeburn, *May the People Live: A History of Māori Health Development 1900-1920* (Auckland: Auckland University Press, 1999).

Langton, Marcia, *"Well, I Heard it on the Radio and I Saw it on the Television": An Essay for the Australian Film Commission on the Politics and Aesthetics of Filmmaking By and About Aboriginal People and Things* (North Sydney: Australian Film Commission, 1993).

Leyden, Michael, *Celebrating New Zealanders* (Auckland: Michael Leyden, 1991).

Macintyre, Stuart, *A Concise History of Australia*, 2nd ed. (Port Melbourne: Cambridge University Press, 2004).

Matheopoulos, Helena, *Diva: Great Sopranos and Mezzos Discuss Their Art* (London: Victor Gollancz, 1991).

Maynard, John, *Aboriginal Stars of the Turf: Jockeys of Australian Racing History*, revised ed. (Canberra: Aboriginal Studies Press, 2003).

McCallum, Janet, *Women in the House: Members of Parliament in New Zealand* ([Picton]: Cape Catley, 1993).

McGregor, Russell, *Imagined Destinies: Aboriginal Australians and the Doomed Race Theory, 1880-1939* (Carlton South: Melbourne University Press, 1997).

McLaren, John, *Writing in Hope and Fear: Literature as Politics in Postwar Australia* (Cambridge: Cambridge University Press, 1996).

McLean, Terry, *All Blacks Come Back: Terry McLean Looks at New Zealand and World Rugby* (London: Pelham, 1975).

Meadows, Michael, *Voices in the Wilderness: Images of Aboriginal People in the Australian Media* (Westport: Greenwood, 2001).

Mein Smith, Philippa, *A Concise History of New Zealand* (New York: Cambridge University Press, 2005).

Mickler, Steve, *The Myth of Privilege: Aboriginal Status, Media Visions, Public Ideas* (South Fremantle: Fremantle Arts Centre Press, 1998).

Miles, Sue, *50 Famous New Zealanders: Portraits and Biographies of 50 of the Most Famous New Zealanders* (Auckland: Burnham House, 1985).

Mitchell, Susan, *Tall Poppies: Nine Successful Australian Women Talk to Susan Mitchell* (Ringwood: Penguin, 1984).

———, *Winning Women: Challenging the Norms in Australian Sport* (Ringwood: Penguin, 1985).

———, *The Matriarchs: Twelve Australian Women Talk About Their Lives to Susan Mitchell* (Ringwood: Penguin, 1987).

Mulgan, Richard, *Politics in New Zealand* (Auckland: Auckland University Press, 1997).

Myers, Virginia, *Head and Shoulders* (Auckland: Penguin, 1986).

Nissen, Wendyl, *Filling the Frame: Profiles of 18 New Zealand Women* (Auckland: Reed, 1992).

Orange, Claudia, *The Treaty of Waitangi* (Wellington: Allen and Unwin in association with Port Nicholson, 1987).

Peris, Nova and Heads, Ian, *Nova: My Story: The Autobiography of Nova Peris* (Sydney: ABC, 2003).

Ramsland, John and Mooney, Christopher, *Remembering Aboriginal Heroes: Struggle, Identity and the Media* (Melbourne: Brolga, 2006).

Robson, Jocelyn and Zalcock, Beverley, *Girls' Own Stories: Australian and New Zealand Women's Films* (London: Scarlet, 1997).

Rose, Lionel and Humphries, Rod, *Lionel Rose: Australian: The Life Story of a Champion* (Sydney: Angus and Robertson, 1969).

Rose, Michael, ed., *For the Record: 160 Years of Aboriginal Print Journalism* (St Leonards: Allen and Unwin, 1996).

Ryan, Lyndall, *The Aboriginal Tasmanians* (St Lucia: University of Queensland Press, 1981).

Ryan, P. M., *P.M. Ryan's Dictionary of Modern Maori* (Auckland: Heinemann, 1994).

Sarti, Antonella, *Spiritcarvers: Interviews With Eighteen Writers From New Zealand* (Amsterdam: Rodopi, 1998).

Sawer, Marian and Simms, Marian, *A Woman's Place: Women and Politics in Australia* (St Leonards: Allen and Unwin, 1993).

Shepard, Deborah, *Reframing Women: A History of New Zealand Film* (Auckland: HarperCollins, 2000).

Sheridan, Susan; Baird, Barbara; Borrett, Kate and Ryan, Lyndall, *Who Was That Woman? The Australian Women's Weekly in the Postwar Years* (Sydney: UNSW Press, 2002).

Shoemaker, Adam, *Black Words White Page* (Canberra: ANU E Press, 2004).

Simons, Dorothy, *New Zealand's Champion Sportswomen* (Auckland: Moa, 1982).

Simpson, Adrienne and Downes, Peter, *Southern Voices: International Opera Singers of New Zealand* (Auckland: Reed, 1992).

Sinclair, Keith, *Walter Nash* (Auckland: Auckland University Press, 1976).

Smith, Bernard, *The Spectre of Truganini* (Sydney: Australian Broadcasting Commission, 1980).

Smith, Terry, *The Champions: Australia's Sporting Greats* (North Ryde: Angus and Robertson, 1990).

Spoonley, Paul and Hirsh, Walter, eds., *Between the Lines: Racism and the New Zealand Media* (Auckland: Heinemann Reed, 1990).

Stell, Marion K., *Half the Race: A History of Australian Women in Sport* (North Ryde: Angus and Robertson, 1991).

The Story of Maureen Kingi: Miss New Zealand 1962 (Dunedin: Joe Brown Enterprises, [1962]).

Sykes, Roberta, *Murawina: Australian Women of High Achievement* (Sydney: Doubleday, 1993).

— — —, *Snake Dreaming* (St Leonards: Allen and Unwin, 2001).

Tatz, Colin, *Aborigines in Sport* (Bedford Park: Australian Society for Sports History, 1987).

— — —, *Obstacle Race: Aborigines in Sport* (Sydney: University of New South Wales Press, 1995).

Taylor, Rebe, *Unearthed: The Aboriginal Tasmanians of Kangaroo Island*, revised ed. (Kent Town: Wakefield, 2008).

Te Awekōtuku, Ngāhuia, *Mana Wahine Maori: Selected Writings on Maori Women's Art, Culture and Politics* (Auckland: New Women's Press, 1991).

Te Kanawa, Kiri, *Land of the Long White Cloud: Maori Myths, Tales and Legends* (London: Pavilion, 1989).

Te Kanawa, Kiri and Wilson, Conrad, *Opera for Lovers* (Sydney: Hodder Headline, 1996).

Thomson, John Mansfield, *The Oxford History of New Zealand Music* (Auckland: Oxford University Press, 1991).

Turner, Graeme, *Making It National: Nationalism and Australian Popular Culture* (St Leonards: Allen and Unwin, 1994).

Walker, Kath, *The Dawn is at Hand* (Brisbane: Jacaranda, 1966).

Walker, Ranginui, *Struggle Without End/Ka Whawhai Tonu Matou*, revised ed. (Auckland: Penguin, 2004).

Williams, John A., *Politics of the New Zealand Maori: Protest and Cooperation, 1891-1909* (Seattle and London: University of Washington Press, 1969).

Woollacott, Angela, *Race and the Modern Exotic: Three 'Australian' Women on Global Display* (Clayton: Monash University Publishing, 2011).

Zavos, Spiros, *The Gold and the Black: The Rugby Battles for the Bledisloe Cup: New Zealand vs Australia 1903-94* (St Leonards: Allen and Unwin, 1995).

Journal Articles and Book Chapters

Abel, Sue, '"Wild Māori" and "Tame Māori" in Television News', *New Zealand Journal of Media Studies* 3, no. 2 (1996), pp. 33-38.

Ashley, Laura and Olson, Beth, 'Constructing Reality: Print Media's Framing of the Women's Movement, 1966 to 1986', *Journalism and Mass Communication Quarterly* 75, no. 2 (1998), pp. 263-277.

Awatere, Donna, 'Wahine Ma Korerotia', *Broadsheet*, no. 101 (1982), pp. 23-27.

Banerjee, Subhabrata Bobby and Osuri, Goldie, 'Silences of the Media: Whiting Out Aboriginality in Making News and Making History', *Media, Culture and Society* 22, no. 3 (2000), pp. 263-284.

Barakso, Maryann and Schaffner, Brian F., 'Winning Coverage: News Media Portrayals of the Women's Movement, 1969–2004', *Harvard International Journal of Press/Politics* 11 (2006), pp. 22-44.

Barclay, Kelly and Liu, James H., 'Who Gets Voice? (Re)presentation of Bicultural Relations in New Zealand Print Media', *New Zealand Journal of Psychology* 32, no. 1 (2003), pp. 3-12.

Barney, Katelyn, '"Women Singing Up Big" The Growth of Contemporary Music Recordings by Indigenous Australian Women Artists', *Australian Aboriginal Studies*, no. 1 (2006), pp. 44-56.

Bartlett, Francesca, 'Clean White Girls: Assimilation and Women's Work', *Hecate* 25, no. 1 (1999), pp. 10-38.

Beaver, Bruce, 'Australian Letters', *Landfall* 19, no. 4 (1965), pp. 368-372.

Beets, Jacqui Sutton, 'Images of Māori Women in New Zealand Postcards After 1900', in *Bitter Sweet: Indigenous Women in the Pacific*, eds. Alison Jones, Phyllis Herda and Tamasailau M. Suaalii (Dunedin: University of Otago Press, 2000), pp. 17-32.

Behrendt, Larissa, 'Cathy Freeman and the Politics of Sport', *Journal of Australian Indigenous Issues* 4, no. 1 (2001), pp. 27-29.

Behrendt, Larissa and Walsh, Stephen, 'From Cairns to the Courtroom', *Polemic* 2, no. 3 (1991), pp. 161-165.

Belich, James, 'Myth, Race and Identity in New Zealand', *New Zealand Journal of History* 31, no. 1 (1997), pp. 9-22.

Beston, John, 'The Aboriginal Poets in English: Kath Walker, Jack Davis, and Kevin Gilbert', *Meanjin* 36, no. 4 (1977), pp. 446-462.

———, 'The Fiction of Patricia Grace', *Ariel* 15, no. 2 (1984), pp. 41-53.

Bowman, David, 'The AJA Code', in *Issues in Australian Journalism*, ed. John Henningham (Melbourne: Longman Cheshire, 1990), pp. 49-68.

Brookes, Barbara, 'Nostalgia for "Innocent Homely Pleasures": The 1964 New Zealand Controversy over *Washday at the Pa*', *Gender and History* 9, no. 2 (1997), pp. 242-261.

———, '"Assimilation" and "Integration": The Māori Women's Welfare League in the 1950s', *Turnbull Library Record* 36 (2003), pp. 5-18.

———, 'Gender, Work and Fears of a "Hybrid Race" in 1920s New Zealand', *Gender and History* 19, no. 3 (2007), pp. 501-518.

Broome, Richard, 'Enduring Moments of Aboriginal Dominance: Aboriginal Performers, Boxers and Runners', *Labour History*, no. 69 (1995), pp. 171-187.

Broughton, W. S., 'Review of *A Breed of Women*, by Fiona Kidman', *Landfall* 34, no. 4 (1980), pp. 365-367.

Bruce, Toni and Hallinan, Christopher, 'Cathy Freeman: The Quest For Australian Identity', in *Sport Stars: The Cultural Politics of Sporting Celebrity*, eds. David L. Andrews and Steven J. Jackson (London and New York: Routledge, 2001), pp. 257-270.

Bryson, John, 'Keri Hulme in Conversation With John Bryson', *Antipodes* 8, no. 2 (1994), pp. 131-135.

Buchan, Bruce, 'Traffick of Empire: Trade, Treaty and *Terra Nullius* in Australia and North America, 1750–1800', *History Compass* 5, no. 2 (2007), pp. 386-405.

Boaden, Craig, 'Interview with Linda Burney', *Public Administration Today*, no. 6 (2006), pp. 4-6.

Bullimore, Kim, 'Media Dreaming: Representation of Aboriginality in Modern Australian Media', *Asia Pacific Media Educator*, no. 6 (1999), pp. 72-80.

Burroughs, Angela and Nauright, John, 'Women's Sports and Embodiment in Australia and New Zealand', in *Sport in Australasian Society: Past and Present*, eds. J. A. Mangan and John Nauright (London: Frank Cass, 2000), pp. 188-205.

Calleja, Paloma Fresno, 'An Interview With Patricia Grace', *Atlantis* 25, no. 1 (2003), pp. 109-120.

Carroll, Susan J. and Schreiber, Ronnee, 'Media Coverage of Women in the 103rd Congress', in *Women, Media, and Politics*, ed. Pippa Norris (New York: Oxford University Press, 1997), pp. 131-148.

Casey, Maryrose and Syron, Liza-Mare, 'The Challenges of Benevolence: The Role of Indigenous Actors', *JAS, Australia's Public Intellectual Forum*, no. 85 (2005), pp. 97-111, 211-215.

Catt, Helena, 'Representation', in *New Zealand Politics in Transition*, ed. Raymond Miller (Auckland: Oxford University Press, 1997), pp. 397-407.

Cauchi, Simon, 'Feminine Persuasive Force', *Islands* 5, no. 1 (1976), pp. 102-105.

Cochrane, Judy, 'Media Treatment of Maori Issues', *Sites*, no. 21 (1990), pp. 5-29.

Conor, Liz, '"This Striking Ornament of Nature": The "Native Belle" in the Australian Colonial Scene', *Feminist Theory* 7, no. 2 (2006), pp. 197-218.

Cooper, Ronda, 'Recent New Zealand Poetry', *Journal of New Zealand Literature*, no. 2 (1984), pp. 23-43.

Craven, Rhonda, 'Oodgeroo: An Educator Who Proved One Person Could Make a Difference', *Australian Literary Studies* 16, no. 4 (1994), pp. 121-130.

Curthoys, Ann, 'Histories of Journalism', in *Journalism: Print, Politics and Popular Culture*, eds. Ann Curthoys and Julianne Schultz (St Lucia: University of Queensland Press, 1999), pp. 1-9.

Daley, Caroline, 'Women Endurance Swimmers: Dissolving Grease Suits and Decentring New Zealand History', *Sporting Traditions* 21, no. 2 (2005), pp. 29-55.

Dalziel, Raewyn, 'Political Organisations', in *Women Together: A History of Women's Organisations in New Zealand: Ngā Rōpū Wāhine o te Motu*, ed. Anne Else (Wellington: Historical Branch, Department of Internal Affairs and Daphne Brasell, 1993), pp. 55-69.

Davidson, Jim, 'Interview: Kath Walker', *Meanjin* 36, no. 4 (1977), pp. 428-441.

Della Valle, Paola, 'The Wider Family: Patricia Grace Interviewed by Paola Della Valle', *Journal of Commonwealth Literature* 42, no. 1 (2007), pp. 131-141.

Dixon, Suzanne, 'The Enduring Theme: Domineering Dowagers and Scheming Concubines', in *Stereotypes of Women in Power: Historical Perspectives and Revisionist Views*, ed. Barbara Garlick, Suzanne Dixon, and Pauline Allen (New York: Greenwood, 1992), pp. 209-225.

Durie, M. H., 'Mana Maori Motuhake: The State of the Maori Nation', in *New Zealand Politics in Transition*, ed. Raymond Miller (Auckland: Oxford University Press, 1997), pp. 372-385.

Elder, Catriona; Pratt, Angela and Ellis, Cath, 'Running Race: Reconciliation, Nationalism and the Sydney 2000 Olympic Games', *International Review for the Sociology of Sport* 41, no. 2 (2006), pp. 181-200.

Ellinghaus, Katherine, 'Indigenous Assimilation and Absorption in the United States and Australia', *Pacific Historical Review* 75, no. 4 (2006), pp. 563-585.

Ellis, Vivienne Rae, 'Trucanini', *Tasmanian Historical Research Association Papers and Proceedings* 23, no. 2 (1976), pp. 26-41.

Else, Anne, 'Not More Than Man Nor Less: The Treatment of Women Poets in Landfall, 1947-61', *Landfall* 39, no. 4 (1985), pp. 431-446.

Fee, Margery, 'Why C. K. Stead Didn't Like Keri Hulme's *the bone people*: Who Can Write as Other?', *Australian and New Zealand Studies in Canada*, no. 1 (1989), pp. 11-32.

Fesl, Eve Mumewa D., 'The Road Ahead', *Australian Literary Studies* 16, no. 4 (1994), pp. 141-146.

Fisher, Robin, 'The Impact of European Settlement on the Indigenous Peoples of Australia, New Zealand, and British Columbia: Some Comparative Dimensions', *Canadian Ethnic Studies* 12, no. 1 (1980), pp. 1-14.

Fleras, Augie, 'From Social Welfare to Community Development: Maori Policy and the Department of Maori Affairs in New Zealand', *Community Development Journal* 19, no. 1 (1984), pp. 32-39.

Fox, Derek, 'The Maori Perspective of the News', in *Whose News?*, eds. Margie Comrie and Judy McGregor (Palmerston North: Dunmore, 1992), pp. 170-180.

Gadd, Bernard, 'Hone Tuwhare in His Poetry', *Landfall* 38, no. 1 (1984), pp. 83-89.

Gale, Fay, 'The Participation of Australian Aboriginal Women in a Changing Political Environment', *Political Geography Quarterly* 9, no. 4 (1990), pp. 381-395.

Gardiner, Greg, 'Running for Country: Australian Print Media Representation of Indigenous Athletes in the 27th Olympiad', *Journal of Sport and Social Issues* 27, no. 3 (2003), pp. 233-260.

Gilbert, Stephanie, '"Never Forgotten": Pearl Gibbs (Gambanyi)', in *Uncommon Ground: White Women in Aboriginal History*, eds. Anna Cole, Victoria Haskins and Fiona Paisley (Canberra: Aboriginal Studies Press, 2005), pp. 107-126.

Godwell, Darren, 'Playing the Game: Is Sport as Good For Race Relations as We'd Like to Think?', *Australian Aboriginal Studies*, no. 1-2 (2000), pp. 12-19.

Goodall, Heather, 'Constructing a Riot: Television News and Aborigines', *Media Information Australia*, no. 68 (1993), pp. 70-77.

— — —, '"Assimilation Begins in the Home": The State and Aboriginal Women's Work as Mothers in New South Wales, 1900s to 1960s', *Labour History*, no. 69 (1995), pp. 75-101.

Goodall, Heather and Huggins, Jackie, 'Aboriginal Women are Everywhere: Contemporary Struggles', in *Gender Relations in Australia: Domination and Negotiation*, eds. Kay Saunders and Raymond Evans (Marrickville: Harcourt Brace Jovanovich, 1992), pp. 398-424.

Goslyn, Annie, 'Patricia Grace on Politics and People', *Broadsheet*, no. 202 (1994), pp. 54-55.

Grace, Patricia and Ihimaera, Witi, 'The Maori in Literature', in *Tihe Mauri Ora: Aspects of Maoritanga*, ed. Michael King ([Wellington]: Methuen, 1978), pp. 80-85.

Greenfield, Cathy and Williams, Peter, 'Bicentennial Preliminaries: Aboriginal Women, Newspapers and the Politics of Culture', *Hecate* 13, no. 2 (1987-1988), pp. 76-106.

Grey, Sandra, 'The New World? The Substantive Representation of Women in New Zealand', in *Representing Women in Parliament: A Comparative Study*, eds. Marian Sawer, Manon Tremblay and Linda Trimble (Abingdon: Routledge, 2006), pp. 134-151.

Grimshaw, Patricia, 'Gender, Citizenship and Race in the Woman's Christian Temperance Union of Australia, 1890 to the 1930s', *Australian Feminist Studies* 13, no. 28 (1998), pp. 199-214.

― ― ―, 'Indigenous Women's Voices in Colonial Reform Narratives – Victoria and New Zealand/Aotearoa', in *Women's Politics and Women in Politics: In Honour of Ida Blom*, eds. Solvi Sogner and Gro Hagemann (Oslo: Cappelen Akademisk Forlag, 2000), pp. 173-196.

― ― ―, 'Settler Anxieties, Indigenous Peoples, and Women's Suffrage in the Colonies of Australia, New Zealand, and Hawai'i, 1888 to 1902', *Pacific Historical Review* 69, no. 4 (2000), pp. 553-572.

― ― ―, 'Interracial Marriages and Colonial Regimes in Victoria and Aotearoa/ New Zealand', *Frontiers* 23, no. 3 (2002), pp. 12-28.

― ― ―, 'Women and the Legacy of Britain's Imperial "Civilising Mission" in New Zealand, 1894-1914', in *Britishness Abroad: Transnational Movements and Imperial Cultures*, eds. Kate Darian-Smith, Patricia Grimshaw and Stuart Macintyre (Carlton: Melbourne University Press, 2007), pp. 169-186.

Haebich, Anna, 'Imagining Assimilation', *Australian Historical Studies* 33, no. 118 (2002), pp. 61-70.

― ― ―, 'Bridging the Gap: Assimilation and Aboriginal Women and Their Households', *Tasmanian Historical Studies* 9 (2004), pp. 4-20.

Hall, Lee-Anne, 'Gesture, Symbol and Identity', in *The Oxford Companion to Aboriginal Art and Culture*, eds. Sylvia Kleinert and Margo Neale (Melbourne: Oxford University Press, 2000), pp. 437-441.

Hannis, Grant, 'The New Zealand Press Association 1880-2006: The Rise and Fall of a Co-Operative Model for News Gathering', *Australian Economic History Review* 48, no. 1 (2008), pp. 47-67.

Havea, Mele-Ann, 'The Need for Critical Reflection on Media Representations of Aboriginal Women', *Journal of Australian Indigenous Issues* 5, no. 1 (2002), pp. 11-22.

Hawke, Sharon, 'Mira Szaszy', *Broadsheet*, no. 114 (1983), pp. 12-17.

Hazlehurst, Kayleen M., 'Ethnicity, Ideology and Social Drama: The Waitangi Day Incident 1991', in *The Urban Context: Ethnicity, Social Networks, and Situational Analysis*, eds. Alisdair Rogers and Steven Vertovec (Oxford: Berg, 1995), pp. 81-115.

Heaven, Patrick and Rowe, David, 'Gender, Sport and Body Image', in *Sport and Leisure: Trends in Australian Popular Culture*, eds. David Rowe and Geoff Lawrence (Sydney: Harcourt Brace Jovanovich, 1990), pp. 59-73.

Heldman, Gladys M., 'The Women's Pro Game', in *The Encyclopedia of Tennis*, ed. Max Robertson (New York: Viking, 1974), pp. 68-71.

Hellyer, Jill, 'Aboriginal Poet', *Hemisphere* 8, no. 12 (1964), pp. 17-18.

'Herea te Tangata ki te Whenua (Bind the People to the Land)', in *Speaking For Ourselves: Echoes From New Zealand's Past From the Award-Winning "Spectrum" Radio Series* A. Owen and J. Perkins eds, (Auckland: Penguin, 1986), pp. 39-60.

Hereniko, Vilsoni, 'An Interview with Patricia Grace', *Contemporary Pacific* 10, no. 1 (1998), pp. 154-163.

Hodge, Bob, 'Poetry and Politics in Oodgeroo: Transcending the Difference', *Australian Literary Studies* 16, no. 4 (1994), pp. 63-76.

Hokowhitu, Brendan, 'Tackling Maori Masculinity: A Colonial Genealogy of Savagery and Sport', *Contemporary Pacific* 16, no. 2 (2004), pp. 259-284.

Holland, Alison, 'To Eliminate Colour Prejudice: The WCTU and Decolonisation in Australia', *Journal of Religious History* 32, no. 2 (2008), pp. 256-276.

Hollinsworth, David, '"My Island Home": Riot and Resistance in Media Representations of Aboriginality', *Social Alternatives* 24, no. 1 (2005), pp. 16-20.

Horn, Pauline; Leniston, Margaret and Lewis, Pauline, 'The Maiden Speeches of New Zealand Women Members of Parliament', *Political Science* 35, no. 2 (1983), pp. 229-266.

Huata, Donna Awatere, 'Walking on Eggs', in *Heading Nowhere in a Navy Blue Suit and Other Tales From the Feminist Revolution*, eds. Sue Kedgley and Mary Varnham (Wellington: Daphne Brasell, 1993), pp. 120-131.

Iorns Magallanes, Catherine J., 'Indigenous Political Representation: Identified Parliamentary Seats as a Form of Indigenous Self-Determination', in *Unfinished Constitutional Business? Rethinking Indigenous Self-Determination*, ed. Barbara Ann Hocking (Canberra: Aboriginal Studies Press, 2005), pp. 106-117.

Jenkins, Cathy, 'A Mother in Cabinet: Dame Enid Lyons and the Press', *Australian Journalism Review* 25, no. 1 (2003), pp. 181-196.

— — —, 'The More Things Change: Women, Politics and the Press in Australia', *Ejournalist* 2, no. 1 (2002), accessed 27 February 2009, available from http://ejournalist.com.au/ejournalist_v2n1.php.

Jenkins, Kuni and Matthews, Kay Morris, 'Knowing Their Place: The Political Socialisation of Maori Women in New Zealand Through Schooling Policy and Practice, 1867-1969', *Women's History Review* 7, no. 1 (1998), pp. 85-105.

Julian, Rae, 'Women: How Significant a Force?', in *New Zealand Politics in Perspective*, ed. Hyam Gold (Auckland: Longman Paul, 1992), pp. 401-409.

Karp, Jeffrey, 'Members of Parliament and Representation', in *Proportional Representation on Trial: The 1999 New Zealand General Election and the Fate of MMP*, eds. Jack Vowles, Peter Aimer, Susan Banducci, Jeffrey Karp, Raymond Miller and Ann Sullivan (Auckland: Auckland University Press, 2002), pp. 130-145.

Keown, Michelle, 'Interview with Patricia Grace', *Kunapipi* 22, no. 2 (2000), pp. 54-63.

Kerin, Rani, 'Charles Duguid and Aboriginal Assimilation in Adelaide, 1950-1960: The Nebulous "Assimilation" Goal', *History Australia* 2, no. 3 (2005), pp. 85.1-85.17.

Kidwell, Clara Sue, 'Indian Women as Cultural Mediators', *Ethnohistory* 39, no. 2 (1992), pp. 97-107.

King, Michael, 'Between Two Worlds', in *The Oxford History of New Zealand*, ed. W. H. Oliver (Wellington: Oxford University Press, 1981), pp. 279-301.

Kinross-Smith, Graeme, 'Lawn Tennis', in *Sport in Australia: A Social History*, eds. Wray Vamplew and Brian Stoddart (Cambridge: Cambridge University Press, 1994), pp. 133-153.

Knudsen, Eva Rask, 'From Kath Walker to Oodgeroo Noonuccal? Ambiguity and Assurance in *My People*', *Australian Literary Studies* 16, no. 4 (1994), pp. 105-118.

Kurtzer, Sonja, 'Is She or Isn't She? Roberta Sykes and "Authentic" Aboriginality', *Overland*, no. 171 (2003), pp. 50-56.

Lake, Marilyn, 'Women and Nation in Australia: The Politics of Representation', *Australian Journal of Politics and History* 43, no. 1 (1997), pp. 41-52.

Lee, S. E., 'Poetic Fisticuffs', *Southerly* 27, no. 1 (1967), pp. 60-71.

— — —, 'Old Verse', *Southerly* 31, no. 3 (1971), pp. 227-240.

Lee, Sandra, 'Tupuna on Our Shoulders', in *Vision Aotearoa/Kaupapa New Zealand*, eds. Witi Ihimaera, Roslie Capper and Amy Brown (Wellington: Bridget Williams, 1994), pp. 218-230.

Lehman, Greg, 'Trukanini', in *The Oxford Companion to Aboriginal Art and Culture*, eds. Sylvia Kleinert and Margo Neale (Melbourne: Oxford University Press, 2000), p. 722.

Lilburn, Sandra, 'Representations of Feminism in the Australian Print Media: The Case of Pat O'Shane', *Demetrius: The Institutional Repository of the ANU*, issued 19 May 2004, accessed 18 June 2008, available from http://dspace.anu.edu.au/handle/1885/41414.

MacDonald, Tui, 'Iriaka Ratana', in *The Book of New Zealand Women/Ko Kui Ma Te Kaupapa*, eds. Charlotte Macdonald, Merimeri Penfold and Bridget Williams (Wellington: Bridget Williams, 1991), pp. 548-549.

MacDonald, Tui and Zister, Ngeungeu, 'Te Puea Herangi', in *The Book of New Zealand Women/Ko Kui Ma Te Kaupapa*, eds. Charlotte Macdonald, Merimeri Penfold and Bridget Williams (Wellington: Bridget Williams, 1991), pp. 664-669.

Manhire, Bill, 'Ready to Move: Interview with Hone Tuwhare', *Landfall* 42, no. 3 (1988), pp. 262-285.

Matt, Gerald, 'An Interview with Tracey Moffatt', in *Tracey Moffatt*, ed. Michael Snelling (Brisbane: Institute of Modern Art, 1999), pp. 64-68.

Maynard, John, 'Vision, Voice and Influence: The Rise of the Australian Aboriginal Progressive Association', *Australian Historical Studies* 34, no. 121 (2003), pp. 91-105.

McGrath, Ann, 'The White Man's Looking Glass: Aboriginal-Colonial Gender Relations at Port Jackson', *Australian Historical Studies* 24, no. 95 (1990), pp. 189-206.

— — —, 'A National Story', in *Contested Ground: Australian Aborigines Under the British Crown*, ed. Ann McGrath (St Leonards: Allen and Unwin, 1995), pp. 1-54.

McGregor, Russell, 'Assimilationists Contest Assimilation: T. G. H. Strehlow and A. P. Elkin on Aboriginal Policy', *JAS, Australia's Public Intellectual Forum*, no. 75 (2002), pp. 43-50, 180-182.

— — —, '"Breed Out the Colour": Or the Importance of Being White', *Australian Historical Studies* 33, no. 120 (2002), pp. 286-302.

— — —, 'Degrees of Fatalism: Discourses on Racial Extinction in Australia and New Zealand', in *Collisions of Cultures and Identities: Settlers and Indigenous Peoples*, eds. Patricia Grimshaw and Russell McGregor (Melbourne: Department of History, University of Melbourne, 2007), pp. 245-261.

— — —, 'Looking Across the Tasman: New Zealand Exemplars in Australian Indigenous Affairs, 1920s-1970s', *History Compass* 5, no. 2 (2007), pp. 406-426.

McKay, Jim, 'Embodying the "New" Sporting Woman', *Hecate* 20, no. 1 (1994), pp. 68-83.

— — —, 'Enlightened Racism and Celebrity Feminism in Contemporary Sports Advertising Discourse', in *Sport, Culture and Advertising: Identities, Commodities and the Politics of Representation*, eds. Steven J. Jackson and David L. Andrews (London and New York: Routledge, 2005), pp. 81-99.

McKee, Alan and Hartley, John, '"Truth, Integrity and a Little Gossip": Magazine Coverage of Aboriginality and the Law in Australia', *Alternative Law Journal* 21, no. 1 (1996), pp. 15-18, 23.

McLeay, Elizabeth, 'Rules, Values and Women's Representation in the New Zealand Parliament', in *Representing Women in Parliament: A Comparative Study*, eds. Marian Sawer, Manon Tremblay and Linda Trimble (Abingdon: Routledge, 2006), pp. 67-82.

McRae, Jane, 'Patricia Grace', in *In the Same Room: Conversations With New Zealand Writers*, eds. Elizabeth Alley and Mark Williams (Auckland: Auckland University Press, 1992), pp. 285-296.

Meadows, Michael, 'A 10-Point Plan and a Treaty: Images of Indigenous People in the Press in Australia and Canada', *Queensland Review* 6, no. 1 (1999), pp. 50-76.

— — —, 'Media Images of Indigenous Affairs in Australia', in *Outer Limits: A Reader in Communication Across Cultures*, ed. J. Leigh and E. Loo (Melbourne: Language Australia, 2004), pp. 273-289.

Mills, Jane, 'A (Filmic) Space Between Black and White', *RealTime + OnScreen*, no. 44 (2001), p. 17.

Mita, Merata, 'The Soul and the Image', in *Film in Aotearoa New Zealand*, eds. Jonathan Dennis and Jan Bieringa (Wellington: Victoria University Press, 1996), pp. 36-54.

Mooney, Christopher and Ramsland, John, 'Growing Up and Breaking Away From the Mission: The Formative Years of Aboriginal Celebrities of the 1950s', *ISAA Review* 6, no. 1 (2007), pp. 6-15.

Moran, Anthony, 'White Australia, Settler Nationalism and Aboriginal Assimilation', *Australian Journal of Politics and History* 51, no. 2 (2005), pp. 168-193.

Moreton-Robinson, Aileen, 'Troubling Business: Difference and Whiteness Within Feminism', *Australian Feminist Studies* 15, no. 33 (2000), pp. 343-352.

— — —, 'Whiteness, Epistemology and Indigenous Representation', in *Whitening Race: Essays in Social and Cultural Criticism*, ed. Aileen Moreton-Robinson (Canberra: Aboriginal Studies Press, 2004), pp. 75-88.

Muir, Kathie, 'Media Representations of Ngarrindjeri Women', *Journal of Australian Studies*, no. 48 (1996), pp. 73-82.

Nairn, Raymond G. and McCreanor, Timothy N., 'Race Talk and Common Sense: Patterns in Pakeha Discourse on Maori/Pakeha Relations in New Zealand', *Journal of Language and Social Psychology* 10, no. 4 (1991), pp. 245-262.

Nauright, John, 'Netball, Media Representation of Women and Crisis of Male Hegemony in New Zealand', *ASSH Studies in Sports History*, no. 11 (1999), pp. 47-65.

Norris, Pippa, 'Women Leaders Worldwide: A Splash of Color in the Photo Op', in *Women, Media, and Politics*, ed. Pippa Norris (New York: Oxford University Press, 1997), pp. 149-165.

Norton, David A., 'Not All Loners and Losers', *Landfall* 30, no. 2 (1976), pp. 150-154.

O'Regan, Tom, 'Documentary in Controversy: *The Last Tasmanian*', in *An Australian Film Reader*, eds. Albert Moran and Tom O'Regan (Sydney: Currency, 1985), pp. 127-136.

O'Shane, Pat, 'Is There Any Relevance in the Women's Movement For Aboriginal Women?', *Refractory Girl*, no. 12 (1976), pp. 31-34.

Onsman, Andrys, 'Truganini's Funeral', *Island*, no. 96 (2004), pp. 39-52.

Oppenheim, R. S., 'Review of *No Ordinary Sun*, by Hone Tuwhare', *Journal of the Polynesian Society* 74, no. 4 (1965), pp. 525-526.

———, 'Review of *Pounamu Pounamu*, by Witi Ihimaera', *Journal of the Polynesian Society* 84, no. 4 (1975), pp. 506-507.

Orange, Claudia, 'An Exercise in Maori Autonomy: The Rise and Demise of the Maori War Effort Organisation', *New Zealand Journal of History* 21, no. 1 (1987), pp. 156-172.

Paisley, Fiona, 'Glamour in the Pacific: Cultural Internationalism and Maori Politics at Pan Pacific Women's Conferences in the 1950s', *Pacific Studies* 29, no. 1/2 (2006), pp. 54-81.

Parekowhai, Cushla, 'Kōrero ki Taku Tuakana: Merata Mita and Me', *Illusions*, no. 9 (1989), pp. 21-26.

Pearson, Bill, 'Witi Ihimaera and Patricia Grace', in *Critical Essays on the New Zealand Short Story*, ed. Cherry Hankin (Auckland: Heinemann, 1982), pp. 166-184.

Perera, Suvendrini, 'Claiming Truganini: Australian National Narratives in the Year of Indigenous Peoples', *Cultural Studies* 10, no. 3 (1996), pp. 393-412.

Pickles, Katie, 'Exceptions to the Rule: Explaining the World's First Women Presidents and Prime Ministers', *History Now* 7, no. 2 (2001), pp. 13-18.

———, 'Kiwi Icons and the Re-Settlement of New Zealand as Colonial Space', *New Zealand Geographer* 58, no. 2 (2002), pp. 5-16.

———, 'Colonisation, Empire and Gender', in *The New Oxford History of New Zealand*, ed. Giselle Byrnes (South Melbourne: Oxford University Press, 2009), pp. 219-241.

Pihama, Leonie, 'Repositioning Maori Representation: Contextualising *Once Were Warriors*', in *Film in Aotearoa New Zealand*, eds. Jonathan Dennis and Jan Bieringa (Wellington: Victoria University Press, 1996), pp. 191-192.

Poata-Smith, Evan S. Te Ahu, 'He Pokeke Uenuku i Tu Ai: The Evolution of Contemporary Maori Protest', in *Nga Patai: Racism and Ethnic Relations in Aotearoa/New Zealand*, eds. Paul Spoonley, David Pearson and Cluny Macpherson (Palmerston North: Dunmore, 1996), pp. 97-116.

Ramsland, John, 'Images of Albert Namatjira in Australian Popular Culture of the 1950s', *Inter-Cultural Studies* 2, no. 2 (2002), pp. 11-26.

Rei, Tania, 'Te Rōpū Māori Toko i te Ora/Māori Women's Welfare League 1951-', in *Women Together: A History of Women's Organisations in New Zealand: Ngā Rōpū Wāhine o te Motu*, ed. Anne Else (Wellington: Historical Branch, Department of Internal Affairs and Daphne Brasell, 1993), pp. 34-38.

Reilly, Alexander, 'Dedicated Seats in the Federal Parliament for Indigenous Australians: The Theoretical Case and its Practical Possibility', *Balayi* 2, no. 1 (2001), pp. 73-103.

Rhode, Deborah L., 'Media Images, Feminist Issues', *Signs* 20, no. 3 (1995), pp. 685-710.

Ricketson, Matthew, 'Newspaper Feature Writing in Australia 1956-1996', in *Journalism: Print, Politics and Popular Culture*, eds. Ann Curthoys and Julianne Schultz (St Lucia: University of Queensland Press, 1999), pp. 168-184.

Rossi, Nick, 'An Interview With Dame Kiri Te Kanawa', *Fanfare* 13, no. 1 (1989), pp. 499-502.

Rowse, Tim, '"Out of Hand" – The Battles of Neville Bonner', *Journal of Australian Studies*, no. 54-55 (1997), pp. 96-107.

———, 'Introduction: Contesting Assimilation', in *Contesting Assimilation*, ed. Tim Rowse (Perth: API Network, 2005), pp. 1-24.

———, 'Global Indigenism: A Genealogy of a Non-Racial Category', in *Rethinking the Racial Moment: Essays on the Colonial Encounter*, eds. Alison Holland and Barbara Brookes (Newcastle upon Tyne: Cambridge Scholars, 2011), pp. 229-253.

Rupa, Mandrika and Tsoulis, Athina, 'Indigenous Filmmakers', *Broadsheet*, no. 199 (1993), pp. 34-38.

Rutherford, Anna, 'Changing Images', in *Aboriginal Culture Today*, ed. Anna Rutherford (Sydney: Dangaroo, 1988), pp. 146-156.

Ryan, Lyndall, 'The Struggle for Trukanini 1830-1997', *Tasmanian Historical Research Association Papers and Proceedings* 44, no. 3 (1997), pp. 153-173.

Saunders, John, 'Skin Deep: The News Media's Failure to Cover Maori Politics', in *Dangerous Democracy? News Media Politics in New Zealand*, ed. J. McGregor (Palmerston North: Dunmore, 1996), pp. 166-180.

Schultz, Julianne, 'The Press', in *The Media in Australia: Industries, Texts, Audiences*, eds. Stuart Cunningham and Graeme Turner (St Leonards: Allen and Unwin, 1997), pp. 23-46.

Sheridan, Susan; Magarey, Susan and Lilburn, Sandra, 'Feminism in the News', in *Feminism in Popular Culture*, eds. Joanne Hollows and Rachel Moseley (Oxford and New York: Berg, 2006), pp. 25-40.

Sinclair, Keith, 'Why are Race Relations in New Zealand Better Than in South Africa, South Australia or South Dakota?', *New Zealand Journal of History* 5, no. 2 (1971), pp. 121-127.

Sinclair, Karen P., 'Maori Literature: Protest and Affirmation', *Pacific Studies* 15, no. 4 (1992), pp. 283-309.

Smith, Elizabeth, 'Are You Going to Come Back Tomorrow?', *Queensland Writer* 2, no. 1 (1990), pp. 13-16.

Stead, C. K., 'Keri Hulme's "The Bone People," and the Pegasus Award for Maori Literature', *Ariel* 16, no. 4 (1985), pp. 101-108.

Stenhouse, John, '"A Disappearing Race Before We Came Here": Doctor Alfred Kingcome Newman, the Dying Maori, and Victorian Scientific Racism', *New Zealand Journal of History* 30, no. 2 (1996), pp. 124-140.

Stevenson, Deborah, 'Women, Sport and Globalization: Competing Discourses of Sexuality and Nation', *Journal of Sport and Social Issues* 26, no. 2 (2002), pp. 209-225.

Strang, Veronica, 'Moon Shadows: Aboriginal and European Heroes in an Australian Landscape', in *Landscape, Memory and History: Anthropological Perspectives*, eds. Pamela J. Stewart and Andrew Strathern (London and Sterling: Pluto, 2003), pp. 108-135.

Struthers, Karen, 'Hands on Parliament: Indigenous Peoples' Participation in Queensland's Democratic Processes', *Indigenous Law Bulletin* 5, no. 27 (2003), p. 4.

Stuart, Ian, 'Tauiwi and Maori Media: The Indigenous View', *Pacific Journalism Review* 3, no. 2 (1996), accessed 25 February 2009, available from http://www.asiapac.org.fj/cafepacific/resources/aspac/Maori.html.

Sullivan, Ann, 'Maori Politics and Government Policies', in *New Zealand Politics in Transition*, ed. Raymond Miller (Auckland: Oxford University Press, 1997), pp. 361-371.

Sykes, Roberta B., 'While My Name is Remembered ...', *Australian Literary Studies* 16, no. 4 (1994), pp. 35-41.

Szaszy, Mira, 'Opening My Mouth', in *Heading Nowhere in a Navy Blue Suit and Other Tales From the Feminist Revolution*, eds. Sue Kedgley and Mary Varnham (Wellington: Daphne Brasell, 1993), pp. 75-84.

Tausky, Thomas E., '"Stories That Show Them Who They Are": An Interview with Patricia Grace', *Australian and New Zealand Studies in Canada*, no. 6 (1991), pp. 90-102.

Terkildsen, Nayda and Schnell, Frauke, 'How Media Frames Move Public Opinion: An Analysis of the Women's Movement', *Political Research Quarterly* 50 (1997), pp. 879-900.

Thomas, Cora, 'From "Australian Aborigines" to "White Australians"', *Australian Aboriginal Studies*, no. 1 (2001), pp. 21-35.

Thomas, Faith, 'From the Shoulder', in *Women of the Centre*, ed. Adele Pring (Apollo Bay: Pascoe, 1990), pp. 28-46.

Tiffen, Rodney, 'The Press', in *The Media in Australia: Industries, Texts, Audiences*, eds. Stuart Cunningham and Graeme Turner (St Leonards: Allen and Unwin, 1997), pp. 191-200.

Turcotte, Gerry, 'Recording the Cries of the People', in *Aboriginal Culture Today*, ed. Anna Rutherford (Sydney: Dangaroo, 1988), pp. 16-30.

Ustinoff, Julie, 'The Many Faces of Political Eve: Representations of Queensland Women Parliamentarians in the Media', *Queensland Review* 12, no. 2 (2005), pp. 97-106.

Ustinoff, Julie and Saunders, Kay, 'Celebrity, Nation and the New Australian Woman: Tania Verstak, Miss Australia 1961', *JAS, Australia's Public Intellectual Forum*, no. 83 (2004), pp. 61-73.

van Acker, Elizabeth, 'The Portrayal of Feminist Issues in the Print Media', *Australian Studies in Journalism*, no. 4 (1995), pp. 174-199.

Van Toorn, Penny, 'Aboriginal Writing', in *The Oxford Companion to Aboriginal Art and Culture*, eds. Sylvia Kleinert and Margo Neale (Melbourne: Oxford University Press, 2000), pp. 313-323.

———, 'Indigenous Texts and Narratives', in *The Cambridge Companion to Australian Literature*, ed. Elizabeth Webby (Cambridge: Cambridge University Press, 2000), pp. 19-49.

Walker, Kath, 'Aboriginals: The Smell of Frustration', *Politics* 1 (1970), pp. 89-93.

Walker, Ranginui, 'The Role of the Press in Defining Pakeha Perceptions of the Maori', in *Between the Lines: Racism and the New Zealand Media*, eds. Paul Spoonley and Walter Hirsh (Auckland: Heinemann Reed, 1990), pp. 38-46.

———, 'The Maori People: Their Political Development', in *New Zealand Politics in Perspective*, ed. Hyam Gold (Auckland: Longman Paul, 1992), pp. 379-400.

Wall, Melanie, 'Stereotypical Constructions of the Maori "Race" in the Media', *New Zealand Geographer* 53, no. 2 (1997), pp. 40-45.

Wallace, Sandra, '"Like Father, Like Daughter"? A Reassessment of the Concept of Male Equivalence in New Zealand', *Women's Studies Journal* 7, no. 1 (1991), pp. 16-28.

Watego, Cliff, 'Aboriginal Poetry and White Criticism', in *Aboriginal Writing Today*, eds. Jack Davis and Bob Hodge (Canberra: Australian Institute of Aboriginal Studies, 1985), pp. 75-90.

Waterhouse, Richard, 'Australian Legends', *Australian Historical Studies* 31, no. 115 (2000), pp. 201-221.

Watson, Geoff, 'Sport and Ethnicity in New Zealand', *History Compass* 5, no. 3 (2007), pp. 780-801.

Wensing, Emma H. and Bruce, Toni, 'Bending the Rules: Media Representations of Gender During an International Sporting Event', *International Review for the Sociology of Sport* 38, no. 4 (2003), pp. 387-396.

Whimpress, Bernard, 'The First Aboriginal Test Cricketer', *Journal of the Cricket Society* 20, no. 4 (2002), pp. 5-12.

Wilkinson, Jane, 'Witi Ihimaera', *Kunapipi* 7, no. 1 (1985), pp. 98-110.

———, 'Do White Girls Rule? Exploring Broadsheet Representations of Australian Women Leaders', *Redress* 15, no. 1 (2006), pp. 16-21.

Wilson, Margaret, 'Women and Politics', in *New Zealand Politics in Transition*, ed. Raymond Miller (Auckland: Oxford University Press, 1997), pp. 418-427.

Wright, Judith, 'The Poetry', in *Oodgeroo*, ed. Kathie Cochrane (St Lucia: University of Queensland Press, 1994), pp. 163-183.

Theses and Unpublished Papers

Bennett, James, 'Redeeming the Imagination: A Trans-National History of Australia and Aotearoa/New Zealand, 1890-1944' (PhD thesis, University of Melbourne, 1997).

Else, Anne, 'On Shifting Ground: Self Narrative, Feminist Theory and Writing Practice' (PhD thesis, Victoria University of Wellington, 2006).

Fox, Karen, 'Dames in New Zealand: Gender, Representation and the Royal Honours System, 1917-2000' (MA thesis, University of Canterbury, 2005).

K. Fox, 'Representing Difference: Celebrated Māori and Aboriginal Women and the Print Media, 1950-2000' (PhD thesis, The Australian National University, 2009).

Hallinan, C.; Bruce, T. and Bennie, J. 'Freak Goals and Magical Moments: Commonsense Understandings about Indigenous Footballers', paper presented at the TASA Conference: The Australian Sociological Association, La Trobe University, 8-11 December 2004, accessed 18 October 2007, available at http://www.tasa.org.au/conferencepapers04/docs/LEISURE/HALLINAN_BRUCE_BENNIE.pdf.

Harris, Aroha, 'Dancing With the State: Māori Creative Energy and Policies of Integration, 1945-1967' (PhD thesis, University of Auckland, 2007).

Taira, Eliana, 'Māori Media: A Study of the Māori "Media Sphere" in Aotearoa/ New Zealand' (PhD thesis, University of Canterbury, 2006).

Wallace, Sandra, 'Powder-Power Politicians: New Zealand Women Parliamentary Candidates' (PhD thesis, University of Otago, 1992).

Websites

'Aboriginal Representation in Parliament', *Hansard and Papers*, Legislative Council, Parliament of New South Wales, updated 5 December 2007, accessed 16 July 2008, available from http://www.parliament.nsw.gov.au/ prod/ parlment/hansart.nsf/V3Key/ LC19950920009.

Australian Government, 'It's an Honour: Australia Celebrating Australians', updated 12 December 2006, accessed 26 February 2009, available from http://www.itsanhonour.gov.au.

Ballara, Angela, 'Mangakahia, Meri Te Tai 1868-1920', *Dictionary of New Zealand Biography*, updated 22 June 2007, accessed 14 May 2008, available from http://www.dnzb.govt.nz/dnzb/default.asp?Find_Quick.asp?PersonEssay=2M30.

— — —, 'Ratana, Iriaka Matiu 1905-1981', *Dictionary of New Zealand Biography*, updated 7 April 2006, accessed 1 December 2006, available from http://www.dnzb.govt.nz/dnzb/default.asp?Find_Quick.asp?PersonEssay=5R7.

Curnow, Jenifer, 'Hinerangi, Sophia 1830-1834?-1911', *Dictionary of New Zealand Biography*, updated 7 July 2005, accessed 28 March 2006, available from http://www.teara.govt.nz.govt.nz/dnzb/default.asp?Find_Quick.asp?Person Essay=2H37.

'The Declaration of Independence of Whaingaroa', accessed 13 May 2008, available from http://aotearoa.wellington.net.nz/imp/whai.htm.

Electoral Commission, 'Maori and the Vote', *Elections New Zealand*, updated 9 April 2005, accessed 19 January 2009, available from http://www.elections. org.nz/democracy/ history/Maori-vote.html.

Foley, Gary, 'Black Power in Redfern 1968-1972', *The Koori History Website*, updated 5 October 2001, accessed 19 May 2008, available from http://www. kooriweb.org/foley/ essays/essay_1.html.

Goldstone, Paul, 'Nehua, Katerina 1903-1948', *Dictionary of New Zealand Biography*, updated 22 June 2007, accessed 6 August 2007, available from http://www.dnzb.govt.nz/dnzb/default.asp?Find_Quick.asp?PersonEssay=4N4.

Head, Lyndsay, 'Te Ua Haumene ?-1866', *Dictionary of New Zealand Biography*, updated 22 June 2007, accessed 14 March 2008, available from http://www. dnzb.govt.nz/dnzb/default.asp?Find_Quick.asp?PersonEssay=1T79.

Hughes, Robin, 'Neville Bonner: Full Interview Transcript', *Australian Biography*, accessed 3 May 2009, available from http://www. australianbiography.gov. au/ subjects/bonner/interview1.html.

Hughes, Robin, 'Rosalie Kunoth-Monks: Full Interview Transcript', *Australian Biography*, accessed 3 May 2009, available from http://www. australianbiography.gov.au/subjects/kunothmonks/interview1.html.

Jones, Philip, 'Unaipon, David (1872-1967)', *Australian Dictionary of Biography*, Online Edition, updated continuously, accessed 19 January 2009, available from http://www.adb.online.anu.edu.au/biogs/A120339b.htm.

King, Michael, 'Cooper, Whina 1895-1994', *Dictionary of New Zealand Biography*, updated 7 April 2006, accessed 7 May 2007, available from http:// www.dnzb. govt.nz/dnzb/Find_Quick.asp?PersonEssay=5C32.

'Kiri Te Kanawa Bio', updated 2008, accessed 27 February 2008, available from http://www.kiritekanawa.org/kiri+te+kanawa.

Matson-Green, Vicki maikutena, 'Tarenorerer [Walyer] (c. 1800-1831)', *Australian Dictionary of Biography*, Online Edition, updated continuously, accessed 2 August 2007, available from http://www.adb.online.anu.edu.au/ biogs/ AS10455b.htm.

Maza, Rachael and Kunoth-Monks, Rosalie, 'Rosalie's Journey', updated 29 April 2005, accessed 27 February 2008, available from http://www.abc.net. au/ message/tv/ms/s1307580.htm.

E. Morrison, 'Newspapers', in *The Oxford Companion to Australian History*, ed. G. Davison, J. Hirst and S. Macintyre, Oxford Reference Online, accessed 8 November 2006, available from http://www.oxfordreference.com/views/ ENTRY.html?subview=Main&entry=t127.e1074.

Oliver, Steven, 'Te Rauparaha, Tamihana ?-1876', *Dictionary of New Zealand Biography*, updated 22 June 2007, accessed 14 March 2008, available from http://www.dnzb.govt.nz/dnzb/default.asp?Find_Quick. asp?PersonEssay=1T75.

Oliver, W. H., 'Te Whiwhi, Henare Matene ?-1881', *Dictionary of New Zealand Biography*, updated 22 June 2007, accessed 14 March 2008, available from http://www.dnzb.govt.nz/dnzb/default.asp?Find_Quick. asp?PersonEssay=1T89.

Parekowhai, Cushla, 'Dennan, Rangitiaria 1897-1970', *Dictionary of New Zealand Biography*, updated 7 July 2005, accessed 28 March 2006, available from http://www.dnzb.govt.nz/dnzb/default.asp?Find_Quick. asp?PersonEssay=4D12.

Parsonson, Ann, 'Herangi, Te Kirihaehae Te Puea 1883-1952', *Dictionary of New Zealand Biography*, updated 22 June 2007, accessed 2 August 2007, available from http://www.dnzb.govt.nz/dnzb/default.asp?Find_Quick. asp?PersonEssay=3H17.

R. Robinson, 'Grace, Patricia', in *The Oxford Companion to New Zealand Literature*, eds. R. Robinson and N. Wattie, Oxford Reference Online, accessed 30 April 2007, available from http://www.oxfordreference.com/ views/ENTRY.html?subview=Main&entry=t200.e472.

Ryan, Lyndall, 'Truganini', in *The Oxford Companion to Australian History*, eds. G. Davison, J. Hirst and S. Macintyre, Oxford Reference Online, accessed 8 September 2006, available from http://www.oxfordreference.com/views/ ENTRY.html?subview=Main&entry=t127.e147.

Ryan, Lyndall and Smith, Neil, 'Trugernanner (Truganini) (1812?-1876)', *Australian Dictionary of Biography*, Online Edition, updated continuously, accessed 8 August 2006, available from http://barney.asap.unimelb.edu.au/ adbtest/biogs/A060326b.htm.

Te Kanawa, Kiri, 'Kiri Te Kanawa Speech to the Rotary Club of Auckland', updated 2008, accessed 25 February 2008, available from http://www. kiritekanawa.org/pdf/2004_ 02_02_rotary_speech.pdf.

Turia, Tariana, 'Being a Maori Woman in Politics', updated 23 September 2006, accessed 22 July 2008, available from http://www.scoop.co.nz/stories/ PA0609/ S00509.htm.

Multimedia

Rymer, Judy, dir., *Standing in the Sunshine: Power* (New Zealand: Isambard Productions, 1993).

Te Kanawa, Kiri, 'Kiri: Maori Songs' (Auckland and London: EMI Records, 1999).

Index

Aboriginal Affairs, Department of 99-100, 147, 149, 159

Aboriginal and Islander Identity 43

Aboriginal-Australian Fellowship 34

Aboriginal Deaths in Custody Royal Commission 100

Aboriginal Development Commission 32, 100, 147

Aboriginal Progressive Association (APA) 34

Aboriginal and Torres Strait Islander Commission (ATSIC) 32, 147, 160

Aboriginalism 115-116

Aborigines' Welfare Board, NSW 43, 53, 83

absorption *see also* assimilation, integration, protection 27-28

ACT Party 160, 199

Advertiser, the (Adelaide) 119, 147, 148, 159, 160, 161, 165

Age, the (Melbourne) 42, 52, 72, 73, 109, 129, 151, 158, 187

Albury, NSW 52, 68

Alliance Party 190, 192, 195, 199

Amery, Mark 113

Amoamo, Jacqueline 87-88

Anderton, Jim 190

Annabell, Ross 97

Aotearoa Māori Tennis Association 60

APN News and Media 46

Arena, Franca 177

Armstrong, Alan 89

Arthur, George 2

Ashley, Laura 157

assimilation

    Australia 17, 21, 28-30, 36, 40, 47, 61, 63-64, 74, 93, 95-96, 104, 106, 115, 118, 125, 147, 186-187, 205, 206, 207, 208

    depiction as exemplars of 61, 63-64, 74, 93, 94-96, 104, 125, 147, 186-187, 207, 208

    gendered aspects 30, 40, 63-64

    and immigrants 93

    New Zealand 17, 21, 30, 40, 47, 93, 94-95, 104, 115, 140, 141, 183, 186-187, 205, 206, 207, 208

    see also absorption, integration, protection

Auckland Multicultural Society 140

Auckland Star, the 162, 163, 164, 191, 193

Auckland University Māori Club 37

Australia Day 37, 157, 165

Australian, the (Canberra) 55, 59, 60, 61, 67, 70, 108, 110, 112, 113, 116, 156, 186

Australian Aboriginal Progressive Association (AAPA) 34

Australian Aborigines' League 34

Australian Broadcasting Commission/Corporation (ABC) 52-53, 100

Australian Journalists' Association 46

Australian Rules football 54, 62

Australian Women's Weekly 13, 22, 40, 43, 63-64, 66, 79, 149, 157, 165, 185

Awatere Huata, Donna 41, 154-155, 160, 169-170, 194, 195

Ayiparinya Aboriginal Hostel 100

Ayrton, Heather 140

Williams, Peter 14, 157

Wilson, Bob 79, 84-85, 95

Wilson, Conrad 101

Wilson and Horton 46

Wimbledon 25, 44, 49, 51, 52, 55, 56, 58, 59, 60-61, 64, 66, 67, 68

Wiradjuri 61, 65

Women's Christian Temperance Union (WCTU) 39

Women's Electoral Lobby (WEL) 40

women's liberation 39, 40-41, 169-170

women's suffrage

Australia 39, 178

New Zealand 39, 177, 178

see also vote

World Tennis 69

World War One 8, 33

World War Two 5, 28, 38, 40, 79, 119

Wright, Judith 111, 113, 119

Wybalenna, Tas 2, 4

Yallop, Richard 71

Yarrabah, Qld 78

Young Māori Party 176

Zalcock, Beverley 128

www.ingramcontent.com/pod-product-compliance
Lightning Source LLC
Chambersburg PA
CBHW061244270326

41928CB00041B/3401

*9 7 8 1 9 2 1 8 6 2 6 1 8 *